'Beautifully written with a hawk-eye for the telling anecdote, *Spain in Our Hearts* constitutes an endlessly fascinating and utterly unputdownable survey of the war to defend democracy in Spain that was not only the first act of the Second World War but also, for many across the world, the last great cause'

Paul Preston, author of *The Spanish Civil War: Reaction, Revolution, and Revenge*

'*Spain in Our Hearts* is narrative non-fiction at its very best. Hochschild's achievement is to make this trial-by-combat story come alive, as if it were happening now. It is impossible for a reader not to identify and feel compassion for those sons and daughters of America who risked and often gave their lives for a cause that could not ultimately prevail against the darker forces of Franco, Hitler, Mussolini, Stalin – and Texaco. A seamlessly woven, unputdownable tapestry of war in Europe; intensely, unforgettably moving'

Nigel Hamilton, author of *The Mantle of Command*

'Adam Hochschild weaves a brilliant tapestry of colourful characters into a story that includes the young Ernest Hemmingway, the charismatic Robert Merriman, the scotch-drinking Milly Bennett, the glamorous reporter Virginia Cowles, and dozens of other Americans whose lives were dramatically altered by the Spanish Civil War. Hochschild's poignant narrative evokes E. L. Doctorow's great historical novel *Ragtime* – but *Spain in Our Hearts* is no novel but a tragic true story about a critical tipping point in the twentieth-century's slide into total warfare. Passionate, evocative, and gracefully written'

Kai Bird, Pulitzer Prize-winning author of *The Good Spy*

'George Orwell once explained that going to Spain, in 1936, "seemed the only conceivable thing to do." As soon as he got there, the right thing t… it was immediat… ricans who

[redacted]
fought in the Spanish [redacted], as Adam Hochschild recounts in this rich and fascinating book. Few writers grapple so powerfully with the painful moral and ethical choices of past actors as does Hochschild, who brings to *Spain in Our Hearts* his exceptional talents – and his moral seriousness – as a reporter, as a historian, and as a writer'

Jill Lepore, author of *The Secret History of Wonder Woman*

'In this beautifully written portrait of Americans caught up in the Spanish Civil War, Adam Hochschild brings to brilliant life the heroism and horror of that fratricidal conflict. His account of the David-and-Goliath fight between the ragtag army of idealistic, pro-democracy volunteers and the mechanized, murderous forces of Franco, Hitler, and Mussolini is one of the most powerful narratives I have ever read'

Lynne Olson, author of *Citizens of London*

'[An] excellent portrait of the war and of the men and women drawn to Spain . . . It is Hochschild's vivid account of what these people witnessed that gives his book its edge. Many other writers have described the Americans who went to Spain, but few have brought to their accounts such an enjoyable and balanced mixture of history and personal narrative . . . Hochschild is good at conveying the barbarity on both sides without letting it swamp the story . . . fascinating'

Caroline Moorehead, *Literary Review*

SPAIN IN OUR HEARTS

Adam Hochschild is an award-winning author of seven books, mostly on subjects related to human rights. *King Leopold's Ghost* was the winner of the prestigious Duff Cooper Prize and *Bury the Chains* was longlisted for the Samuel Johnson Prize. He lives in Berkeley and teaches at the Graduate School of Journalism at the University of California, Berkeley.

BOOKS BY ADAM HOCHSCHILD

Half the Way Home:
A Memoir of Father and Son

The Mirror at Midnight:
A South African Journey

The Unquiet Ghost:
Russians Remember Stalin

Finding the Trapdoor:
Essays, Portraits, Travels

King Leopold's Ghost:
A Story of Greed, Terror, and Heroism in Colonial Africa

Bury the Chains:
Prophets and Rebels in the Fight to Free an Empire's Slaves

To End All Wars:
A Story of Loyalty and Rebellion, 1914–1918

Spain in Our Hearts:
Americans in the Spanish Civil War, 1936–1939

SPAIN IN OUR HEARTS

Americans in the Spanish Civil War, 1936–1939

Adam Hochschild

PAN BOOKS

First published 2016 by Houghton Mifflin Harcourt

First published in the UK 2016 by Macmillan

This paperback edition published 2017 by Pan Books
an imprint of Pan Macmillan
20 New Wharf Road, London N1 9RR
Associated companies throughout the world
www.panmacmillan.com

ISBN 978-1-5098-1060-4

1 3 5 7 9 8 6 4 2

A CIP catalogue record for this book is available from the British Library.

Printed and bound by CPI Group (UK) Ltd, Croydon, CR0 4YY

For Rosa and Sonia

Contents

Maps

Author's Note

Where place names have a common rendering in English, I have used them, such as Majorca, Navarre, Seville, Aragon, Cordova, Catalonia, and Saragossa. Where today's maps show Basque or Catalan town or street names, I have nonetheless used the Spanish version when that is how the name appears in writings from the civil war era; hence Guernica, Marsa, the Ramblas, and so on. Some errors in Spanish words or phrases quoted by American journalists and volunteers have been silently corrected, but I have not altered the occasionally erratic English spelling and punctuation of their letters and diaries.

Prologue: Far from Home

DAYBREAK, APRIL 4, 1938. Shivering, exhausted, and naked, two bedraggled swimmers climb out of the freezing water and onto the bank of Spain's Ebro River, which is swollen with melted snow from the Pyrenees. Both men are Americans.

The country is in flames. For nearly two years, the fractious but democratically elected government of the Spanish Republic has been defending itself against a military uprising led by Francisco Franco and backed by Nazi Germany and Fascist Italy. Franco, who has given himself the title of Generalissimo, has a framed photograph of Adolf Hitler on his desk and has spoken of Germany as "a model which we will always keep before us." The skies above the Ebro this dawn are dark with warplanes, state-of-the-art fighters and bombers, flown by German pilots, that the Führer has sent the Generalissimo. On the ground, tanks and soldiers from Italy, some of the nearly 80,000 troops the dictator Benito Mussolini will loan Franco, have helped launch the greatest offensive of the war. A powerful drive from the western two thirds of the country, which Franco controls, its goal is to reach the Mediterranean, splitting the remaining territory of the Spanish Republic in two.

Franco's prolonged battle for power is the fiercest conflict in Europe since the First World War, marked by a vindictive savagery not seen even then. His forces have bombed cities into rubble, tortured political opponents, murdered people for belonging to labor unions, machine-gunned hospital wards full of wounded, branded Republican women on their breasts with the emblem of his movement, and carried out death sentences with the garrote, a medieval iron collar used to strangle its victim.

Battered by the new offensive, the Republic's soldiers are retreating chaotically, streaming eastward before Franco's troops, tanks, and bombers. In some places, his rapidly advancing units have leapfrogged ahead. The Republican forces include thousands of volunteers from other countries, many of them Americans. Some have already been killed. Franco has just announced that any foreign volunteers taken prisoner will be shot.

Cutting through rugged mountainous country in Spain's northeast, the fast-flowing Ebro, the country's largest river, marks the line between death and safety: the east bank is still in Republican hands. Small clusters of American volunteers, trapped behind the lines, have succeeded in slipping past Franco's troops by night, navigating by the North Star. After three days with little sleep, pursued by soldiers, tanks, and cavalry guided by spotter planes circling overhead, they reach the Ebro before dawn, near a point where a bridge appears on the map. The bridge, they discover, has been blown up, and there are no boats. A few of those who cannot swim desperately tear a door from an abandoned farmhouse to use as a raft; other nonswimmers enter the river clinging to a log. Swept away by the current, at least six—four of whom are wounded—will drown.

Three remaining Americans who can swim strip off their boots and all their clothing and plunge into the icy water. One of them lands far downstream, but two young New Yorkers, John Gates and George Watt, who has a sprained ankle and a shrapnel wound in his hand, wade out of the water together on the far side. As morning breaks, they head east, hoping to find someone who can tell them where the remnants of their unit might be. "We walk stark naked and barefoot over a seemingly endless stretch of sharp stones and burrs that cut our feet," Watt remembered. "We are shivering from the cold, and our feet are bleeding when we reach the highway. . . . A truck comes down the road. I wonder what must be going through the mind of the driver, seeing two naked men standing on the highway. He hands us a couple of blankets and drives away."

Gates recalled the next moment this way: "Hungry and exhausted, I felt I could not take another step. . . . We lay down on the side of the road, with no idea of who might come along, too beat to care. . . . Suddenly a car drove up, stopped and out stepped two men. Nobody ever looked better to me in all my life. . . . We hugged one another."

In the black two-seater Matford roadster are a *New York Times* correspondent, Herbert L. Matthews, and Ernest Hemingway, who is covering the war for the North American Newspaper Alliance. "The writers gave us the good news of the many friends who were safe," Gates wrote, "and we told them the bad news of some who were not." Hemingway and Matthews had often reported on the American volunteers in Spain and knew some of them well. Many are now missing, including Major Robert Merriman of California, chief of staff of the XV International Brigade, last seen some ten miles away leading a party of soldiers about to be encircled by Franco's troops. None of the four men by the river have any news of his fate.

"There are hundreds of men still across the Ebro," wrote Watt. "Many are dead; some are drowned. How many captured? We have no idea. Matthews is busy taking notes. Hemingway is busy cursing the Fascists." The novelist's notorious strut and bluster were on full display, though his audience consisted only of two wet, shivering men wearing nothing but blankets. "Facing the other side of the river," as Gates remembered it, "Hemingway shook his burly fist. 'You fascist bastards haven't won yet,' he shouted. 'We'll show you!'"

The war in which these four Americans encountered each other near a riverbank so far from home was a pivotal event in Spain's history. At the time it was also seen as a moral and political touchstone, a world war in embryo, in a Europe shadowed by the rapid ascent of fascism. Roughly 2,800 Americans fought in the Spanish Civil War, an estimated 750 of them dying there—a far higher death rate than the US military suffered in any of its twentieth-century wars. For many veterans it would be the defining experience of their lives, as it would be for some American correspondents. “Wherever in this world I meet a man or woman who fought for Spanish liberty,” Herbert Matthews wrote years later, “I meet a kindred soul.” Despite the conventions of American journalism, reporters can feel as partisan as anybody else. In this war all pretense otherwise often vanished: as Republican troops fled Franco’s deadly offensive that spring, Matthews and his counterpart from the *New York Herald Tribune* both sent personal telegrams to President Franklin D. Roosevelt begging him to send the Republic arms.

The Second World War has largely eclipsed the earlier conflict in our collective memory, but at the time, tens of millions of Americans followed news of it intently. While the fighting lasted, from mid-1936 to early 1939, the *New York Times* ran more than 1,000 front-page headlines about the war in Spain—outnumbering those on any other single topic, including President Roosevelt, the rise of Nazi Germany, or the calamitous toll of the Great Depression. While their government adamantly refused to intervene in Spain, many Americans were deeply involved—on both sides. For example, the fuel for those Nazi aircraft bombing and strafing the American volunteers came from Texas, sold to Franco by a swashbuckling American oilman with a penchant for right-wing dictators.

My own introduction to the war came in the mid-1960s when I was a cub reporter on the *San Francisco Chronicle*. Two older journalists at the paper were veterans of the Abraham Lincoln Brigade, as the several units of American volunteers informally came to be called. I remember asking one of them, who had driven an ambulance in Spain, how he looked back on the war. Over the clatter of manual typewriters and teletype machines and the whoosh of pneumatic tubes that carried our stories to the typesetters, he said with great feeling, so unlike the usual banter of the newsroom, “I wish we’d won.”

The Spanish Republic lost the war, of course, and that loss has cast a certain shadow over the conflict ever since. The aura of knowing things will end in defeat pervades the best-known novel of the war, Hemingway's *For Whom the Bell Tolls*, published the year after Franco's victory. More than any other event of its era, the Spanish Civil War invites "What if?" questions. What if the Western democracies had sold Republican Spain the arms it repeatedly, urgently tried to buy? Might these have been enough to defeat the aircraft, submarines, and troops dispatched by Hitler and Mussolini? And if so, would Hitler still have sent his troops into Austria, Czechoslovakia, and finally some dozen other countries? Could the Second World War in Europe, with its tens of millions of deaths and untold suffering, have been avoided? Or might it at least have unfolded in some different, more limited way?

Few American volunteers doubted that they were fighting the first battle of a world war to come, and they were right: where else, after all, were Americans being bombed by Nazi pilots more than four years before the United States declared war on Germany and Japan? In other countries as well, many felt the Spanish war to be the era's testing ground. "Men of my generation," wrote the French novelist Albert Camus, "have had Spain in our hearts. . . . It was there that they learned . . . that one can be right and yet be beaten, that force can vanquish spirit, and that there are times when courage is not rewarded."

There seemed a moral clarity about the crisis in Spain. Rapidly advancing fascism cried out for defiance; if not here, where? This is why so many men from around the world volunteered to fight, and why, decades later, I saw Lincoln Brigade veterans enthusiastically cheered when they appeared in demonstrations for civil rights or against the Vietnam War in the 1960s, or against US intervention in Central America in the 1980s. Over time, I met half a dozen former volunteers, and was friends with two for many years. (Only in writing this book did I realize that yet another, Dr. Jacques Grunblatt, who appears only briefly in these pages, was the surgeon who once stitched me up after an accident when I was a boy.) Imagining myself in their shoes became still easier when I discovered that the couple whom you'll meet in the first chapter lived, when the husband was a graduate student at Berkeley in the 1930s, only a few blocks from where I do today, in a building I've walked past hundreds of times. All of us who care about social justice feel a need for political ancestors, and surely, it seems, that's what these men and women—some 75 American women, mostly nurses, volunteered in Spain—were.

I felt this as strongly as did other members of the '60s generation. Anyone's interest in a time and place usually springs from wondering: what would I have done then? I often liked to believe that, had I been alive in that era, I, too, would have gone to Spain. Yet I also knew that the story had a darker, less romantic side. For the only major country that did sell arms to the Spanish Republic was the Soviet Union, and it exacted a considerable price in return. Some Spaniards became victims of the ruthlessness against his enemies, real and imaginary, that was such a hallmark of Joseph Stalin's dictatorship.

In a most unexpected place, I once encountered a vivid reminder of the toll that his paranoia took. In 1991, I was researching a book on how Russians were coming to terms with Stalin's legacy. Just that year, as the Soviet Union was swiftly falling apart, the authorities finally lifted decades of restrictions on where foreign journalists could travel, so I was able to visit a place few Westerners had previously seen, Karaganda, in Kazakhstan. That remote, decrepit city of crumbling gray and brown concrete had once been the center of a huge network of *gulag* labor camps for prisoners put to work mining coal. In a desolate rural cemetery, some miles outside of town, years of freezing and thawing had left stark, homemade metal crosses tilted or flat on the ground. Electric power lines crossed above them, and scraps of plastic bags and garbage blew in the constant wind of the Central Asian steppes. To my surprise, many graves had Spanish names.

The USSR, I learned, had taken in several thousand Republican refugees, many of them children. In addition, when the war ended, Spanish sailors on ships in Soviet ports and several hundred Spanish pilots in training were unable to return home. Like millions of

Soviets, a number of these Spaniards fell victim to Stalin's suspicions. An estimated 270 Spanish Republicans were sent to the *gulag*, many dying there of starvation, exhaustion, or exposure. At least 60 were imprisoned near the cemetery I saw, in a crowded labor camp surrounded by three high, concentric fences of barbed wire.

How do we reconcile these two pictures of the Spanish Civil War? Surely Spaniards were right to resist a coup backed by Hitler and Mussolini. But did the Republic become doomed by its entanglement with the Soviet Union, whose government was at least as murderous as the Franco regime? Defenders of the Republic were, in short, fighting for one of the finest of causes beside one of the nastiest of allies. How did they experience this? How much were they even aware of it? Or, if you're in a desperate battle for survival, do you have the luxury of worrying about who your allies are? These were among the questions that long made me want to explore this period of history.

Most of the Americans who went to Spain considered themselves Communists, and we cannot understand them without understanding why communism then had such a powerful appeal and why the Soviet Union seemed a beacon of hope to so many. The funeral of one of my Lincoln Brigade friends, 65 years after he left Spain and 45 years after he left the US Communist Party, was the first time I ever heard the "Internationale." Once it had been the anthem of the world Communist movement; now it was a tune sung by a few old men struggling to remember the words and, perhaps, the youthful dream they had once evoked.

Today communism, Trotskyism, and anarchism have generally lost their hold, and the old arguments among their followers can sometimes feel as remote as medieval religious disputes. Vanished also is the widespread conviction that the capitalist system was in crisis and could endure no longer, and that a blueprint for the future existed, even if there were quarrels over whose blueprint was right. While much of that feels distant now, other aspects of 1930s Spain still seem all too similar to many countries today: the great gap between rich and poor, and the struggle between an authoritarian dictatorship and millions of powerless people long denied their fair share of land, education, and so much more. These things make Spain of the 1930s, a crucial battleground of its time, a resonant one for ours as well.

I wondered about something else too. For more than half a century now, many members of my own political generation have been strongly opposed to war, and especially to American intervention in the civil wars or internal affairs of other countries, whether in Vietnam, Nicaragua, El Salvador, Iraq, or almost anywhere else. Yet most of us have long thought the world would have been better off if our government had not stood aside from the Spanish Civil War. We've regarded as heroes an earlier generation of Americans who went off to fight in it. This raises the question: are there times when military involvement in a distant conflict is justified?

This was certainly the only time so many Americans joined someone else's civil war—and they did so even though their own government made strenuous efforts to stop them. They came from nearly every state in the Union and included rich and poor, Ivy League graduates, and men who had ridden freight trains in search of work. What made them go? What did they learn—about themselves, about war, about the country they had signed up to defend and the one they had left? Did any have later regrets?

There were also Americans, I discovered as I began exploring this era, who were drawn to Spain not by the fight that the Lincolns were waging, but by a far less publicized social revolution happening behind the lines. One, who reached Spain months before any of the Lincoln volunteers, was a fiery young Kentucky woman on her honeymoon.

I was curious about another group of people as well. As a journalist who has often reported from abroad, on occasion from conflict zones, I wanted to take a close look at the much-mythologized American reporters who covered the war. Did Matthews, Hemingway, and their colleagues get the story right? Did their passionate feelings—it's normally unheard of for correspondents in the field to send telegrams to the White House—skew their reporting? What did they miss?

And so I decided to explore the lives of Americans involved in the

Spanish Civil War. I have widened the circle slightly to include three Englishmen: one fought with the Americans, one against them, and a third is familiar to all American readers. What follows is not a full history of the war, or even of American involvement in it. It is, rather, the story of a collection of people whose paths took them an ocean away from home during a violent time. History does not come neatly packaged, and some of these men and women, however courageous, had beliefs that seem illusions to us today; idealism and bravery, after all, are not always synonymous with wisdom. Still, it was deeply moving to get to know them, and to wonder again what I might or might not have done in their place and time. Looking into their lives took me to meetings with their descendants, to libraries and archives, to a few documents long tucked away in closets or drawers, and finally to the banks of the Ebro River.

PART I

1

Chasing Moneychangers from the Temple

In a state that was largely brown desert, the wide lawns of the University of Nevada stood out like a green oasis. On a bluff overlooking Reno, tree-shaded red-brick buildings were laced with vines and dotted with cupolas and windows in white frames. Spread around a small lake, the school had an Ivy League look that would make it a favorite location for Hollywood films set on campuses.

Six feet two and a half inches tall, sandy-haired, rangy, and handsome, Robert Merriman was working his way through college. He held jobs at a local funeral home, as a fraternity house manager, and as a salesman at J. C. Penney, where he used his employee discount to buy his clothes. Growing up in California, he had already spent several years in a paper mill and as a lumberjack—his father's trade—between high school and college. Along the way, he had also worked in a cement plant and on a cattle ranch. Once enrolled at Nevada, he discovered he could earn an extra $8.50 a month by signing up for the Reserve Officers' Training Corps, or ROTC, whose cadets wore cavalry-era dress uniforms including riding boots and jodhpurs. He also found time to play end on the campus football team, and then, when an injury forced him to stop, to become a cheerleader. Indeed, for the rest of his life there would remain something of the clean-cut cheerleader about him.

Bob Merriman met Marion Stone at a dance just before their freshman year. On the first day of school he spotted her as he was driving by in a small Dodge convertible, braked, and called out, "Climb in! We're going places." Slender, attractive, and half a head shorter than he, Marion was the daughter of an alcoholic restaurant chef. She, too, had worked for two years after high school and, like millions of other people, had then lost her savings in a bank failure. She was supporting herself as a secretary and by cooking and cleaning for the family who owned the mortuary where Bob worked.

Marion lived most of her college years in a sorority house. By her account, campus courting was a chaste affair: dancing, kissing, and perhaps an occasional daring visit to a Prohibition-era speakeasy. She was chosen "Honorary Major" of the University Military Ball that Bob staged with his ROTC friends, and he splurged some of his hard-earned money to buy her slippers and a taffeta gown. On the morning of graduation day in May 1932, they received their degrees and Bob his commission as a second lieutenant in the Army Reserve. They were married that afternoon. Afterward they drove through the Sierra Nevada to a borrowed cottage on the shore of Lake Tahoe and went to bed together at last. It was, she says, the first time for each of them.

That fall, encouraged by one of his Nevada professors who had spotted his talent, Bob Merriman enrolled as a graduate student in economics at the University of California at Berkeley. In a country gripped by the worst depression in its history, with nearly a quarter of the population out of work, no subject seemed more vital. Berkeley leaned to the left, but with millions of homeless Americans living in "Hooverville" shacks of corrugated iron, tarpaper, cinderblocks, or old packing cases—in New York, one Hooverville sprouted close to Wall Street and another in Central Park—you didn't have to be a leftist to wonder: was there a better way?

Franklin D. Roosevelt entered the Oval Office during Merriman's first year at Berkeley, voicing in his inaugural address a near-biblical radicalism seldom heard from an American president before or since: "Practices of the unscrupulous moneychangers stand indicted.... The moneychangers have fled from their high seats in the temple of our civilization. We may now restore that temple to the ancient truths. The measure of the restoration lies in the extent to which we apply social values more noble than mere monetary profit." Some of the moneychangers seemed uneasy. The financier J. P. Morgan Jr., heir to a vast banking fortune, put his yacht in mothballs, writing a friend, "There are so many suffering from lack of work, and even from actual hunger, that it is both wiser and kinder not to flaunt such luxuriant amusement."

Funds were tight for the newlyweds. For several months, Marion could not afford to leave a new job she had in Nevada. A stream of letters and an occasional love poem from Bob to his "Dearest girl of all" assured her of how much he missed her: "Love and please hurry. I'm tired of living alone and need you and you alone." At the same time, he kept a wary eye on their finances: "I am very much in favor of your coming down over the holidays if you can make it. However, if there is any possibility of spending much money doing it we had better not try."

He shared with her his excitement at being on a far more sophisticated campus: "One room in the library is like a handsome club room of some sort. Soft armchairs and all." It was thrilling for him to become an instructor of undergraduates and to get to know fellow graduate students who had come long distances to study in his department, including a young Canadian named John Kenneth Galbraith. "The most popular of my generation of graduate students at Berkeley" was how Galbraith would remember Merriman. "Later he was to show himself the bravest."

Bob took a bed in a rooming house while searching for an affordable place for the couple to live. "Since my arrival here," he wrote to Marion, "I have looked at, at least, fifty apartments.... Last nite I left the library early ... and searched some more. I found one that I consider we can't beat.... So I put down $5 deposit and shall move in tomorrow afternoon.... They charge $20 a month so it is no palace neither is it a shack. . . . I have been a trifle skimpy on rations but I'm eating more now all of the books are paid for. I am feeling like a million and just dying to have my sweetheart join me soon."

Before long she did, in the one-room studio Bob had found five minutes' walk north of the campus, equipped with a Murphy bed that unfolded from the wall. Despite the Great Depression, Marion seemed to have a knack for landing on her feet and finding work. She first took a job as a bank secretary, then clerked at a housewares store in San Francisco, to which she commuted by trolley car and ferry. Even with little money, married life was a delight. "Bob invented a mischievous game in which we would sneak into the luxurious Nob Hill hotel, the Mark Hopkins, by pretending to be meeting someone at the bar. Once inside we danced for hours, never spending more than the price of the first drink. We got so good at it that we sometimes didn't even order a drink." Among their favorite tunes were "Stardust" and "Tea for Two."

Soon three more people were crowded into the tiny apartment: on a cot in the kitchen was a graduate student without a place to live whom Bob had taken pity on; sleeping on another cot and the living room couch were Marion's eight- and eleven-year-old sisters. Their mother had died and their hard-drinking father was incapable of caring for them. "You walked in the door and you had to crawl over a bed to get anywhere," Marion remembered. "Bob was unflappable. He simply figured my sisters, the graduate student, and, God knows, maybe even someone else eventually, were in need; he had room, we ought to share it." His infectious good spirits made her feel "as though I were a child running and laughing in a wild game of Follow the Leader."

Meanwhile, the country around them simmered in misery. Thirty-four million Americans lived in households with no wage earner. In every city, long lines of jobless men in cloth caps or Homburgs waited outside soup kitchens, but the churches and charities operating them sometimes ran out of funds and had no food to serve. Families rummaged in trash bins and garbage dumps for anything edible and tried to keep warm in winter over sidewalk hot-air grates. In Pennsylvania, homeless unemployed steelworkers and their wives and children lived inside idled coke ovens. The economic abyss was deepened by a drought of historic proportions that sent millions of people streaming westward from the Great Plains under vast clouds of topsoil turned to dust. Midwestern farmers who managed to harvest a crop sometimes could find no grain elevator willing to buy it. The city of Detroit slaughtered the animals in its zoo to provide meat for the hungry. When the Empire State Building opened to great fanfare, it could rent only 20 percent of its space. For the jobless, telephones became an unaffordable luxury: between 1930 and 1933, the number of households with phone service shrank by more than three million.

A mood of national despair was punctuated by moments when the desperate tried to seize what they needed to survive. Some 300 men and women gathered on the main street of the town of England, Arkansas, and refused to move until shop owners distributed bread and other food. In Oklahoma City, people forced their way into a grocery store and took food off the shelves, while in Minneapolis it required 100 policemen to break up a crowd doing the same thing.

Labor turned militant. More than 300,000 textile workers walked off the job in 1934 in the largest strike America had yet seen. From Maine to Georgia, clothing mill employees clashed with police, strikebreakers, and the National Guard in violence that left some dozen people dead. The Georgia governor put the whole state under martial law. Elsewhere, by the hundreds of thousands, small farmers and homeowners lost their property to foreclosure—or sometimes gathered neighbors with shotguns and refused to move.

In the summer after his first year at Berkeley, Bob Merriman worked on a Ford auto assembly line in the nearby industrial city of Richmond and was appalled to find that the workers, not even allowed bathroom breaks, were routinely splashed by battery acid. The next summer, in 1934, he would be swept into a far more political world than the one he had known in Nevada. Some 15,000 West Coast longshoremen had formed a union and, when shipping firms refused to recognize it, walked off the job. Sailors, harbor pilots, and truck drivers carrying cargo to the docks joined them. In a display of solidarity rare for that era, the strikers and their allies—whites, blacks, Chinese and Filipino Americans—marched eight abreast up San Francisco's Market Street under a union flag.

The maritime companies hired replacements, sometimes housing them on shipboard to keep them beyond reach of the fists and boots of angry longshoremen. At Berkeley, hundreds of professors and students, like Merriman, fervently backed the strikers, while the football coach—William Ingram, an Annapolis graduate known as "Navy Bill"—organized players to work as strikebreakers.

All major Pacific coast ports were shut down, but the heart of the battle was in San Francisco, then a rough-edged, blue-collar city and the country's biggest union stronghold. A thousand men at a time blocked the waterfront in 12-hour shifts. Tensions rose, and any truck that tried to drive through the line of picketing workers was met by fusillades of rocks and bricks. From the hills that overlooked the wharves, thousands of San Franciscans watched the ensuing street fighting and listened to police gunfire. When tear gas grenades lit a hillside of dry grass on fire the city looked even more like a war zone. In several days of fighting, two strikers were killed and well over 100 injured people were taken to hospitals. A solemn crowd of 15,000 escorted the bodies of the dead along Market Street in silence. The San Francisco Labor Council voted, for only the second time in American history, to call a general strike. Throughout the Bay Area, nearly 130,000 people stopped working.

Some 500 special police were sworn in, and vigilante groups joined them in wrecking union offices and a kitchen feeding the strikers. The attackers smashed furniture, threw typewriters out of windows, and beat up union members and other radicals. "Reds Turn Black and Blue" ran the triumphant headline in the *San Francisco Chronicle*. Well over 250 unionists and their sympathizers were arrested, and the governor mobilized 4,500 National Guardsmen. Along the waterfront, helmeted soldiers manned sandbag barricades and a machine-gun nest.

The conflict did not bring on the revolution that many dreamed of, but the strikers won some of their demands. The union took firm root among longshoremen, and until cranes for shipping containers replaced dockworkers' cargo hooks several decades later, it would be one of the country's strongest. Working as a volunteer in the strike publicity office, Bob Merriman had a front-row seat at a historic labor victory.

Just as the strike was one part of Merriman's introduction to the political strife of his day, his surroundings at Berkeley were another. Teaching in his department, for instance, was the economist Paul Taylor, husband of the photographer Dorothea Lange; the couple went into sunbaked fields to research and publicize the dire conditions of California's migrant farmworkers, among the poorest of the country's poor. Berkeley was home to many others on the left: Democrats who wanted Roosevelt's New Deal to be more far-reaching, Socialists who advocated a peaceful transition to public ownership of industry, Communists, and members of a host of smaller sects.

It was hardly surprising that the Merrimans became interested in the Soviet Union. Nor were they the only Americans to feel that the USSR was worth a sympathetic look. Surely, many felt, there must be an alternative to an America where workers trying to organize risked bloody beatings and an economic system drove so many to depths of despair. Every day brought more headlines that underscored the enormity of the national crisis. Ten paroled prisoners asked to be readmitted to a penitentiary in Pennsylvania because they couldn't find jobs. Chicago ran out of money to pay its schoolteachers. In Appalachia, men, women, and children survived on wild grass, roots, and dandelions. Capitalism, it seemed, was at last experiencing the death throes that Karl Marx had predicted. Couldn't a planned economy, by contrast, put the unemployed to work building much-needed housing, schools, and hospitals? And wasn't that just what they were doing in Russia?

Today we remember the American Communist Party as the handmaiden of a ruthless and ultimately failed Soviet dictatorship. But as the historian Ellen Schrecker has written, it was also "the most dynamic organization within the American Left during the 1930s and '40s." Thanks to its influential role in great labor battles like the San Francisco waterfront strike and its pioneering efforts to organize farmworkers, the Party had won respect from many far beyond its small membership. In a highly segregated and sexist age, it campaigned to get black Americans onto jury and voter rolls and fought for the rights of women. A New York trade unionist, who would later cross paths with Merriman in Spain, joined the Party after he saw members of its youth league defiantly carrying the belongings and furniture of newly evicted tenement dwellers back upstairs to their apartments. "There was an organization that didn't just talk, but actually did something."

The national sense of crisis was so deep that, in the presidential election of 1932, 52 prominent American writers—including Sherwood Anderson, Theodore Dreiser, John Dos Passos, Langston Hughes, and Edmund Wilson—announced their support for the Communist candidate for president. Even that very non-Communist chronicler of high society F. Scott Fitzgerald urged Marx on his daughter: "Read the terrible chapter in *Das Kapital* on *The Working Day*, and see if you are ever quite the same."

As the '30s went on, it only became clearer that the New Deal was doing little to pull the country out of the Depression. And elsewhere things seemed even worse. Riding a deadly wave of street violence by his brown-uniformed storm troopers, Adolf Hitler had taken power in Germany, burned books, fired Jewish professors, pulled his country out of the League of Nations, and thrown more than 50,000 Germans into "protective custody" in prisons and concentration camps. In 1934, in the "Night of the Long Knives," he personally led the contingent of SS men who gunned down more than 100 of his enemies inside and outside the Nazi movement, including a former German chancellor; one man was murdered with pickaxes. The next year Germany dramatically stepped up its military spending and stripped citizenship and civil rights from the country's Jews, whom propaganda chief Joseph Goebbels called "syphilis" infecting the people of Europe. In Italy, Benito Mussolini's paramilitary Blackshirts terrorized anyone who resisted his Fascist dictatorship. On the other side of the world, a militarized imperial Japan had brutally occupied the Chinese region of Manchuria.

In many countries hit by the Depression, right and left clashed violently—and the right seemed to be winning. When revolution-minded Spanish coal miners armed with dynamite seized mines, factories, banks, and other businesses in the province of Asturias in the fall of 1934, at least 1,000 of them were slaughtered by government troops and artillery. The soldiers included the much-feared Spanish Foreign Legion, whose men sported the sliced-off ears of their victims on wire necklaces and sometimes cut off miners' hands, tongues, and genitals. Rebellious miners saw their wives raped, and thousands of them were thrown in prison. The victorious troops were led by one of Europe's youngest generals, the tough-talking Francisco Franco, whom the Associated Press referred to as "Spain's 'man of the hour.'"

By comparison, events in the Soviet Union sounded promising. In these apocalyptic times, it became a place onto which millions of people projected their hopes. There were no strikes—at least none that anyone in the United States heard of—and whatever other problems the new society might have, unemployment was not one of them. The Soviet economy appeared to be booming, enough so that Joseph Stalin ordered 75,000 Model A sedans from Henry Ford.

More than that: the Russians were hiring. When the government posted job openings for American engineers and technicians, in an eight-month period more than 100,000 applied. Thousands more headed for the country on tourist visas hoping to find work when they got there—enough American and British newcomers so that the weekly English-language *Moscow News* went daily. Two brothers who would later become major labor leaders, Walter and Victor Reuther, were among the tens of thousands of foreigners who found jobs in Russia, working in an auto factory in the city of Gorky. A book originally written for Soviet schoolchildren, *New Russia's Primer: The Story of the Five-Year Plan,* spent seven months on the American bestseller list. "In the great financial storm that has burst on us your own ship is sinking," the Irish playwright George Bernard Shaw told American radio listeners after returning from a visit to the USSR, "and the Russian ship is the only big one that is not rolling heavily and tapping out SOS on its wireless."

Although he had become head teaching fellow in Berkeley's economics department, Bob Merriman was an activist at heart. He was more interested in a society that was remaking itself than in texts about supply and demand curves that seemed to have little relevance to a world caught in the Depression. Though not a Communist Party member, he began to move in its circles. The chair of the economics department was a conservative, but told Bob that he believed it was important to understand the new Soviet system. Why not, Merriman thought, do his doctoral dissertation on some aspect of the subject? By the end of 1934, he had finished his course work and, as Galbraith wrote, "was awarded one of the rare traveling fellowships in the gift of the university." Although the decision must have been painful for her, Marion placed her two sisters, now ten and thirteen, in the most enlightened children's home she could find (a professor of Bob's was on the board). The fellowship provided $900 for study abroad, and that was enough, with the couple's savings, to set the Merrimans on their way to Moscow.

2

Promised Land, Black Wings

For ambitious young Americans in the years between the two world wars, one of the most glittering of all professions was that of foreign correspondent. A select group of journalists, telegraphing their reports by underwater cable, interpreted the wider world for readers back home. To be a member of this elite seemed to Louis Fischer a miraculous leap from his origins in the Philadelphia slums.

"My father worked as a laborer in a factory and then graduated to selling fish and fruit from a pushcart," he later wrote. "I can still hear his cry, 'Peaches, fresh peaches.' Sometimes I hauled the empty pushcart to the stable. My mother took in washing. The family moved whenever it could not pay rent—which was often. Until I reached the age of sixteen, I never lived in a house with electricity, running water, or an inside lavatory, or any heat except from a coal stove in the kitchen–living room." Food often ran out.

Restless to escape, Fischer identified journalism as his path to a more glamorous life. In the aftermath of the First World War he persuaded the *New York Evening Post* to pay him by the article for pieces he would send from Berlin—where Germany's ruinous inflation meant the dollar went a long way. His skill in cultivating edi-

…s and a knack for quickly mastering languages soon found him in Moscow, where he began churning out books as well as hundreds of freelance articles for the venerable New York liberal weekly the *Nation* and newspapers like the *New York Times* and the *Baltimore Sun.* By the late 1920s he was taking a steamship home each year to profit from the American appetite for authoritative-sounding speakers on foreign affairs. His books and lectures made him enough of a minor celebrity that when touring the United States he was sought out by other reporters for interviews.

In 1922, Fischer married a Russian woman and before long they had two sons, who would grow up in Moscow. With as much of an appetite for women as for travel, he had numerous affairs on several continents, fathering at least one additional child. But he remained fond of his wife, and later in their lives, even long after they had parted ways, they regularly traded warm letters. By the mid-1930s, Fischer had developed a sideline: for several weeks each summer, he took tour groups of Americans through the USSR. Although he sometimes wore a Russian peasant's blouse and sandals to show his solidarity with the working classes, he enjoyed the extra money these trips earned him and was particularly proud one year that his "star pupil" was Maurice Wertheim, a "millionaire investment banker" with a New York penthouse, a Connecticut estate, a private salmon-fishing river in Canada, and a collection of Picassos. (Wertheim's daughter would later win wide renown as the historian Barbara Tuchman.)

Like so many others in these years scarred by war and depression, Fischer was searching for a creed that would make sense of the world and hold out the promise of a better future. "I cannot imagine life without something higher than myself in which I can have faith," he wrote. After a youthful flirtation with Zionism, he found that faith in the Soviet Union. "I too was swept away by it. . . . A whole nation marched behind a vision. . . . I had stood at train windows during night hours of horrid wakefulness crossing the flat face of Russia. No light. Hundreds of miles of darkness. People lived in that all their lives. I had done high-school lessons by kerosene lamp. It doesn't kill you, but bright light is better. To this day I hate to turn off a light. . . .

Now the electric bulb was invading the bleak black village. . . . Russia was trying to lift itself out of an ancient mire."

Communism seemed to be magically sweeping a backward country into the industrial age. Like many creeds, this one had its living prophet. Accompanying an American delegation in 1927, Fischer spent the better part of a day in the company of Joseph Stalin, whose soft-spoken, simple-soldier manner charmed many a foreign visitor. "As he talked to us hour after hour my respect for his strength, will and faith grew. . . . His calm voice reflected inner power."

In photographs Fischer is never smiling. Intense, broad-shouldered, with a shock of black hair and imposing dark eyebrows, he was not to everyone's taste. The British writer Malcolm Muggeridge, then a young correspondent in Moscow, found him a "sallow, ponderous, inordinately earnest man . . . who had never once through the years veered from virtuously following the Party Line." When the two of them were talking to an engineer at a dam-building site who dropped an impolitic hint that the construction workers were, in fact, prisoners, Fischer quickly changed the subject.

What drew Fischer to his role in Moscow was not just naïve idealism but the hunger for recognition and closeness to power of someone who had grown up with neither. In the many photos he saved, the other person in the picture is often a premier, general, or cabinet minister. Most reporters request an interview to hear someone else's views, but after returning to Moscow from one trip to Western Europe, Fischer wrote to Stalin asking for a meeting so that "I . . . could give you my impressions of that journey . . . and talk with you about the international situation." There is no record of whether the dictator replied, but Soviet officials clearly knew how to satisfy Fischer's ego. In 1932, he was one of three foreign correspondents honored for their "fairness and impartiality in presenting the news" at a banquet given by the Commissariat of Foreign Affairs. Such flattery paid off: "Sun over the Kremlin: Mr. Louis Fischer Finds Russia a Busy, Happy Nation" ran the headline in the *Washington Post* a few years later over a review of one of his books.

In the Soviet Union and on reporting trips elsewhere, Fischer artfully cultivated politicians in his fluent Russian, French, or German. By sharing news and gossip, he was able to fill his black leather notebooks with comments from them that lent his articles the air of being inside the great game of global politics. He yearned to be an influential figure on that stage himself and was forever giving advice to those who were. "The Prime Minister . . . looked at me and measured his words," he wrote in one of many similar passages in his memoirs. "'. . . I am glad you have spoken frankly with me. . . . If you have more criticism write me again, or come see me.'" He proudly described how one prominent Soviet general summoned a stenographer to take notes on suggestions Fischer was giving him. Clearly those he interviewed sensed that the path to favorable coverage in Fischer's stories was enthusiastic listening.

Foreigners searching in the Soviet Union for a future that worked, in the journalist Lincoln Steffens's famous phrase, usually found it. Fischer was no exception. The Soviet secret police, he wrote in a 1935 book, "is not merely an intelligence service and militia. It is a vast industrial organization and a big educational institution" operating, among other things, the Dynamo Athletic Club of Moscow, to which it generously gave outsiders access. The camps it maintained across the country were efforts to reform criminals through healthy outdoor work. In the same book, he devoted a rapturous chapter to Bolshevo, a bucolic Potemkin-village penal colony near Moscow where hundreds of foreign visitors were shown how Soviet criminals were generously provided with sports facilities, a movie theater, an art studio, and courses of study. The inmates were treated so well, Fischer wrote, that "many of them have told me that they love the place too much to give it up."

Friendships form quickly among compatriots in a foreign country, and on tennis courts a few blocks north of the Kremlin Fischer soon became a regular partner of the athletic young economist who had just arrived from Berkeley, Bob Merriman. This "smiling, shy, tall person," Fischer wrote, was "always eager to assure me, when he defeated me on the courts, that I really played better than he did."

In January 1935, when Bob and Marion had left California, it was the first time either of them had been east of Nevada. They crossed the United States by decrepit jitney, their fare reduced because Bob helped with the driving. Along the way were constant reminders of the millions of Americans hungry, homeless, and out of work: shuttered factories, long lines of people on sidewalks waiting to turn in job applications or collect bowls of soup. In Philadelphia and New York they saw men warming themselves around open fires in Hoovervilles. Then came a liner across the Atlantic with music to dance to every night, stops in London and Copenhagen, an icebreaker voyage to Helsinki, and finally the train to Moscow, capital of the promised land.

A Berkeley friend had given them an introduction to a Russian woman who edited a government newspaper for Soviet peasants. When she learned that Bob planned to write his doctoral dissertation on Soviet farming, she asked him to send her articles from his travels to collective farms around the country. Bob also studied Russian and took classes at Moscow's Institute of Economics, while Marion did secretarial work for British and American businessmen.

The handsome, likable young couple quickly became popular figures in the American expatriate community. Bob was appreciated for his skill at bridge and poker, and friends at the US embassy pumped him for information from his travels to places that were off limits to diplomats. As one consular official reported to Washington, Merriman's enthusiasm for the USSR was so great that he would "engage in conversation with visiting Americans with the purpose of persuading them to agitate for a change in American policies towards the Soviet Union. He even went so far as to make formal speeches to several groups of tourists"—probably those being shepherded by Louis Fischer.

Bob sent a stream of upbeat articles back to the *Pacific Weekly*, a small left-wing newspaper in California: Moscow had built 72 new schools and a subway system; the Soviet leadership had "greater real support from the people than any other government in the world"; rest homes for workers were spacious and clean; 99,000 new tractors and 25,000 new combines have "given the peasants greater improvements and opportunities than they had ever dreamed possible."

In reality, of course, what Soviet peasants had never dreamed possible was one of history's most catastrophic man-made famines. It had happened in the winter of 1932–33, two years before the Merrimans' arrival, and was sparked by the forced collectivization of agriculture. Better-off farmers saw their land confiscated and, under the eyes of troops with machine guns, were deported in freight cars to distant parts of the vast country. Other peasants were moved off their tiny individual plots and onto large collective farms—which the authorities were confident would rapidly increase the production of food for the nation's fast-growing cities. They didn't. Peasants slaughtered and ate more than 70 million cattle and sheep rather than see them go to the new collectives.

That winter and spring, starvation claimed at least five million lives. Snow drifted over the bodies of those who dropped from hunger on village streets or rural roads. As usually happens in famines, the birth rate plummeted too. When preliminary census returns later found 15 million fewer people in the Soviet Union than expected, Stalin ordered some census officials shot. The next round of statistics proved far brighter.

If Bob Merriman was aware of any of this, he gave no indication in anything he wrote; his only reference to the famine was a denunciation of "the deliberate lies" about Soviet hunger that appeared in the jingoistic Hearst newspapers. Famine survivors, like any Soviets with dark stories to tell, would have known that it was unsafe to say anything critical to a foreigner. If Merriman ever asked his friend Louis Fischer about the rumors of famine, the correspondent, judging from what he wrote on the subject, would have assured the young economist that they were wildly exaggerated, and that collectivization was the biggest step forward since Russia freed the serfs in 1861. That a star Berkeley graduate student should be so capable of ignoring a monumental human disaster in precisely the field he was studying may seem strange today. But many people then experienced the world in black and white: if you were outraged by the hunger, joblessness, and inequality of the West, then Russia had to be the shining path to a better way.

The Merrimans got a more jaundiced view from another new friend in Moscow, someone destined to share the next phase of their lives as well. Thirty-seven-year-old Milly Bennett had been born in San Francisco and at nineteen had gone to work as a newspaper reporter—something unusual for a woman in those years. She soon won attention for a series of articles about working as a maid: "'Milly' on New Job Overturns Bowl of Soup," "'Milly' in Berkeley Home Rebels at Cap," "'Milly' Quits." Another series chronicled jobs elsewhere: "Milly Bennett Gets Acquainted with Girls Working in Factory." Next came five years on a paper in Honolulu, a marriage and divorce, and several years as a journalist in China, then in the midst of revolutionary turmoil. In 1931, she began work in Russia as a reporter for the government's English-language *Moscow Daily News* and soon afterward married a Russian ballet dancer. Sassy and irreverent, she lost her job for a time when Soviet officials thought an article she wrote for a magazine back home had poked too much fun at the naïveté of American pilgrims to Moscow, but she managed to win it back.

"We got along from the first moment," recalled Marion Merriman, who, with Bennett's help, found work at the newspaper as a proofreader. Milly, she wrote, "was a homely woman, but . . . her shapely figure turned the head of many a man with a roving eye. . . . Her face reflected her travels, her features craggy and rough-hewn. She was regarded as 'one of the boys' in the newspaper office and at the cafe bars where the journalists, a crowd that included few women, gathered."

Despite her adventurous career, Bennett's letters from this time—largely bereft of capitals and usually on the newsprint paper that served reporters' manual typewriters—show her often yearning for something that seems out of reach. Sometimes it was domesticity:

writing to a friend who had just given birth, she asked timidly, "Did it hurt?" Sometimes what she found missing from her life was the grounding in Marxist theory the times seemed to require: "I'm attending classes in Leninism; and classes in dialectic materialism . . . i sat in a study group last night, trying to figure out a chapter of Engel's . . . and i want to say that only a small part of it, oh, a very small part, seem[s] to mean anything to me." And sometimes she merely yearned for a more secure position in journalism. While she was able to place an occasional magazine piece, rejection letters were more common, and what assignments she got from American newspapers seemed to come only when a regular correspondent needed extra help or was on vacation.

However marginal her perch in the world, Bennett made a strong impression. "Hair like a Hottentot, thick glasses, heavy features," wrote one newspaperman. Bennett, he said, could "cover any kind of story, fight with anybody who didn't have her radical notions, brave bullets, cuss you from hell to breakfast or captivate you with her gruff graciousness. She had a way of putting a man ill at ease by peering at him steadily through the wall-like lenses of her glasses and saying, 'I hate handsome men,' until he didn't know whether to be complimented or insulted."

The great shock of Bennett's Moscow life came when her Russian husband, Evgeni "Zhenya" Konstantinov, was arrested in her presence and thrown into a Siberian labor camp for the crime of homosexuality. Whether this trait of his took her by surprise, or whether the marriage was meant to give him cover, is unclear. In any event she seemed very attached to him, for in one 1934 letter she wrote, "i would grab tomorrow's boat [home], except for zhenya and his mother. and i am in love with my young husband. so what do i do. . . . i have just returned from a trip to the concentration camp to visit him—and that almost completely put me down." Although the marriage broke up, for years afterward she would send money to his family.

Such experiences left her with a more grim view of the country than Bob Merriman's, and according to Marion, "their arguments at the American embassy bar were legendary." Years later, Marion reconstructed one such conversation:

"'Jesus Christ, Bob,' Milly said in her peppery, usually profane way, 'how can you find any value in what you see out there with those peasants? Why, for Christ's sake, they aren't any better off now under these Soviets than they were under the tsars . . .'

"'Milly,' Bob responded with signs of exasperation, 'this country is in the middle of the most massive change of any country on earth right now. And, I'm telling you, I have seen the Russian peasants working their way into what is, without question, a new and improved life.'

"'Aw, bullshit,' Milly said, sipping her scotch whiskey. . . . 'I've been out there and seen 'em too, and so they have gotten rid of a few wooden plows and replaced 'em with steel, so what?'"

Bennett had come to the Soviet Union less as a pilgrim than as a wanderer. She still had some pilgrim in her, however, and even that visit to a prison camp—an almost unheard-of experience for a foreign journalist—seems not to have entirely eradicated it. Life under communism, she wrote to a friend, "can be bitter . . . and dark, past understanding. but the thing you have to do about Russia is what you do about any other 'faith.' you set your heart to know they are right . . . and then, when you see things that shudder your bones, you close your eyes and say . . . 'facts are not important.'"

For those who had faith, any hint of problems in the Soviet Union was easy to dismiss by looking at the other nations of Europe. When the Merrimans traveled west for a summer vacation in 1936, they saw men and women everywhere without jobs or enough to eat. In Vienna they found people fearful that Austria would soon be within Hitler's grip. They traced the scars that bullets and artillery shells had left on the walls of a famous model Socialist housing complex, the Karl Marx Hof, from attacks on it by right-wingers, police, and paramilitary forces two years earlier. Clearly, this was the scene of a class struggle more violent and bitter than the San Francisco waterfront strike.

Bob and Marion returned to Moscow sobered, feeling, as the

French writer André Malraux would soon say, that "Fascism has spread its great black wings over Europe." The Treaty of Versailles after the First World War had banned German military installations in the Rhineland, a slice of western Germany on either side of the Rhine River, but in 1936 Hitler brazenly violated the agreement, sending troops across the river and building military bases there. In response, the democracies issued only faint protests. Hitler had powerful admirers among the British elite and in North America as well: an obviously entranced Canadian Prime Minister W. L. Mackenzie King would pay a state visit to Berlin the following year and write in his diary that the Führer "will rank some day with Joan of Arc among the deliverers of his people." Whatever faults the Soviet Union might have, to the Merrimans, Louis Fischer, Milly Bennett, and millions of others, it seemed the only major nation taking a strong stand against the most dangerous development on the planet: fascism.

Even in the United States, proto-Fascist movements were flaunting their presence. Twenty thousand Americans of German descent joined the German-American Bund and went to summer camps for military drill in brown storm-trooper uniforms. The group staged mass rallies at Madison Square Garden and elsewhere modeled on those of the Nazis. The great majority of Italian-American newspapers and organizations were enthusiastic backers of Mussolini, and several hundred young Italian Americans sailed for the home country to volunteer for his army. In Atlanta alone, 20,000 whites joined the Order of the Black Shirts, also known as the American Fascisti, which terrorized people of color. Meanwhile, 16 million Americans, most of them non-Catholics, listened to the "radio priest" Father Charles E. Coughlin, a fist-shaking anti-Semitic orator with a voice of gold. "He could carry an audience, rub their emotions raw and juggle them at will," wrote one reporter who watched him address a huge crowd ringed by young male followers in uniforms and puttees. "His voice was a clear tenor with an operatic ring, there was a pent-up savagery in each of his sentences which he punctuated with his arm like the downward thrust of a stiletto." Although Coughlin had started off on the left, as the 1930s went on he found ever more to admire in Hitler and Mussolini, and attacked President Roosevelt for being in thrall to both Jewish Communists and Jewish bankers.

At a time when ominous forces seemed on the march on both sides of the Atlantic, people were unexpectedly cheered by one piece of good news. It came from Spain.

In February 1936, a coalition of liberal, Socialist, and Communist parties known as the Popular Front narrowly defeated lavishly financed right-wing opponents to win a majority in the country's parliament. Surprisingly, the scene of this unexpected triumph was the Western European nation closest to feudalism, for Spain's economy and distribution of wealth lagged far behind most of the Continent. Huge changes at last seemed possible in a country where the major powers were wealthy industrialists, big landowners with holdings sometimes larger than 75,000 acres, and the Catholic Church—whose bishops had warned congregations to vote for the right. "It has been many months," the *Nation* exulted in New York, "since Europe has furnished news as encouraging for democracy as are the results of the Spanish elections."

The bitter tensions that simmered throughout Europe in the 1920s and '30s had nowhere boiled over more than in Spain, with general strikes and peasant risings, hundreds of political killings by both left and right, bank robberies by revolutionaries and torture by the authorities, mass arrests, jailbreaks, and street fighting. Paramilitary forces and mounted police in dark cloaks beat starving farm laborers found with acorns stolen from pigs' troughs and clashed with rebellious urban workers. In the months after the election, strikes and turmoil continued, with several hundred people dying in political violence.

Now, with their election victory, members of the Popular Front cabinet, precariously riding a tiger, promised dramatic changes, while army officers seethed at the new government's plans to divert some of the military budget to programs for the poor. The stock market fell as emboldened leftists occupied factories and draped them with red or black banners. Too impatient to wait for legislation, landless peasants began to occupy some of the big estates and start to plow, and jubilant crowds burned churches (a feature of past popular uprisings) and wrecked the offices of right-wing newspapers. Without waiting for a formal amnesty decree, activists marched on jails to release thousands of political prisoners from the miners' revolt of 1934.

Louis Fischer visited Spain on a reporting trip soon after the election. "The reactionaries," a trade union leader told him, "can come back into office only through a coup d'état." To guard against that possibility, Fischer found, generals known for their far-right politics were being reassigned to remote posts in the provinces or colonies. General Francisco Franco, for example, the man who suppressed the 1934 miners' revolt, was removed as army chief of staff and assigned to command a military base in the Canary Islands off the coast of Africa, more than 800 miles from the Spanish mainland.

A large proportion of Spain's 24 million people lived on the land, but most had only tiny plots, and millions had none at all. Until a modest land reform program had begun a few years earlier, a mere 2 percent of Spaniards owned 65 percent of the land. Wanting to see the countryside, Fischer and another American correspondent set off on a 1,200-mile trip around Spain by car. What they found was a state of near war between peasants living in thatch-roofed shacks and estate owners determined to hold on to land that they feared the Popular Front government would take from them. Women with worn, leathery faces, kerchiefs, and long, ragged skirts tilled fields by hand as they had for centuries, bent-over men carried huge bundles of branches for firewood on their backs, and political divisions were stark. "As we drove along the highway and through villages, some people gave us the outstretched-arm Fascist salute.... Elsewhere adults and children greeted us with the clenched fist"—the sign of the Popular Front. Arriving at one political meeting where the scheduled speaker failed to show up, the unashamedly partisan Fischer took over the gathering and began questioning the audience of peasants. When he asked if any of them ate meat as often as once a week, not a single hand was raised. Then he inquired what would happen if right-wing forces tried to take away their newly acquired plots of land. "They will have to kill us first!" was the reply.

Outside Spain, however, fascism was on the march. In 1935, eager for territory to fit his dreams of a new imperial Rome, Benito Mussolini launched an invasion of Ethiopia. As one of the few parts of Africa that remained uncolonized, the territory appeared ripe for conquest. Backed up by tanks, bombers, and poison gas, nearly half a million Italian soldiers steadily gained ground against an ill-equipped Ethiopian army. Since the victims were Africans, in Europe and North America the reaction was muted, amounting to little more than disapproving newspaper editorials. Black Americans, however, felt strongly: some 3,000 people packed a Harlem church for a protest rally; black communities raised funds and sent bandages and supplies for a 75-bed field hospital. Several thousand men enlisted in a "Black Legion" of volunteers and began training to fight for embattled Ethiopia, although logistics and opposition from the US government would make this impossible. Several American cities saw street fighting between blacks and Italian Americans, and angry crowds in Harlem wrecked or boycotted shops and bars with Italian names.

By mid-1936 the Italian dictator's black-shirted troops controlled the entire territory, and the war was over. The civilian and military death toll, estimated at 275,000, was so high that it was said Mussolini wanted Ethiopia with or without Ethiopians. Despite an eloquent plea by the bearded, diminutive Emperor Haile Selassie, the major powers did nothing. "It is us today," the emperor told the Assembly of the League of Nations. "It will be you tomorrow."

3

"Those Who Do Not Think as We Do"

TOMORROW ARRIVED SOONER than anyone expected—and with shocking violence.

On July 17, 1936, the United Press office in London received a telegram from its bureau in Madrid that began: MOTHERS EVERLASTINGLY LINGERING ILLNESS LIKELY LARYNGITIS AUNT FLORA OUGHT RETURN EVEN IF GOES NORTH LATER EQUALLY GOOD IF ONLY NIGHT . . . The bizarre wording signaled that a correspondent was trying to evade suddenly imposed censorship. When his London colleagues strung together the first letter of each word, the message read: MELILLA FOREIGN LEGION REVOLTED MARTIAL LAW DECLARED.

Melilla was a city in the North African colony of Spanish Morocco. In a carefully coordinated uprising, hundreds of army officers commanding tens of thousands of troops were making a grab for power in that territory and in Spain itself. The nation was no stranger to military coups by an army notoriously top-heavy with generals, but this one was different, planned with unprecedented thoroughness, with orders discreetly dispatched across the country via a network of messengers in civilian clothes. The attempt to seize power would be carried out with a scorched-earth ferocity that Europeans had often wielded in colonial wars but that had seldom been seen in Europe itself since the Middle Ages. The code word signal to the officers to start the rising was "Covadonga"—the name of an eighth-century battle regarded as the beginning of the *Reconquista*, or reconquest of Spain from Muslims. The conspirators felt they had a similarly historic mission to reconquer the country from new rulers equally alien to them: the left-leaning government of the Popular Front.

In addition to Nazi Germany and Fascist Italy, many European countries, including Portugal, Poland, Greece, Lithuania, Romania, and Hungary, were under dictators, military rule, or regimes of the far right, most of them with a blatant streak of anti-Semitism. Spain, however, was a democracy, albeit a wobbly and imperfect one, born five years earlier with enormous hopes, at home and abroad, that the nation would at last join the modern age. An experiment with republican rule in the late nineteenth century had been short-lived. Only in 1931, amid street demonstrations and tumbled statues, had the king fled the country and centuries of monarchy and military strongmen been replaced by a Spanish Republic with an elected government, a new constitution, and the promise of far-reaching reform.

To the coterie of generals leading the new revolt, however, democracy itself was profoundly threatening and the victory of the Popular Front coalition in the latest election was anathema. They were convinced it would lead to a Spanish version of the Russian Revolution. The military rebels called themselves *Nacionales*, a term "rather stronger," the historian Paul Preston explains, "in its connotations of 'the only true Spaniards' than the usual English rendition of 'Nationalists.'"

Although not yet the revolt's leader, a key plotter was General Francisco Franco. A cautious man, he had waited to join the planning for the coup until it appeared certain of success. In part to compensate for his short stature (five feet four inches), unmilitary potbelly, double chin, and high-pitched voice, he had early on earned a reputation for cool mastery of detail and iron discipline, even when it meant ordering disobedient soldiers shot.

Franco was widely regarded as the army's most competent general. As the first director of the national military academy—which, to the army's rage, the Republican government had shut down—he was well known to hundreds of younger officers. Ambitious and puritanical, an architect of the elite Spanish Foreign Legion, he was driven by a fierce belief that he was destined to save Spain from a deadly conspiracy of Bolsheviks, Freemasons, and Jews (no matter that King Ferdinand and Queen Isabella had expelled the latter from their realm in 1492, during the Inquisition, and that few had ever returned). The Popular Front government's decision to dispatch him to the Canary Islands, and additional right-wing generals to other distant outposts, had been a disastrous mistake, for it merely allowed them to better conceal their plans for the uprising.

Most of the coup's organizers had already spent much of their military lives in the colonies; they were *Africanistas*, veterans of bloody fighting in the 1920s against defiant Berbers in the mountainous Rif region of Spanish Morocco. Some had even been born in the colonies to army families. They thought of themselves as tough and battle-tested guardians of traditional Spanish values against both colonial rebels and the corruptions of the modern world. "Without Africa," Franco declared, "I can hardly explain myself."

These officers brought the colonizer's mentality back to Spain: one prominent general contemptuously referred to impoverished Spanish peasants as "Rif tribesmen." During the more than ten years he spent in Morocco, Franco himself had once proudly returned from an expedition against guerrillas with 12 severed heads. Other *Africanistas* fighting Moroccan rebels sometimes used bombs and artillery shells filled with deadly mustard gas, purchased from Germany after the end of the First World War. As Franco and his fellow conspirators now embarked on an equally brutal campaign to seize control of Spain, the most professional force at their command was the Army of Africa, which included the notorious Foreign Legion. Despite its name, the legion was mostly made up of Spaniards, many of them criminals whose sentences had been commuted in return for enlisting.

The larger share of the Army of Africa were Arab or Berber recruits, or Moors—*moros*, as Spaniards called them. Muslims, they were led by Spanish officers who told them that they would be fighting against infidels and Jews who wanted to abolish Allah. They would go into battle, ironically, alongside monarchist Spanish militiamen in red berets whose war cry was *¡Viva Cristo Rey!* ("Long Live Christ the King!")

With the help of sympathizers in London, the coup's leaders hired a British airplane to secretly fly Franco from the Canaries to Spanish Morocco, where he took command of the Army of Africa. These more than 40,000 experienced troops were the plotters' strongest force, but they were stranded in Morocco. Plans to swiftly transport them to Spain, where they could be the decisive factor in sweeping the Nationalists into power, were derailed when sailors on many Spanish naval vessels refused to join the rebels, killed some of their officers, and remained loyal to the Republic. The coup plotters were dismayed, for in Spain itself their attempt to seize control was running into unexpected resistance, while their best troops were marooned on the other side of the Mediterranean. Few aircraft were available to fly them to Spain because most of the Republic's air force had refused to take part in the coup. What was to be done?

Franco promptly dispatched envoys to the two European leaders he was confident would help, Benito Mussolini and Adolf Hitler. The emissaries to Germany were received just after Hitler had attended a performance of Wagner's *Siegfried* at the opera festival in Bayreuth. The Führer was wearing his brown storm-trooper's uniform; the rest of his entourage, in evening dress, were kept waiting for their supper while he met with Franco's representatives. They gave him a handwritten letter and map from the general. After several hours' talk—much of it a monologue from Hitler, who was still annoyed that Spain had stayed neutral in the First World War—the dictator agreed to supply whatever Franco needed. He then summoned Air Marshal Hermann Göring and ordered him to send more planes than Franco had asked for.

Within a few days the first of them were on their way to Spanish Morocco, and soon they were ferrying Franco's troops, and before long the general himself, across the Strait of Gibraltar to Spain. In a bow to the opera the senior Nazis had just watched, in which the fearless Siegfried passes heroically through flames to wake Brünnhilde from a deep sleep, the dispatch of German transport planes would be called Operation Magic Fire. For Hitler, resentful of being disdained by the Western democracies since he had come to power three and a half years earlier, it was a delight to have another country's military ask for his aid.

Mussolini similarly agreed to help, eager to have himself, rather than Hitler, viewed as the Spanish Nationalists' primary benefactor. This would give him a chance to expand Italy's influence in the Mediterranean, which he sometimes referred to, echoing the Romans, as "our sea." He dispatched a squadron of a dozen trimotor Savoia-Marchetti bombers, with one of the Nationalist envoys hitching a ride home in a tail-gunner's turret.

Hitler sent more planes, however: 20 Junkers Ju-52s, three-engined workhorses nicknamed "Three Marías" by the Spanish, which doubled as bombers or transports, along with German pilots and mechanics. Although each aircraft's nominal capacity was 17 passengers, once its seats were removed up to 40 heavily tattooed Foreign Legionnaires or Moors in flowing robes and turbans or red fezzes could be packed in, crouching in rows on the floor, knees pulled up to their chests. Many Moors had never seen a plane before, much less traveled on one. In a matter of days, flights ferried 15,000 troops to Seville, the jumping-off point for a Nationalist drive to the north. It was history's first major military airlift. Without it, the coup might have been swiftly defeated.

High-ranking Nazis had crossed paths with the Spanish generals before the July uprising. Wilhelm Canaris, Hitler's Spanish-speaking military intelligence chief, knew and liked Franco, who had toured military installations in Germany some years before. General José Sanjurjo, a key figure in the conspiracy, had visited Berlin with a small retinue in early 1936, staying at the elegant Hotel Kaiserhof, but exactly what he did or whom he saw remains unknown. Though Hitler himself apparently did not know of the coup in advance, it would prove a marvelous opportunity for him.

Portugal, a right-wing dictatorship conveniently next door to Spain, would also offer help and provide the launching ground for another Nationalist offensive. Some 8,000 Portuguese volunteered for Franco's Foreign Legion, and their government let the Nationalists send convoys of troops and supplies from the port of Lisbon to the Spanish border, provided radios, munitions, and bases for Nationalist warplanes, and even handed over Republican refugees to be shot.

A shiver of terror ran through Spain, for the entire Nationalist campaign was designed to maximize bloodshed. In a foretaste of what Europe was to experience in years to come, commanders spoke of *limpieza*, or cleansing, as they ordered somber columns of captives in everyday clothes marched off with their hands in the air. Some firing squads operated at night, their victims lined up in the glare of car headlights. Trade union officials and Republican politicians, including 40 parliamentary deputies from the governing coalition, were bayoneted or shot, as were army officers who refused to take part in the conspiracy. For military dissenters, rank was no protection—seven generals and an admiral reluctant to join the coup were shot. Family ties were swept aside: when one officer would not allow the Nationalists to take over a military airfield, the order to execute him was approved by his first cousin and childhood playmate, General Franco.

If the targeting of those killed made no sense, as in Huesca, for example, where 100 supposed Freemasons were shot in a town where the order boasted less than a dozen members, it hardly mattered: the resulting panic still inspired fear. (Spanish Freemasons were in the plotters' sights because they had long been anticlerical.) Such massacres happened everywhere, whether the advancing Nationalist forces met resistance or not.

"It is necessary to spread terror," declared the *Africanista* General Emilio Mola, the coup's initial leader. "We have to create the impression of mastery [by] eliminating without scruples or hesitation all those who do not think as we do. . . . Anyone who helps or hides a Communist or a supporter of the Popular Front will be shot." Although Spanish Communists loomed large in right-wing propaganda, there were relatively few of them. Millions had supported the Popular Front, however. Mola's orders were put into effect with chilling thoroughness. In the northern province of Navarre, one out of every ten Popular Front voters was summarily executed. An elderly Navarre priest who protested the killings had his head chopped off. Liberal or left-wing newspapers were shut down. Workers who went on strike faced the death penalty. Sometimes the nature of the terror varied sadistically according to the victim. In Cordova, where an imprisoned Socialist parliamentary deputy was diabetic, Nationalist jailers force-fed him sugar until he died.

One of the best known of "those who do not think as we do" was the poet and playwright Federico García Lorca, who had declared, "I will always be on the side of those who have nothing," and who took his traveling theater company to the poorest of rural villages. He was shot in his hometown of Granada, along with an eventual total of some 5,000 others in that city alone. Overwhelmed by the mass of corpses, the caretaker of the local cemetery suffered a mental collapse and had to be committed to an asylum.

If you had taken part in any movement that wasn't purely Spanish, whether it was vegetarianism, learning Esperanto, teaching in a Montessori school, or joining a Rotary club, you were immediately suspect. Just wearing a red necktie could be considered a sign of Communist leanings and cause for arrest. In León, one man was denounced by an informer for having attended a lecture on Darwin's theory of evolution and asked questions that sounded knowledgeable; he was shot. In Mérida, a Nationalist officer identified targets for arrest by repeatedly walking one of his prisoners, a Republican doctor, around town and making note of who greeted him. Then he shot the doctor.

Within several weeks of the uprising, the Nationalists, aided by a generous flow of German and Italian arms and ammunition, had seized control of roughly one third of Spain, mainly in the country's south and west. Their killings mounted into the tens of thousands, far outstripping anything Hitler or Mussolini had done when they took power. As gruesome warnings, bodies of slaughtered Republicans were left on streets, in plazas, and at crossroads. As would soon be clear, however, by no means was all of the killing done by the Nationalist rebels. Centuries of pent-up social tensions had erupted in a murderous fury.

Like millions of other people around the world, Bob and Marion Merriman were horrified at the news of Spain's military coup and of one town after another falling to the Nationalists. At the *Moscow Daily News,* where she was reading proofs, employees contributed to a food relief fund for civilians in the Spanish Republic. Bob chafed that there seemed little more they could do. Their friend Louis Fischer, however, soon set off on a trip to Republican-held Spain. For journalists like him, the war had quickly become the biggest story on the Continent, and two months after the uprising began, he found himself plunged into reporting a struggle more "rich, thrilling and interesting" than he had ever known, in Russia or anywhere else. When he landed in Barcelona, he found workers with rifles slung on their backs running the airport; in Valencia, his next stop, people laughed when he asked for the bill at the airport canteen: for foreign comrades the food was free. He traveled onward by train to Madrid, passing a large gasoline storage tank belching black smoke after an air raid by German planes.

Despite such damage, Fischer, writing for the *Nation* and an assortment of European and American dailies, was encouraged by much that he saw. Although its fighter aircraft were obsolete biplanes, the Republican air force mounted raids on rebel strongholds, and the French novelist André Malraux organized a squadron of volunteer pilots from other countries. The plans of the coup plotters to instantly seize power throughout Spain had been stymied, and a long war would raise supply problems they had not stopped to consider. Where, for example, would the Nationalists get the oil to fuel their armies? Their allies Hitler and Mussolini were oil importers, not exporters.

Fischer stepped out of his reportorial role even more than usual to bombard politicians with advice. He wrote a long letter to the Republic's prime minister: Why not stop all civilian construction and build an impregnable defense line 30 kilometers outside Madrid? Why not form partisan units to fight behind enemy lines? When he saw the foreign minister, he suggested that since the Nationalists held Spanish Morocco, the Republic "could proclaim its independence. That would make trouble for Franco among the Moors." He also poured out a steady stream of suggestions to the Soviet ambassador, who, probably to get Fischer off his back, finally replied, "Write me a memo. I'll send it to Moscow."

Despite such encounters, Fischer's diary reveals a man far different from the self-important correspondent he had been in the Soviet Union. In Spain, he was moved by the spectacle of a bountiful idealism, by a fervor that was not the product of propaganda, and by people who were risking their lives to save the country's infant democracy. He also tasted the experience of combat for the first time when he covered an event making headlines all over the world: the siege of the Alcázar. In this fourteenth-century fortress in Toledo, Nationalist rebels had been holding out for two months against surrounding Republican forces.

Although the battle would end with a much-trumpeted victory for Franco, as a column of his troops fought its way into the fortress and relieved the 68-day siege, for Fischer it was a heady baptism of fire. Riding on the back of a tank in his tennis shoes, he accompanied Republican forces trying to capture the Alcázar. "I understood then how soldiers go over the top with zest and animal passion. There is something exhilarating in the combination of danger and muscular exertion." In the middle of a firefight, the air filled with smoke and bullets, he joined two soldiers in carrying a bleeding comrade to a stretcher, and later helped move the man onto the operating table at a first-aid station. "Over his heart the wet red patch grew bigger and bigger. . . . [He] moaned for water. There was none available. Part of

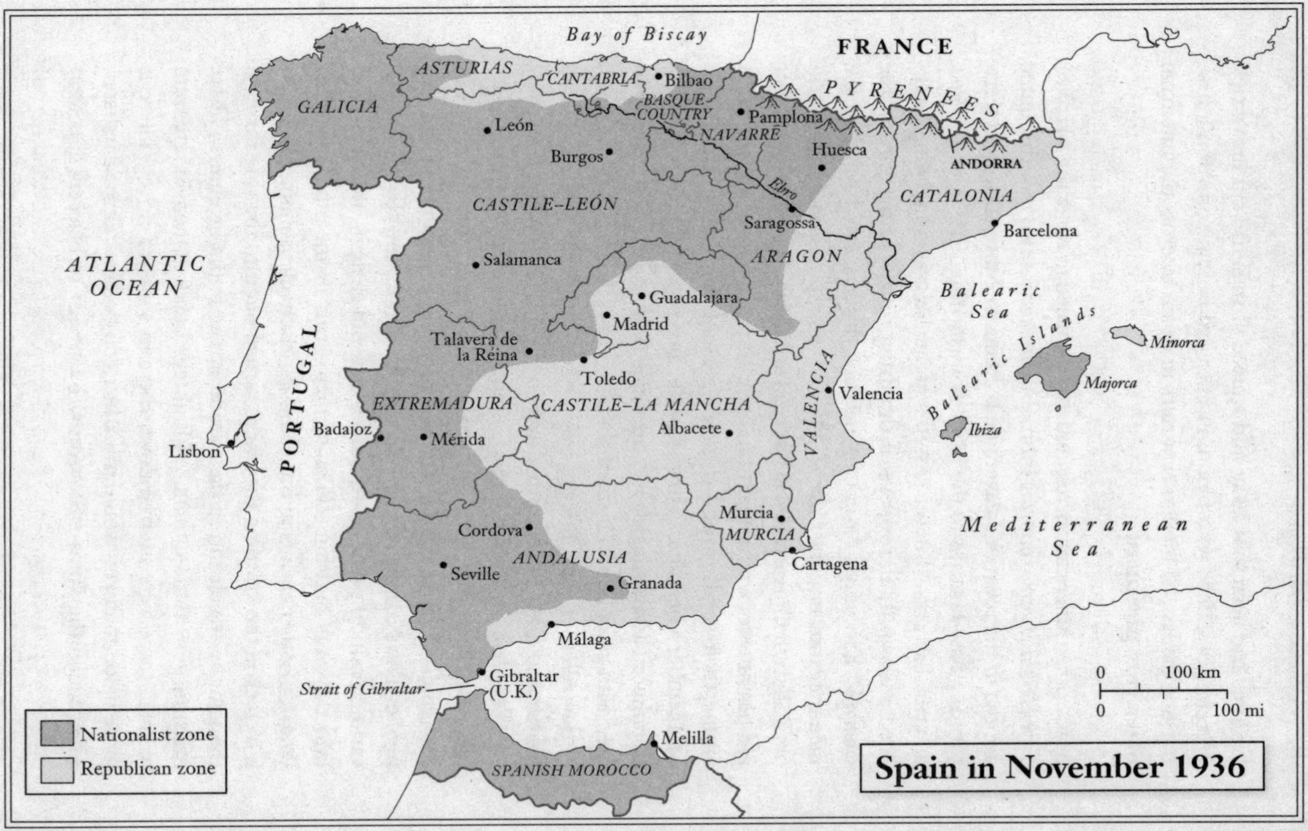

Spain in November 1936
Nationalist zone
Republican zone
Bay of Biscay
FRANCE
PYRENEES
ATLANTIC OCEAN
PORTUGAL
GALICIA
ASTURIAS
CANTABRIA
BASQUE COUNTRY
NAVARRE
CASTILE–LEÓN
ARAGON
CATALONIA
ANDORRA
EXTREMADURA
CASTILE–LA MANCHA
VALENCIA
MURCIA
ANDALUSIA
SPANISH MOROCCO
Balearic Sea
Balearic Islands
Mediterranean Sea
Minorca
Majorca
Ibiza
Bilbao
Pamplona
Huesca
León
Burgos
Ebro
Saragossa
Barcelona
Salamanca
Guadalajara
Madrid
Talavera de la Reina
Toledo
Valencia
Badajoz
Mérida
Albacete
Lisbon
Murcia
Cartagena
Cordova
Seville
Granada
Málaga
Gibraltar (U.K.)
Strait of Gibraltar
Melilla
0 100 km
0 100 mi

his knee had been shot away, and a piece of steel had cut into a rib." His clothes stained with blood, Fischer had become one of the first, but not the last, of foreign reporters in Spain to cross the line from observer to participant.

Many other American correspondents hastened to cover the war. *New York Herald Tribune* reporter John T. Whitaker for two months rented a room in the town of Talavera de la Reina in Nationalist-held territory as a base for trips to the front. It was within earshot of a *cuartel*, an army barracks. "I never passed a night there without being awakened at dawn by the volleys of the firing squads in the yard of the *Cuartel*." Executions "averaged perhaps thirty a day. I watched the men they took into the *Cuartel*. They were simple peasants and workers." Signs of more executions were everywhere. "You could find four old peasant women heaped in a ditch; thirty and forty militiamen at a time, their hands roped behind them, shot down at the crossroads. I remember a bundle in a town square. Two youthful members of the Republican assault guards had been tied back to back with wire, covered with gasoline and burned alive."

Jay Allen of the *Chicago Daily Tribune* reported that a Moorish soldier had tried to sell him a human ear for one peseta. The story by Allen that attracted the most attention, however, was from Badajoz, near the border with Portugal and in a province where tens of thousands of farmworkers had occupied big estates under the Republic. The Nationalists now seized the region, and Republicans of various political parties, both militiamen and civilians, were marched into the city's bullring. "Files of men, arms in the air. They were young, mostly peasants in blue blouses, mechanics in jumpers. . . . At 4 o'clock in the morning they were turned out into the ring through the gate by which the initial parade of the bullfight enters. There machine guns awaited them. . . . Eighteen hundred men—there were women, too—were mowed down there in some 12 hours. There is more blood than you would think in 1,800 bodies." Three days later, Allen found the arena still covered by a layer of blackened, coagulated blood several inches thick. The Spanish war laid bare political divisions everywhere: Allen's coverage of the atrocities in Badajoz so angered the archconservative owner of the *Tribune*, Colonel Robert McCormick, that he was fired.

In talking to foreign journalists, the Nationalists maintained no veneer of public relations. "Of course we shot them," the commanding general at Badajoz told John T. Whitaker. "What do you expect? Was I supposed to take 4000 reds with me as my column advanced, racing against time?" Whitaker heard more of the same from Captain Gonzalo de Aguilera y Munro, Count of Alba de Yeltes, a press officer with a handlebar mustache. "You know what's wrong with Spain?" he told the American reporter. "Modern plumbing! In healthier times—I mean healthier times spiritually, you understand—plague and pestilence could be counted on to thin down the Spanish masses. . . . Now with modern sewage disposal and the like they multiply too fast. The masses are no better than animals, you understand, and you can't expect them not to become infected with the virus of bolshevism. After all, rats and lice carry the plague." The count, a cavalryman and an ardent polo player, claimed that when the coup began, he lined up the workers on his estate and shot half a dozen of them just to show who was boss.

It was clear which classes backed the military rebellion. As Nationalist soldiers swore fealty to their cause by kissing the Spanish flag, they were blessed by bishops and cheered by elegantly dressed women in black lace mantillas. At another mass execution near Badajoz in front of a large crowd of spectators, a band played and a priest said Mass before the shots rang out. "Sons of landowners," writes the historian Antony Beevor, "organized peasant hunts on horseback. This sort of activity was jokingly referred to as the '*reforma agraria*' whereby the landless *bracero* was finally to get a piece of ground for himself."

Ten weeks into the coup, with several potential rivals out of the way—one popular right-wing politician had been assassinated by leftists before the rising, another was in a Republican prison, and General

Sanjurjo, slated to lead the march on Madrid, was killed in an airplane crash—the forty-three-year-old Franco became the revolt's supreme leader. His diminutive, unprepossessing figure belied a boundless ambition and a quiet bureaucratic skill at outmaneuvering competitors. With a uniform bedecked with gold tassels, he took on the title of Generalissimo of the Nationalist armed forces, and then, at an elaborate ceremony whose guests included diplomats from Germany, Italy, and Portugal, head of state. (This startled several fellow generals, who thought they had merely elected him head of government—in most European countries these are separate positions.) His tightly controlled propaganda apparatus began referring to him as "Caudillo [Leader] by the grace of God." Later, he would also name himself Captain-General, a rank previously held only by Spain's monarchs. Throughout the Nationalist hierarchy, everyone flaunted symbols of rank and status: Franco himself donned a broad scarlet-and-gold sash on special occasions; officers of the General Staff wore one of blue and gold; and one senior general, a tough *Africanista* named José Varela, even kept his military medals pinned to the dressing gown he wore over his pajamas.

Delighted at the recognition of his regime by the Fascist powers, Franco declared extravagantly, "This moment marks the peak of the life of the world." With these allies, the Generalissimo had an inside track. Hitler would deal only with him, something that allowed him to direct the flow of weapons and ammunition from abroad, doling them out to other generals as he wished. Along with the command of the crucial Army of Africa, this had enabled him to swiftly elbow aside all the others. The only possible remaining rival, General Mola, the rising's original leader, would, fortuitously for Franco, be killed in another air crash the following year.

As with many fundamentalist movements, the Nationalists were fiercely determined to keep women in their place. They forbade women to wear trousers. Skirts and sleeves had to be long. Schooling, which had become secular under the Republic, was handed back to the Church, where, for girls, it was strong on sewing and religion.

Coeducation was banned; one prominent Nationalist believed it to be a Jewish plot. Toward female supporters of the Republic, Nationalist ferocity knew no bounds. General Gonzalo Queipo de Llano, commander in the south, another Africa veteran with a fondness for dress uniforms, medals, and mounted escorts, in radio broadcasts repeatedly promised his Moorish troops the women of Madrid: "Kicking their legs about and struggling won't save them." From a maternity hospital in Toledo, 20 pregnant women deemed Republican sympathizers were taken to a local cemetery and shot. Near Seville, Nationalist soldiers raped and shot a truckload of women prisoners, threw their bodies down a well, and then paraded through a nearby town, their rifles draped with the murdered women's underwear.

Whitaker of the *Herald Tribune* was with Nationalist troops at a crossroads on the highway to Madrid when two teenage girls were brought before a major. Their only crime: one, a textile factory worker, was carrying a union card. After interrogating them, the major "had them taken into a small schoolhouse where some forty Moorish soldiers were resting. As they reached the doorway an ululating cry rose from the Moors within. I stood horrified in helpless anger." When Whitaker protested, the major replied, "Oh, they'll not live more than four hours."

Rapes like this were standard procedure, and playing on centuries of racial feeling that was shared across the political spectrum, Nationalist officers deliberately compounded the terror by choosing Moorish troops to do the raping. To Noel Monks of the British *Daily Express*, Nationalist soldiers bragged of what they'd done with women they captured. "But they weren't *atrocities.* Oh no, señor. Not even the locking up of a captured militia girl in a room with twenty Moors. No, señor. That was fun."

"The wisdom of this policy was debated by Spanish officers in a half-dozen messes where I ate with them," wrote Whitaker. "No officer ever denied that it was a Franco policy. But some argued that even a Red woman was Spanish and a woman." Such reasoning did not prevail. Advancing Nationalist troops scrawled on walls: "Your women will give birth to Fascists." Beyond the rapes, in town after town, women whose only crime was to be supporters of Popular Front parties had their heads shaved. In a practice borrowed from Italian Fascists, they were then force-fed castor oil (a powerful laxative) and paraded through the streets, sometimes naked or half naked, to be jeered as they soiled themselves.

In mobilizing to resist the revolt, Spain's government moved with agonizing slowness, badly hobbled by tensions within the Popular Front coalition. A majority of army officers had thrown in their lot with the Nationalists, and this left the Republicans with a mixture of loyal soldiers and ill-trained militia units that left-wing political parties and labor unions had begun forming in the previous few years. Most militiamen had no uniforms, almost none had boots, and their mismatched array of headgear—garrison caps, berets, hats with brims or tassels, First World War–surplus helmets—seemed to symbolize both Republican ardor and disorganization.

In addition, given the country's long history of labor unrest, many government officials were at first uneasy about arming the militias. Once they finally decided to do so, 60,000 of the 65,000 rifles the Ministry of War handed out to trade unionists in Madrid couldn't be fired because they lacked bolts. Long fearful of workers raiding armories, the authorities had stored the bolts elsewhere—in barracks that were now occupied by the Nationalists. When militiamen managed to find three artillery pieces with which to attack the barracks, they had to be drawn into position by a beer truck.

The news from Spain, however, was not entirely grim. Despite Nationalist hopes of a quick coup, fierce popular resistance in the first several months of fighting kept in Republican hands an irregularly shaped territory comprising a little more than half of the country. And this included the three biggest cities, Madrid, Barcelona, and Valencia. Louis Fischer was moved to find the capital's defenses largely in the hands of impromptu militias. One day he stumbled onto a battalion of athletes: bullfighters, boxers (the ring name of one was Tarzan), a skier, the nation's 5,000-meter track champion, and a whole soccer team. And 1,300 barbers joined a unit that took its name—Batallón de los Figaros—from the chief character of the opera *The Barber of Seville.*

Spain's Communist Party was small, but its tight top-down discipline quickly won its militia regiment a reputation as the most effective of such forces. Anarchist militias grew to an estimated 100,000 men, and some women, their ranks strengthening as several thousand foreign sympathizers, including a few Americans, made their way to Spain to join them. Workers came to the defense of the Republic in other ways as well. When fighting disrupted the national telephone system, for instance, Socialist railwaymen used the rail network's telephone lines to gather information on Franco's troop movements. The main force resisting the Nationalists in the early months of the war was not a professional army, but citizens who had managed to arm themselves.

And they did more than that. Throughout Republican Spain, workers took over hundreds of factories, promptly converting some to make urgently needed munitions. One plant that had manufactured lipstick cases began turning out cartridges. Banners appeared—THE LAND IS YOURS, WORKERS—and peasants divided up the vast estates they had worked as farm hands. Word of such events thrilled radicals abroad. Wasn't this what they had long dreamed of: the people at last seizing the means of production? Except for the short-lived Paris Commune, little like it had ever happened in Western Europe. Nor was this a revolution orchestrated by a single party that monopolized all power, as in Russia, but one being made from the bottom up. The conflict in Spain, remarkably, was at the same time both a right-wing military coup and a left-wing social revolution.

Among the millions of people riveted by such news were a young American couple who, in a striking parallel to Bob and Marion Merriman, were also a university economics instructor and his wife. Lois and Charles Orr were in Europe on their honeymoon. Five feet six inches tall, Lois had light brown hair and spoke with a Kentucky drawl. A sophomore at her hometown University of Louisville, she had met Charles, who was a decade older, at a political meeting on campus, and earlier in the year she had married him.

Lois's father was a building contractor. She credited her mother, who subscribed to the liberal *New Republic*, with giving her a sense of social justice. Both Lois and Charles were supporters of the Socialist Party. Like so many others in the Depression years, American Socialists were convinced that the existing economic system had failed. The new society they believed in, however, would be built democratically and not, like the Soviet Union, through dictatorship. It was with such eyes that the newlyweds embarked to see the world. After a stay in Europe for a firsthand look at the Nazi menace, they planned to travel on to India to study the effects of colonialism. In the photograph of the two of them in their joint passport, Lois wears a floral-print blouse and Charles a jacket and tie. Both gaze at the camera with great solemnity, as if to say that their wedding journey was serious business.

While visiting Germany and France, the Orrs followed events in Spain with increasing fascination. At the center of the Spanish social revolution were anarchists, adherents of a creed that thrived in Spain as nowhere else in the world. The anarchists believed in *comunismo libertario*, libertarian or stateless communism. The police, courts, money, taxes, political parties, the Catholic Church, and private property would all be done away with. Communities and workplaces would be run directly by the people in them, free at last to exercise a natural human instinct for mutual aid that, anarchists fervently believed, exists in us all. This was not exactly the Socialist utopia the Orrs had imagined, but it seemed excitingly close in spirit.

Anarchism was really a preindustrial ideology, and exactly how its vision was to be realized in a complex modern economy remained hazy at best. Still, it was a dream that inspired millions of Spaniards, and anarchists were rapidly putting their ideas into practice. They had, for example, a deep hatred of prisons, where many of them had been confined, and in a number of cities they now controlled anarchists had thrown open the prison gates, releasing both political prisoners and common criminals. In an echo of the French revolutionary attack on the Bastille, a particularly notorious prison in Barcelona was triumphantly demolished. Several hundred former inmates of one penitentiary even served in an anarchist militia unit known as the Iron Column—proof, it seemed, that thoroughgoing revolution could leave human beings transformed.

The most tantalizing reports that Charles and Lois Orr heard came from Catalonia, in Spain's northeast, particularly its major city, Barcelona. The great Liceu opera house—one of Europe's largest—had been turned into a people's theater; political murals several stories high covered the outsides of buildings; pawnshops were forced to give objects back to their poorer customers. Mansions confiscated from the wealthy had been converted into housing for the homeless; factories were starting literacy classes; and unionized cooks and waiters at the restaurant of the city's Hotel Ritz, with its elaborate chandeliers, white linen, and monogrammed china, had pushed the tables together into long rows and turned it into a people's cafeteria for working-class families and the city's poor.

Hearing of such doings was not enough. In September 1936, the Orrs, then in France, suspended the rest of their honeymoon plans and began hitchhiking to Barcelona, the epicenter of what people like them were jubilantly calling the Spanish Revolution. It was Lois, the more adventurous of the two, who insisted they make the journey. She was nineteen years old.

As news of the civil war flashed around the globe, the Spanish Republic pleaded for help. Members of trade union or party militias, marching off to battle with rifles, blanket rolls, and the flimsiest of shoes, sleeves rolled up in the summer heat, might be wildly cheered by crowds offering clenched-fist salutes, but they had almost no training, no heavy weapons, and no concept of how to maneuver in the field against an experienced army. One column of men left Barcelona for the front only to send back a messenger several hours later to say that they had forgotten to bring any food.

It was not for aid that the government begged so urgently, but for the right to buy arms. It could afford to do so, for Spain's treasury possessed the world's fourth-largest gold reserves and these were still in Republican hands. While the other major nations of Europe had gone deep into debt and privation to fight the First World War, neutral Spain had enjoyed an export boom. It sold food, clothing, military equipment, and more to both sides, traded profitably with the rest of the world in a way the warring countries could not, and tripled its gold supply. In 1936, the Spanish Republic had 635 tons of gold backing its national currency, worth more than $12 billion in purchasing power today.

Surely, the Republic's leaders hoped, democracies like the United States, Britain, and France would be willing to sell weapons to an elected government trying to defeat a military uprising fueled by Nazi arms. France was also under a liberal-left Popular Front government and, already bordered by Italy and Germany, would certainly not want yet another such state next door. The Republic's prime minister, José Giral, rushed off a telegram to his French counterpart: SURPRISED BY DANGEROUS MILITARY COUP STOP BEG YOU TO HELP US IMMEDIATELY WITH ARMS AND AEROPLANES STOP FRATERNALLY YOURS GIRAL. At rallies in Paris, thousands of French leftists chanted, "*Des avions pour l'Espagne!*"

The French right was powerful, however, and some of the country's senior generals quietly favored Franco. Even without the Spanish war to complicate matters, France was bitterly divided, riven by strikes, with political passions so high that fistfights erupted in the national legislature while crowds battled outside. One outburst of Paris street fighting had left a ministry building on fire, some 2,000 people injured, and 15 dead. Under fierce attack by right-wing newspapers and worried about a civil war of its own, the French cabinet was reluctant to intervene in someone else's. It allowed the Spanish Republic to buy small quantities of munitions, including several dozen unarmed or obsolete military aircraft, some of them at grossly marked-up prices, but, for the time being, no more.

Britain had even less interest in helping. The British companies that mined much of Spain's copper, sulfur, and iron had tangled badly with the Republic's militant labor unions and were far more comfortable with the prospect of Franco. Right-wing British military officers went out of their way to be helpful to Franco's forces. The commander of the British fortress at Gibraltar, bordering Spain, let the Nationalists use his communications equipment to stay in touch with their allies in Rome, Lisbon, and Berlin. At one point he apparently supplied them with ammunition. Much of the British elite considered the Spanish Republic to be little better than the USSR: "If there is somewhere where fascists and bolsheviks can kill each other off," said Prime Minister Stanley Baldwin, "so much the better."

The only country to swiftly offer Spain aid was distant, impoverished Mexico, whose left-wing regime sent a gift of 20,000 rifles, ammunition, and food. (The Republic insisted on paying, but Mexican President Lázaro Cárdenas would only accept a sum considerably less than the arms' true value.) The rifles proved crucial, arriving six weeks into the fighting, at a point when the Republic had only one working firearm for every three soldiers.

The enormous economic might and modern aircraft industry of the United States made it the most promising source of desperately needed weapons. But some Americans were horrified that the Republic had distributed arms to labor union militias. What a precedent! Secretary of State Cordell Hull warned President Roosevelt that this move would lead to "mob rule and anarchy." Washington's ties with Spain were weak, and for the moment Roosevelt was far more concerned about battling the ravages of the Great Depression at home. Acutely aware that voters felt this way too, two weeks after the Spanish war began he gave a speech promising to keep the United States clear of the kind of carnage he had witnessed touring the front as assistant secretary of the navy during the First World War: "I have seen war on land and sea. I have seen blood running from the wounded. . . . I have seen the dead in the mud. . . . I shall pass unnumbered hours thinking and planning how war may be kept from this Nation."

Instead, he called for a global "moral embargo" on arms sales to either side. FDR's ambassador to Spain was a longtime friend, the loquacious Indiana journalist and popular history writer Claude Bowers, an eccentric who, as Louis Fischer described him, "first ate half of his cigar and then lit and smoked what remained of it." When Bowers began besieging Roosevelt with long missives banged out with two fingers on a typewriter and filled with haphazard spelling ("propoganda," "facists," "socilolist") which urged him to help the Republic, the president replied noncommittally, "Do write me some more marvelous letters like that last one." FDR faced his first reelection campaign in November 1936. Perhaps after that, supporters of the Republic hoped, he would feel freer to act on the deep-seated antipathy he clearly felt toward fascism.

For now, however, despite its ready supply of gold, the Republic found the doors of the United States, France, and Britain closed, as well as those of smaller countries under their influence. And so, in the fall of 1936, as more patches of territory fell under Franco's control—on newspaper maps it looked as if a Nationalist inkblot were closing in on Madrid from several sides—the embattled Republican government faced an extraordinary paradox. The only major nation willing to sell it arms and ammunition was not another democracy. It was Joseph Stalin's Soviet Union.

Although reporting almost nothing about the anarchist-led revolution in Catalonia that so inspired people like Lois and Charles Orr, the Soviet press devoted much space to the war. In the Communist Party's *Pravda*, news of the fighting sometimes filled a full page out of the paper's six. Rumors reached the Merrimans that volunteers were heading to Spain to fight for the Republic, and Bob began to talk of joining them. Marion was dismayed, not just at the prospect of danger and separation, but because in a Moscow notoriously short of housing they at last had a decent place to live: an American businessman friend had loaned them his spacious penthouse while he and his family went on a long home leave.

As Bob and Marion argued about whether he should go to Spain, the Kremlin leadership debated what to do about the Republic's ever more urgent pleas to buy arms. Stalin faced a dilemma. A Spain under Franco would be an ally for Hitler, who had started rearming and made no secret of his desire to expand his country's power to the east, clearly threatening the USSR. Furthermore, if the Soviet Union failed to help Republican Spain, that would make a mockery of its claim to be the leader of the progressive forces of the world—and just at a moment when Stalin felt himself in deadly competition for that role with his archenemy Leon Trotsky, the great Communist heretic he had exiled from Russia. On the other hand, if the Soviet dictator appeared to support the far-reaching social revolution emerging in Catalonia and other parts of the Republic, it would horrify Britain and France, the allies he would need in case of war with Germany. It was obviously in the Soviet interest to help the Republic survive, but, as Stalin put it in a letter to the Spanish prime minister, to "prevent the enemies of Spain from regarding her as a Communist republic." That would prove a delicate balancing act.

Treading this tightrope, Stalin carefully orchestrated public shows of support for the Republic, gathering more than 100,000 Muscovites in Red Square for one solidarity demonstration, while he delayed selling it arms. To satisfy the British and French, the Soviet Union joined them and two dozen other countries in signing a formal agreement not to give or sell military supplies to either side in Spain. Despite the diplomats who arrived in their bowlers and fedoras for long, solemn meetings of a Non-Intervention Committee in London, the agreement, which included Germany and Italy among its signatories, was a sham. The cynical German foreign minister, Joachim von Ribbentrop, joked that the body should be renamed the Intervention Committee. But participating allowed various governments to claim that they were working to prevent another continent-wide war. The Non-Intervention Committee was a diplomatic backwater, and at least one member seemed to have other matters on his mind. Baron Erik Palmstierna, the Swedish representative, was busy composing a book, *Horizons of Immortality*, that featured conversations with "messengers from the other world."

British Prime Minister Baldwin also had his mind elsewhere. "I hope," he told Foreign Secretary Anthony Eden soon after the Spanish war began, "that you will try not to trouble me too much with foreign affairs just now." Far more worrisome to him were newspaper headlines about the shocking romance between King Edward VIII and the svelte American socialite Wallis Simpson, who had already divorced one husband and seemed to be separating from a second.

Meanwhile, Hitler's support for Franco only grew. The Germans, like the Italians, were very happy at gaining an ally and at the opportunity for their military to have battle experience in preparation for a future European war. When that war came—and Hitler was already dreaming of the day—having a friendly regime in power in Spain would also provide the Nazis with the prospect of something they now lacked: U-boat bases on the Atlantic coast.

In sending Franco arms, however, Hitler bargained harder than Mussolini; for him Nationalist Spain was also a crucial source of raw materials. He demanded payment for his aid in copper, in iron ore, which Germany was acutely short of, and in pyrites, which yield sulfur and other minerals. These were supplies he wanted for building up his armed forces, the Wehrmacht. The very first ship from Germany to carry mechanics and parts for the planes airlifting Franco's troops from Africa returned home with a cargo of copper ore. In the nearly three years of warfare to come, Hitler and Mussolini would provide Franco with an immense amount of military help, some of it on credit but much of that from Germany paid for with Spanish minerals. It is hard to put a precise price tag on the value of these arms, because on the open market no one can easily find, for instance, 100 of the most modern fighter planes with highly trained pilots. A recent authoritative study by the Spanish scholar Ángel Viñas puts the value of German and Italian aid to Franco at between $432 and $692 million in currency of the time. Depending on how it is calculated, that would be the equivalent of $7 billion to more than $11 billion in today's dollars. One hundred seventy shiploads of supplies came from Germany alone, with still more arms transported in four cargo flights every week.

Seeing Germany and Italy jumping into the fray, Stalin waited in vain for Britain or France to provide weapons to the Republic. This did not happen. Several months after the coup, he finally dispatched the first shiploads of Soviet arms to Spain. Little was said about what he expected in return. But at last one of the world's great military powers was sending help. Across the political spectrum of the Republic, people hoped that they would now have the tools to win the war.

By autumn the Soviet Union was not just quietly selling the Republic arms, but also sending military advisors, pilots, and tank crews. Eager to make use of the tremendous sympathy for the Republic among leftists throughout the world, the Communist International, or Comintern, through which Stalin controlled Communist parties in other countries, passed the word to begin recruiting special brigades of volunteers to help fight Franco. This was the news that men like Bob Merriman were waiting for. Some foreign supporters of the Republic, however, had not waited for anyone's orders. They had already arrived in Spain.

4

A New Heaven and Earth

"THE FAIR, RED-CHEEKED Gallic customs officer touched the brim of his blue cap and raised the white road barrier as we left France," wrote Lois Orr. It was September 15, 1936, a rainy morning two months after the start of the Nationalist uprising. The two American honeymooners, the youthful Lois and her older, taller, bespectacled husband, walked across the border and into the most revolutionary corner of Spain. "We found ourselves surrounded by a crowd of dark, unshaven militiamen in wrinkled blue coveralls, with red and black neck scarves. . . . Each anarchist had a heavy black rifle on his shoulder and a pistol at his belt. . . . 'Why have you come to Spain? . . . What are these German visas? How do we know you aren't Nazi spies?'"

A letter attesting to Charles Orr's membership in the Socialist Party of Kentucky was no help. In a car whose door was emblazoned CNT–FAI—for Confederación Nacional del Trabajo (the National Labor Confederation, of anarchist unions) and Federación Anarquista Ibérica (the Iberian Anarchist Federation)—the couple were driven away for further questioning. "Most of the young comrades of the Frontier Control Committee came along with us for the ride," Lois remembered. "Jammed together, rifles sticking out the windows, we tore off at top speed. The narrow road wound back and forth around hairpin turns, like the all-too-familiar roads in Harlan County, Kentucky. In the valleys far below us were wrecked cars bearing the red initials, CNT–FAI. Not an encouraging sight."

What Spanish they understood—Charles had lived in Mexico for a few months—was largely useless, for they were surrounded by speakers of Catalan, "a language," as Lois described it, "of hissed sibilants and clipped final x's and t's." After a long round of suspicious questions and an overnight stay in a flea-ridden inn, the two Americans thought they were free to go, only to find themselves arrested again and taken off in another car full of armed men to a new interrogation. Finally a local anarchist English teacher examined Lois's diary and assured her comrades that the Orrs were not Nazi spies.

Traveling onward to Barcelona, the couple were thrilled when they boarded a bus. "I held out my pesetas," Charles wrote, "to pay the fare. . . . The driver ostentatiously refused my filthy money. This bus, he proudly announced, was operated 'in the service of the people.'" On the next stage of the journey, by train, the Orrs were delighted to find that first and second class had been abolished; only the hard benches of third class remained.

When they reached Barcelona at last, a big banner at the railway station read WELCOME FOREIGN COMRADES. Anarchist flags—red and black, divided by a diagonal line—hung from balconies or ropes strung across streets. They also fluttered from small poles fastened to automobiles and were painted on every imaginable surface, Charles noted, from subway cars to shoeshine boxes. Everyone in the city seemed to be wearing party badges pinned to their shirts. Taxis and trolleys were repainted red and black, and the sides of street-cleaning trucks sported quotations from the nineteenth-century anarchist writer Mikhail Bakunin. Bunches of flowers or ribbons nailed to trees marked spots where, two months earlier, people had been killed in street fighting when Barcelona's workers prevented Nationalists in the local army garrison from taking over the city. Even a sidewalk barrel organ played the "Internationale."

The couple were awed by a city that seemed to be transforming itself. More than a quarter of Spain's population was illiterate, one of the highest percentages in Europe, but political posters in bold designs could be understood by all, a profusion of evening adult literacy classes were available for free, and new schools were opening everywhere. The number of children in Barcelona's schools would more than triple during the first year of revolution. Spanish women had long hoped for day care centers and kindergartens, and several of the city's newly collectivized textile factories were now installing them. On the Ramblas, a central boulevard with a wide pedestrian walkway lined with plane trees—"the only street in the world which I wish would never end," said García Lorca—hats had largely disappeared. "Pirates, buccaneers, princes, señoritos [young gentlemen], priests—these are the hatted folks of history," an anarchist newspaper proclaimed. "What has the free worker to do with this outworn symbol of bourgeois arrogance? . . . No hats, comrades, on the Ramblas and the future will be yours." (Not at all happy about this, however, was the anarchist hatters' union.)

Anarchist thinkers like Bakunin, who idealized Russian village society, had long found a ready audience in Catalonia. The anarchist hostility to government echoed Catalan resentment against Madrid's rule as well as the region's growing labor militancy. And the philosophy's disdain for private property resonated with the strong communal traditions of northeastern Spain's rural villages and of the fishing cooperatives on its Mediterranean coast, where nets, boats, and pastureland were sometimes collectively owned. A Barcelona factory worker might be only one generation removed from such a way of life. Spanish anarchists also proudly claimed still older roots, pointing, for example, to where, in Miguel de Cervantes's seventeenth-century novel, Don Quixote tells Sancho Panza about "the times called golden by the ancients" when "all things were owned in common." The good knight was famously not the best guide to reality, of course, but it is hard to think of another national epic in which someone voices such a dream.

Anarchists hated the Catholic Church as passionately as other

Spaniards on the left, bidding farewell to each other with *salud* rather than *adiós*, because that word is short for "I entrust you to God." Nonetheless, they mirrored Christianity in their vision of a judgment day when priests, capitalists, and bureaucrats would be struck down, and of a heavenly future when, in place of greed and exploitation, cooperation and love would reign supreme. They referred to this moment to come as the "anarchist millennium." Indeed, decades later, this would be the final title of the unpublished manuscript that Lois Orr would rewrite many times about the life-changing months she spent in Spain.

"Barcelona's Ramblas was dazzling," she wrote there. "Red, yellow, green and pink handbills and manifestos floated about our feet. Bright lights on . . . cafes, restaurants, hotels and theaters lit up red or red and black banners saying Confiscated, Collectivized, CNT–FAI or Union of Public Performances." Throughout Republican Spain, more than a million urban laborers and some 750,000 peasants were now in businesses or on farms newly controlled by their workers. In towns and cities the 2,000 enterprises involved included not just factories but ranged from warehouses to flower shops. Thousands of big landowners and urban businessmen fled to France. Nowhere had the old order been overturned more thoroughly than in Catalonia, where workers had taken over more than 70 percent of all places of employment. There was still a Catalan regional government, but real power lay in the hands of thousands of workers' collectives. It seemed to Charles Orr that these collectives ran everything: "They opened clinics and hospitals in lush private villas. . . . Every automobile in the street was decorated with the initials and colors of one or another workers' organization. There were no more private cars."

Almost everything they saw delighted the couple, from the bullfight held to raise funds for the militias—the matadors entered the ring offering the Popular Front's clenched fist—to a collectivized restaurant they dined in. One of the two brothers who owned it had fled, a waiter told them; the other, whom the waiter pointed out, had remained behind and, because he knew bookkeeping, had been elected cashier by the workers. Even the absurd and incongruous charmed

Lois, who, for all her fiery radicalism, had a keen eye for the unexpected detail: "The Anarchist trade unions have adopted Popeye as their own pet mascot. . . . Everywhere they sell pins, scarves and statues of Popeye waving an anarchist flag of black and red. Betty Boop is also much in favor among the Anarchists, but Mickey Mouse, who is the idol of the people, is so popular that [it] is necessary that he be non-partisan. The anarchists all wear tiny silk triangles instead of neckties, printed red and black with various designs—a victory wreath, pictures of dead comrades, a clenched fist, and, most popular of all, a nude woman."

To new arrivals like the Orrs, here to taste life in what seemed a radical utopia, it might appear that the anarchists controlled Barcelona and the surrounding region, but this was a movement that, in principle, did not believe in control. Anarchists were opposed to bureaucracy of any kind, and their rallying cry was "Too many committees!" Some of their powerful labor unions had won strikes but were opposed to union contracts, for they believed workers and management were doomed to be in eternal conflict. The CNT, the anarchist union federation, claimed some two million members but employed only a single paid officer and a small clerical staff, so committed was it to the idea that officials should remain on the job as workers. (This made, of course, for endless evenings of political meetings.) Its national committee could be recalled at any time by a vote of the federation's members, and was elected each year from a different town or region so that no person would serve more than one year or gain permanent power.

The Spanish anarchists blamed the emerging tyranny in the Soviet Union not on the one-party nature of its government, but on the fact that it had a government at all. "All governments are detestable," one anarchist newspaper wrote, "and it is our mission to destroy them." The anarchists were, nonetheless, the dominant force in Catalonia. When Lluís Companys, the president of the regional government, recognizing this, proposed a power-sharing agreement with them, they somewhat uneasily agreed. They took no part, however, in the Republic's national government, and ran no candidates for the nation's parliament. Could the Spanish Revolution be preserved if its makers refused to put their hands on the traditional levers of power?

In other ways as well, Spain was more confusing than the American newcomers expected. When Charles went to the headquarters of what sounded like a possible political home, the United Socialist Party of Catalonia, "I was received by a lady who spoke English. . . . I tried to impress upon her that I was not only a socialist, but a revolutionary who had come to offer my services. . . . 'There is no revolution,' she answered sharply. 'This is a people's war against fascism'. . . . I then realized I had been sent to communists."

Charles had stumbled upon a major political fault line. Catalonia and other pockets of the country were indeed in the midst of a social revolution without parallel. But it was one opposed by much of the Republic's political spectrum: the Moscow-oriented Communists, most Socialists, and the middle-class liberal parties. The mainstream parties were no enthusiasts of revolution to begin with, while the Communists were leery of one spontaneously erupting from below and not orchestrated by the Party, Soviet-style. Both groups were convinced that Britain, France, and the United States would never sell arms to a Spanish Republic that appeared too radical.

This was not an unreasonable fear. From their diplomats in Spain, Western governments were already receiving alarmed messages about factories seized by their employees. Would Washington, for instance, want to do business with the Republic now that armed anarchists had taken over the Barcelona auto plants owned by Ford and General Motors? The Ford workers even sent their own 30-man militia unit to the front—and continued to pay them out of the company's confiscated bank account. The workers at GM defied orders from corporate headquarters in the United States to shut the plant down, and converted it to make trucks for the war effort.

Most anarchists did not care what capitalist governments or corporations thought of their actions, for without a revolution, they believed, they would lose the war. One of their posters showed a cannon barrel crossed with a factory chimney flying the anarchist flag, and below them the slogan "The Revolution and the War Are Inseparable." Unless they had a new, egalitarian society to fight for, why would working-class men and women be willing to risk their lives? Who, after all, in a matter of days had defeated the Nationalist coup throughout Catalonia—perhaps the single most embarrassing setback suffered by the plotting generals? Anarchist workers.

When the cautious regional government had at first refused to arm them against the military's July 1936 rising, Barcelona's anarchists broke into armories, stormed a prison ship in the harbor to seize its warders' weapons, and cleaned out the city's gun shops. Catalan metalworkers quickly fashioned armored cars that looked like giant boxes on wheels by welding steel plates to the frames of trucks and automobiles. Others fashioned homemade bombs and hand grenades, and thousands pitched in to build street barricades of everything from dead horses to massive rolls of newsprint to paving stones passed hand-to-hand along a chain of people. Office clerks in white shirts and neckties took up rifles behind the barricades. Union members sounded the alarm with factory sirens and persuaded wavering soldiers to join them. "At one moment during the fighting" in Barcelona in July, writes Antony Beevor in his history of the war, "a small group of workers . . . rushed across to [a Nationalist] artillery detachment with two 75 mm guns. They held their rifles above their heads to show that they were not attacking as they rushed up to the astonished soldiers. Out of breath, they poured forth passionate arguments why the soldiers should not fire on their brothers, telling them that they had been tricked by their officers. The guns were turned around and brought to bear on the [Nationalist] forces."

The most popular anarchist leader, the stocky, dark-haired, charismatic former railwayman and machinist Buenaventura Durruti—a Che Guevara figure for his day—personally led the final charge that captured some Nationalist-held barracks near Barcelona's port. In the attack, this legendary survivor of two decades of uprisings, imprisonments, a bank robbery, the assassination of an archbishop, escapes, exile, and troublemaking on three continents saw his closest comrade fatally shot beside him. But victory was his, and seemed to underline his famous statement, "We carry a new world in our hearts." No wonder sympathizers like the Orrs felt that only the dream of that new world would rally the people to defeat Franco.

"If only," Lois wrote wistfully, "they would make their revolution in some other language." As the Orrs soon discovered, the defense of the Republic was complicated by intense regional feelings. This was especially true of prosperous Catalonia and the iron-rich Basque country of Spain's northern coast, where people spoke languages other than Spanish and had long thirsted for autonomy or independence. Such feelings had only deepened as these two areas became the country's most industrialized and Basques and Catalans came to resent the disproportionate share of taxes they paid to the national government.

For hundreds of years, however, the country's monarchs and then the military men and conservative politicians who shared power with them in the nineteenth and early twentieth centuries had insisted on a centralized, authoritarian nation where the language of government and education could only be Castilian Spanish. The Republic had been far more responsive to demands for autonomy, and under it Catalonia had enjoyed its first regional parliament in modern times.

As a proper internationalist radical, however, Lois was shocked that for many Catalans, region mattered more than class. She was further disconcerted to find that even if they knew Spanish well, they often refused to speak it. "These people here are fiends on this subject of Catalanism," she wrote to her family in Kentucky. "This spirit of nationalism has no place in a workers' world, of course." When her mother wrote back asking about local customs, Lois replied, "The most important thing about Catalan workers at this particular moment is not that they wear red hats and drink wine from such funny bottles, but the fact that they are the vanguard of the world working class."

Although Lois eventually learned to understand both tongues, for months the Orrs' rudimentary Spanish and lack of Catalan meant that the people they talked to were mainly other foreigners. Besides a handful of other Americans, their friends in Barcelona soon included men and women from Britain, France, Canada, Germany, Belgium, and Cuba. The newcomers to the city quickly bonded. "Those all-night sessions at the Café Ramblas," Lois wrote, "were my first initiation into the political realities of Europe's concentration camp universe."

Before long both Orrs found paying work. Lois began writing English-language press releases for the Catalan regional government. The twelve pesetas a day she was paid (worth perhaps $25 today) was "the first money I ever earned in my life," she exulted in a letter home. Charles produced English-language shortwave radio broadcasts and edited a newspaper, the *Spanish Revolution*, for the Partido Obrero de Unificación Marxista, or POUM, the Workers' Party of Marxist Unification, a small group that was as left-wing as its name but was vigorously anti-Stalinist. It had become part of the regional government's Popular Front coalition just as the Orrs arrived in Barcelona, and it shared the anarchists' conviction that revolution was essential to winning the war. Lois also sometimes went on the radio for the POUM's daily 15- or 20-minute English broadcast, but the transmitter was so weak that she never knew if anyone abroad could hear her.

At first the couple were housed in a confiscated hotel where, as workers for the revolution, their meals were free. "Every day," Lois wrote, "a truck brought huge rounds of bread to the manager's office, to be stacked next to 100 kilo bags of potatoes." Miraculously, it seemed, in a cashless barter system, peasants supplied the city with truckloads of vegetables, rabbits, and chickens in return for goods from Barcelona's factories. It surely helped that it was the fall harvest season. Breakfasts, Charles reported, "came from an inexhaustible supply of large sardine tins. Our noon-day meals were enhanced by floods of really excellent bottled wine. These supplies, it was said, had been 'liberated' from the cellars of the rich." More goods appeared like magic. Lois could never figure out the source of the seemingly unending river of newsprint that fed the eight daily newspapers and numerous weeklies produced by Catalonia's fractious array of political parties.

Sharing the space with other foreign leftists, the Orrs were eventually given quarters in a luxurious apartment in the hills above the city confiscated from the consul of Nazi Germany. With a view of the harbor from its balcony, it was still full of fine paintings and furniture—although all chair and sofa cushions had been taken away for use in hospitals. Some of the consul's papers, Charles reported, were being put to good use in the bathroom. "You should see our 10 room magnificent appt! . . . We have hot water, electricity & all. No one collects! I don't know how long it can last."

Parades and rallies took place almost daily. At the headquarters of the CNT, the union federation—a building seized from the Chamber of Commerce—Lois found unionists using stock certificates for scratch paper. "We were living the revolution instead of our own personal lives, an incredible expansion of consciousness. . . . Everything was new and different, anything was possible, a new heaven and a new earth were being formed."

Lois imagined the new heaven and earth in all she saw. "I completely lost myself in the life of the revolution, leaning on the railing of the tall balcony-window . . . and watching the black-clad women below drawing water from the plaza fountain for their cooking. Their menfolks stood under the lamppost listening to a literate comrade read aloud from *Solidaridad Obrera* ('Workers' Solidarity,' the CNT daily). It was the regular *tertulia* of the neighborhood. The *tertulia* is a conversation group which meets for years in the same café, village square, or here, barrio plaza to sift out the meaning of the events of the day, of the decade, the generation or even life itself."

Perhaps. On the other hand, these neighbors could well have been talking—in the language this visitor from Kentucky knew barely a word of—not of the meaning of life itself, but of the price of bread. Or, for that matter, of their resentment over the endless political rhetoric on all sides, for not everyone in Barcelona shared Lois's excitement. Thousands of workers tried to shirk service in the militias. A surge in membership in the CNT's unions may have been due less to hope for a new millennium than to the fact, as one scholar points out, that "life in revolutionary Barcelona was quite difficult without a union card." Lacking such identification, you had a much harder time obtaining housing, welfare payments, medical care, or food. Records show that large numbers of union members were loath to attend meetings or pay dues.

For the moment, though, Lois lived in a bubble of exhilaration. "I'm having the time of my life here," she wrote her family. She had no doubt that all she saw around her would eventually be universal. As she told her disapproving father, "For any good revolutionary . . . Spain is the most valuable place in the world to be. . . . Some day someone will have to make a revolution in the United States and people who know anything about it will be vitally necessary."

Such confidence was easy to have in Barcelona in the autumn of 1936. Just walking from the former German consul's apartment to her job in the Catalan government office, she could see churches that had been converted into cooperative workshops, cultural centers, refugee shelters, or public dining halls. Elsewhere a liqueur distillery was being transformed into a hospital, and a monastery into a children's TB sanitarium. From the countryside came news of even greater changes. More than 40 percent of the Republic's arable acreage had been taken over by peasants who previously had little or no land, and more than half of that had been turned into collectives, where what had once been a large estate was now cultivated communally. In hundreds of these collectives people expressed their politics by making bonfires of property deeds—and of paper money.

"Here in Fraga," an anarchist newspaper boasted of a town in Aragon, just west of Catalonia, "you can throw bank notes into the street and no one will take any notice. Rockefeller, if you were to come to Fraga with your entire bank account you would not be able to buy a cup of coffee. Money, your God and your servant, has been abolished here, and the people are happy." Sometimes, replacing money, a collective issued coupons that symbolized the value of a certain number of hours of labor worked, with families who had more children receiving more coupons. (The system often came to grief when the coupons were not honored in the next village.) Bourgeois items like lipstick were disapproved of, and sometimes alcohol, tobacco, and even coffee were banned. While they lasted, some of these collectives successfully produced more food than the estates they replaced. In Aragon, the equal to Catalonia in radical fervor and with a much higher percentage of collectivized farmland, food production increased by 20 percent.

Anarchist beliefs were reflected in names given to newborns: one activist christened his daughter Libertaria. The movement's hatred of bureaucracy extended to marriage. In a coastal village south of Barcelona run by an anarchist committee, an observer came upon this scene:

"Four couples have been united since the beginning of the revolution. Accompanied by their families and their friends, they appeared before the secretary of the committee. Their first and last names, their ages and their desire to unite were recorded in a register. Custom was respected and the festivity was assured. At the same time, in order to respect libertarian principles, the secretary pulled out the page on which all these details were inscribed, tore it into tiny pieces while the couples were descending the stairway, and, when they were passing under the balcony, threw the pieces at them like confetti. Everyone was happy."

For Lois, as an upper-middle-class radical, it was a heady thrill to imagine herself part of a proletarian movement. "The main reason I like [Barcelona]," she wrote to her sister-in-law, "is because it's a workers' city, not because of the 'luminous flood of light' or its reserved delicate soul. Hell, if it's got a soul, it's an anarchist one, a suspicious underdog one, dark and dangerous and ready to fight to the last drop of blood or the last stone for their first chance for any kind of decent life. Not dainty and reserved and delicate, but strong and crude, and rough, just like any worker."

However much she romanticized the workers of Barcelona, Lois and Charles were indeed living in a city that had turned the normal social order on its head. No one knew how long this extraordinary moment would last, but while it endured it drew independent-minded leftists from all over Europe. One of those political pilgrims, who ate in the same communal dining room as the Orrs and worked in the same building as Charles, was a twenty-three-year-old political exile named Willy Brandt. Several decades later he would become chancellor of West Germany. Someone who would win even more renown was soon to arrive.

Although Charles Orr had seen more of the world than his nineteen-year-old wife, neither of them seems to have paid much attention to a disturbing part of the history they were living through.

The anarchist tradition was curiously contradictory. The movement's prophets held out an inspiring, gentle vision of a millennium when men and women would live together cooperatively, free at last from exploitation. Some anarchists embodied this spirit in their own lives. The Russian theorist Pyotr Kropotkin, for instance, was beloved by nearly everyone he met, from workers and peasants to curious business leaders and philanthropists. (It helped that he was a superb raconteur in five languages, played the piano, and had been born a prince.) At the same time, he and almost every other anarchist thinker of note were in love with the idea of "the propaganda of the deed"—the great, shocking act that would cause people to rise, feel their power, and bring closer the millennium, when parasitic bureaucracies like armies, churches, corporations, and governments would all vanish. What was the deed? Much of the time it turned out to be assassination.

Between 1894 and 1914, anarchists assassinated no less than six heads of governments, including President William McKinley of the United States and two prime ministers of Spain. One of the latter, something of a reformer, in fact, was shot dead from behind in 1912 while looking into a bookstore window in Madrid. Dozens of other business and political leaders, and yet more passersby who happened to be in the way when a bomb was thrown, fell victim as well. In the 1920s, Spanish anarchists, reacting to the killings of union leaders by the police, assassinated yet another prime minister, an archbishop, and many other officials, and tried unsuccessfully to kill the king.

Now, with Spain at war, this idealization of killing had reached an apocalyptic scale. "We must burn much, MUCH, in order to purify everything," declared an anarchist newspaper some two weeks after the coup. Not only the anarchists and the POUM, to whom the Orrs felt politically close, but also the Communists whom they hated had been responsible for much bloodshed throughout Republican Spain. Most of these killings happened before the Orrs arrived. Charles noticed a few clues, however, that they might be continuing: "There were two Italian comrades, tall and handsome, attached to the POUM. They came around our offices from time to time, but had no obvious jobs. They carried pistols in their belts. My colleagues told me that they were the POUM's trigger men . . . hinting that they knew more than they cared to tell."

He saw other signs of recent violence: "Churches were closed and most of them burnt out. The walls and sometimes the roofs still stood, but the interiors were charred, the entrances boarded up. Workers' militia, during the first days, as they advanced from Barcelona towards Aragon, had stopped along the way to destroy churches." The violence had, in fact, gone far beyond this. In the first few months of the war, reported one American correspondent in Barcelona, "every morning saw bodies scattered about in outlying parts of the city." And then, as word of Nationalist rapes and murders reached Republican-controlled territory, more mass killings took place in revenge—something that only accelerated once Hitler's planes began bombing Republican towns. In city after city, right-wing prisoners were taken out of their cells and shot in direct reprisal for the indiscriminate Nationalist air raids.

The people targeted in these early months were Nationalist supporters of all sorts: landowners, shopkeepers, businessmen—particularly those known for acting harshly toward the poor. As in the French Revolution, the Catholic clergy was also a prime target: radical workers murdered priests, flaunted bishops' robes, assembled a firing squad to "execute" a famous statue of Christ, and dug up clerical graves and displayed opened coffins full of bones to mock the Church's promise of eternal life. The Church was seen as a handmaiden of the big employers and landlords, promising abundance in the next world to workers denied their fair share in this one. Altogether, nearly 7,000 clergy were put to death, one of the largest such massacres in modern times.

The anarchist practice of throwing wide the prison gates didn't help matters. The most principled leftists of various persuasions then went off to fight at the front, leaving behind less disciplined comrades, as well as just-freed common criminals, to settle old scores. All told, scholars estimate today, more than 49,000 civilians were killed in Republican territory during the war, the vast majority of them in the first four months.

A far larger number of people were murdered in Nationalist-controlled Spain: some 150,000, with at least 20,000 more executions after the war. But in a European and American press dominated by conservative media barons—the Hearst newspaper chain, for example, enthusiastically backed Franco—it was the killings in the Republic, especially of the clergy, that were splashed across front pages. By the end of 1936, the Republican government succeeded in largely bringing such deaths to a halt, but they had done great damage to its chances of getting help from abroad.

"Early one morning—that is about 10 a.m. Spanish office time—in December 1936," remembered Charles Orr, "I was working at my office in the administrative building of the POUM on the Barcelona Ramblas. A little militiaman, in his blue coveralls and red scarf, trudged up the stairs to my office on the fourth floor. The lifts, as usual, bore the familiar sign NO FUNCIONA. . . .

"There was an Englishman, he reported to me, who spoke neither Catalan nor Spanish. . . . I went down to see who this Englishman was and what his business might be.

"There I met him—Eric Blair—tall, lanky and tired, having just that hour arrived from London. . . . I invited him in and we climbed those long stairways, back up to the fourth floor.

"Exhausted, but excited, after a day and a night on the train, he had come to fight fascism, but did not know which militia he should join. . . . At first, I did not take this English volunteer very seriously. Just one more foreigner come to help . . . apparently a political innocent." The visitor, wearing a corduroy jacket, mentioned a book he had written about his experiences living as a tramp in England and washing dishes in Paris restaurants. Neither Charles nor Lois had heard of it.

"To us he was just Eric . . . one of a small band of foreigners, mostly British, fighting on the Aragon Front." Talking with Charles and a British colleague in the POUM office, Eric Blair decided to abandon his plan to enlist in the International Brigades—the force being recruited by the world's Communist parties—and instead join the POUM militia, which was manning the front line against Franco's troops in nearby Aragon.

"Eric," Charles wrote, "was tall, lean and gangling, to the point of being awkward. . . . He was tongue-tied, stammered and seemed to be afraid of people." Tongue-tied the newcomer might be in conversation, but he was not so in print, where he wrote under the name of George Orwell.

It is unsurprising that the Orrs were not familiar with his name, for at this point in his life—he was thirty-three—Orwell was little known even in England. He had been supporting himself mostly by working part-time in a bookstore and by running a small grocery shop out of his home. (On his POUM militia enlistment papers, he put down his occupation as "grocer.") The work that would first bring him wide public notice, *The Road to Wigan Pier*, a close-up look at poverty in the industrial north of England, he had finished before he left for Spain, but it was not yet published. The book he would write about his experiences in the Spanish Civil War, *Homage to Catalonia*, would eventually become the most widely read memoir of this conflict in any language.

However ill at ease and diffident he may have appeared, Orwell had a quick grasp of all he was seeing and the ability to bring it alive in a few brushstrokes. Like the Orrs, he found himself under the spell of a transformed Barcelona:

> Waiters and shop-walkers looked you in the face and treated you as an equal. Servile and even ceremonial forms of speech had temporarily disappeared. Nobody said '*Señor*' or '*Don*' or even '*Usted*'; everyone called everyone else '*Comrade*' and '*Thou.*' . . . Almost my first experience was receiving a lecture from an hotel manager for trying to tip a lift-boy. . . . The revolutionary posters were everywhere, flaming from the walls in clean reds and blues that made the few remaining advertisements look like daubs of mud. . . . All this was queer and moving. There was much in it that I did not understand, in some ways I did not even like it, but I recognized it immediately as a state of affairs worth fighting for.

Orwell was also struck by what seemed to him a touching innocence:

> In the barbers' shops were Anarchist notices (the barbers were mostly Anarchists) solemnly explaining that barbers were no longer slaves. In the streets were coloured posters appealing to prostitutes to stop being prostitutes. . . . Revolutionary ballads of the naïvest kind, all about proletarian brotherhood and the wickedness of Mussolini, were being sold on the streets for a few centimes each. I have often seen an illiterate militiaman buy one of these ballads, laboriously spell out the words, and then, when he had got the hang of it, begin singing it to an appropriate tune.

By this time, Lois Orr had become increasingly aware of the deep tension within the Republic between the POUM and the anarchists on the one hand, and on the other, the parties that wanted to suppress the revolution. "We tried to explain to the newcomers that the war would be decided by politics, not personal *valor.* There was more than enough of that. . . . Deafest of all was Eric Blair. . . . He had come to Spain for a clear moral confrontation of good vs. evil, and did not want a lot of politics to confuse him. He wanted only to carry his ideals and his feelings into . . . action, and soon left Barcelona." Orwell's introduction to Republican Spain's political conflicts would come later. For now, he was eager to fight. After only a week of training, he was sent off to the front.

The Orrs, however, remained in the revolutionary city. "This is a gloriously exciting place to be," Lois wrote to her family, calling Barcelona "the most interesting spot in the world at this particular moment." Indeed, for the time being, except for occasional air-raid drills and increasing food shortages, it was almost possible to forget that there was a war on.

5

"I Will Destroy Madrid"

As Franco's forces steadily gained ground, sweeping up from southern Spain and eastward from the Portuguese border, the Generalissimo made it clear that his aim was to turn the country into a military dictatorship. Before long he would order all his supporters—the Spanish Fascists, several Catholic and right-wing parties, and two monarchist factions supporting rival branches of the royal family—merged into a single movement. From this point on, it would be the only political party allowed in Nationalist Spain. Franco put his brother-in-law in charge of it, and any public dissent was punished with immediate arrest. The movement's role was to support his dictatorship; there was no pretense that he served at its pleasure. His system was closely modeled on those of Hitler and Mussolini: the posters that quickly appeared, proclaiming, "One Fatherland, One State, One Chief," echoed Hitler's *Ein Volk*, *Ein Reich*, *Ein Führer.* Scholars quibble about whether Franco should be called a Fascist, usually reserving the word for the blue-shirted followers of the Falange Española, the openly Fascist party that had been absorbed into his movement. Mussolini, however, who for several years before the coup had secretly financed military training in Italy for both the Falange and other right-wing Spaniards, did not hesitate to speak of the "Fascist sword" being "unsheathed" in Spain.

Although the German aircraft bombing cities in the path of his troops were the most modern of weapons, Franco's eye was on the past. His was a war of earlier centuries against modernity, of traditional Catholicism against the secular world, of an ancient rural order against urban, industrial culture. His aim was to restore the glories of an age-old Spain and the key pillars of a highly authoritarian state: the army, the Church, the big estates, and the overseas Spanish empire that had once spanned continents—although it remained foggy just how that would be regained. There would be no elections, no independent trade unions, no democratic trappings of any sort. The very symbol the Nationalists used, an ox yoke superimposed on crossed arrows, came from the reign of Ferdinand and Isabella more than four centuries earlier. The yoke stood for an all-powerful realm—Aragon and Castile united and subservient under the dual monarchy, like two oxen under one yoke—and the arrows were for hunting down heretics. Among the many humiliations to which the Nationalists subjected captured Republican women was the branding of this symbol on their breasts.

Heresy was indeed on the minds of Franco and his followers, for one striking aspect of his regime was the extraordinary position given the Church. Spain's Catholic hierarchy was the most reactionary in Europe. Its Jesuits, for example, published a translation of the infamous anti-Semitic forgery *The Protocols of the Elders of Zion* and serialized it in one of their magazines. To see how the Germans dealt with troublemakers, one priest known for his zealous attacks on Jews and Freemasons, Father Juan Tusquets Terrats, had paid a visit in 1933 to the new concentration camp at Dachau.

The great majority of Spain's Catholic bishops embraced Franco wholeheartedly, and were rewarded in return. Various reforms enacted under the Republic, including a law permitting divorce, were reversed. Textbooks were purged of anything deemed contrary to Christian morality, and all teachers were ordered to lead their children daily in praying to the Virgin Mary for a Nationalist victory.

Bishops joined Franco and his generals in giving the straight-armed Fascist salute. The Church burned thousands of books. To Cardinal Isidro Gomá, Archbishop of Toledo and Primate of All Spain, the war was the "clash of civilization with barbarism," and the Nationalists were bravely fighting "dark societies controlled by the Semite International." When 65 Republicans were shot by a Nationalist firing squad near Pamplona, the coup de grâce was administered to each by a Catholic priest. Another, Father Juan Galán Bermejo, proudly displayed to an officer his "little pistol which has rid the world of more than a hundred Marxists." One of them he shot when the victim, a Republican militiaman fleeing Franco's troops, knelt next to him in a cathedral's confessional booth; five others he deliberately buried wounded but alive.

The war had not reached Barcelona, where Lois and Charles Orr continued to work, but by late 1936 it was fast closing in on Madrid, where Louis Fischer was reporting from. Nationalist troops now controlled roughly the western half of Spain. When the Republic's new prime minister, Francisco Largo Caballero, telephoned his military commander in Illescas, a mere 20 miles southwest of the capital, he found himself talking to the Nationalist general whose troops had just taken the town. That Franco would capture Madrid seemed so certain that congratulatory telegrams addressed to him began pouring in to the Telefónica, the headquarters of the telephone monopoly. Over the radio, the Nationalist General Mola laughingly placed an advance order for a cup of coffee at the Café Molinero on Madrid's Gran Vía. He boasted that he would enjoy it before October 12, Columbus Day. The date marks, of course, the start of Spain's conquests in the New World, just the sort of imperial triumph the Nationalists so dreamed of.

In a dispatch to the *Nation* in New York, Fischer gave a straightforward account of how some Republican soldiers, poorly armed and trained, panicked and fled when they came under artillery fire from Franco's troops, and how officers had drawn revolvers to stop them. Soon afterward, he ran into Mikhail Koltsov, a correspondent for *Pravda* and Stalin's chief pair of eyes in Spain, accompanied by the British journalist Claud Cockburn, a Communist Party stalwart. Koltsov knew of the article and was furious. He refused to shake Fischer's hand, while the American protested that he had only reported the facts.

"Yes," Koltsov answered cuttingly. "Those are the facts. How extraordinarily observant and truthful you are. . . . You've done more harm than thirty British M.P.'s working for Franco. And then you expect me to shake hands with you." Fischer's only interest was his own reputation, the Russian said, not the cause of the Republic. "You, as the French say, have lost an excellent opportunity to keep your mouth shut." Koltsov and Cockburn insisted that the duty of a committed journalist was to write whatever was necessary to win the war.

(On Party orders, a year and a half later, Cockburn would do just that. He wrote a supposedly eyewitness account of a completely imaginary battle, a massive anti-Franco mutiny of Moors in Spanish Morocco. Impossible to verify, for foreign correspondents were seldom allowed to visit the territory, the piece was filled with names of streets and plazas gleaned from guidebooks. It was meant to influence the French prime minister, who had closed the border to all arms destined for the Republic, leaving a large shipment of artillery halted at the frontier. The hoax story, which made the Nationalists appear far shakier than they were, appeared just as a delegation was about to lobby the prime minister on behalf of the Republic to open the border and let the guns through. It worked.)

The outskirts of the capital became the new front line, and much of Madrid came under artillery fire. In early November 1936, as ammunition and supplies ran low, the government feared the city lost and relocated to Valencia, well behind the lines on the Mediterranean coast. Its departure in a long convoy of trucks was so precipitous that in scores of ministry offices the lights were left on, and desks were still piled high with papers. The Republic's army remained, however, to attempt to defend Madrid. Half a million refugees flooded the city, camping in parks and cooking over open fires on the street. Some were trying to herd their sheep and donkeys to safety with them.

Municipal buses were commandeered to rush troops to the front. Ever more buildings lay in ruins or were pockmarked by shrapnel. With Spain's richest farmland rapidly falling under Nationalist control, food ran short, and the remains of any horse or donkey killed by Franco's shells or bombs quickly found its way into soup bowls. Madrid's defenders built barricades out of anything they could find, including suitcases left in a railway station's checkroom. "Streets had been torn up and the granite blocks used to build walls across streets and in front of big buildings," Fischer wrote. "Avenues were dug up to obstruct tanks. Most Madrileños refused to leave the city. The government actually arrested several noted artists and professors and took them to the coast where they were released. It did not want them to be hurt or killed. The art treasures of the Prado and other museums were moved out." Also dispatched to Valencia for safekeeping was a first edition of *Don Quixote*.

Panic spread. One day a Republican pilot had to make an emergency landing behind Nationalist lines. Shortly afterward, a Nationalist airplane flew over the Republican air base near Madrid and dropped, by parachute, a box containing his body, cut into pieces, accompanied by insults scrawled in Italian. On the radio the Nationalist General Queipo de Llano continued gloating: "Three militia girls to every Moor: what a time we're having!" He promised vengeance against more than just Republican women. "Our war is not a Spanish Civil War," he declared, "it is a war of western civilization against the Jews of the entire world." Queipo was rumored to be a heavy drinker; at the end of one broadcast, not realizing the microphone was still turned on, he shouted to an aide, "Bring wine for fuck's sake."

With each new wave of frightened refugees, more chilling news filtered into the city. They told how some of the death sentences in territory Franco captured were being carried out by the iron collar of the garrote, which an executioner tightens—slowly, if he is so inclined—around the victim's neck. In Palma del Río, near Cordova, peasants had collectivized the land of Félix Moreno Ardanuy, a wealthy landowner and breeder of fighting bulls, and had eaten some of his bulls. As the historian Paul Preston describes it: "The news infuriated Moreno. When a Nationalist column captured the town . . . he drove behind in a black Cadillac. . . . The village menfolk who had not fled were herded into a large cattle-pen. For each of his slaughtered bulls, he selected ten to be shot. As desperate men pleaded with him on the grounds that they were his godson, his cousin or linked to him in some way, he just looked ahead and said, 'I know nobody.' At least eighty-seven were shot on that day and twice that many over the following days."

The Republicans, too, were carrying out a reign of terror, killing thousands of people in Madrid alone. Paranoia about spies spread through the city, spurred by reports that the Nationalist General Mola claimed to have four columns of troops attacking Madrid, and a "fifth column" of secret supporters inside it. It is not clear that Mola made such a boast, but such was the tension in the air that the rumor was treated as fact. When driving a car, wrote the filmmaker Luis Buñuel, "it was dangerous even to hold out your hand to signal a turn, as the gesture might be interpreted as a Fascist salute and get you a fast round of gunfire." Even bombs from German planes were sometimes blamed on fifth columnists, since Spaniards who had not experienced World War I at first had trouble grasping that the explosions around them could be caused by aircraft barely visible in the sky.

"The city was nervous," Fischer wrote. "In the evenings, the blackout made everything gruesome. Several times, militiamen fired from the street into house windows where a light shone. Zeal and folly." At the sound of aircraft engines, everyone's faces anxiously scanned the sky. Private telephone lines were turned off, to prevent sympathizers from phoning information to Nationalists on the city's outskirts. Such fears were not unjustified: a workers' demonstration had been called for 8 a.m. on November 14 in the plaza by the Atocha railway station, then canceled when officials realized it would be an ideal air-raid target. But German Junkers bombers showed up right on time to bomb the square.

Just two days after the Republican government fled town, Madrileños took heart when the first troops of the International Brigades arrived at that station and with blanket rolls over their shoulders marched along the Gran Vía to the front, now in the city's western districts. Most had no helmets. The crowds who cheered them wildly did not realize they also had little training and that their rifles and machine guns dated from before 1914. Despite the ecstatic shouts of "*¡Viva Rusia! ¡Vivan los Rusos!*" this first group of volunteers was mostly from Poland, Britain, and France—the country that contributed by far the most men to the Internationals—or leftist refugees from Italy and Germany. Not marching in the parade were any of the Soviet military advisors who had also begun quietly arriving in Madrid.

Crucially, the Soviets had also started providing the Republic with tanks and fighter aircraft and the crews to operate them. The fighters were dramatically visible as they dueled with German and Italian planes. Crowds cheered if a plane with the large black X of Franco's air force on its tail was shot down by a Republican fighter with red wingtips. Most of the Soviet fighters were fast, up-to-date, snub-nosed I-16 monoplanes, nicknamed *Mosca*, or "the Fly," by Spaniards. For the moment they were more advanced than the aircraft supplied by Hitler and Mussolini, giving sudden superiority to the Republican air force and unexpected hope to those on the ground. Without such help, Madrid would have been doomed.

In an upsurge of popular enthusiasm for all things Russian, the city's cinemas screened Soviet classics like Sergei Eisenstein's *Battleship Potemkin.* Even the reception room of a Madrid brothel sported large pictures of Marx, Lenin, and Stalin. The Western arms embargo that had forced Republican Spain to depend on Soviet weapons also greatly increased the membership of the Spanish Communist Party.

Spurring the Party's growth as well was the country's most charismatic orator, the Communist parliamentary deputy Dolores Ibárruri, known to all as La Pasionaria, "the Passionflower." The daughter, sister, and wife of Basque coal miners, she had worked as a seamstress before entering politics and passed several spells in prison. Her fervent speechmaking on the radio and at rallies provided just the image of defiance the Republic needed. No matter that most of her slogans—"*¡No pasarán!*" ("They shall not pass") or "It's better to die on your feet than live on your knees!"—were borrowed from other wars and that some of her speeches were written for her by Party functionaries. Bold and erect, with a melodious voice and dark flashing eyes, wearing the rope-soled sandals and black dress of working-class women and without makeup or jewelry, she quickly became legend.

When she visited troops in frontline trenches and behind barricades, a helmet covering black hair that was pulled back in a bun, the press followed her every move. At one point, in a loudspeaker truck blaring the "Internationale," La Pasionaria personally rallied several hundred retreating soldiers to save the key Segovia Bridge into the city from falling to the Nationalists. The power of this fiery figure shouting "*¡No pasarán!*" stemmed in part from the fact that no Spanish man wanted to appear cowardly before a woman.

As Franco's troops drew ever closer, Fischer and the other foreign correspondents could see the progress of the war from the upper floors of the 14-story Telefónica building, Madrid's tallest. Feet propped on windowsills or a terrace railing and eyes glued to binoculars, they watched fierce aerial dogfights that seemed almost at eye level. Its cellars packed with refugees and its ground floor surrounded by sandbags, the building itself was a prime target for Nationalist artillery fire. Reporters called it "the dart board." They went to the Telefónica every evening to cable their news home in a babel of languages, sometimes dozing on cots while waiting for overworked censors and telephone operators.

It was, wrote a colleague of Fischer's from the Associated Press, as if the fighting "were being staged in a giant open-air theatre for our benefit." The infantry "could be seen as small dots on the landscape, now moving forward under cover of an artillery barrage, now being forced back. . . . Tanks and Moorish cavalry stood out in relief against the crazy-quilt pattern of zig-zag trenches, then scurried for cover in the wooded patches. Enemy artillery could be located by flashes bright even in the brilliant sunlight. Shellbursts made small puffs on the slopes of the gentle rises." This was not the first war to

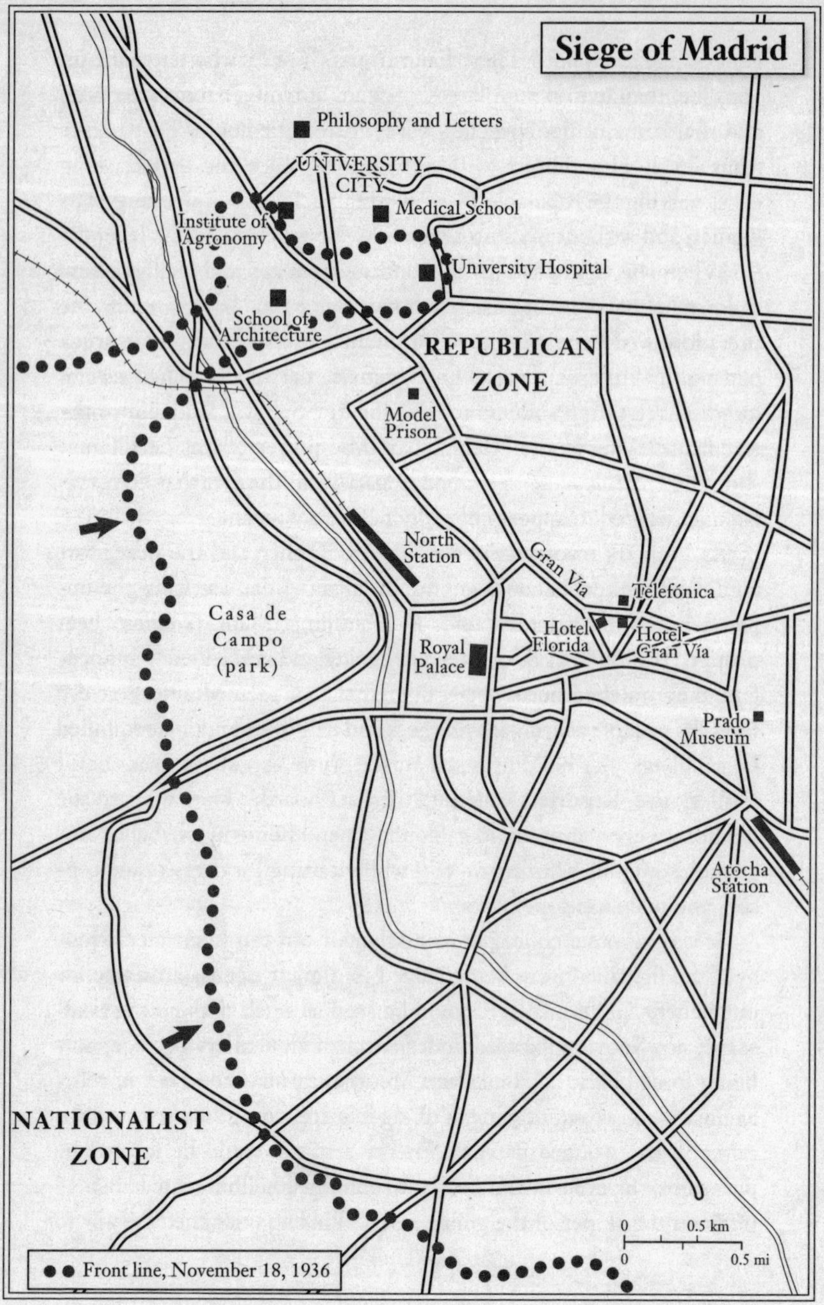
Siege of Madrid
Philosophy and Letters
UNIVERSITY CITY
Medical School
Institute of Agronomy
University Hospital
School of Architecture
REPUBLICAN ZONE
Model Prison
North Station
Gran Vía
Telefónica
Casa de Campo (park)
Hotel Florida
Hotel Gran Vía
Royal Palace
Prado Museum
Atocha Station
NATIONALIST ZONE
0 0.5 km
0 0.5 mi
Front line, November 18, 1936

be reported and photographed, but it was the first where journalists could be literally in sight of the front lines and then have their words and pictures—thanks to the new wirephoto technology—reach other continents within minutes.

"I will destroy Madrid," Franco declared, "rather than leave it to the Marxists." His airplanes and artillery, however, spared the elegant Salamanca district, where many upper-class Nationalist supporters lived and where thousands had taken asylum in foreign embassies and additional buildings the Republic had allowed the embassies to put under diplomatic protection. Instead, the artillery deliberately targeted the Gran Vía—now nicknamed "Shell Avenue"—at hours when crowds would be emerging from its movie houses. The Capitol Theater, screening Charlie Chaplin's *Modern Times*, stretched a tarpaulin across a shell hole in its ceiling. "Every evening when the noise of the city traffic ceases," Fischer told American readers, "I hear from my hotel window the incessant boom of cannon and the sharp firing of machine-guns, which sounds like cavalry galloping over cobblestones." Trolleys still ran, and people joked that they were the safest way to get to the front line, because if you took the Metro, the city's subway system, you might well find yourself emerging on the other side.

With his usual name-dropping about access to the high and mighty, Fischer claimed that he had attended a meeting of a subcommittee of the Republic's cabinet. But what he concentrated on bringing his readers was the experience of being in the first European capital to be under heavy, sustained aerial bombardment. A fleet of motorcycles with sirens roared through the streets to warn of each impending air raid, and people ran for shelter in the overcrowded Metro stations, which could hold only a fraction of the city's population. At one point Fischer found himself in a raid carried out by 28 of Hitler's Junkers and two Italian Capronis.

> There is nothing so harrowing and so criminal in all the world.
>
> I was riding in an automobile just before two o'clock in the af-

> ternoon when I noticed people running. . . . Suddenly there was a crash, and before one could think a mountain of smoke rose above a five-story building down the street. We turned the corner; there was another deafening bang, and the bricks of the cornices mixed with wood and glass separated from a huge apartment house and fell across our path. . . . A military motor cyclist asked for my car to transport the wounded. He was commandeering all automobiles for this purpose. Presently they began to return with people who had lost limbs or parts of their faces. . . .
>
> From the lower floors of bombed houses women, old men, and little children started to creep out. All was white; white hair, white faces, white clothes—powdered by crumbling plaster. . . . A wrinkled old woman wrapped in a blanket, every feature on her face trembling uncontrollably, stood on the pavement dazed and asked repeatedly, "Where can I go?"

Things looked hopeless. "Automobiles packed with occupants and laden high with mattresses and suitcases dashed toward the exits of the city." Fischer's hotel ran out of food. Franco's troops were less than 45 minutes' march away. A senior Soviet advisor urged him, "Leave as soon as possible!"

All over the world, the Republic's sympathizers anxiously tracked the city's fate. People posted maps in shop windows in Mexico, in trade union offices in Paris, and in a ward of the US Public Health Service Hospital in San Francisco, where the first question a gravely ill patient who had been unconscious for a day asked on awakening was "Has Madrid fallen?"

In the city itself the wreckage of bombed-out buildings filled the streets: shattered concrete, bedsteads, pots and pans, smashed bureaus, the twisted iron grillwork from fallen balconies. Madrid's loss seemed so certain that 19 foreign journalists formed a betting pool over dinner one night. Eighteen picked dates for the city's surrender during the next few weeks. Only one, from the United Press, chose "never." Trying to beat the competition, one American reporter even sent a dispatch saying that Madrid had fallen, only to have it stopped by the Republican military censor.

Meanwhile, Louis Fischer moved into a new role. He had been reporting the biggest story of his life while simultaneously enjoying another of his love affairs, this time with a young Norwegian journalist who, when they were apart, sent him passionate letters in German. But for a man who always kept a shrewd eye on his earning power and his career, he now made an uncharacteristic leap. Being a correspondent, he declared in a memoir written a few years later, "was not enough. . . . For fifteen years I had written and spoken about what other people did. This limitation always irked me. . . . Now men were dying; I wanted to do something." He headed for Albacete, a city some 150 miles southeast of Madrid in La Mancha, the part of the country from which Don Quixote had set off on his travels. In what their organizers hoped would be a more productive endeavor, this was where the International Brigades were assembling. Fischer became the first American to enlist.

Eventually, between 35,000 and 40,000 men from more than 50 countries would fight in five International Brigades. At this point, however, the new force still had to be trained and equipped, and its supply system was as chaotic as the cacophony of different languages spoken by the volunteers. Fischer presented himself to the man who was organizing the International Brigades for the Comintern: André Marty, a heavy-jowled Frenchman with a gray walrus mustache. He asked what he could do. "We need a quartermaster," Marty told him. Fischer took on the job, and soon his dark-haired, stocky figure was dressed in the uniform of a *comandante*, or major.

"I had to feed the brigade. . . . I had to clothe the new arrivals from head to foot, keep the barracks clean, and distribute arms. Each one of these tasks was a nightmare. . . . To add to my troubles, the battalions at the front would send emissaries to me announcing that they had lost cooking utensils, clothing, and bedding in a battle. But I had nothing to give them. Once a battalion commander threatened to send an armed guard from the front to arrest me for failing to deliver the equipment he demanded. What could I do? I begged everywhere."

Along with Marty and other top officials, Fischer lived in a hotel, while the volunteers streaming in from across Europe were jammed into old barracks, whose iron balconies overlooked a central courtyard, near the city's bullring. Spanish soldiers had left behind an array of garbage, and the pit latrines gave off a perpetual stink. Some ground-floor rooms bore bloodstains from fighting between Nationalists and Republicans in July. Nor was there much charm in Albacete itself, whose many unpaved streets turned to mud in the winter rain. From a smelly slaughterhouse a trail of blood ran into the gutter, and several brothels lay near the market square. Notices in shop windows reminded customers of the increasing shortages. The sign *No Hay Tabaco* would later prompt one American volunteer to say, "Who cares? No one wants to smoke hay."

Despite the squalid surroundings, Fischer was stirred by the sense of solidarity among volunteers from countries that had been enemies only two decades before. For the true-believing Communists who flocked to Albacete, the new heaven and earth were not Spain's experiments with social revolution, of which the Party so disapproved; it was the sense of comradeship across national barriers. Fischer found a French major and a German recently released from a Nazi prison who discovered that they had been on opposite sides of the Somme front 20 years earlier. An Italian and a Hungarian volunteer learned that they, too, had faced each other across a First World War battlefield, in northern Italy. The great spectrum of languages in the barracks was proof to believers that the Communist dream was something that transcended nationality. It promised to transcend class barriers too: one day Fischer was visiting a brigade headquarters at the front when a delegation from the Spanish shoemakers' union appeared carrying great rolls of leather, ready to make boots for any Internationals who needed them. In Madrid, meanwhile, taxi drivers had offered 3,000 taxis to the government to help fight the rebellion.

Boots and taxis were one matter, finding adequate arms quite another. Promised Soviet weapons were slow to arrive, and the small existing stock of rifles available to the brigades dated from 1896 and was no match for the Nationalists' modern sniper rifles with German telescopic sights. Although the major Western democracies refused to sell arms to Spain, on occasion some slipped in anyway. As Fischer and his helpers unpacked bales of clothing sent by the French Communist Party, they were at first exasperated to find one bundle containing baby clothes and a silk blouse—until they saw the machine gun and several dozen pistols these were wrapped around. The Republic's government, he wrote, bought "arms wherever it could get them. . . . Any Spaniard who said he had a friend in Antwerp or Athens or Amsterdam or Stockholm, who once knew a man who had worked for an arms merchant was given . . . money to try to buy whatever was available. Some of these Spaniards were fraudulent adventurers who made off with a lot of funds."

Fischer soon crossed swords with André Marty, a suspicious martinet who would be disliked by virtually everyone who met him in Spain. A former sailor in the French navy, he was a hero to Communists because he had led a mutiny when his ship was ordered to fight against revolutionaries in the Russian Civil War, and spent four years in prison for doing so. Because of this, it was said, he was one of the few foreigners whom Stalin trusted. Although he outranked Fischer, Marty was jealous that the journalist knew so many prominent Soviets and could speak Russian to the officers sent by the USSR, some of whom were now commanding troops. "Marty wanted to be the only boulder on the beach," Fischer wrote. The Frenchman's opinion of Fischer was equally low. "He muddled up the little that had been done," Marty reported to Moscow, "emptied the stores, brought the 2,000 men of the International Brigades base to the brink of lacking provisions, and set the entire staff against himself."

Their relationship only grew worse. Fischer was horrified when five brigade volunteers, including a Polish assistant of his, were taken away by armed men at night, accused of being followers of Leon Trotsky. The five were never seen again. Far from Moscow, Fischer was face-to-face with the Soviet repression he had avoided recognizing in Russia itself. Soon after this episode, Marty suggested that Fischer could make a greater contribution to the cause by returning to journalism. He took the hint and resigned.

For Spain's ancient capital to fall to the Nationalists was such a potential disaster that it briefly lessened the tension between the revolution-minded anarchists and the Socialists, Communists, and mainstream liberals who composed the Republic's Popular Front. In a symbolic unity gesture, in November 1936, four anarchist leaders put aside their longtime opposition to all governments and joined the cabinet. One, Federica Montseny, a feminist writer and publisher, was the first woman in any Spanish cabinet and as minister of health introduced reforms that led to sex education, legal abortion, and greater availability of birth control. Another anarchist, who became minister of justice, dismayed his more traditional colleagues by undertaking the destruction of all prison records.

As the siege continued, some of the most intense fighting took place on the northwest side of town, where a Nationalist spearhead had penetrated the sprawling grounds of University City, Madrid's new campus. Each of its red-brick dormitories and majestic Bauhaus classroom buildings, spread across a hillside, became separate fortresses. At one point the Republicans held the medical school; the Nationalists, the Institute of Agronomy. Buildings, sometimes single floors, changed hands over weeks of fighting. British volunteers found themselves quartered amid the marble corridors, ornate doors, and paneled lecture rooms of the Philosophy and Letters building until dispatched to fight nearby. Franco's troops took the building; French volunteers recaptured it with a bayonet charge.

The anarchist leader Buenaventura Durruti, who had played a major role in saving Barcelona, was summoned to Madrid with the 3,000 troops he commanded. He and his men made four costly attacks on Nationalist positions in University City, repeatedly beaten back by artillery and machine-gun fire. Franco's troops took the School of Architecture; Durruti was ordered to take the university hospital. In the midst of confusing, floor-by-floor fighting that raged through the building, Durruti headed for the scene, brandishing a pistol, to rally his exhausted troops. A bullet—apparently fired accidentally when the cocking lever of a comrade's weapon caught on a car door—hit him in the chest. Bleeding severely, he remained conscious, occasionally murmuring the anarchist lament, "Too many committees!" He died early the next morning.

Two days later, a vast funeral procession accompanied his body to the grave in Barcelona. "For five hours," wrote Lois Orr, who was there, "innumerable mobs, clumps, masses of people walked past Durruti's bier, three hundred thousand souls, the whole proletariat of Barcelona, in black berets [and] black dresses carrying black libertarian banners. The occasional red and black flag looked bright. One by one, free individual spirits, each came to say farewell to Durruti and the lost revolutionary innocence of July 19, when he had led them off with roses in their rifles to find the fascists and safeguard the dawning age of brotherhood."

Back in Madrid, where the battle continued on the university campus, British volunteers took over the job of clearing the hospital of Moorish troops, aided by the fact that some of the hungry Moors had poisoned themselves by eating rabbits, guinea pigs, and other laboratory animals injected with viruses for medical experiments. Shattered lab equipment littered the floors. In another campus building, other Internationals used elevators to dispatch bombs timed to explode when they reached floors held by the Nationalists. It was in this fighting at the university that the mobile blood unit of the Canadian surgeon Norman Bethune gave its first transfusions, a landmark in military medicine.

Returning to their Philosophy and Letters headquarters, the Britons, including John Cornford, a great-grandson of Charles Darwin, set up sniping positions in the windows of a lecture hall, behind barriers that included the thickest books they could find: metaphysics texts, nineteenth-century German philosophy, and the *Encyclopaedia Britannica.* (In another building, French volunteers were sheltering behind parapets of Kant, Goethe, Voltaire, and Pascal.) A bullet, the British found, would penetrate an average of 350 pages before coming to a stop. In the building's basement they discovered a large selection of books in English, and lugged copies of Thomas De Quincey, Charlotte Brontë, and others up four flights of stairs to their strongpoint to read during lulls in the fighting. The precocious Cornford had already won highest honors at Cambridge, published poetry, joined the Communist Party, fathered a child, separated from its mother and taken up with another woman, and seen combat with the POUM militia before joining the International Brigades. He would be killed in December, within a day of his twenty-first birthday.

The siege of Madrid spurred more massacres in the city itself, where prisons were filled with right-wingers. The biggest of them, the Model Prison, held thousands of Nationalist sympathizers, many of them army officers, only 200 yards from the front line. In the largest such mass murder in Republican Spain, over the course of several weeks somewhere between 2,200 and 2,500 prisoners were tied together in pairs, taken away in red double-decker buses, and shot. Communists and anarchists collaborated in this particular killing and made little attempt to keep it secret. Thousands more people in Madrid lost their lives in the frenzied, suspicious atmosphere when they were accused, rightly or wrongly, of being Nationalist agents or sympathizers. Sometimes victims were hauled before a makeshift tribunal, sometimes simply put up against a wall and shot. Many lived in fear of the nighttime sounds that signaled an arrest: a car screeching to a stop, men pounding on a house or apartment door, the car starting up again.

Some high Republican officials risked their lives to try to stop the headlong rush to kill. Juan Negrín, a cabinet member who would become prime minister the next year, walked Madrid's streets at night confronting militiamen who appeared to be making unnecessary arrests. Lluís Companys, president of Catalonia and a devout Catholic, saved the life of a cardinal, and his regional government arranged for some 11,000 right-wing civilians and clergy to leave the country. Melchor Rodríguez, a former bullfighter, was nonetheless a member of a small group of anarchists who were opposed to violence where humans were concerned. Just outside Madrid, an angry mob marched on a prison holding more than 1,500 right-wingers, demanding blood in revenge for a Nationalist air raid. Prison officials fled, but Rodríguez confronted the crowd and told them that they would have to kill him first. The crowd backed down.

By late November, it was clear that Madrid was saved. This was a significant setback for Franco and a stunning triumph, although at a heavy cost in lives, for the hastily organized International Brigades. To the merriment of all, the cup of coffee General Mola had ordered over the radio at the Café Molinero was left cold and untouched on a table with a "Reserved" card in his name. A cable to the Telefónica from a South American sympathizer of Franco's, congratulating him on his conquest of the city, was returned with the message UNKNOWN AT THE ABOVE ADDRESS. The United Press correspondent who had placed his money on Madrid not falling won the reporters' betting pool. "The die is not yet cast," Louis Fischer told his American readers. "This affair may last longer than anybody now believes."

In December, Fischer returned to his wife and children in Moscow. He had begun to question everything that had drawn him to Russia. Although it had been clear for years that the Soviet Union was a dictatorship, in 1936 it became much harder for anyone to believe it was a benevolent one. This was the year, Fischer would write later, when he first "sensed the oncoming night." Stalin's repression became dramatically more public with the first big show trial of what would become known as the Great Purge, a cataclysm that within a few years would result in the death or imprisonment of millions.

Two former high officials, Grigory Zinoviev and Lev Kamenev, were already in prison. In August, they had been put on trial, beneath the crystal chandeliers of what had once been Moscow's Nobles' Club. Along with 14 others, they were charged with plotting against the regime in league with Trotsky and the Nazis. A banner on the court-room wall read, TO THE MAD DOGS—A DOG'S DEATH. After a week-long trial, all 16 were shot. The accused in such cases, we know now, were routinely tortured or deprived of sleep until they confessed. The spectacle of well-known leaders abjectly admitting to being part of a counterrevolutionary conspiracy shocked Communists everywhere. Could it really be that Kamenev and Zinoviev—lifelong revolutionaries, and Jews—had conspired with representatives of Hitler? Across the world, some staunch Party members began to lose the faith; others to echo Stalin's paranoia.

The trial had already shaken Fischer before he left for Spain. Once in that country, he encountered the same ferocity toward imagined internal enemies from Stalin's man in the International Brigades, André Marty. The mustachioed Frenchman was becoming notorious for his purges of suspected Trotskyists and other dissidents, and in time would become quite open about it, telling the central committee of the French Communist Party the following year that "I did not hesitate and ordered the necessary executions. The executions ordered did not go beyond 500." Although the actual number seems to have been several dozen, that was chilling enough.

In Moscow, Fischer dared speak about his doubts to almost no one—and not just because it meant questioning the Communist dream and the pro-Soviet journalism on which he had built his career. As an American he could come and go as he pleased, but his wife was a Soviet citizen without such protection. For her sake, and that of their two young sons, he stepped carefully and maintained his friendly contacts with high Soviet officials.

Like many other conflicted Communist sympathizers around the world, Fischer found the crisis in Spain a welcome distraction from his disillusionment. People in his circles were learning Spanish songs and reading Spanish poets. "Everyone talked Spain. My boys asked me to come to their schools and give little speeches on Spain. . . . The apartment was filled with people all the time, and no one let me ask questions about Russia. 'Spain is more important,' they said. 'If we win in Spain we will be happy here.'"

The Spanish war filled Fischer's mind. "Can't you organize a committee to send relief, medicines. . . . You mustn't allow America to get away with passivity in this great fight," he wrote to his editor at the *Nation* in New York. In his articles, he railed against the Western democracies for looking the other way while Germany and Italy funneled arms and men to Franco. Increasingly uncomfortable in Moscow, where he came to feel that "it would have been mental torture to live," he made plans to return to Spain, and then embark on one of his American lecture tours, this time to rouse support for the Republic that could make President Roosevelt change his mind about not selling Spain arms. "The alternative would have been to go away and attack the Soviet regime in my writings and lectures. I was not yet ready to do that. . . . Every nation was kicking Spain, and only Russia helped. It did not help enough but it helped."

If Fischer's tennis partner Bob Merriman shared any doubts about the Soviet Union, he never confided them to anyone. Within days of Fischer's return to Moscow, Merriman telephoned him to ask, Where should you go to volunteer for Spain? For weeks, Bob and Marion had been arguing about whether he should join the International Brigades. She pleaded against it, for they had never been separated for long and had been planning to return to the United States and try to have a child. But Bob was increasingly adamant: others were risking their lives. And in October and November 1936 ominous portents appeared when Hitler first declared an "axis" binding him to Mussolini and then forged an alliance with Japan. Wouldn't it be better to set a precedent by dealing fascism a decisive defeat in Spain instead of waiting passively for another world war?

All the Americans in Moscow seemed to know and like Merriman, and the US Army attaché gladly pored over maps of the fighting with him. Another embassy friend, who quietly shared the Merrimans' left-wing politics, argued vigorously that Bob could better fight fascism as a teacher and scholar; it was best to leave combat to soldiers. But news arrived that the first group of American volunteers for the International Brigades was to sail from New York. Bob was in torment, and one evening, most uncharacteristically, he got very drunk at an embassy party. One night soon after, the couple argued until 5:30 in the morning. "But why you, Bob?" Marion kept asking him. "Why you?" He left their apartment to pace the frozen streets.

Finally, just after Christmas, he told her, "I'm going." He took one small suitcase, insisting that the war could not last more than three or four months, after which he would be back and they could get on with their life together. Marion accompanied him to Moscow's Byelorussia station and waved from the platform as the train pulled out. "For days," she wrote, "I was in something of a trance. I was unable to concentrate on anything. . . . I read every word I could find on the war in Spain. I prayed for some word from Bob that he was all right."

Stopping over in Paris to change trains, Merriman was browsing in Brentano's bookstore on the Avenue de l'Opéra when he heard a familiar voice: "Hell's bells, Bob Merriman! You're on your way to Spain! I can see it all over you! Well, so am I!"

It was his adventurous journalist friend from Moscow, Milly Bennett, with whom he had had so many arguments over Soviet politics. "Bob said he expected to do some work on the new collective farms" in Spain, Bennett recalled, "but he didn't look me in the eye when he said it."

She, too, tried to talk him out of fighting: "'You'll get killed. The foreign brigades are the shock troops. They have the highest casualties.' . . . But nothing I could say would change his mind. If Marion couldn't, how could I." They agreed to travel together. Her Russian marriage at an end, Bennett was going to Spain to cover the war and to search for a former boyfriend among the American volunteers. She and Bob went shopping for a revolver and cartridges for him, and for gas masks for them both. Given vivid French memories of the First World War, these items were stocked by the Paris department store Galeries Lafayette. Bennett had also promised to bring some masks for the Associated Press bureau in Spain. For themselves, they bought models that fitted over the horn-rimmed glasses each wore. Then they headed for the Gare d'Orsay on the banks of the Seine and beneath its high, vaulting glass roof boarded the train that had already carried many a left-wing volunteer southward, nicknamed "the Red Express."

"*Salud España!*" Merriman wrote in his diary the next day. "From Paris with Milly. . . . Unusual united front. 1:40 pm crossed border."

PART II

6

"Don't Try to Catch Me"

SOME SEVEN WEEKS after the war began, La Pasionaria traveled to Paris to plead for French arms and help. Speaking to a crowd of thousands who packed an indoor stadium near the Eiffel Tower, she echoed Haile Selassie's words to the League of Nations. "It is Spain today," she said, "but it may be your turn tomorrow." Half a dozen years later, the very arena where she spoke, the Vélodrome d'Hiver, would be filled with 13,000 French Jews, including 4,000 children, on their way to Nazi death camps.

The fighting in Spain made people everywhere wonder if it would be their turn next. Across the English Channel in London, for example, recalled Jason "Pat" Gurney about the war, "for myself, and a great number of people like me, it became the great symbol of the struggle between Democracy and Fascism everywhere." Gurney had gone to an elite British boarding school, which he left to live on his own in South Africa. He then worked two seasons on Norwegian whaling vessels in the Antarctic and with the money he earned returned to England to pursue sculpture. "For me, the human body was an unending source of delight. I spent hours stripped naked in front of a mirror, with a drawing board on one side and an anatomy book on the other, moving the various bones and muscles of my body, studying exactly how the whole thing worked."

With a tall, burly physique, "the donkey work of roughing-out large carvings in wood or stone . . . was never a hardship for me." He described a daily routine that sounds like many a man's dream: "During the day I worked and made love; in the evening I went out drinking and talking endlessly with my friends, usually starting at the Six Bells and Bowling Green in the King's Road." This Chelsea pub was also frequented by Dylan Thomas, the young actor Rex Harrison, and "an apparently unlimited supply of young women. . . . The majority of them soon tired of the dirt and discomfort of a poverty-stricken life and settled for a good, solid bourgeois marriage, while treasuring the memories of a year spent in exploring the beds of Bohemia."

Despite the attractions of this life, the twenty-six-year-old Gurney felt the urgency of the times. In England, as in the United States, millions were jobless. In the slums on the edge of Chelsea, "houses which had been built for one family now provided shelter for six," while in nearby Sloane Square "were the very rich, who lived a life of great elegance with large houses, staffs of servants and magnificent cars." Meanwhile, the demagogic Sir Oswald Mosley led an increasingly aggressive British Union of Fascists, its militants dressed in black tunics, black trousers, and wide black leather belts with brass buckles. Whenever Mosley was heckled at one of his rallies, he stopped speaking and searchlights focused on the heckler as jackbooted men beat him and then threw him out of the hall. With trumpet fanfares and flags showing a bolt of lightning, ranks of Mosley's followers marched through Jewish neighborhoods of London, shouting insults, giving the Fascist salute, and violently attacking anyone in their way. The group boasted 50,000 members.

"The war in Spain," Gurney wrote later, "had started at a time when the apparent danger of Mosley's Fascist movement was at its height. . . . The Spanish people were fighting desperately . . . and their courage was, in a sense, a reproach to those in England who saw the danger but did nothing." He made his way to the Communist Party office behind Covent Garden market and volunteered.

Among the tens of thousands who joined the International Brigades from Europe, North America, and elsewhere, Gurney was in a distinct minority. He merely thought of himself as an "old-fashioned radical" and had an astute skepticism about the Party. The problem with Communists, he felt, was that they "were always right. There were never two ways about anything. They had studied the works of Marx, Engels and Lenin, which held the correct answer to any subject under the sun, and that was the end of the matter. Since they believed this as implicitly as any of the most bigoted religious sects believed in their scripture, the Party was not for me." Moreover, the members he knew had no sense of humor. "Any hint of levity was treated like farting in church."

At the same time, Gurney fully understood the Party's appeal: "The chap who sold the *Daily Worker* outside the Underground station was not merely the chap who sold the *Daily Worker* outside the Underground station—he was the assistant Agit. Prop. Sec. of the Branch. . . . He made reports and his superiors listened to him with sympathy and encouragement. At the weekly meetings he proposed resolutions aimed at increasing the sales and readership of the *Worker*, which were then disputed and argued over, as if the world depended on the outcome."

That the International Brigades were organized by the Party did not bother him. He spoke for many when he wrote: "I realized perfectly well that the Communists were taking advantage of the opportunities presented by the War to forward their own interests, but if I had to ally myself with them to fight against the ultimate tyranny of Fascism, I would do so, and deal with subsequent problems when the time came." No one else, after all, was recruiting large numbers of men to fight at a time when Spain was battling for its life.

A mere 24 hours after signing up, Gurney was on his way to Paris. When his group of British volunteers arrived at the Gare du Nord, leftist taxi drivers gave them free rides to the trade union office that served as the assembly center for those going to fight. Soon he was on the Red Express heading southward. It was January 1937 when he reached Barcelona, "unmistakably a revolutionary city." Like Orwell and the Orrs before him, he was exhilarated by the sight of working-class militiamen in red or red-and-black scarves guarding all the public buildings, and above all "the glorious feeling of optimism; the conviction that anything that was not right with society would assuredly be put right in the new world of universal equality and freedom which lay ahead. It may have lacked realism, but it was heady stuff to a young man who was by nature a romantic, and I drank deeply of it." To the question of whether making a revolution would help win the war, Gurney at this moment believed the answer was yes.

A thoughtful observer to begin with, by the time he wrote his memoir of the war several decades later Gurney could see his youthful self with perspective. He came to understand, for instance, part of the appeal of being in Spain to so many foreign volunteers like him. "The position of a middle-class person in a working-class movement is always anomalous, particularly in such a class-obsessed country as England. It involves an elaborate pattern of pretence on both sides. . . . But here in Spain one was free of the whole thing. A Spanish working man does not—and cannot—distinguish between one class and another amongst a group of foreigners. . . . The sun shone and we all felt that we were at the centre of one of the great events of history."

He could not help but notice the political tensions in the air, especially the hatred the Communists felt for the POUM, which the Kremlin had branded Trotskyist. "Like the religions of old, the heretic was infinitely more abominable than the heathen." Ironically, the POUM was not, in fact, part of the Trotskyist movement, which was weak and shattered. The rigid, acid-tongued Trotsky had himself attacked some of the POUM's positions. But the party was heretical in Stalin's eyes, because its leaders included former Communists who had publicly broken with the Soviet Union.

Gurney's only disappointment on his stopover was that, because most of Barcelona's churches were destroyed, damaged, or closed, he could not enter the famous multispired Sagrada Familia basilica, which as an artist he had long yearned to see. (Even Lois Orr put aside her revolutionary zeal long enough to write home a description of this "absolutely fantastic" Gothic wedding cake of a church designed by Antoni Gaudí.) After a few days, he and his contingent of Internationals traveled on by rail to Albacete. The new arrivals were promptly harangued by André Marty, whom Gurney liked no better than Louis Fischer had. "He was both a sinister and a ludicrous figure. He was a large, fat man with a bushy moustache, and always wore a huge, black beret. . . . He always spoke in a hysterical roar, he suspected everyone of treason, or worse, listened to advice from nobody. . . . He now stood yelling away at us in French, which the majority of those present did not understand."

Gurney and his fellow volunteers were each issued brown corduroy trousers and a jacket too light for the January weather, a flimsy blanket, bulky ammunition boxes attached to a belt, and a helmet. "In spite of its dashing appearance, it was made of very thin metal and was quite useless as a protection against anything more lethal than kids throwing stones."

There were no rifles.

Nonetheless, in a small farming village an hour's truck ride from Albacete, the British battalion went into training. Like many an International Brigades volunteer who would follow him, Gurney was overwhelmed by the near-medieval life of Spanish peasants: "There was no fuel for heating and everyone in the village lived in a permanent condition of damp clothes and damp houses, breathing in the awful moisture-sodden air." Meager cooking fires were made from "pieces of last year's vine-prunings chopped into half-a-dozen four-inch lengths a pencil thick." The church, however, "was a very large building for such a small village, with a tower tall enough to be seen for miles."

It had been turned into the British battalion mess hall, with kitchens in the chancel and dining tables in the nave. Had clergy been killed here? "I never saw any village people enter it," Gurney wrote, "and they even seemed to avoid looking at the place, as if they had a sense of guilt about it. I never discovered what had actually happened there, but it left me with an uneasy feeling that something had occurred which everybody preferred to forget."

Gurney had an eye for irony. "Everybody was addressed as Comrade . . . Comrade Battalion Commander, Comrade Political Commissar, down to just Comrade," he wrote. This produced strange moments such as "the occasion when two dishevelled figures arrived at the Battalion HQ. They had obviously been engaged in a fight and the less severely damaged of the pair was dragging along his badly-battered opponent shouting 'This comrade has stolen my watch.'"

The British volunteers trained for six weeks, but only a day before they were sent to the front did a shipment of Russian rifles arrive. Ominously, the same day word came that Málaga, a city on Spain's south coast, had fallen to Franco's troops, heavily supported by Italians manning tanks and armored cars.

Franco, however, had so far conspicuously failed to capture Madrid. He now planned for Nationalist forces to encircle the city in a giant pincer movement. This was a war with few brilliant generals on either side, and though the troops making up one of the arms of Franco's pincers were not yet ready to attack, he nonetheless ordered those forming the other arm to do so. They were to cross the Jarama River south of the city and then strike toward the northeast to cut the road from Valencia, the lifeline on which Madrid depended for arms, ammunition, and food.

The majority of the attackers would be Moors and Spanish Foreign Legionnaires, the two much-feared groups that formed the core of the Nationalist army. Although the Moors were demonized by the Republicans, they were themselves victims of extreme privation. Almost entirely illiterate, with few prospects of employment, they had been drawn to the army from impoverished Moroccan villages in a time of severe drought by a hefty enlistment bonus of cash and food that promised survival for their families.

The Foreign Legion was famous for its battle cry, "*¡Viva la muerte!*" ("Long live death!"), and its brutal discipline. All officers and sergeants carried a small whip, and if a commander deemed a soldier disobedient or cowardly, he had the right to execute him on the spot. The attacking Nationalist troops would be equipped with the latest German arms, including 88 mm artillery pieces. This extremely accurate gun, originally developed as an antiaircraft weapon, was being used in battle for the first time in Spain. The Nationalists and their Nazi allies would quickly learn that with the proper shells it could be just as effective for long-range bombardment or penetrating the armor of tanks. Firing 15 to 20 high-velocity rounds a minute, it would become the most famous artillery piece of the Second World War, a versatile weapon Allied soldiers dreaded. The Spanish war was turning out to be a superb laboratory for Hitler.

Franco's attack was launched on February 6, 1937, and in the first few days the Nationalists managed to kill or wound well over 1,000 Republican soldiers and to come dangerously close to the Madrid–Valencia road. Republican commanders rushed new troops, principally the International Brigades, to defend the road's threatened flank. It was here that Pat Gurney and his comrades were sent, ordered forward through rain-soaked olive groves under heavy Nationalist artillery fire. The volunteers were relieved to have rifles at last. "We began to feel like men again and something of the spirit of the crusade came back into us," Gurney wrote. "Had I realized that one half of our company would be dead within the next twenty-four hours, I might have felt differently."

As Gurney's British battalion marched to the front, American volunteers were being rushed into training. The Communist Party had begun quietly enlisting men in late 1936, and the recruits came from across the social spectrum. James Yates's grandmother had been a slave. A fifteen-year-old when blue-uniformed Yankee troops arrived at her Mississippi plantation, she would die in her eighties while her grandson drove supply trucks in Spain. Of the roughly 90 other black American volunteers, some had hoped to fight against Mussolini's seizure of Ethiopia, and one coined the phrase "This ain't Ethiopia, but it'll do." The faces and hands of other volunteers bore telltale blue marks where carbon dust was embedded in a healed cut or scratch—the sign of a coal miner. Frank Alexander had grown up on a Nebraska Indian reservation speaking both English and Sioux; his father had been a Pony Express rider. Irving Goff was a vaudeville acrobat. Len Levenson and Bob Colver had both been fingerprint technicians for the FBI (and secret Communists). Hyman Katz was a rabbi. David McKelvy White's father had just finished a term as governor of Ohio.

About three quarters of the American volunteers were members of the Communist Party or its youth league, and some had known each other as children in the Party's summer camps. Their average age was twenty-nine. Many were labor unionists who would find themselves sharing trenches with men who had once walked the same picket lines. Because of strikes on the New York waterfront and in the garment industry, many early volunteers were unemployed sailors, longshoremen, or clothing workers. A third or more were from the greater New York City area—some 60 were students, faculty, staff, or graduates of City College alone. Close to half were Jewish and in Spain could speak Yiddish with volunteers from other countries; at least ten were alumni of a single institution, the Hebrew Orphan Asylum of Brooklyn. "For us it wasn't Franco," said New Yorker Maury Colow, "it was always Hitler."

None of the Americans came from illustrious lineages like John Cornford, the descendant of Charles Darwin killed at Madrid, or fellow Briton Julian Bell, a nephew of Virginia Woolf, who would be fatally wounded on another Spanish battlefield, or Lewis Clive, who could claim as an ancestor Clive of India, the eighteenth-century general who helped bring the wealth of the subcontinent under British control. None had the political perspicacity of someone like George Orwell, and the future writers among them were not the equals of volunteers like him or André Malraux. The Americans in Spain win a place in history not for who they were or what they wrote but for what they did. By the end there would be men from 46 states and all walks of life fighting there, but if there was a prototypical volunteer, he was a New Yorker, a Communist, an immigrant or the son of immigrants, a trade unionist, and a member of a group that has almost vanished from the United States today, working-class Jews.

The only other systematic attempt to recruit Americans to fight in Spain was made by the Socialist Party, but it netted a mere handful of men. The Communists were far better organized, and turned few applicants down. Indeed, as the historian Peter N. Carroll writes, "One volunteer went to Spain with a metal knee brace; another was blind in one eye. Still another served in combat with a wooden leg! (It was discovered when a machine-gun bullet shattered the 'limb.')" Even so, "most American volunteers were better fed and consequently healthier than their European counterparts."

Communist Party officials were worried about being prosecuted for recruiting for a foreign army on American soil, and members of the first group of volunteers were told to say they were traveling to Europe as tourists, students, or hikers. Each of them, however, was given an identical cheap black cardboard suitcase with yellow straps containing First World War uniforms from a New York army surplus store owned by a Party sympathizer. The nearly 100 young men boarding the French Line's triple-funneled flagship *Normandie* on December 26, 1936, were also told not to associate with each other on shipboard, an instruction they found easier to obey once they discovered that among the passengers were the chorus girls from Paris's famous Folies Bergère.

Despite precautions, everyone else seemed to guess where the men were heading. A friendly passport officer told volunteer Bill Bailey, a hulking sailor and longshoreman who traveled on a later ship, "Keep your head down." One volunteer would find that the crew slipped him extra food; another, who stayed discreetly silent whenever the dinner conversation touched on the war in Spain, was startled at the end of the voyage when a New York businessman at his table whispered, "Good luck where you're going," and gave him an envelope of cash.

When the *Normandie* docked at Le Havre, customs officials in their round pillbox hats smiled at the identical suitcases and exclaimed, "*Vive la République!*" The volunteers found French newspapers filled with accounts of the unprecedented General Motors sit-down strike that had begun that week, in which tens of thousands of autoworkers would occupy more than half a dozen GM plants in Michigan. Nearly five million Americans would go on strike in 1937. On both sides of the Atlantic, it seemed, revolution was in the air.

It was a heady experience to travel through France, the third-class compartments of the Red Express packed with people singing the "Internationale" and other songs in languages ranging from Swedish to Hungarian. Americans, Austrians, Italians, Danes, Germans, and men from a dozen other countries shared wine, cheese, salami, and long loaves of French bread. The volunteers leaned from the windows to exchange exuberant clenched-fist salutes with laborers in the fields, truck drivers, and railway track workers. As the train pulled out of stations, people ran along the platform cheering and blowing kisses.

After traveling across the Pyrenees into Spain on an ancient school bus, one of the Americans raised a clenched fist and shouted to some men at the roadside, "*¡Viva la República!*" Back came, instead, the anarchist salute (clasped hands over the head, symbolizing brotherhood) and the cry, "*¡No, viva la revolución proletaria!*" Still, whatever their differences, Spaniards of all the left factions cheered and embraced these new arrivals who had crossed an ocean to fight beside them. Bands played, people shouted "*¡No pasarán!*," and a banquet was laid on.

A few days later, the US consul general in Barcelona was astonished to see a mass of men — 15 fewer than had embarked in New York: some had too good a time in Paris, missed the train, and were sent on later — marching four abreast in First World War khaki, through the Plaza de Cataluña in front of his office. Carrying an American flag, they stopped beneath the consulate windows to sing "The Star-Spangled Banner." Most extraordinarily, they also sang the words to the seldom-heard later verses. The third, for instance, begins:

And where is that band who so vauntingly swore
That the havoc of war and the battle's confusion,
A home and a country should leave us no more!
Their blood has washed out their foul footsteps' pollution.

The startled consul undoubtedly did not know the common left-wing joke, "How can you tell who's a Y.C.L.er [member of the Young Communist League]? Anyone who knows the third stanza of 'The

Star-Spangled Banner.'" The Communist Party was always eager to prove it was thoroughly American. The next day, more men trooped through the spacious plaza, this time under a red banner that read 1ER BATALLÓN AMERICANO ABRAHAM LINCOLN. That name, too, was an attempt by the Party to stanch any suspicion that it wasn't fully American. After all, Lincoln led the victorious side in a civil war ignited, like Spain's, by a military uprising against an elected national government.

More groups of Americans soon arrived to join the Abraham Lincoln Battalion, under instructions, should anyone ask about their politics, to merely say "anti-Fascist." By mid-February 1937, nearly 400 of them had reached Albacete, where one likened André Marty's oversize beret to "a soggy black flapjack." In a speech to the US volunteers, Marty boomed a warning that they must search out and expel any Trotskyists or other "political deviates." Sour enough to begin with, the Frenchman was angry that the US Communist Party had sent him few men with military experience. But the situation was dire: these inexperienced newcomers would have to be trained and thrown into battle in a hurry. When they were told to go and select boots that fit them, they found a pile some two feet high. None were new and many had bloodstains. These were the boots of soldiers who would be fighting no more.

One American was already at the front. He had arrived in Spain before the Lincoln Battalion was formed, and had joined the British volunteers.

Joseph Selligman Jr. was from Louisville, Kentucky, Lois Orr's hometown. The mothers of the two, in fact, appear to have known each other. Selligman and his two sisters had grown up in an unusual home: their father was a former chairman of the Republican Party of Kentucky, but their mother voted Socialist. Only a few months earlier, Joe had begun his senior year at Swarthmore College in Pennsylvania, where he was editor of the campus literary magazine and a member of the debating team. He hoped to go on to Harvard as a graduate student in philosophy. A doodle later found among his college papers, however, provides a clue to what was increasingly on his mind. He had drawn a rough map on which Germany, Italy, Portugal, and Nationalist Spain were colored black. It was captioned, "Europe: Again Victim of the Black Plague."

On December 11, 1936, the day, as it happened, that King Edward VIII announced to his people that he was abdicating the British throne to marry "the woman I love," Joe's mother telephoned her son at Swarthmore. She was told, to her shock, that he had disappeared.

His parents finally received a letter from him, mailed by a friend after a week's deliberate delay, that began, "By the time you get this letter I will be in Europe. I am going to Spain. . . . I am really too excited and angry . . . to do anything else. . . . Besides, a lot of good a diploma would do in a Fascist era—and Spain seems to me to be the crucial test." Frantic, his father sent a telegram to the father of a college friend of Joe's, whose home in Vermont Joe had visited for Thanksgiving: JUST LEARNED OUR SON JOSEPH LEFT SWARTHMORE COLLEGE DECEMBER THIRD FOR SPAIN STOP RUMORED YOUR SON GONE WITH HIM STOP . . . WIRE ANY INFORMATION YOU HAVE. But this was not the case; Joe had confided nothing to the other family of his plans, said a telegram of reply. The Vermont father followed up with a letter. "We found Joseph a very agreeable guest," he wrote. ". . . After his trip up here, he wrote us a very kind and courteous note of thanks."

In the letter to his parents, Joe added, "Please don't try to follow or catch me or anything." But Selligman's father, a prominent lawyer who had argued cases before the Supreme Court, did try. He hired a New Jersey private detective with international contacts and brought him to his Louisville law office, where the man fired off cables and phone messages to steamship lines, passport offices, and American consulates. Through an agent in France, the detective managed to locate Joe in Paris, where he had gone to enlist. Selligman Sr. then sent a young law partner racing across the Atlantic, to try to persuade Joe to come home. The family also mobilized the American ambassador to France, who was the cousin of a Louisville attorney they knew, and Joe was somehow talked into coming to the embassy to receive a phone call from his parents. Their efforts were in vain.

The International Brigades recruiters first turned Joe down, telling him that at nineteen he was too young. He solved the problem by trying again, after paying $15 for the identity documents of an Irishman, Frank Neary. Once accepted, he traveled on to Spain, happy to join the British battalion under Neary's name because, he confessed in one letter, "an alias rather adds to the adventure-feeling, romance, etc." He would be far from the only volunteer to fight under a name he was not born with. In such times, changing your name felt like a sign that you could remake yourself as you were remaking the world.

In letters home Joe Selligman mentioned proudly that he was growing a beard and a mustache, and in one he included a photograph of himself in uniform with a beret. "Quit worrying," he wrote his family before he began training with the British volunteers. "I am in no danger." He would work as a driver or an interpreter, he said, and so stay out of the line of fire. After all, he knew French, German, a little Spanish, and "also I am learning to speak British." Selligman's father, not at all reassured, wrote to Louis Fischer, knowing he was covering Spain for the *Nation*, pleading with him to make inquiries about Joe.

February 11, 1937, was the day that Selligman, the London sculptor Pat Gurney, and the rest of the hastily trained British battalion marched to the front line. In the battle for Madrid, Selligman would be the first American to go into combat.

The soldiers were relieved to leave their ramshackle training base behind. The next day dawned clear and cold. As Franco's artillery boomed and fighters dove and wheeled in a dogfight overhead, the British received orders to move forward. The landscape into which they advanced was a lovely one of pine, oak, cypress, and olive trees scattered across a plateau and valley, carpeted here and there with fragrant marjoram and sage. For a moment, positioned on hills with a view of the countryside, feeling part of a great international effort (French and Belgian volunteers were to their right), "we looked mag-

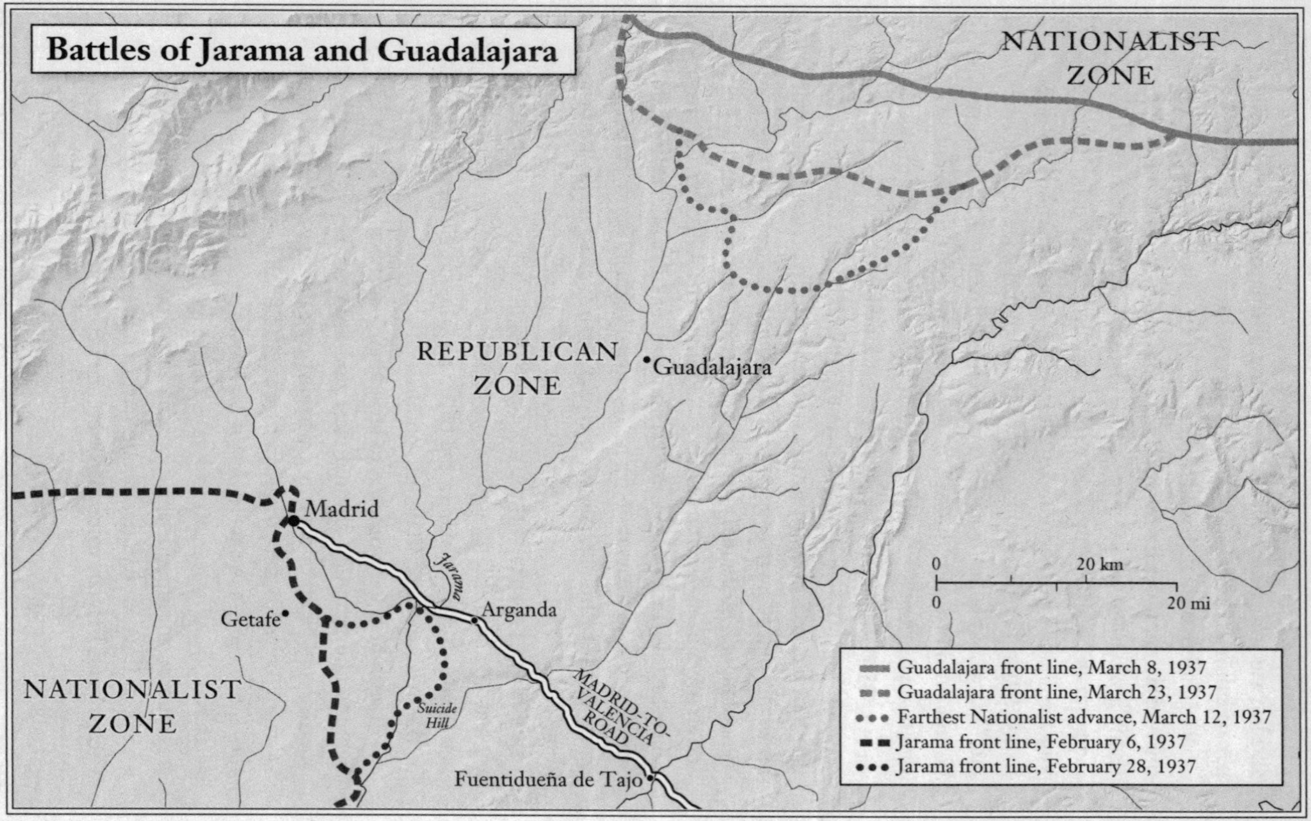
Battles of Jarama and Guadalajara
NATIONALIST ZONE
REPUBLICAN ZONE
Guadalajara
Madrid
Jarama
Arganda
Getafe
NATIONALIST ZONE
Suicide Hill
MADRID-TO-VALENCIA ROAD
Fuentidueña de Tajo
0
20 km
0
20 mi
Guadalajara front line, March 8, 1937
Guadalajara front line, March 23, 1937
Farthest Nationalist advance, March 12, 1937
Jarama front line, February 6, 1937
Jarama front line, February 28, 1937

nificent, we felt magnificent," remembered one battalion member, "and we thought that if only our colleagues back home . . . could see us now, how proud they would be."

But "not even the Brigade staff," according to Gurney, "possessed maps . . . and they were dependent on reports arriving in four different languages." Furthermore, the unit's machine guns—most of them prone to quickly jam—required four kinds of ammunition, and its rifles a fifth. Some belts of bullets didn't fit any of the battalion's machine guns. One advantage the British theoretically had was that part of their position was on higher ground. When a three-hour Nationalist artillery barrage began, however, they christened the place Suicide Hill. They had no training in digging trenches and foxholes—and there were no shovels.

Then came an attack by thousands of Moors, "their uniform," wrote Gurney, "covered by a brownish poncho blanket with a hole in the middle which appeared to flutter around them as they ran. . . . It was terrifying to watch the uncanny ability of the Moorish infantry to exploit the slightest fold in the ground which could be used for cover. . . . It was a formidable opposition to be faced by a collection of city-bred young men with no experience of war, no idea of how to find cover on an open hillside, and no competence as marksmen." The superior number of Nationalist troops and the relentless pounding of German artillery took a terrible toll on the battalion, against which a stream of exhortations from brigade headquarters in French and Russian was little help.

Enemy shelling cut the battalion's telephone lines, so Joe Selligman was assigned to be a message runner. As the day wore on, the toll continued to mount. By evening only 125 out of the battalion's 400 riflemen had not been wounded or killed. "Everywhere men are lying," remembered one survivor. "Men with a curious ruffled look, like a dead bird."

Near dusk, Pat Gurney unexpectedly came upon a group of wounded. They had been carried "to a non-existent field dressing station from which they should have been taken back to the hospital, and now they had been forgotten. There were about fifty stretchers all of which were occupied, but many of the men had already died and most of the others would die before morning. . . . They were all men whom I had known well, and some of them intimately—one little Jewish kid of about eighteen whose peculiar blend of Cockney and Jewish humour had given him a capacity for clowning around and getting a laugh out of everyone . . . now lay on his back with a wound that appeared to have entirely cut away the muscle structure of his stomach so that his bowels were exposed from his navel to his genitals. His intestines lay in loops of ghastly pinkish brown, twitching slightly as the flies searched around over them. He was perfectly conscious, unable to speak."

The experience seared Gurney. "I went from one to the other but was absolutely powerless to do anything other than to hold a hand or light a cigarette. . . . I did what I could to comfort them and promised to try and get some ambulances. Of course I failed, which left me with a feeling of guilt which I never entirely shed. . . . They were all calling for water but I had none to give them."

One British battalion member who may well have been in this group of wounded was Joe Selligman, for during the day's fighting he received a bullet in the head from the attacking Moors. Finally evacuated by mule—a jolting nightmare for a soldier with a head wound—he ended up in a hospital near Madrid.

When his family heard this news they immediately began sending panic-stricken messages to American diplomats in both Spain and Washington. URGENTLY REQUEST EFFORT BE MADE TO REMOVE HIM FURTHER FROM FIGHTING ZONE OR INTO FRANCE IF POSSIBLE AND HIS CONDITION PERMITS, his father telegraphed Secretary of State Cordell Hull, I WILL BEAR ALL NECESSARY EXPENSE. On what happened next the record is contradictory. A flowery letter from Harry Pollitt, chief of the British Communist Party, assured Mr. Selligman that young Joe had been "taken to hospital where he was given every available treatment, and expressed his own appreciation of the kindness and solicitude of all those who came in contact with him." But a British survivor of the battle, a fellow message runner, told a family friend that Joe never regained consciousness. Whatever the case, within two weeks of being wounded—or possibly less; no medical records survive—he was dead.

The same letter from Pollitt spoke of how well liked Joe was, of "the sublime self-sacrifice of so many fine sons such as your own," and said that Joe had been "buried with full military honours." But when his grieving father asked American diplomats to see if Joe's body could be sent home, again offering to pay all expenses, a telegram from the secretary of state suggested a different story, saying that the remains CANNOT BE REMOVED FOR REBURIAL AS HE WAS BURIED WITH SOME SEVEN OR EIGHT MEN WHICH WOULD MAKE INDIVIDUAL IDENTIFICATION IMPRACTICABLE. The secretary was actually softening news received from an American diplomat in Spain. Two days earlier, he had reported to Washington that at the time of Joe's death THERE WERE SOME 250 OTHER SOLDIERS WHOSE BODIES HAD TO BE REMOVED FROM THE HOSPITAL AND BURIED AT ONCE.

Unable to recover his son's body, Joe's father asked the State Department's help in sending home his belongings. All that could be found, however, fitted into a single envelope: two billfolds containing a Kentucky driver's license and an ID card from the Swarthmore College gym.

As trucks and ambulances full of Republican wounded were taken to the rear, an Australian volunteer nurse wrote in her diary, "We seem to wade about in a river of blood without a break." The shortage of adequate helmets meant that many soldiers, like Joe Selligman, had succumbed to head wounds. But the Nationalists had failed to cut the critical Madrid–Valencia road. While the surviving British and other Internationals established a new defensive line, the American battalion, whose members had little idea of the carnage the British had suffered, was sent to the front.

For Pat Gurney, deeply shaken by all he had seen and by being unable to help the wounded men, the next ten days passed in an exhausted blur. "I must," he wrote, "have recovered considerably by the 22nd February because I distinctly remember my first encounter with the Lincoln Battalion. They came marching along the road, only about three hundred yards from the Fascist lines [which were] concealed by a shoulder of the hillside. . . . There were about five or six hundred men. . . . They had imagined that they would hear the thunder of a battle, long before they arrived. But it so happened that there was nothing more than a desultory sniping fire at that particular moment. What would have happened to them if they had gone on around the bend of the road, I dread to think. They were led by a tall, bespectacled character who looked like a schoolmaster, draped in pistols, binoculars and all the panoply of war. He was very indignant when I came screaming down off the hill, shouting at them to stop."

Gurney later heard other Americans refer to the tall officer leading them as "the college boy." It was Bob Merriman.

When Merriman had arrived in Spain in early January 1937, he had trouble at first finding anyone willing to let him fight. Unlike most volunteers, he had come alone, not in a group recruited by his country's Communist Party. Only on January 22—a month before Gurney saw him on the road—was he allowed to join up. "Lonesome for Marion," he wrote in his diary the next day, "but in general satisfied."

Even in the suspicious eyes of André Marty, Merriman had two things going for him. One was that, despite showing up as a loner, he had arrived from Moscow. An American soldier heard a rumor that he had come from the Frunze Military Academy, the Soviet staff college; another wondered if he was a Party VIP, because he was receiving telegrams from the Soviet capital (these actually came from Marion). Had he perhaps been sent by the Kremlin to report back on brigade officials? The other factor in Merriman's favor was that, unlike almost all the other American volunteers, he'd had ROTC training and was an officer in the US Army Reserve.

In the biographical statement he wrote on enlisting in the International Brigades, Merriman exaggerated both points. He promoted himself to captain in the Reserve and claimed that he had spent a year at a "Communist Academy" in Moscow—which sounded more impressive than the eight months of classes he apparently took at the Institute of Economics.

Immediately, he was appointed the Lincoln Battalion's second-in-command. The commander, a US Army veteran who had come over on the *Normandie*, proved given to drink, incoherent monologues, and disappearing at crucial moments. Before long, Merriman was ordered to replace him. It was during these early weeks that he finally joined the Communist Party—of Spain.

In little time he would come to be admired even by those not following Party discipline. "Merriman was universally liked and respected . . . one of those rare men who radiate strength and inspire confidence by their very appearance," recalled battalion member Sandor Voros, though by the time he was writing, Voros had become a vocal anti-Communist. "He was tall and broad-shouldered with a ruddy bronze complexion. . . . The physical strength of the athlete combined with the reserved manners of the scholar and the introspective expression in his eyes bespoke great inner power."

As he took over the training of the Americans, Merriman lectured them on what he could remember from ROTC: scouting, signaling, map reading (though they had no proper maps), throwing grenades, and digging trenches. He showed the recruits how to take apart and reassemble machine guns and some bulletless Canadian rifles, more than 30 years old, they had been given for training.

The unit's morale was low: endless lectures about politics were no substitute for live ammunition, there were too few blankets for the winter nights, and some men were beginning to feel uneasy because Marty's staff had confiscated their passports "for safekeeping." A few weeks earlier, Pat Gurney, more savvy than these newcomers, had managed to hide his own. Eventually, some 580 American volunteers would report "lost" passports to the State Department. The Soviets wanted these for their own purposes. A Canadian volunteer's passport, for example, would be used by the Soviet agent who assassinated Leon Trotsky in Mexico in 1940.

At meals, the Americans were given mule or burro meat "so tough it defied chewing," one volunteer wrote. "It was elastic like an old auto tire and snapped back when one tried to take a big bite out of it. It had to be swallowed and left for the digestive juices to do the rest." The petty rivalries and tensions that afflict any group living in close quarters were exacerbated by the fact that few of the men had ever been under military discipline, though many of them, as union members, had plenty of experience in loudly demanding their rights. Furthermore, the International Brigades had a confusing dual structure modeled on the Red Army: in addition to its commanding officer, each unit at every level also had a commissar, whose duties were to watch morale and keep everyone on the correct political path, and who could sometimes overrule the commander.

In the evening, Americans who had had their eye on the opposite sex found themselves sorely frustrated. If a couple went for a walk holding hands, her parents would follow along behind. "The only time you'll receive a picture of me with a *señorita* on my knee," one man wrote home, "is if her mother is seated on the other one." Doctors handed out condoms, but most soldiers could use them only as tobacco pouches. When volunteer Harry Fisher invited an attractive girl of about eighteen to the movies, her entire family came along, taking the seats between them. Another soldier thought he had found gold when he discovered an organization of young anarchist women called Mujeres Libres, but "it soon transpired all they were interested in was talking politics."

American volunteers discovered that villagers assumed they were there because President Roosevelt—said to be a friend of the poor—had sent them. What did the Spaniards make of these foreigners among them? It is risky to generalize, but many Lincolns remembered moments of warmth. "The Spanish peasants had never seen a Negro before," wrote Tennessee-born Vaughn Love, who would be twice wounded, "and I happened to be at the village fountain one day, while a group of peasant women were getting water and gossiping. They surrounded me and gave me a good examination. They rubbed my face to see if the color would come off. . . . One of the women embraced me and said, 'los esclavos' (the slaves). I was very much impressed when each and every one of the women took their turn and embraced me."

There were usually 500 or more men in each battalion, and the Lincolns were one of four that made up the XV International Brigade. (At this point, the others were the ill-fated British battalion, a French-Belgian one, and a battalion mainly of Eastern Europeans.) The Republic was throwing all available Internationals into the battle to defend the Madrid–Valencia road, and one by one, ahead of the Americans, other battalions had been dispatched to the front. The Americans had little idea how badly the British had been mauled.

Late one afternoon, a motley convoy of trucks with the three-pointed red star of the International Brigades on their sides appeared at the Lincolns' training base, collected the men, and took them to the bullring in Albacete. After dark, with the *plaza de toros* lit by the trucks' headlights, Marty and other high commanders told them that defending the road was the greatest task facing the Republic and that once again the Internationals were needed to save Madrid. British and French officers also spoke, the men shouted "*¡No pasarán!*," and the senior officers shook hands with the soldiers and departed.

From a supply truck the Americans were ordered to unload wooden crates. Pried open, these yielded Remington bolt-action rifles still in packing grease, wrapped in Mexico City newspapers. Some were old enough to bear the double eagle of tsarist Russia. The men were also issued needle-like "pig-sticker" bayonets, but many of the rifles had no place to attach them. They had nothing with which to clean off the grease, so Merriman told them to tear strips of cloth from their shirts.

The Lincolns cannot have been feeling confident when he then ordered them onto the canvas-covered trucks, which carried them under a single swinging light bulb above the bullring's massive gates and out into the night. After many freezing, bumpy hours on the road to the front, they were allowed out of the trucks to test-fire their new rifles at the wall of a quarry: five cartridges apiece. For most of them—city boys from places like Brooklyn or Detroit who had never hunted—these were the first shots they had ever fired. Then disaster struck: no one had maps, the disorganized Republican army had not posted any guides at road junctions, and the first two trucks in the convoy, carrying more than a dozen American volunteers, at least one Canadian, and all the battalion records, missed a turn and ended up driving straight into Nationalist territory. The men were never heard from again.

The remaining trucks made the correct turn, and when they stopped the men in them were ordered to dig trenches in the rocky soil. "Marion dear I love you!" Merriman scribbled in his diary in a rare burst of feeling. "I am willing to die for my ideas—May I live for them and you! Received orders to go into action." After digging through the night with helmets and bayonets—there were still no shovels—at dawn the Americans found themselves under heavy machine-gun and artillery fire. It turned out that they had dug themselves into dangerously exposed positions on a skyline. The battalion artillery observer, Charles Edwards, poked his head up to survey the situation and promptly died with a sniper's bullet through his skull.

It was after the Lincolns had endured several more days under fire that Pat Gurney encountered Merriman leading his troops down a road to new positions—and new setbacks. Several men broke under the stress; one, disturbingly, was Merriman's second-in-command: "Steve Daduk cracked up and I recommended him to rest home." On February 23, 1937, the Lincolns made their first attack, advancing through olive groves, but none of the battalion's eight machine guns turned out to work. Twenty men were killed and more than 40 wounded. A fresh group of some 70 untrained Americans arrived, some still wearing civilian clothes and Keds sneakers. Desperately, as the troops dug trenches, Merriman tried to reorganize the battalion and make sense of logistical chaos, since his men were equipped with no less than 17 different types of firearms. To match them with the right bullets, he set up a wooden table with sample cartridges taped to it, each labeled.

On top of everything else, it began to snow.

As February 27 dawned, loaves of bread and jars of coffee, already cold, were delivered to the trenches. To Merriman's horror, the Lincolns were again ordered to attack. But the barrage of Republican artillery that was supposed to soften up the Nationalist trenches had come three hours late and missed its target. Of the 20 Republican aircraft scheduled to support the attack, only three briefly appeared. Promised new machine guns and armored cars did not materialize. A Spanish battalion that was to move forward side by side with the Lincolns tried to advance, met heavy enemy fire, then abruptly pulled back. Worst of all, Nationalist machine-gunners had the Lincolns' trenches squarely in their sights. "They pitted the sand-bags all along the line in a constant staccato," one volunteer later recalled. The streams of bullets "sprayed in our direction like the heavy pounding of a riveting machine."

On a field telephone, Merriman called brigade headquarters to protest that an advance would be suicidal. He was shouted down by the brigade commander, an imperious Yugoslav who demanded that the Americans attack "at all costs." Against all evidence, the commander insisted, in a rage, that the Spanish battalion had advanced far ahead of the Lincolns. He then dispatched two officers on a motorcycle to Merriman's post to make sure his order was carried out. All four of these men undoubtedly knew that two months earlier, after Republican reverses on a different front, an angry André Marty had seen to it that a French battalion commander whom he thought too timid was accused of being a spy, court-martialed, and shot by a firing squad. Bob Merriman was not only facing the harsh discipline of the Communist International, where any dissent risked an accusation of espionage, but facing war itself, for the firing squad was common to many armies of this era. In the First World War, the British military alone executed more than 300 soldiers for desertion, cowardice, the casting away of arms, or disobeying orders. The French shot roughly twice that number.

Now a world away from being merely a graduate student gathering dissertation material, Merriman felt he had no choice. Reluctant and agonized, he gave the order for the Lincolns to attack, and stepped out of the trench to lead the men forward himself.

• • •

In Moscow, a second big show trial was under way, with more wild accusations that high officials were secret accomplices of Trotsky, Germany, and Japan. In her memoirs Marion Merriman refers only to the "frightening rumors" that swept the city, commenting that "most Russians were guarded in any conversation that led to the subject of politics." Her main fears were for Bob in Spain.

While he was in training, letters had arrived sporadically. He talked about the country's poverty, and about the hospitality the volunteers received, and said how much he missed her. Only once did he mention political issues, dutifully echoing the Party line about going slow on revolutionary change.

"Then," she wrote, "the shattering news arrived."

It was a four-word telegram: WOUNDED. COME AT ONCE.

7

Rifles from the 1860s

Of all nations on earth in the late 1930s, the one that possessed the most mismatched array of weaponry was the Soviet Union. Modern arms were coming off new assembly lines, but a huge assortment of more antiquated munitions filled armories and warehouses spread across the vast country. Some were left over from prerevolutionary Russia. Others were weapons the Tsar's army had captured from the even more decrepit Austro-Hungarian military in the early days of the First World War. And still more had been left behind by the defeated counterrevolutionary White forces in the Russian Civil War of 1918–21, which had been supplied by the United States, Britain, Canada, France, Italy, Japan, and some half-dozen other countries, each with its own equipment.

Franco's propagandists made much of the fact that Stalin was sending arms to the Republic. But the Nationalists little knew that some of these much-vaunted Soviet weapons were barely usable. Only when Moscow archives were opened more than half a century later did a British military historian, Gerald Howson, discover many of the details.

Equipping an army is much easier, of course, if everybody has the same models of rifles, machine guns, and artillery, all using the same kinds of ammunition. What was being unloaded with such great anticipation from Soviet ships arriving in Spain in late 1936 and early 1937, however, included German grenade throwers that had become obsolete 20 years earlier and a variety of clumsy single-shot rifles more than 60 years old. Of 9,000 American Winchesters, some had left the company's Connecticut factory in the 1860s. More than 13,000 Italian rifles firing a bullet 11 mm in diameter had apparently been captured by Russia in an 1877 war with Turkey. Some 11,000 more 11 mm rifles of French and Austrian manufacture used bullets not interchangeable with the Italian ones, and in any case, ammunition of this caliber had not been manufactured for four decades. Once the paltry supply included was exhausted, the rifles would be useless.

Heavy weapons were little better, another multinational potpourri chosen, as Soviet Defense Commissar Marshal Kliment Voroshilov wrote to Stalin, "to rid ourselves, once and for all, of the artillery of foreign—British, French and Japanese—manufacture." The Spaniards called one set of artillery pieces from tsarist times "the battery of Catherine the Great."

Among the machine guns delivered were more than 300 French Saint-Étiennes dating from 1907, whose gunner perched on a raised bicycle-style seat. A group of Internationals who unpacked the first batch were bewildered, remembered a British volunteer: "We looked blankly at one another. . . . There were men who had been in half a dozen wars, in half a dozen armies . . . but none of them had ever come across a machine-gun remotely like this.

"They were the most extraordinary machines—beautifully made, insanely complicated, the lock (whose principles we never really understood) working on a system of cogs and slides that had the complexity of one of those old-fashioned clocks whose mechanism also indicates the days of the month and eclipses of the moon. But what worried us most was their weight." With seat and tripod, each was more than 120 pounds. Moreover, they jammed regularly—one reason why they had been withdrawn from the French army in 1914.

It was no wonder that Bob Merriman had been frustrated by the bewildering variety of ammunition his men had to contend with at Jarama. A postwar inventory would find among Republican armaments 49 different types of rifles, 41 models of machine guns, and an astonishing 60 varieties of artillery. Once these antique weapons had been cleared out of Soviet warehouses, the quality of arms sent to Spain would improve, and top-of-the-line Soviet tanks and aircraft, in particular, were already an essential part of the hard-pressed Republic's arsenal. In the first months, however, there was less to Soviet support than met the eye—though the Spaniards paid dearly for it, shipping to Russia some three quarters of the Republic's enormous gold reserves.

The government had little choice. The Soviets were the only major nation willing to sell it arms, and the gold was at risk of capture not only by the Nationalists, but also by the anarchists, experienced as they were in bank robberies. At one point in late 1936 they actually planned a raid on the Bank of Spain, but then dropped the idea. It certainly would not have been safe to store the gold in Britain or France, whose governments might well have frozen it. (Under pressure from the French right, the Bank of France, in fact, had done just that for a time with some Spanish Republic gold it had on deposit.)

The Soviets treated the gold as an account to be gradually debited for the arms being sent to Spain. Disguised in wooden ammunition boxes, the gold was first moved to tightly guarded caves on a naval base at the port of Cartagena. "This is the heavy artillery of the Republic!" soldiers were told. "Handle it carefully!" In the course of three nights in October 1936, while Hitler's bombers raided the blacked-out city, drivers trucked the gold to docks where it was loaded onto four small Soviet freighters for the voyage to Odessa. Under the eyes of secret policemen, railway boxcars carried the treasure onward to Moscow. In addition to boxes of ingots, the normal form in which national banks hold gold, thousands of cloth sacks tied shut with twine contained an estimated 60 million coins—francs, dollars, marks, lire, florins, pesos, escudos, pesetas, and more that Spain's government had accumulated over the centuries. Using an old Russian expression, Stalin told his entourage that the Spanish would never see their gold again "any more than they can see their own ears." They wouldn't, but without the arms that came in return, the Republic's army might well have been defeated by the end of 1936.

Not all of the outdated weaponry arrived directly from Soviet warehouses. Much of it was purchased in nations that ranged from Bolivia and Paraguay to Estonia and Poland, where dealers, by acquiring some of the Soviet stock of antiquated arms, prepared to take full advantage of Republican Spain's urgent need. Even under the best of circumstances, buying arms is not a trade for amateurs, which the Republic's representatives distinctly were. Con men took advantage of them. One favorite tactic of black market merchants was to suddenly raise the price, claiming that a Republican offer for a shipment of weaponry was being outbid by an agent of Franco's. Shrewd dealers also played off political factions against one another or undermined a hard-bargaining Republican arms buyer in Copenhagen or Brussels by whispering in the right ear in Madrid that the man couldn't be trusted. Many of the arms the Republic paid for were never delivered. Fighter planes arrived without machine guns, and artillery pieces without sights. Customs officials delayed shipments and demanded bribes or storage fees, other countries charged high sums for export licenses, and mysterious transit fees were added to bills. And there was little help to be had from the world's greatest manufacturing power, the United States.

President Roosevelt's desire to stay out of the Spanish war was making it harder for Americans even to go to the country, as a frightened Marion Merriman discovered. On the way to Spain, she sought help from a friend at the US consulate in Paris. He immediately walked her out of the building, beyond earshot of his colleagues, and said, "If I see your passport, I have to stamp it, 'Not Valid for Travel in Spain.'" This was the US government's attempt to discourage volunteers for the Lincoln Battalion; the State Department was granting exemptions only to journalists, medical or relief workers, and the occasional VIP.

Marion traveled first to Valencia, where Milly Bennett had found work in the Republican government's news bureau. About Bob, Bennett told her, "He's in the Hospital Internacional in Murcia."

To a young Englishwoman, Kate Mangan, who worked with Bennett, Marion said: "I'll do my damnedest to get Bob right out of Spain and the whole business. The worst of it is he believes in the cause." Marion, Mangan would remember, "seemed so young, from a different world, still believing in normal human happiness which we had all forgotten." In Valencia, Marion found a flood of anxious cables from home, for American newspapers had reported that Bob had been wounded and many Lincolns killed.

In Murcia, a city in southeastern Spain, she found him. He was "encased from waist to left shoulder, his left forearm frozen in a crooked position just above his belt buckle. The doctors lacked [lightweight] cast plaster and were forced to bind Bob's shattered shoulder, broken in five places by the impact of a bullet, in regular housing plaster." In his diary, normally a laconic record of political and military meetings, Bob wrote, "Marion came . . . walked around in a dream with her."

Bob was "broad as [a] house in the shoulders and strong as an ox," recalled Bennett, who also visited him, "but he was never able to stay on his feet more than 15 minutes at a time when the arm was mending. The weight of the . . . cast wore him down." The doctors promised him a full recovery, but it would clearly take time.

Marion volunteered for work at the hospital, and soon was writing letters home for wounded Americans unable to hold a pen. "I even sat on top of an English volunteer with two fractured vertebrae who was determined to get out of bed and walk." Medicines were limited. "We had aspirin but not much else."

From Bob she heard the story of the disastrous morning in the Jarama valley when he had been wounded, a battle he was refighting in angry memos from the hospital to XV Brigade headquarters. After being shouted at and threatened over a field telephone by the brigade's Yugoslav commander, Colonel Vladimir Copic, he had led his men out of their trench for the doomed attack. He was hit before he had gone more than a few steps.

Others tried to run forward through an olive grove, but the machine-gun fire was relentless. Some men threw themselves flat on the ground, frantically piling up dirt for protection, which snow and rain quickly turned to mud. Soon mortar shells began dropping among them. After Merriman was carried to the rear, things only became worse. Dutch stretcher bearers were shot when they tried to bring in more wounded. A British lieutenant who temporarily took over as commander only made things worse by threatening reluctant Americans with his revolver, first initiating another attack and then ordering the pinned-down men to pull back to their trench while it was still light. Those who followed the order were fatally exposed to the Nationalist machine-gunners.

In the chaos, it was unclear how many Lincoln Battalion volunteers died. Digging graves in the freezing, rocky soil was impossible, so many of the bodies were burned in a pyre and the remains left under a memorial cairn of rocks, earth, and helmets. Estimates vary, but one calculation puts the toll at 120 killed, 175 wounded. No ground was gained, and the attack was in any case unnecessary, for the Nationalist drive to cut the Madrid–Valencia road had already stalled.

While the disaster was still unfolding, the wounded Merriman felt determined "to have it out with Copic," as he would later write in his diary. But when the stretcher bearers brought him to brigade headquarters, Copic, something of a dandy who wore polished boots and sported a pistol, binoculars, and leather map case, refused to talk to him. Merriman was taken off to a medical aid station. It was "a butcher shop," he jotted down later. "People died on stretchers in yard." Painkillers ran short. His arm taped to a board, he bounced for three and a half hours on the floor of an ambulance, which lost its way before finally delivering him to an American field hospital that had been rushed into operation only a few days earlier.

The Communist Party had recruited medical volunteers as well as soldiers, and Dr. Edward Barsky and his 17-member team had arrived in Spain only a few weeks earlier. An intense, chain-smoking surgeon with a small mustache from New York City's Beth Israel Hospital, Barsky had a reputation for stoical calm and boundless energy despite being in constant pain from a stomach ulcer. As the Jarama battle began, he was handed an order: "Set up one hundred bed emergency hospital and be ready to receive patients in forty-eight hours." The doctors and nurses took over a schoolhouse and pried open the crates of American medical equipment they had brought with them. They were shaken to find that a dozen crates had disappeared en route, probably swiped by other units in an army desperately short of supplies. But nothing could be done.

Students and teachers moved out desks, books, and blackboards, while Barsky frantically mobilized local craftsmen to knock out a wall and build wooden bedsteads from scratch. Townspeople with baskets of earth and stones filled potholes in the road, to give the wounded a less jarring ride. There was no telephone, no running water, no kitchen, no toilets. "We did not put a red cross on our roof because it would have meant annihilation," wrote a nurse, "as had happened in Madrid, where hospitals had been bombed by German planes." For the same reason, ambulance drivers painted out the red crosses on their vehicles.

The medical team had been getting the place ready for two days and a sleepless night when the first load of wounded arrived. "Inside the truck on the floor were mattresses upon which about 25 wounded lay," remembered a pharmacist. "Two were already dead. Several others were very low. The rest suffered excruciating pain due to fractures and the ride over the torturing road." Soon, six more trucks rolled in, and wounded men quickly occupied all the beds, sometimes two to each, then mattresses on the floor, and still more lay on stretchers in the building's courtyard.

Within a day 200 wounded men—American, French, German, Spanish—filled a hospital equipped for 75. For 40 hours surgeons and nurses worked nonstop. Some men were in shock, and to keep them warm—the building had no heat—nurses lit small cooking stoves beneath beds or stretchers. One freezing night the feeble electricity failed, and Dr. Barsky had to finish removing a shattered kidney by the glimmer of hand-held flashlights. "Each instrument made the hand ache as in handling ice," he would remember.

"Wounded kept coming day and night. . . . While assisting at operations I used to hop first on one foot and then on the other to keep warm," recalled nurse Anne Taft. "The instruments were so cold they stuck to my hands. . . . You could see clouds of vapor rising from our patients' abdomens and other wounds." The medical unit had crossed the Atlantic on the same ship with some of the Lincoln volunteers. Lini Fuhr, another nurse, "cut through clothing of boys I had danced with on our way to Spain."

Bitter recriminations over the attack continued long after Merriman had been sent on from Barksy's hospital to convalesce in Murcia. Some soldiers put the onus on him, others on the incompetent British lieutenant who took command later in the day; Merriman himself blamed Copic; Copic blamed his superior, a much-disliked Hungarian general. The general tried to put the best face on things, claiming to a reporter that some of the American dead had been found with their fists still clenched in the Popular Front salute.

The Lincolns turned surly and suspicious, and some men deserted. One large group of furious survivors, showing their trade union background, posted sentries in their trenches and marched to the rear to demand to see the XV Brigade's commissar. It was more of a protest meeting than a mutiny, for one of their demands was for several weeks of training under officers with real military experience. Brigade officers from European countries and their Soviet advisors, unused to this kind of backtalk, were horrified. Resentment lingered for months, and one American survivor told a visiting newspaper correspondent, "You can say that the battalion was named after Abraham Lincoln because he, too, was assassinated."

What was it like to be a soldier on the other side at Jarama? As it happens, English was the native language of one of them, for Franco's army also had its foreign volunteers. Twenty-one-year-old Peter Kemp of Britain arrived at the front some ten days before Merriman was wounded. An ardent monarchist and anti-Communist who also admitted to "a feeling for adventure," Kemp had just graduated from Cambridge. With a father who was a retired judge of the High Court in Bombay, he came from a world of English country houses, private schools, titled friends, and colonial grandeur. Although speaking little Spanish, Kemp found various Nationalist noblemen or other officials who knew people he knew and charmed his way into being appointed an officer.

The Nationalist army, Kemp found, had a strict class hierarchy. Like other officers, he was given a batman, or personal servant, who fetched his food and tidied his quarters. When his unit was sent by train to new positions, the officers traveled first class, five to a compartment, the sergeants were in second class, and the ordinary soldiers, despite winter weather, in cattle cars.

Throughout the Nationalist army there were priests. One, to Kemp's amusement, was "deeply shocked when I once told him clergymen of the Church of England were permitted to marry." On his first day at Jarama, Kemp met his company's chaplain, "a stern-faced, lean Navarrese with the eyes of a fanatic gleaming behind his glasses. . . . He was the most fearless and the most bloodthirsty man I ever met in Spain. . . . '*Hola*, Don Pedro!' he shouted to me. 'So you've come to kill some Reds! Congratulations! Be sure you kill plenty!' The purple tassel of his beret swung in the candlelight."

The next day, a column of Nationalist tanks sent the Republican troops reeling in retreat. "I was conscious of Father Vicente beside me . . . he was bent on seeing that we did not allow the fleeing enemy to escape unpunished. He kept on pointing out targets to me, urging me shrilly to shoot them down. . . . He could barely restrain himself from snatching my rifle. . . . Whenever some wretched militiaman bolted from cover to run madly for safety, I would hear the good Father's voice raised in a frenzy of excitement: 'Don't let him get away—Ah!

don't let him get away! Shoot, man, shoot! A bit to the left! Ah! *that's* got him,' as the miserable fellow fell and lay twitching."

In a later battle, Father Vicente actually "led one wing of the assault, mounted on a white horse and still wearing his scarlet beret with the purple tassel."

Purple tassels notwithstanding, the Nationalist army in which Kemp was fighting was rich in modern weapons. Over the course of the war Germany alone would send Franco antiaircraft batteries that helped cripple the Republican air force, the newest field artillery, some 200 tanks, and more than 600 military aircraft. Most equipment was of the latest models, since the Wehrmacht was eager to try them out in battle. Altogether, some 19,000 German troops, aviators, instructors, and advisors would see action in Spain or take part in training thousands of Nationalist officers and NCOs.

Most important was the Condor Legion, an elite, khaki-uniformed German unit kept permanently supplied with between 99 and 132 state-of-the-art fighters, bombers, and reconnaissance aircraft. Spanish trainees were often taken along on the legion's missions. Its planes were turned over to the Nationalists when still newer models arrived. For much of the war, the unit's commander met with Franco several times a week. The Nationalists treated Condor Legion fliers as VIPs, putting an entire hotel at their disposal in Seville and arranging hunting trips, shopping excursions to Spanish Morocco, and special brothels supervised by physicians. At one of these, housed in a villa, the prostitutes received German officers in blue bedrooms and enlisted men in green cubicles.

Among the many German aviators who honed their skills in the Condor Legion was Werner Mölders, who shot down 14 Republican aircraft in Spain and, a few years later, over France, England, and Russia, would become the first Luftwaffe pilot to down 100 planes. The charismatic Adolf Galland, another pilot who would have more than 100 such victories and succeed Mölders as chief of the Luftwaffe's fighter command, spent months piloting a Heinkel He-51 fighter in Spain, flying in swimming trunks because of the heat. Twenty-seven other Germans who would become aces during the larger war to come received their first taste of combat in Spanish skies. Condor Legion veterans would also train many of the bomber crews who later took part in the blitzkrieg against Poland.

Mussolini's airplanes were less advanced, but he would send the Nationalists 762 of them by the war's end, as well as 1,801 artillery pieces, at least 149 tanks, 223,784 rifles, 3,436 machine guns, and large quantities of bombs and ammunition. Nearly 80,000 Italian troops would eventually fight for Franco. Small wonder that, in an article published on March 27, 1937, several years before newspapers around the world would begin capitalizing the phrase, Louis Fischer spoke of the coming of the "second world war."

With Franco still trying hard to encircle Madrid, most other sectors of the front were relatively quiet. It was to one of them, some 140 miles west and a little north of Barcelona, in the hilly, impoverished countryside of the Aragon region, that George Orwell and his POUM militia unit of young Spaniards were sent. When rifles were distributed, he was dismayed. His own "was rusty, the bolt was stiff, the wooden barrel-guard was split; one glance down the muzzle showed that it was corroded and past praying for. . . . The best rifle of the lot, only ten years old, was given to a half-witted little beast of fifteen." The irony was that, unlike his fellow militiamen, Orwell actually knew something about firearms, having spent nearly five years as a colonial policeman in Burma.

His unit's commander was Belgian and its doctor was from New York, but the impatient Orwell had arrived a few weeks ahead of a group of several dozen volunteers from England and at first his fellow soldiers were nearly all Spanish. In group photographs, the writer is a full head taller than the youthful recruits around him.

"You cannot possibly conceive what a rabble we looked. We straggled along with far less cohesion than a flock of sheep. . . . And half of the so-called men were children—but I mean literally children, of sixteen years old at the very most. . . . It seemed dreadful that the defenders of the Republic should be this mob of ragged children carrying worn-out rifles they did not know how to use. I remember wondering what would happen if a Fascist aeroplane passed our way—whether the airman would even bother to dive down and give us a burst from his machine-gun. Surely even from the air he could see that we were not real soldiers?"

Orwell impressed his comrades by mastering some Catalan and remained a keen observer of everything around him, jotting down his impressions in a diary. (He "was always writing," remembered an Irishman who joined his unit. "In the daytime he used to sit outside the dugout writing, and in the evenings he used to write by candlelight.") His experience of the world had been oddly mixed. A passionate commitment to radical politics had brought him to Spain, yet he had spent much of his life in hierarchies: class-conscious Britain, an education at Eton and at another exclusive boarding school before it, and then the colonial police. What fascinated him was to see how the POUM and anarchist militias were attempting to create what most people would have considered a contradiction in terms: an egalitarian army.

> Everyone from general to private drew the same pay, ate the same food, wore the same clothes, and mingled on terms of complete equality. If you wanted to slap the general commanding the division on the back and ask him for a cigarette, you could do so, and no one thought it curious. . . . Orders had to be obeyed, but it was also understood that when you gave an order you gave it as comrade to comrade and not as superior to inferior. There were officers and N.C.O.s but there was no military rank in the ordinary sense; no titles, no badges, no heel-clicking and saluting. They had attempted to produce within the militias a sort of temporary working model of the classless society. . . .
>
> I admit that at first sight the state of affairs at the front horrified me. How on earth could the war be won by an army of this type? . . . [But] a modern mechanized army does not spring up out of the ground, and if the Government had waited until it had trained troops at its disposal, Franco would never have been

> resisted. . . . The discipline of even the worst drafts of militia visibly improved as time went on. In January the job of keeping a dozen raw recruits up to the mark almost turned my hair grey. In May for a short while I was acting-lieutenant in command of about thirty men, English and Spanish. We had all been under fire for months, and I never had the slightest difficulty in getting an order obeyed.

What Orwell said was perhaps true for himself, but many officers in POUM or anarchist units did have trouble getting orders obeyed without debate—or at all.

While his POUM unit may have been striving to be a microcosm of a classless society, its living conditions were less than utopian. Daily life in the trenches was a matter of lice and "the smells of urine and rotting bread, the tinny taste of bean-stews wolfed hurriedly out of unclean pannikins." Key supplies were nonexistent, from flashlights to telescopes, and Orwell had to grease his rifle with olive oil, bacon fat, cold cream, or Vaseline. There was so little water that he shaved with wine. "The issue of candles had ceased, and matches were running short. The Spaniards taught us how to make olive oil lamps out of a condensed milk tin, a cartridge-clip, and a bit of rag. . . . These things would burn with a smoky flicker, about a quarter candle power, just enough to find your rifle by."

After he had been several months on the front line, he finally took part in his first attack, a night raid on a Nationalist position. The POUM militia by now included more than 600 foreigners from 14 countries, and among the men joining the raid were German volunteers as well as the Spaniards and Britons of his own unit. The "best of the bunch," he felt, was Bob Smillie, grandson of a famous Scottish labor leader, a Glasgow university student who entertained his fellow soldiers with lilting Scottish ballads.

Orwell's vivid description of the attack evokes the terror of floundering through muddy beet fields, of crossing an irrigation ditch "in water up to your waist, with the filthy, slimy mud oozing over your boot-tops," surrounded by fellow soldiers he could barely see in the dark: "a bunch of humped shapes like huge black mushrooms gliding slowly forward." He feared that the sucking sound of his feet in the mud would alert the enemy to their presence. Thirty men had only a single pair of shears to cut the Nationalist barbed wire. Would the enemy hear them snipping? Suddenly they were tossing grenades and exchanging rifle fire in the pitch black: "Every loophole seemed to be spouting jets of flame. It is always hateful to be shot at in the dark—every rifle-flash seems to be pointed straight at yourself." The POUM raid succeeded in breaking into the Nationalist trench, killing some defenders and forcing the others to flee.

"I remember feeling a deep horror at everything: the chaos, the darkness, the frightful din, the slithering to and fro in the mud, the struggles with the bursting sand-bags—all the time encumbered with my rifle, which I dared not put down for fear of losing it. . . . Bob Smillie, the blood running down his face from a small wound, sprang to his knee and flung a bomb." In the midst of the fighting, several German volunteers came racing down the enemy trench from a point where they, too, had broken through. But they spoke no English or Spanish and could communicate with Orwell and his comrades only in frantic sign language.

The booty from the raid: a box of ammunition, a box of hand grenades, and several rifles, all of which had to be dragged back to the POUM trenches through the mud under fire. In an army without sufficient arms, this was valuable loot.

Far to the south, in the hospital in Murcia, Bob Merriman was able to have Marion move into his room as he recuperated—a luxury enjoyed by few wounded soldiers in this or any other war. Then, while still weighed down by the cast on his shoulder and arm, he went back to work training new American volunteers. She accompanied him on visits to Madrid, where they came under shellfire, and to the trenches at Jarama. When she saw that he was determined to go back to front-line duty once he recovered, and that there was no chance of them leaving the country together as she had hoped, she decided to stay. "I would do anything to remain with Bob. So I enlisted, was issued my official papers, and became a corporal. . . . I immediately found a seamstress who would make a uniform with culottes for me of khaki wool, the same material used for the men's uniforms." Unlike most foreign volunteers, she spoke some Spanish, and before long was doing clerical work at the International Brigades headquarters in Albacete, paid six pesetas a day, the sole American woman there.

8

Over the Mountains

As the ocean liner *President Harding* approached the French port of Le Havre one day in the spring of 1937, the pilot boat that came out to meet the ship carried an American consular official. He asked the three dozen Lincoln volunteers among the passengers to assemble in the vessel's salon. "The government knows where you intend to go," he warned them, "and it is my duty to inform you that you are making a very serious and costly mistake. If you enlist in the armed forces of another country, you will forfeit your American citizenship." This was not true, but the secretary of state had advocated this position, and such proposals were being discussed in Congress. The consul added: "The U.S. government has very generously arranged to pay for your return passage to New York." There were no takers.

For the first wave of Americans, reaching Spain had been easy. A major obstacle appeared, however, in March 1937 when, under pressure from a British government sprinkled with Franco sympathizers, France closed its border to all military assistance for Spain. Crossing points were equipped with machine guns and searchlights. Armed guards with dogs began patrolling the frontier. For nearly all International Brigades volunteers from now on, reaching Spain meant a long, clandestine, arduous climb, guided by Basque smugglers, over an ever-changing network of snowy footpaths that crossed the Pyrenees.

These mountains, which rise to more than 11,000 feet, are the most formidable natural wall in Western Europe outside the Alps. Their crest forms the border between France and Spain. For most of their expanse, only a few passes allow the traveler to cross from one country to the other at less than 6,500 feet, and these all had border control posts. Carved by glaciers—and the site of ski resorts today—the forbidding terrain ensured that some American volunteers would die before they even reached the war zone.

When Sandor Voros, a Hungarian American from Ohio, crossed the mountains that spring, his group began walking at nightfall on a circuitous route far above the timber line. At one point "the guide stopped abruptly and held up his staff. We all halted. . . . Lights were bobbing hundreds of feet below us in the dark—the border patrol! . . . We pleaded with the guide to slacken the tempo but he shook his head and climbed relentlessly on. Inside my chest a fiery iron band was crushing my lungs and the pressure tightened with every breath I drew. My eyes were beginning to swell and an artery behind my ear started throbbing with the roar of a subway train."

As the group briefly stopped to rest, Voros was too exhausted to move out of the rivulet of melting snow in which, it turned out, he had lain down. "We continued climbing all through the night, and daybreak found us up in the snow belt. . . . We were in a land where few feet ever trod, a land of crags and snow-covered peaks that bore no sign of vegetation, birds, or animals. . . . Suddenly the guide sprang to his feet in great alarm. He asked us to stand up and took a rapid count. There were only sixteen of us. One comrade was missing, a German."

The guide retraced the group's steps for more than an hour, then returned. The German could not be found. Against protests, he insisted they move on. The volunteers ate snow to quench their thirst but had no food. Most had only ordinary city shoes, and their soaked feet were raw with blisters. When they gathered around a fire the second night, a shepherd appeared with news that a French patrol was in close pursuit. The men could barely get their shoes back on over swollen feet. As they were traversing a narrow ledge in the dark, Voros heard a scream: a Polish volunteer had fallen over the edge. They waited for daybreak; this time the guide was gone for two hours, but again was unable to find the man or his body. At the day's end they were able to buy some bread and cheese at a tiny settlement, then they pushed on for a third night.

Crossing a patch of crumbling snow beneath a mountain crest, Voros slipped off the path and slid down the slope, stopping his fall only by grabbing a bush sticking out of the snow. He was appalled to see the rest of group move off, and he had fallen too far to hear what they were shouting. Finally, after giving up hope, he spotted two fellow Americans making their way toward him. Climbing back up to the trail, and then racing along it to catch up with the remainder of the volunteers, the three several times had to wade, waist-deep, across mountain streams, their shoes tied by the laces around their necks. Just before nightfall at the end of the third day, a road and huts came into sight: Spain. In the months ahead, this journey across the mountains would claim the lives of an estimated 200 volunteers.

In the wake of the fighting at Jarama, when Merriman and so many other Americans were casualties, it was some weeks before new arrivals were taken to the front to replace the dead and wounded of the Lincoln Battalion. During their training, well behind the lines, no one dared reveal to the newcomers the extent of the February 27 debacle. "Our boys were victorious in a very important battle near Madrid," an officer told them, "a defensive battle in which they stopped the fascists dead in their tracks. . . . I know you are waiting to hear about the casualties. . . . Only one American was killed and only four were wounded." The roomful of recruits erupted in cheers. This was hardly the first or the last occasion in wartime that propaganda got the better of truth, but it would prove a particularly morale-sapping one, because as soon as the men arrived at the front, they learned of the February battle's horrendous toll.

When enough Americans had trekked over the Pyrenees to form an additional unit, they at first voted to name themselves the Tom Mooney Battalion, after a well-known California labor martyr serving a life sentence in prison (who would later be the subject of a Woody Guthrie song). A telegram from the Communist Party in New York, however, barred the name as too provocative. Instead, the unit became the George Washington Battalion. The Lincoln machine-gunners did succeed in calling themselves the Tom Mooney Company, but the Party remained resolutely patriotic in such matters; at home the special pins it gave to family members of those volunteering in Spain showed the Liberty Bell. When enough new arrivals had crossed the Atlantic to form a third battalion, it was thought politic to give a nod to the many Canadian volunteers, and so—though most of its officers and men were from the United States—it became the Mackenzie-Papineau Battalion, after two nineteenth-century patriots who were as respectable in Canadian terms as Lincoln and Washington. Bob Merriman, still recovering from his wounds, supervised the training of the newcomers. After more than two months, the heavy plaster was at last removed from his shoulder. "So long cast!" he jotted in his diary.

More doctors and nurses arrived. Eventually, about 140 American medical workers would serve in Spain. Like the other volunteers, many had been politically active, some in a New York group that provided medical help to strikers and their families. Dr. Barsky and his team soon found themselves transferred from their temporary schoolhouse hospital to more opulent quarters. These were at Villa Paz, a luxurious country home confiscated from the Infanta—as Spanish princesses were known—María de la Paz de Borbón, an aunt of the last king. Her portrait still hung on the mansion's wall and her books, paintings, and antique furniture still filled its grand rooms. Barsky was thrilled with his good luck: "The Infanta's villa was an enchanting place. There were most romantic gardens with rare trees and sweet flowers, and there were nightingales in the trees. . . . Around the grounds wandered huge wolf-hounds. The peasants said that these ghostly hounds would not leave the estate. They were incredibly thin . . . wandering in and out among the great trees and overgrown hedges, they gave the greenery a tapestry-like look.

"There were vast stables and grain lofts which we turned into wards. Inside the villa there was an enormous bed draped in regal brocade . . . the whole middle of it covered with a gigantic royal crest. Three of our nurses used to sleep in that bed together." When nurses discovered glass jars etched with the royal crown and filled with preserved peaches, they ate the peaches and sterilized the jars so they could hold surgical sutures. Word that the Americans were installed at Villa Paz rapidly spread. "Peasants come to us," an ambulance driver wryly noted, ". . . with the ills which have afflicted them for centuries, expecting miracles."

Farmworkers had taken down fences and begun plowing some of the Infanta's land. A small building in a poplar grove had served as "the Infanta's private jail," they told the Americans. Nurse Salaria Kea, who was black, was stunned by the contrast between the Infanta's lavish accommodations and the way "the peasants attached to the estate, impoverished and illiterate, still lived in the same cramped, poorly lit quarters they had before. In a corner of the usual one-room hut, on top of a tile they burned dried dung from the cattle. This was their only source of heat." Though the Infanta's family was long gone, the peasants had not dared move into the villa; some even lived in nearby caves. "This was my first concrete example of discrimination where race was not the basis."

Kea would become head nurse of a ward, with five white nurses under her—something unheard of at the time in the United States. In short order the medical team set up an operating room and 250 beds. They would see much use.

Deeply shaken by losing most of his British friends in the fierce fighting at Jarama in February 1937, Pat Gurney asked to be transferred to the Lincoln Battalion. His new comrades seemed amused by this

Englishman who had joined them: "He was a tall man, blond with a slight mustache," recalled one American soldier, "and an overwhelming upper class English accent, which he employed effectively in telling humorous stories and in the rendition of the London version of Salvation Army songs." Gurney developed a reputation for retelling Old Testament tales with a bawdy twist. "He was funny and as an entertainer was well received." But he showed the aftereffects of the terrible day when the British battalion had seen most of its men killed or wounded. The same soldier remembered the way Gurney "would repeat, time and again how scared he was." Although the memoir he later wrote was reserved on this score, others also noticed the emotional scars. "His nerves cracked," recalled an American nurse. When he talked about what he had seen at the front, he was "sobbing, spitting out words."

Gurney was suffering from what we now call post-traumatic stress disorder. He was one of two dozen Britons and Americans treated for such symptoms by Dr. William Pike, a New York psychiatrist who doubled as a general doctor at the front. Pike believed that work was the best therapy, so he set his patients to building a road designed both to shorten the arduous hourlong scramble from the front lines to the nearest medical aid station and, using the contours of the terrain, to better shelter travelers from shellfire. Gurney was able to employ his sketching skills to help draw up the plans for "Pike's Turnpike" and gradually regained some of his equilibrium.

Meanwhile, the Lincolns endured months of intermittent Nationalist sniping, machine-gun fire, and trench raids, but no major battles. They were, however, engaged in a struggle familiar to soldiers from many wars. "Everyone up in the line was infested with lice," wrote Gurney, "large, translucent, yellow brutes which looked like sugar ants. They lived principally in the seams of any garment where they remained comparatively quiescent during the day, becoming violently active at night. Their bite produced large, raised weals that itched like hell. . . . There was no insecticide and the only effective method of dealing with the lice was to run all the seams of your clothing through a candle flame at regular intervals. The lice popped and hissed in a most disgusting way as they and their eggs hit the flame."

Nor was this the only misery. At the bottom of every trench were inches of mud, which found its way into food, tobacco, and blankets. Worse yet, March 1937 saw constant rain, requiring the men to repeatedly drain or bail out the trenches. Icy winds howled across the hills. And while their own weapons were still inadequate, the Nationalists had mortars, which could lob a shell in a high arc ending in an almost vertical descent into a trench. All the International Brigades had was a single, risky homemade mortar that a British soldier had devised out of a steel pipe.

Dead bodies in no-man's-land began to stink and had to be retrieved at night for burial, a job the soldiers loathed. Despite the pleas of medical workers, the troops had little enthusiasm for digging latrines in the freezing rain, and the resulting contamination of food left everyone with diarrhea. This, one soldier wrote home, "is one of my constant companions. We know each other inside & out in every little variation & mood, from the subtle, unexpected moods (the slight sputterings) to the more virile, forceful firehose type of moods."

Dr. Pike made valiant efforts to get the Americans to build better latrines and clean their dirty dishes with sand and scarce water. He noticed that Spanish soldiers, whose sanitation was no better, did not suffer diarrhea and thought he saw the reason: long braids of garlic on the walls of their dugouts, which they chewed daily. But he could not persuade the Lincolns to do the same.

Signs with New York street names—Broadway, Union Square—popped up on many trenches. On the downhill slopes behind them, the men built temporary shelters for sleeping or keeping warm, often with underground rooms hollowed out of the red clay soil, with sheets of corrugated iron for roofing and sometimes planks for walls and floors. These shelters were not so different from the hundreds of thousands of Hooverville huts in clusters all over the United States. "We aren't going to pay any rent after this war," said one New York soldier to a visiting journalist. "We'll just build dugouts in Battery Park."

One moonless night, Gurney went with several others "to cut down the young vine growth which obscured our view of the enemy trenches. We were creeping around in the pitch dark, breaking off the sap shoots, when we realised that our numbers appeared to have doubled. No word was said but both sides suddenly realised that they were working alongside each other on a mutual task. . . . Each [group] of us headed for home as fast as we could go."

The Americans had a moment of terror and triumph on March 14, when Moorish troops following small Italian Fiat tanks tried to break through a nearby section of the front lines held by Spanish conscripts. In what was later informally known as the Battle of Dead Mule Trench, the Republicans rallied and drove the Moors back. For a moment the ideal of international solidarity seemed made flesh, with British and American volunteers storming down a trench together, a French officer joining in as a sniper, and Soviet tanks moving up in support. Afterward, the Spanish came to thank the Americans, while the bodies of dead Moors littered no-man's-land.

Most of the time, however, nothing much happened. Unlike the trench-bound armies of the First World War, the International Brigades were too shorthanded to rotate troops to the rear every few days for rest, showers, dry clothes, and better food. As a result, wrote Gurney, "none of us had enjoyed a night's sleep out of uniform or a decent hot meal for several months. There was no relief from the continual fear of snipers and occasional mortar shells. We were filthy and full of body-lice and began to feel that we were in a trap from which there was no escape. This situation produced a series of desertions. . . . If a man disappeared for a short time it was safer to pretend that nobody had noticed his absence for fear of making an official issue of it."

Compounding the morale problem was ambiguity about how long the men had enlisted for. Some, confident of swift victory, had signed up without asking. Others had been told six months, but as that time elapsed without an end to the war in sight, protest delegations and grievance committees sprang up, leading the XV Brigade newspaper, *Our Fight*, to plead, "Comrades, let us not grumble."

The food only made things worse. "No real attempt was made at cooking," recalled Gurney, "beyond chucking everything available into a tub of water and boiling it. The result was a whitish-looking fluid consisting principally of potatoes and dried beans with occasional vestiges of meat and olive oil. It was cold by the time it got up to the line and usually looked so unappetizing that it was barely worth the effort to eat."

On this score, things finally began to improve at the end of April with the arrival of Steve Nelson as the new Lincoln Battalion commissar. He was one of a group of experienced activists the US Communist Party dispatched to Spain in the wake of the Jarama disaster. Thirty-four years old, Nelson was a soft-spoken, unassuming-looking man who projected quiet authority, a rare figure who was trusted by both the Party brass (he had worked for the Comintern in Moscow) and the American volunteers.

Nelson soon spotted someone who could help him raise the unit's morale: Jack Shirai. A Japanese-American chef from San Francisco, Shirai and two fellow volunteers often talked of opening a restaurant together after the war, where anyone who had fought in Spain could eat for free. Shirai had insisted on serving as a rifleman. Nelson placed him in the battalion kitchen with the proviso that he could keep his rifle on hand for crises. His cooking made one grateful soldier call him "a miracle worker."

The glamour of the International Brigades made them a favorite stop for touring dignitaries. "Most of these occasions," Gurney wrote, "had something of the character of a Board of Guardians paying their annual visit to an orphanage. They were clean, decently dressed, well fed, and in no real danger, while we were dirty, ragged, hungry and desperately unsure of our future. But above all, we were there to stay, while they only had to put up with the dirt and stink for half an hour—an occasional shot overhead to remind them of the realities provided an extra excitement. . . .

"Most annoying of the visitors were the type that said, 'God, I wish I was able to stay out here with you fellows'—the implication presumably being that their activities were so important that their presence could not be afforded, while us lucky chaps had the leisure to enjoy the real fun." An extraordinary parade of VIPs came to see the American and British troops in their trenches. By all accounts, the most welcome was the singer Paul Robeson, whose willingness to perform stirring bass-baritone renditions of "Ol' Man River" and other songs everywhere from barracks to hospital wards brought wild cheers from Americans and Spaniards alike.

Other visitors included British Labour Party leader Clement Attlee (who mistakenly called out "*¡No pasaremos!*"—"We shall not pass!"—instead of "*¡No pasarán!*"—"They shall not pass!"); Indian independence leader Jawaharlal Nehru; the actor Errol Flynn; and writers like Stephen Spender, Theodore Dreiser, Archibald MacLeish, and Langston Hughes, who gave a poetry reading for the drivers and mechanics of the XV Brigade's motor pool. "Everybody was there but Shakespeare," commented one volunteer.

"The most controversial of them all," in Gurney's words, was "full of hearty and bogus *bonhomie*. He sat himself down behind the bullet-proof shield of a machine-gun and loosed off a whole belt of ammunition in the general direction of the enemy. This provoked a mortar bombardment for which he did not stay."

The visitor was Ernest Hemingway, thirty-seven years old and already one of the most celebrated authors alive. Having written his first two novels and classic short stories in the 1920s, his life had become partly taken over by the persona he had developed for himself, as brash and flamboyant as his early work was spare and understated. He was now profiled and photographed big-game hunting, hanging out with bullfighters, machine-gunning sharks, and landing giant marlin. Some of this he-man façade crept into his writing as well. It had been eight years since he had published a novel, two recent nonfiction books had drawn some bad reviews, and critics—and perhaps Hemingway himself—were wondering if he had lost his touch. "He appears," wrote the poet John Peale Bishop, "to have turned into a composite of all those photographs . . . sunburned from snows, on skis; in fishing get-up, burned dark from the hot Caribbean; the handsome, stalwart hunter crouched smiling over the carcass of some dead beast."

Although until then one of the least political of American writers—in the midst of the Great Depression he had written a book about safaris in Africa and he had not bothered to vote in the 1936 election—Hemingway had an almost proprietary love for Spain. A trip there had been the basis for *The Sun Also Rises*, the novel that first made the world notice him, and he had returned often, seeing Spanish friends and gathering material for *Death in the Afternoon*, his book about bullfighting. He was enraged by the Nationalist coup, which he saw as an act of great violence against a culture he loved. He also identified with the young Americans who had volunteered to fight, just as he had volunteered, less than a year out of high school, as a Red Cross ambulance driver in the First World War.

The Spanish war seemed made for him. "In Spain maybe it's the big parade starting again," he wrote to a journalist he knew. He even dressed the part, as if to recapture the days of his youth. When his friend the novelist Josephine Herbst met him in besieged Madrid, she found him wearing "a kind of khaki uniform with high polished boots." He saved fragments of shells that hit the city's Hotel Florida, where he stayed, marking on them the numbers of the rooms they had destroyed, and making one dud shell into a lamp.

"He was bigger than life," wrote the Lincoln physician William Pike, "—generous, scrupulously honest and dedicated to his work but lurking somewhere was a mean-spirited, uncertain, frightened, aggressive child, overly impressed with physical courage, [with] a need to, over and over again, prove himself a 'man.' . . . He told me he had no use for psychiatry, others needed it, not he—to go to a psychoanalyst was a confession of weakness."

For all his chip-on-the-shoulder bluster, which occasionally led to fistfights with those he thought had insulted him, Hemingway was a shrewd judge of character. He made friends with Lincoln Brigaders he particularly respected, including Pike. His warmth toward the American volunteers shines through the newspaper reports he wrote from the front. He raised money for the American medical unit, contributing enough himself for an ambulance, paid for the passage to Spain of several volunteers, and visited wounded Lincolns in the hospital. After the war, he remained in touch with many veterans, loaning or giving money to some in need. Despite a penchant for anti-Semitic outbursts and writing fiction that celebrated rugged outdoorsmen, he came to feel deep affection for the Lincolns, of whom a majority had spent their lives in big cities, were Jews, or both.

Hemingway had signed a contract with the North American Newspaper Alliance (NANA) syndicate, made up of some 50 leading dailies, to cover what he felt certain was "the dress rehearsal for the inevitable European war." His very acceptance of this assignment was a news event, and before he published a word, the press noted his arrival in Europe and his crossing the border into Spain. He would make four long trips there during the war; NANA paid him $1,000—the equivalent of more than $15,000 today—for each dispatch he mailed home, and $500 for each he sent by the expensive transatlantic cable. For Hemingway Spain offered a chance to recapture not only the experience of war, but another part of his youth. In the early 1920s he had been a foreign correspondent, and something of the terse economy of language forced by telegraph transmission had become a permanent part of his style. However little he impressed Pat Gurney, he would leave his mark on the American memory of the Spanish Civil War. And, despite his braggadocio, he would never write a word about one remarkable night when he would cross the line from writer to soldier.

George Orwell, of course, had long since crossed that line, and after four months at the front was returning to Barcelona on leave:

> The train . . . was invaded by more and more peasants at every station on the line; peasants with bundles of vegetables, with terrified fowls which they carried head-downwards, with sacks

> which looped and writhed all over the floor and were discovered to be full of live rabbits—finally with a quite considerable flock of sheep which were driven into the compartments and wedged into every empty space. The militiamen shouted revolutionary songs which drowned the rattle of the train and kissed their hands or waved red and black handkerchiefs to every pretty girl along the line. Bottles of wine and of anis, the filthy Aragonese liqueur, travelled from hand to hand. With the Spanish goat-skin water-bottles you can squirt a jet of wine right across a railway carriage into your friend's mouth, which saves a lot of trouble. Next to me a black-eyed boy of fifteen was recounting sensational and, I do not doubt, completely untrue stories of his own exploits at the front to two old leather-faced peasants who listened open-mouthed. Presently the peasants undid their bundles and gave us some sticky dark-red wine.

Orwell, still known to all as Eric Blair, was eager to reach Barcelona, because his wife, whom he had married less than a year earlier, had recently moved there to be closer to him. She was now working as Charles Orr's secretary in the office where he produced the POUM's English-language newspaper. Like so many women of that era, Eileen O'Shaughnessy Blair appears in the written record mostly in terms of her appearance and whom she was married to; even in Orwell's memoir of Spain she is only "my wife" and not a fully drawn character. Charles Orr described her as attractive and vivacious, "a round-faced Irish girl, prim and pretty, with black hair and big dark eyes." A woman friend also remembered the eyes, which "could dance with amusement, like a kitten's watching a dangling object." When she could manage to find them in Barcelona's shops, Eileen dispatched scarce items like cigars and margarine to Orwell and his grateful colleagues in the party's militia. Yet he had seen her only a few times since her arrival, one of them when she, Charles, and a British friend had visited his unit's trenches for a day.

When Orwell's train got to Barcelona, he found a city visibly changed from the one he had seen when he first arrived in Spain.

"The militia uniform and the blue overalls had almost disappeared; everyone seemed to be wearing the smart summer suits in which Spanish tailors specialize. Fat prosperous men, elegant women, and sleek cars were everywhere." It was, in short, a place where "the normal division of society into rich and poor, upper class and lower class, was reasserting itself. . . . My wife and I went into a hosiery shop on the Ramblas to buy some stockings. The shopman bowed and rubbed his hands as they do not do even in England. . . . In a furtive indirect way the practice of tipping was coming back."

As she walked to work each day, Lois Orr noticed the same thing: men were again wearing neckties, and many collectivized shops and businesses were, by government decree, being quietly returned to their prewar owners. "It is terrible to realize that the things that the workers took over for themselves, after years of oppression and misery," she wrote to her sister, "are slowly being given back."

Beyond these changes, Barcelona was under stress: factories were turning out weapons instead of household goods, and peasants on many collectivized farms tended to keep meat and vegetables for themselves, sending urban food prices soaring. An underground economy began to appear. Lois felt guilty when the kindhearted Eileen Blair, or someone else who had newly arrived with foreign currency, "would take me out for 30 peseta meals at one of the black market restaurants . . . but I was always so hungry I ate the food gladly."

Orwell blamed the changes on the hostility of the Republic's government and its Soviet advisors toward Catalonia's social revolution. In this he was not wrong, but it was far from the only reason the anarchist dream was running onto shoals. Charles Orr, for instance, eventually came to question the triumphal decree that everyone—worker, manager, secretary, idle capitalist, or foreign sympathizer—should receive the same wage of ten pesetas a day. "Simple and obvious though this system of distributing money income seemed to be, a closer look revealed problems." Those who worked for some factories or enterprises collected all sorts of benefits—from free meals to blankets and housing (as did he and Lois)—while others received little or nothing extra, at a time when rapid inflation meant that those ten pesetas could be exhausted by the cost of a day's food alone. He foresaw additional obstacles as utopian dreams met complex reality: "As a democratic socialist, I was attracted by the idea of workers' direct ownership. . . . But, as an economist, I was worried about coordination at the top. . . . Would the decision making for the economy as a whole be organized by central planning, or would that be left to the competitive market?"

Other complications made things difficult as well. The Orrs were not the only people who hadn't been paying their electric bill. Nor was the hard-pressed local electric utility the only enterprise—worker-controlled or not—that had trouble collecting money owed to it. After the first flush of revolutionary enthusiasm, the ideal of "from each according to his abilities, to each according to his needs," however splendid in theory, proved hard to enforce, especially when many workers felt what they needed was more time off. Factory absenteeism rose, and the city's warehouses were empty of the food and raw materials that had been on hand months before.

A deeper problem was one faced by any society that tries to stage a revolution overnight. Changing who owns a factory or business is one thing, but changing centuries-old habits is quite another. "A people as a whole . . . cannot abandon their inherited ways," Charles observed, though "thousands turned out to celebrate any occasion and to shout themselves hoarse to the most revolutionary slogans." He recounted one such event: "a mass meeting to 'free the women.' It was held in an auditorium and was attended by a thousand workers—*all men of course*—because who had ever heard of bringing women to a meeting on a Thursday evening?"

Despite her revolutionary fervor, Lois eventually had to acknowledge something similar: "The woman question was a vexed one for the libertarians [anarchists]. Their women seemed to be more interested in sewing machines and learning about child nutrition than in the great abstract ideals of The Revolution. . . . The first major campaign of the anarchist Free Women . . . was for the abolition of prostitution. The Libertarian Youth joined them in this, but it never seemed to shorten the block-long lines before the collectivized houses when the militia returned to Barcelona on leave."

Although the front was still far from the city, the increasing shortages were a reminder that Spain was at war. And Hitler's ominous buildup of the German military made clear that before long the whole Continent might be at war as well. From home, Lois heard the news that her fellow Kentuckian, young Joe Selligman, had been killed in the defense of Madrid. His parents were still trying to recover his personal belongings and asked Lois's family for her help. "I was very sorry to hear about the death of this comrade," Lois wrote home, "and I wish you would tell his mother for me that he died fighting for something worthwhile. I'll do all I can to get anything he has left to her."

The Orrs still had time for an occasional day off. They both enjoyed Eileen Blair's warmth and good humor, and one Sunday they went for a picnic in the country with her and an Italian friend. Charles spoke of Mexico, where he had once lived, and Eileen said that if a world war came, perhaps they could all go to Mexico together. And while Orwell seemed chronically awkward and ill at ease, his wife, wrote Charles, "was friendly, gregarious and unpretentious. . . . At the office, Eileen just could not resist talking about Eric—her hero husband, whom she obviously loved and admired. It was my privilege to hear about him day after day. Not that I paid much attention. He was still just an unknown would-be writer who, like others, had come to Spain to fight against fascism." Charles felt that Orwell "needed, no doubt, a socially extrovert wife as a window to the world. Eileen helped this inarticulate man to communicate with others. Though married for less than a year, she had already become his spokesman."

As this little group of foreigners were getting to know one another, political tensions in the city were rising. "I felt as if I were living in a powder-keg," wrote Lois. Behind the changes, as Orwell put it, lay "the antagonism between those who wished the revolution to go forward and those who wished to check or prevent it—ultimately, between Anarchists and Communists." A startled foreign visitor found two posters on the walls of a Communist Party office: "Respect the Property of the Small Peasant" and "Respect the Property of the Small Industrialist." The Spain that promised an anarchist millennium was receding from sight.

Meanwhile, something else added to the tension. The Republic's government was urgently trying to build a national army to replace the ill-trained hodgepodge of militia units loyal to different political parties and trade unions. As one Communist journalist observed, implicitly including his own party in the indictment, "Battalion commissars and quartermasters used political influence in Madrid to obtain what they needed. By packing a department with a staff of its own political faith, a party might switch the precious ammunition, machine guns, rifles, etc., toward its own column." If they were going to defeat the Nationalists, Republican cabinet members believed—not illogically—that they needed a unified, disciplined army under a strong central command. "Given this alignment of forces," Orwell wrote, "there was bound to be trouble."

With no further major fighting in the Jarama valley, Hemingway had little to report from there. But before long the other arm of Franco's planned pincer movement belatedly swung into action. Nationalist forces attacking from the north aimed first to capture the provincial capital of Guadalajara and then to complete the encirclement of Madrid and cut—while coming from another direction this time—the vital Madrid–Valencia road. On March 8, 1937, 50,000 Nationalist troops launched their assault, advancing some 20 miles in several days. Significantly, however, only 15,000 of the soldiers were Spanish or Moroccan. The other 35,000 were Italian, supposedly volunteers—the Corpo Truppe Volontarie—sent by Mussolini. This was by far the largest force that either Italy or Germany had yet sent into battle in Spain.

Opposing them were a much smaller number of Republican troops, including two International Brigades, one of which had a battalion composed mainly of Italians. Thirty years later, one of its company commanders, Pietro Nenni, would become his country's foreign minister. Most of its soldiers had fled Italy as political refugees, which made promising copy for foreign correspondents: Fascist and anti-Fascist Italians fighting each other on another country's soil.

The battle soon became an embarrassing rout for Mussolini's badly trained troops, who were much stronger on Blackshirt bravado than military prowess. One of the divisions the Italian dictator had dispatched to Spain was composed of conscripts, not volunteers, who thought they were heading for Italy's newly acquired colony, Ethiopia. Many had been issued only lightweight tropical uniforms, inadequate for the snow and freezing rain of Spain in March. When taken prisoner, others claimed they thought they were to be extras in an epic film about a Roman general.

Mussolini's commander was operating with a Michelin map that showed little more than the dirt roads now turned to mud on which his fleet of 2,000 trucks quickly bogged down. In addition, his men faced constant loudspeaker broadcasts from Republican lines—in Italian: "Brothers, the Spanish people are fighting for their freedom. Desert the ranks of their enemies! Come over to us!"

Many of the troops did so—and then took to the Republican loudspeakers in turn to urge their comrades to do the same. The Nationalist attack soon stalled, with thousands of men fleeing to the rear and 6,000 more killed, wounded, or taken prisoner. As bombastic and mercurial as ever, the furious Mussolini recalled some of his generals and declared that no Italian soldier could return home until a final victory in Spain had wiped away the shame of this failure. The Battle of Guadalajara, as it became known, was something the Spanish Civil War had not yet seen: a resounding Republican victory.

"Along the roads were piled abandoned machine guns, anti-aircraft guns, light mortars, shells, and boxes of machine gun ammunition, and stranded trucks, light tanks and tractors," Hemingway jubilantly told his newspaper readers, along with "letters, papers, haversacks, mess kits, entrenching tools and everywhere the dead."

The result of the battle, he wrote, was "to unite the people in its fury against foreign invasion. . . . A wave of enthusiasm is sweeping over the population." The Republican victory at Guadalajara, he extravagantly claimed, "will take its place in military history with the other decisive battles of the world."

Despite the hyperbole, Hemingway and other correspondents did have a tale to tell, of the civil war within the civil war, of Italians versus Italians. Among the journalists, however, there was a civil war of a different sort. It was within America's most influential newspaper, the *New York Times*.

9

Civil War at the *Times*

His head covered by a beret and his lanky frame dressed in gray flannels, the soft-spoken, thirty-seven-year-old Herbert L. Matthews was the principal correspondent covering Republican Spain for the *Times.* To Pat Gurney's English eyes, Matthews "looked and behaved like a Yankee banker. He was a tall, thin, angular man, whose clothes hung on him as on a clothes horse, with a long, thin, bony face which always carried a faintly disapproving expression. It was quite an experience to meet Matthews walking through the trenches. He always wore a city suit with a collar and tie, looking as if he had just stepped out of an office. His clothes were rather old-fashioned and he wore the kind of lace-up boots which were the approved footwear for city gents of my grandfather's generation. He was rather coldly treated by the Battalion, who felt that the representative of the . . . *New York Times* must necessarily be antipathetic to our cause. In the event, we were entirely wrong."

Much to the annoyance of the American volunteers, some bureaucrat at International Brigades headquarters had made up a list of reading material judged suitable for the Lincolns: the *Daily Worker,* the *Negro Worker, Soviet Russia Today,* and the like; the capitalist *Times* was on a list of "Newspapers and Periodicals NOT to be sent." But clippings arrived in mail from home, and before long the soldiers welcomed Matthews with far greater enthusiasm than they did the *Daily Worker* correspondent.

Nothing in his background suggested that Matthews would become a passionate supporter of the Republic. He had studied in Italy during the 1920s and found much to admire in Mussolini. A visit to Asia in 1929 left him no less impressed with the dynamism of Japan. For the *Times*, he accompanied Italian troops to Ethiopia in 1935, as what we would now call an embedded reporter, finding it a "thrilling experience" to be covering a war in a part of the world new to him. Quite conventionally for an age that took colonialism for granted, he felt that "the Italians did bring a measure of civilization to Ethiopia," whose native inhabitants were "pure savages, with a vicious lust for blood." Italian soldiers, he told *Times* readers, fought a "brilliant campaign." No matter that Ethiopia had few modern weapons with which to defend itself against Mussolini's bombers and poison gas. And did the Ethiopians mind being conquered, after suffering hundreds of thousands of military and civilian deaths? Hardly at all, he claimed: "a vast majority of the native population now favors the Italian occupation." Not surprisingly, Mussolini's new Viceroy of Ethiopia awarded Matthews a medal, making him the first journalist covering the war, Italian or foreign, so honored.

In Republican Spain, however, he was transformed—as were other hard-boiled reporters who saw bombs and shells falling not on African "savages" but on Europeans. "Such human beings they are, these Spaniards!" Matthews wrote. Feeling that "the immediate fate of this world of ours is being settled right here," he came to identify with the besieged people of Madrid in a way he never had with Mussolini's African victims. Oddly, he never sensed any contradiction: a memoir he wrote about covering both conflicts is jauntily titled *Two Wars and More to Come*. But he left no doubt where he stood on Spain. Defending the Republic, he wrote a decade later, "made men ready to die gladly and proudly. It gave meaning to life; it gave courage and faith in humanity; it taught us what internationalism means. . . . There one learned that men could be brothers."

Naturally, such effusive partisanship would never do for the long, gray columns of the *Times*, where his articles were far more restrained. Then as now, however, the supposedly opinionless reporters of American daily journalism had ways to show what they felt, from the words they chose to which stories they picked to report. Everyone knew where Matthews stood.

The *Times*, it was said in this era, was a newspaper owned by Jews, edited by Catholics, and read by Protestants. The managing editor, Edwin L. James, was a bon vivant who wore flashy suits, carried a walking stick, and liked his evenings on the town, so he tended to leave work early and to give great latitude to the "bullpen" of editors on the paper's night desk. The man among them who routinely laid out the front page, Neil MacNeil, was an active Catholic layman who wrote books and gave speeches about the decline of morality; the deputy who took over on his nights off, Clarence Howell, was a Catholic convert whom Matthews called "almost fanatically religious." They both edited incoming foreign news, decided which stories should get front-page play, and sometimes rewrote headlines to suit their political tastes. (One first-edition story, "Priest Defends Fascist Nations," became for the late edition, "Priest Sees Soviet as Real Foe of U.S.")

Careful readers soon noticed that the Spanish Civil War was being fought not just on battlefields in Spain but inside the *Times*. In New York James sometimes summarized the week's war news for the Sunday edition. On February 14, 1937, for example, he wrote, "General Franco is making an effort to cut off Madrid from the seacoast, which is to say, from its source of supplies. . . . The main highway from the capital to Valencia has been rendered practically useless. . . . It is even claimed that Franco's men are across the road at the Arganda bridge."

A furious Matthews saw this as a direct affront. A story of his had been published only the day before, reporting that Franco's troops had *not* cut the vital road. He and another correspondent had actually driven across the Arganda bridge in a decrepit taxi under shellfire. Tweaking James, whom he despised, Matthews sprinkled his subsequent stories with references to the highway being in Republican hands.

Then in March came the Battle of Guadalajara. *Times* editors, who were receiving angry protests against Matthews's stories from the Italian embassy in Washington, began removing from them some references to how Franco's forces in this battle had been predominantly Italian, and to how incompetently they had fought. And where he wrote of the battle's aftermath, "The dead bodies, the prisoners, the material of every kind . . . were Italian and nothing but Italian," the bullpen editors changed the sentence to read, "Insurgent and nothing but Insurgent" (a word often used to refer to Franco's Nationalists), then dropped it entirely from later editions.

Matthews was enraged. His memoirs—he wrote several—are filled with fulminations against James and the bullpen editors. He even includes exchanges of angry telegrams with them, typically calling one message from James "weaseling." Among the papers he would leave to Columbia University on his death are carbon copies of his dispatches as he cabled them to the *Times*, so history would have a record of what was edited out. A careful look at these, however, reveals only the lightest of censorship; nothing else is as egregious as the substitution of "Insurgent" for "Italian." In fact, the real civil war at the newspaper was not between the thin-skinned Matthews and his editors in New York, but between him and a rival sometimes only a few miles away, the *Times* correspondent covering the war from the Nationalist side.

William P. Carney, known as "General Bill" to his fellow journalists, was a Texan, a devout Catholic, and an open Franco enthusiast. Separated by the battlefront, for several years the two reporters carried on an indirect duel. Matthews would emphasize the civilian casualties of Franco's bombing and shelling and the help he was getting from Hitler and Mussolini; Carney would write about the good cheer of the population in Nationalist Spain and the Republic's killings of priests. While Matthews was covering the humiliating Nationalist defeat at Guadalajara, Carney traveled to Seville, in southern Spain, to produce a lengthy report on the city's "fiesta spirit." He also painted a flattering portrait ("popularity firmly established . . . unmistakable military bearing . . . smiling, cordial greeting and affability") of General Gonzalo Queipo de Llano, the man so notorious for his gloating radio broadcasts about the rapes the women of Madrid would face at the hands of his Moorish troops.

Some of Carney's articles were republished as pamphlets by supporters of Franco in the United States. At one point, according to American ambassador Claude Bowers, Carney even made a propaganda broadcast for a Nationalist radio station, ending it with the Francoist war cry, "*¡Arriba España!*" In the Spanish Republic, Carney wrote, "all semblance of democratic forms and usages of government has disappeared," and luckless workers were "terrorized" into joining labor unions. In this same dispatch, written after a brief stay in Madrid early in the war, Carney infuriated those fighting against Franco by revealing the exact locations of more than half a dozen Republican artillery and antiaircraft batteries.

Carney made amazingly little attempt to disguise his political sympathies: as he traveled around Nationalist Spain, he used as his mailing address the embassy of Nazi Germany. The Knights of Columbus, the Catholic fraternal organization, gave him a gold medal "for distinguished services to journalism." At the same time, Catholics launched an assault against Matthews. Dr. Joseph Thorning, a priest and educator, called him a "rabid Red partisan" and joined other prominent Catholics in a campaign to make the *Times* recall him from Spain. But Matthews had the support of the paper's owners—the *Times*'s publisher, Arthur Hays Sulzberger, and his wife were godparents to his son—and he kept his post.

Some months down the road, as the duel between the two correspondents became more direct, Matthews would score a journalistic bull's-eye hit on Carney.

Ten days after the Guadalajara fighting ended, a small car made its way up the winding road from Valencia to besieged Madrid. Two of the passengers were Americans: a newly arrived journalist, twenty-six-year-old Virginia Cowles, and Milly Bennett, who was freelance reporting while continuing to work in the Republic's press office. Bennett, Cowles would later write, "had a monkey-like face and wore thick horn-rimmed spectacles. She had a strong provocative personality and I liked her at once. . . . She had left-wing convictions, but on this particular morning her outlook was sour." Bennett filled Cowles in about a third passenger in the car, who didn't speak English, an elderly priest with nicotine-stained fingers. "I know the old humbug: he's a show piece," said Bennett, despite her job in the Republic's publicity effort. "He goes around France doing propaganda lectures—saying the priests are well treated in Republican Spain. He's made a packet."

Among foreign correspondents women were rare. If Milly Bennett's brassy, one-of-the-boys manner was one path to a tenuous foothold in the profession, Virginia Cowles took another. The daughter of a prominent psychiatrist, Ginny, as her friends called her, grew up in Boston and had been a debutante in the 1928–29 "season," the last before the stock market crash that ushered in the Great Depression. By temperament she was no rebel, but, ambitious to see the world and to write, she quickly grasped that as a woman that would not be easy. Starting to pen newspaper pieces, she discovered that "the trouble is, they're always looking for a woman's angle." The result was stories like "Miss Cowles Dissects Types of Husbands Debs May Choose." She was determined, however, to report on the war in Spain. "The only way a girl can cover the War," she later said, "is to tell the paper of her choice that she is going anyway and would they like some articles." This was the strategy she tried with a top executive of the Hearst chain, and it worked.

Once in Spain, she showed no shyness in asking other reporters—nearly all of them men—for advice, and they competed to help her. It didn't hurt that she bore a resemblance to the actress Lauren Bacall, dressed elegantly, and had a slender figure and long, dark hair topped with a fetching beret. Her large brown eyes, set far apart, "held one's own steadily," remembered one smitten man. Of one moment in her career when there were no cars or taxis available and a male photographer volunteered to carry her suitcase for a mile, Cowles wrote, "I thought what a fine thing it was to be a female of the species."

The youthful debutante who had, as she put it, "no qualifications as a war correspondent except curiosity," would turn out to be one of the finest journalists on the scene. Her autobiographical *Looking for Trouble*, parts of it drawn closely from the articles she wrote from Spain, still seems crisp and subtly observed today, while the many memoirs of the war by other American reporters mostly have a musty feel.

Virtually everyone who wrote about meeting Cowles in Spain, man or woman, referred to her dazzling good looks, her high heels, and her past as a debutante. That she had been, but her early life—which she seldom talked about—was an odd combination of privilege and privation, and perhaps helps explain the unusual resourcefulness she would show as a journalist. After her parents went through a bitter divorce and custody battle, following which her father paid no alimony, Virginia and a sister were raised by their mother, who had to go to work as a typesetter for the *Boston Herald* to support them, picking up extra money by writing on the side. Only later did she become an editor at another paper. With her earnings she sent the eleven-year-old Virginia off to a private girls' school. Despite Virginia's appearances on Boston society pages as a guest at this or that benefit or ball, in the early years of the Depression she had to support herself selling advertising and magazine subscriptions. A life insurance payment on her mother's death in 1932 finally gave her enough money to travel around the world—a journey she was able to parlay into newspaper articles, launching herself as a writer.

One of the first men who volunteered to show her the ropes in Madrid was Sefton "Tom" Delmer of the London *Daily Express*.

> As we were walking down the Gran Vía on the way back to the hotel I asked Tom how often the city was shelled and he stopped and looked meditatively at his watch. 'It's past noon now. They usually drop a few before lunch.' Scarcely a moment later I heard

> a noise like the sound of cloth ripping. It was gentle at first, then it grew into a hiss; there was a split second of silence, followed by a bang as a shell hurtled into the white stone telephone building at the end of the street. Bricks and timber crashed to the ground and dust rose up in a billow. A second shell plunged into the pavement thirty yards away and a third hit a wooden block of flats on a corner. Everyone started running, scattering into vestibules and doorways, like pieces of paper blown by a sudden gust of wind.
>
> Tom and I took cover in a perfume shop and the explosions continued one every minute. My heart pounded uncertainly; the crash of falling bricks and breaking glass and the thick dust that rose up to blot out the sunshine seemed like some fearful Bible plague tuned up and mechanized for the twentieth-century. . . .
>
> The bombardment lasted about half an hour. When it was over we walked down the street; the pavements were strewn with bricks and shrapnel and a telephone pole leaned drunkenly across one of the buildings, the wires hanking [*sic*] down like streamers. The second floor of a hat-shop had a gaping hole and at the corner an automobile was a twisted mass of steel. Nearby, the pavement was spattered with blood where two women had been killed. . . . I had never before felt the sort of fear that sends the blood racing through your veins.

Cowles stayed with other foreign correspondents at the art nouveau, marble-clad Hotel Florida—where rooms that were once less expensive because they overlooked a side alley now cost more because they faced away from Nationalist shellfire. She soon became a regular at the late-night gatherings in Hemingway's suite, where journalists enjoyed beer, whiskey, and scarce canned ham and pâté brought in from France. Occasionally they could share a hare or partridge the novelist had proudly shot and had a hotel maid cook for him. (With roads to Madrid under fire, the once posh hotel restaurant offered little besides bread, onions, and beans.) The reporters ate and drank to the Chopin records Hemingway was fond of. They usually kept their overcoats on, for much of Spain's coal was on the other side of the front line, and the city had little heat.

Hemingway was the sun around which the Hotel Florida coterie revolved. The group included Delmer of the *Daily Express*, Matthews of the *Times*, and Martha Gellhorn, who wrote for the popular weekly *Collier's*. Hemingway was beginning a soon-to-be famous romance with her, and several years later she would become his third wife.

For the novelist, the Spanish war was raw material, but it was also a grand stage where he was always performing. His ever-changing audience included other writers, generals, foot soldiers, diplomats, cabinet ministers, and visiting VIPs. At all times he seemed compulsively working to make an impression. Hemingway, remembered Kate Mangan of the Republican press office, "always came with an entourage. . . . He was a huge, red man, in hairy speckled tweeds, with a crushing handshake. . . . One always had the feeling that there were several shadowy, unidentifiable, obsequious figures in the background while Hemingway, the great man, was in the foreground." Being seen with the glamorous blond Gellhorn, who was impeccably dressed in chiffon scarf and Saks Fifth Avenue clothes, was part of his performance. "She had an elegant coiffure, a linen dress and a perfectly even sun-tan. She wore her skirt rather short, and sat on the table swinging her long, slim legs in a provocative manner. The Spaniards disapproved of this. They believed that sexuality should be directed only at one person at a time, preferably in private."

To the correspondents, the Hotel Florida, just down the street from the Telefónica building where they sent off their dispatches, seemed like the center of the world. Representing a Paris daily was the aviator-author Antoine de Saint-Exupéry, and the novelist André Malraux, who had organized foreign volunteers to fly for the Republic, came and went. In the Florida's lobby might be glimpsed an American poet, a Swedish labor leader, a British member of Parliament. For those at the hotel, being close to the front and in danger was a powerful aphrodisiac. Whenever there was shelling or an air raid at night, as Delmer wrote, "all kinds of liaisons were revealed as people poured from their bedrooms to seek shelter in the basement, among them Ernest and Martha." Couples rushing out of their rooms could be seen from other floors because a central glass-roofed atrium rose the full height of the ten-story hotel.

Some of the trysts in the Hotel Florida's rooms, as a British visitor discovered, were with professionals. The Very Reverend Hewlett Johnson, Dean of Canterbury, was an enthusiastic backer of left-wing causes. The novelist Josephine Herbst described him as "black-frocked . . . a well-meaning man, no doubt, with a large, pink, saccharine face, the head of a Humpty-Dumpty, bald and fringed with a little babyish skirt of lacy hair." The previous occupants of his suite at the hotel, two Moroccan prostitutes who did a lively business with International Brigades soldiers, had checked out one morning. Delmer described what happened next. "The Dean had hardly settled into his rooms when there was a knock on the door. He opened it. Outside in the corridor stood a small group of Britons who had come from the front to visit the Moorish girls. This, of course, the Dean was not to know. He assumed that these young fellows whom he had heard talking English were a delegation of Freedom Fighters wishing to honour their eminent comrade, the Red Dean. So he talked to them very kindly, praised their readiness for service and sacrifice, and gave them a little impromptu homily on the Christian virtues of the cause for which they were fighting. Then he blessed them and withdrew once more into his room."

A Scottish volunteer, however, "had been drinking downstairs and had reeled up to the Dean's door only just in time to see the party break up and the Dean disappear inside what Jock thought was Fatima's room. Jock completely misunderstood the situation. . . . He waited and he waited, and he waited. At last his patience was exhausted. In a fury of righteous indignation he went up to the Dean's door and hammered on it with his fists. 'Come oot, yer old bustard!' he roared. 'Ye've been mair nae twenty minutes in there! Yer time's oop. Come oot!'"

The two Moroccans were not the only members of the oldest profession at work in Madrid. They had many competitors, and legends spread. The ribald Milly Bennett used to entertain other journalists with a tale of an American volunteer who sought female company but, she claimed, demanded a 50 percent discount—because he had had one testicle shot off.

At the Hotel Florida, "Hemingway's room was presided over by Sidney Franklin," Virginia Cowles wrote, "a tough young American bull-fighter. . . . When I asked him how he had happened to come to Madrid, he said: 'Well, see, one day Ernest rings me up and says: "—'lo, kid, want to go to the war in Spain?" and I says, "Sure, Pop. Which side we on?"'"

Hemingway relished his role of leader of the pack. When Martha Gellhorn was along, Delmer remembered, "he lectured her on how to observe things as a writer." Sometimes, proud of his expertise, he would take Cowles, Gellhorn, and others to see the ongoing fighting from a half-ruined eight-story building, its gutted apartments strewn with everything from wedding pictures to hair curlers. "The 'Old Homestead,'" Cowles wrote, "was a house which Hemingway found on the outskirts of the capital. The front had been ripped away by a bomb, so it provided an excellent vantage-point from which to watch the battle. . . . Against the wide panorama of rolling hills the puffs of smoke were daubs of cotton and the tanks children's toys. When one of them burst into flames it looked no bigger than the flare of a match. . . .

"Hemingway, however, followed the combat eagerly. 'It's the nastiest thing human beings can do to each other,' he pronounced solemnly, 'but the most exciting.'"

By the spring of 1937, the people of Madrid had learned to live under what seemed a permanent state of siege. Buildings were pocked by shrapnel, and glass panes not yet shattered were crisscrossed with tape. Workers at a large bookstore piled up a protective wall of books by the front window. The Palace Hotel had been turned into a hospital, and what was once its restaurant, replete with gilt-framed mirrors and crystal chandeliers, now held eight operating tables. The nurses, Cowles noticed, were former prostitutes: "peroxide blondes with dirty hands and nails painted vermilion. I learned that the nursing profession had been almost entirely restricted to the nuns; since they were on the Franco side the doctors had been forced to use whatever help they could find."

The two sides remained entrenched in their positions at University City, the campus buildings pummeled into skeletons by shellfire. It was remarkably close to the Hotel Florida: "You took a tram halfway, walked the other half, and you were there," Cowles wrote. In neither of the world wars were reporters and photographers so free to plunge into the thick of the fighting at will. Whenever Cowles wanted to do so, a man, it seems, was eager to accompany her. "A few days after I arrived in Madrid I met Professor J.B.S. Haldane, an English scientist and former don at Cambridge University, who was lunching at the *Gran Vía* restaurant. 'Think I'll hop down to the battlefield and have a look round,' he said casually. 'Do you want to come?'"

As they neared the front line,

> guards in sweaters and corduroy trousers, with rifles propped up beside them, said *Salud* and asked to see our passes. Most of them could not read, and some even held the papers upside down, but they all studied them with knitted brows, raised a clenched fist in the Popular Front salute, and let us pass.
>
> At the end of the avenue the streets grew desolate and blocks of houses were gutted and empty. Some . . . looked like stage sets with whole fronts ripped off. High up on one was a table all set for dinner, napkins in place, chairs pulled up, but for a wall it had only a piece of blue sky. . . .
>
> Suddenly . . . we found ourselves in the front line. Long streams of soldiers were firing through the openings in the sandbags. Their faces were unshaven and their jackets and khaki trousers were smeared with grease and mud. Some looked not more than sixteen or seventeen years old. . . .
>
> One of the soldiers handed me a rifle and asked if I did not want to take a shot at los facciosos, and then a young boy with pink cheeks and large brown eyes stepped up and held a peri-

scope over the trench so I could see the enemy lines. They were a jumble of stones and grass only fifty yards away. On the no-man's land in between lay three twisted bodies.

"Los muertos nuestros," the boy said softly.

Cowles made other trips to the front, including one with Hemingway, where Republican soldiers "considered [it] a friendly gesture to take us for a drive in an armoured car and run us down a road which was under enemy fire in order that we might hear the bullets cracking up against the steel sides." The novelist showed off his familiarity with violence of a different sort at a lunch with Cowles and Josephine Herbst one day in the basement restaurant of the Hotel Gran Vía, where a large table was reserved for the press.

Shells were dropping on the street outside the café and it was impossible to leave, so we sat lingering over our coffee. At the next table I noticed a fastidious-looking man dressed from head to toe in dove grey. He had the high forehead and long fingers of the intellectual and wore horn-rimmed spectacles which added to his thoughtful appearance.

"That," said Hemingway, "is the chief executioner of Madrid." [His name was Pepe Quintanilla, and he was chief of staff of Republican counterespionage.]

Ernest invited him to join us and he accepted on the condition we would allow him to buy us a carafe of wine. His manner was ingratiating to the point of sycophancy, but I shall never forget the look in his bright, marble-brown eyes. . . . Hemingway was passionately interested in details of death and soon was pressing the man with questions.

"Have many people died in Madrid?"

"A revolution is always hasty."

"And have there been many mistakes?"

"Mistakes? It is only human to err."

"And the mistakes how did they die?"

"On the whole, considering they were mistakes," he said

meditatively, "very well indeed; in fact, magnifico!" It was the way he said it that sent a shiver down my spine. His voice rose on the last word to a note of rapture and his eyes gleamed with relish. He reached out for the carafe of wine and filled my glass. It gurgled into the tumbler, thick and red, and I could only think of blood.

When we got out of the restaurant, Hemingway said: "A chic type, eh? Now remember, he's mine."

Months later, when she read "The Fifth Column," Hemingway's Spanish Civil War play, Cowles recognized lines in it from this conversation.

Herbst also left an account of the meal, writing of Cowles, "She is young and pretty; dressed in black, with heavy gold bracelets on her slender wrists and wearing tiny black shoes with incredibly high heels. I often wondered how she navigated over the rubble."

The executioner, like so many other men, took a shine to Cowles. As other diners abandoned the restaurant amid the noise of shells exploding on the streets outside and windows shattering, "he pats her knee reassuringly and says: 'We will all go to my house. I will divorce my wife and marry you. There are plenty of beds, plenty of room, even for Hemingway. . . . I have a son,' he tells Virginia, 'and you won't have to make another. Just be my wife. My wife can be the cook. . . .'

"'I'm afraid when you get tired of me you'll make me be the cook,' says Virginia."

During this spring in Madrid, Cowles also saw Hemingway and his entourage at work on a project for which he had great expectations. It was a documentary, to be called *The Spanish Earth*. Joris Ivens, the director, was a Dutch filmmaker with close ties to the Comintern. Backers of the Republic fervently hoped that the film, with the famous novelist participating, might help mobilize support abroad. Hemingway, who was writing the narrator's script, had contributed $4,000 toward production costs, and was happy that the project included many friends. Among those involved were his bullfighter sidekick Sidney Franklin, his new lover Martha Gellhorn, and his longtime fishing companion, the writer John Dos Passos, whom he had first met in Italy when they were young ambulance drivers in the First World War. The two had often traveled together and shared a deep love of Spain.

For more than a month, Hemingway and a changing array of hangers-on accompanied Ivens and his crew. The husky writer sometimes lent a hand carrying camera equipment as they filmed the trenches at University City, battle scenes near Madrid, air raids in progress, shells landing, wounded soldiers being carried off on stretchers, and even a German plane crashing. At one point the film crew's car was hit by shrapnel. With his usual onstage swagger, Hemingway wrote in one of his newspaper dispatches about bullets smacking into the walls of a building from which they were filming. Virginia Cowles joined the camera crew one day at a farming village on the Madrid–Valencia road that figured in the script. Sidney Franklin was also along, but the crew could not get much filming done, Cowles wrote, because "a few minutes after our arrival some one identified him as a matador, and the entire village poured out to get a look at him. . . . The Mayor brought out a jug of wine, the children crowded into the room and for the rest of the afternoon we discussed the technicalities of the bullfight." When the shooting was completed in May 1937, Ivens rushed to New York to edit the results. Everyone involved had high hopes for the impact the documentary could have where it counted most—the United States.

Cowles left Spain after spending several months there. "For weeks, in Paris, the sound of a car backfiring, or the drone of a vacuum cleaner, gave me a foolish start. . . . Spain had left a deeper mark than I had realized." Nonetheless, she began preparing for her next goal: reporting the war from the Nationalist side.

10

The Man Who Loved Dictators

The glamorous collection of foreign correspondents who chronicled the ordeal of Madrid have been celebrated in a score of memoirs, novels, histories, and even a 2012 made-for-television movie, *Hemingway and Gellhorn,* in which an abandoned California railway station was transformed into the lobby of the Hotel Florida. Nearly 1,000 journalists from other countries reported from Spain at some point during the war, filing hundreds of thousands of words in a dozen or more languages describing this majestic, beautiful city under siege, suffering the ravages of prolonged aerial bombing. Yet, strangely, these reporters missed a huge story.

Not one of them, it appears, looked up at the droning, V-shaped formations of Hitler's Junkers in the sky above Madrid and wondered: whose fuel is powering those aircraft?

It should have been an obvious question. Not just planes, but tanks, armored cars, trucks, and much else vital to fighting a modern war run on oil: more than 60 percent of the oil going to Spain during the war was consumed by the rival armies. Yet for Hitler and Mussolini, who had rushed to send Franco troops, aviators, and arms of all kinds, oil was the one thing they lacked. Germany, in fact, imported more than two thirds of what it used. Nationalist Spain could not easily have afforded to purchase oil on the world market, because the country's gold reserves were in the hands of the Republic. It would have added greatly to Germany's and Italy's expenses as Franco's major arms suppliers for them to also put up the money for him to buy oil. As it turned out, they didn't have to do so.

Franco's oil came on credit. And it came from Texas.

The man who made this happen could often be seen at the '21' Club, a favorite haunt of New York café society. This former speakeasy was known for its red leather banquettes, wood-paneled bar, and flamboyantly expensive menu. A variety of brightly colored jockey statuettes had been donated by patrons who owned racehorses, and certain diners had their own private wine collections in the restaurant's cellars. The regulars included everyone from big-time gangsters to Humphrey Bogart and the Marx Brothers. Sometimes an item on the menu honored a favored customer, and one hamburger-and-egg dish bore the name of a barrel-chested, square-jawed figure whose presence dominated any gathering.

By the time he was fifteen, Norwegian-born Torkild Rieber had gone to sea as a deckhand on a full-rigged clipper ship. This was before the Panama Canal was completed, and the vessel took six months to make its way from Europe around Cape Horn to San Francisco. For the next two years he signed on with ships carrying indentured workers from Calcutta to the sugar plantations of the British West Indies. Their crews won bonus money for every worker they delivered, and this echo of the slave trade made "coolie ships" some of the most crowded and brutal vessels afloat. All his life, Rieber thrived on telling stories in his deep, gravelly voice about his sailing days: climbing to a high yardarm to furl sails far above a rolling, pitching deck, forecasting storms from the look of the sky at dusk, riding out Atlantic hurricanes in a ship packed with desperately seasick Indian laborers. Onshore, however, he liked wearing a tuxedo when he went out to dinner at '21' or elsewhere, because, he said, "that's the way the Brits ran the colony in Calcutta."

After surviving a knifing by a drunken crewman, the youthful Rieber was naturalized as an American citizen and became the captain of his first vessel, a tanker. From then on he was known as "Cap." By the time the Spanish Civil War began, he was long gone from the sea. What he now captained, from an elegantly wainscotted office high in New York's Chrysler Building, with a globe behind his desk and roll-down maps on the wall, was an oil company.

After the tanker he commanded was bought by the Texas Company—better known by its service-station brand name, Texaco—Rieber had realized that in oil the big money to be made was on dry land. As the company expanded, and the red Texaco star with a green T spread to gas stations across the world, he married his boss's secretary and rose rapidly up the corporate ladder. "He cannot sit at a desk," wrote an awestruck reporter from *Life* magazine. "He bounces up and down, fidgets and jumps up to pace the floor as if it were a deck. He is perpetually restless, on a terrestrial scale. He cannot stay long in one office or in one city or on one continent." *Life*'s sister publication, *Time*, was no less susceptible to Rieber's rough-diamond charm, calling him a "hard-headed, steel-willed" corporate chieftain with "horse sense, a command of men and the driving force of a triple-expansion engine."

Texaco long had the reputation of being the most brash and aggressive of the big oil companies; its founder, who hired Rieber, proudly flew a black skull-and-crossbones flag atop his office building. "If I were dying at a Texaco filling-station," a Shell executive once said, "I'd ask to be dragged across the road." For the company, Rieber muscled his way into oil fields around the world, making under-the-table deals with local strongmen everywhere from the Persian Gulf to Colombia. There, a new city called Petrólea arose in the midst of a Rhode Island–sized expanse of land where Texaco had won the right to drill. Pumping the oil to a Colombian port where tankers could collect it required building a 263-mile pipeline through jungle and mountains, crossing the Andes over a mile-high ridge at Captain Rieber Pass. Workers died building it, and German friends nicknamed Rieber *Leichenfänger*, scavenger of corpses. Rieber's ambitions

The enormous gulf between rich and poor was a major tension underlying the Spanish Civil War.

Spain's Catholic hierarchy fervently backed the Nationalists. The bishop of Salamanca (left) and other church dignitaries salute alongside General José Millán Astray y Terreros, founder of the Spanish Foreign Legion and Franco's propaganda chief.

In Republican-controlled territory, mobs killed nearly 7,000 members of the clergy and burned hundreds of church buildings.

The dining room of Barcelona's Hotel Ritz, converted to People's Cafeteria No. 1.

International Brigade volunteers in Madrid defending the university's Philosophy and Letters building. Note the protective piles of books.

Marion and Bob Merriman, November 1937, just before she left Spain, with Dave Doran (left), who went missing in action with Bob.

Moorish troops in Morocco awaiting transport to Spain in Nazi aircraft.

The author with Lucy Selligman Schneider, sister of Joseph Selligman Jr., the first American casualty in the battle for Madrid.

Lois Orr, nineteen-year-old American eyewitness to social revolution in Barcelona.

Franco's favorite oilman, Torkild Rieber of Texaco.

Citizens man a Barcelona barricade against the Nationalists two days after the start of the coup.

Barcelona militia members hold a wedding.

Anarchist militia atop a makeshift armored car, summer 1936.

October 28, 1938: the International Brigades march through Barcelona in farewell.

Ebro River swimmers George Watt (left) and John Gates.

Journalists Louis Fischer and Virginia Cowles.

spanned the earth, as did his travels: in 1936, he managed, along with an explorer, an opera singer, the lord mayor of Frankfurt, and various other celebrities, to get a coveted cabin on the first voyage of the dirigible *Hindenburg*, from Germany to the United States.

Like many executives of his day, the hot-tempered Rieber had no love for unions or for Franklin D. Roosevelt's New Deal. But beneath his broad shoulders, iron handshake, sailors' oaths, and the up-from-the-lower-decks persona that played so well at '21' lay something darker. Although not particularly anti-Semitic—"Why," he would say, "some of my best friends are goddam Jews, like Bernie Gimbel and Solomon Guggenheim"—he was an admirer of Adolf Hitler's. In later years he would downplay such sympathies by claiming that they were purely a matter of business. "He always thought it was much better to deal with autocrats than democracies," a friend recalled. "He said with an autocrat you really only have to bribe him once. With democracies you have to keep doing it over and over again."

Texaco had become Spain's principal oil supplier the year before the Nationalist coup. When Franco and his fellow conspirators made their grab for power, Rieber decided not to follow his contract with the Republican government's state oil company, but to make a deal with the new autocrat on the scene. Knowing that military trucks, tanks, and aircraft need not only fuel but a range of engine oils and other lubricants, he quickly ordered a supply of drums and cans of these on hand at the French port of Bordeaux to be loaded into an empty Texaco tanker and shipped to the Nationalists.

As often happens, political feelings were reinforced by a personal tie. The friendship was between Rieber and a much younger man, José Antonio Álvarez Alonso, a twenty-eight-year-old English-speaking official of the Spanish government oil company. When that organization had signed its contract with Texaco in 1935, it bought a Texaco tanker, and the Spaniard traveled to the corporation's pipeline terminal at Port Arthur, Texas, to mark the occasion and meet Texaco's new chairman. Álvarez Alonso was an enthusiast of his country's Fascist movement, the Falange Española, and as Rieber showed him around the ship, the two men hit it off, realizing they saw the world the same way. The Texaco chieftain invited his new friend back to the United States a few months later, to attend an oil industry meeting in Los Angeles. After the Nationalist uprising began in 1936, Republican-held Madrid became a dangerous place for Fascists, and Álvarez Alonso fled to France. He knew the Nationalists would be short of oil, and from Marseille sent a telegram to William M. Brewster, Texaco's representative in the French capital. Immediately a reply came back: COME TO PARIS. CAPTAIN RIEBER IS HERE AND WOULD LIKE TO SEE YOU.

When Álvarez Alonso met with the two men, "Mr. Rieber told me that his company would side with Nationalist Spain." Álvarez Alonso then traveled to Burgos, the Spanish city where Franco had set up his headquarters. From there, he sent messages to an impatient Rieber in Paris, explaining that although the Nationalists urgently needed oil, they lacked tankers and cash. Rieber replied with a telegram that would long be celebrated in Franco's inner circle: DON'T WORRY ABOUT PAYMENTS. Soon afterward, Álvarez Alonso invited Rieber and Brewster to Burgos. It was agreed that Texaco would supply Franco with all the oil he needed—on credit. Juan March, a banking, tobacco, and newspaper magnate who was the Nationalists' biggest financial backer, stepped in as the guarantor. Ties were further cemented when, after a short period as a volunteer at the front, Álvarez Alonso was put in charge of Nationalist oil imports. (After the war, he would be rewarded with a job as president of the Spanish subsidiary of Texaco.)

On the other side of the Atlantic, when a Republican tanker docked at Port Arthur in the fall of 1936, its captain expecting the contract with Texaco to be honored, he was dismayed to discover that Rieber had sent orders that no more Texaco oil was to be sold to the Republic. Since both Nationalist Spain and its allies were short of oil, and the United States had an apparently bottomless supply, this lifeline from Texaco ensured that Franco could continue to wage war. If the US government intervened to stop the flow, the Nationalist war effort could be seriously disrupted.

• • •

Spanish Republicans fervently hoped that President Roosevelt would soon change his mind about staying neutral in Spain, and so did their supporters everywhere. Surely, more than any other Western leader, he would not want to see Hitler and Mussolini gain another ally. And surely Eleanor Roosevelt, who in visiting coal mines, farmers struggling with Dust Bowl drought, and shack dwellers in Appalachia had shown such concern for working people and the dispossessed, must be on their side too.

In fact, she did send a personal contribution to a Quaker fund for Spanish children's relief. Although she was careful never to directly criticize American policy in her widely read newspaper column, supporters of the Republic were encouraged by her repeated references to the suffering caused by the war. In the end, however, the power was the president's, and whatever was in his heart, for the time being he remained, on this issue, a very cautious man. Aiding the Spanish Republic would win him few votes, and was certain to infuriate Catholic bishops and the editors of hundreds of Catholic newspapers and magazines across the country. When running for reelection in 1936, FDR was believed to have quietly promised the American Catholic leadership that he would not take sides in Spain. The radio preacher Father Coughlin called Franco a "rebel for Christ, a rebel for humanity's sake," and spoke of the murders of thousands of Spanish priests "beneath the crimson cross of Communism upon which the brothers of Christ had been crucified."

Roosevelt was intrigued by the relatively new practice of opinion polling, and he followed polls closely. In February 1937, one poll found that, though Americans who sympathized with the Republic outnumbered Franco supporters by nearly two to one, 66 percent of the population favored neither side or had no opinion at all. That figure, wrote the pollster George Gallup, "will warm the heart of any isolationist." By contrast, a majority of the American people knew exactly what they thought about King Edward VIII giving up his throne so he could marry Mrs. Simpson: he was right.

Working from a townhouse in Manhattan, Jay Allen, fired from the conservative *Chicago Daily Tribune* for his exposés of Franco's massacres, had become a passionate lobbyist for the Republic. Eleanor Roosevelt was always ready to hear him out and at one point arranged for him to put the case for helping Republican Spain to her husband at their country retreat on the Hudson River. Paul Preston tells the story:

"When the day came, he went to Hyde Park and delivered his speech. When he finished, believing that he had said it all, and said it well, he was thrown into confusion by Roosevelt's laconic response: 'Mr. Allen, I could not hear you!' Jay was nonplussed. Had the president really not heard him? Had he not spoken loudly enough? . . . Seeing his dismay, the president explained: 'Mr. Allen, I can hear the Roman Catholic Church and all their allies very well. They speak very loudly. Could you and your friends speak a little louder, please?'"

Roosevelt continued to listen to those who spoke the loudest. By US law, the export of "arms, ammunition, and implements of war" to other countries at war was prohibited. Early in 1937, a congressional resolution made clear that any weapons destined for "the unfortunate civil strife in Spain" were included in the ban. The Senate voted in favor, by 80 to 0, as did the House of Representatives, by 411 to 1. The 1 was John T. Bernard of Minnesota, a stubborn, Corsican-born opera lover and former iron miner. On the floor of the House, he kept raising procedural objections until the *Mar Cantábrico*, a Spanish Republican ship with a cargo of a dozen secondhand civilian aircraft, some airplane engines, and other supplies could make it out of New York harbor and into international waters. The vessel was being trailed by a Coast Guard cutter, a New York City police plane, and several planeloads of reporters and photographers. When Bernard got word that the ship was beyond the territorial limit, he stopped talking in midsentence, and the resolution passed. The *Mar Cantábrico*'s journey, however, did not end well. As it approached Spain, it was intercepted at sea by a Nationalist warship. The captain, five passengers, and ten crewmen were shot; the rest were sentenced to life in prison at hard labor. Franco's air force happily helped itself to the aircraft on board—one of which would eventually carry two important American visitors around Nationalist Spain.

The toughened American neutrality legislation was welcomed by Franco, who said Roosevelt had "behaved like a true gentleman." The dictator was doubtless pleased as well that—bizarrely—the new law did not prohibit the export of crude oil, gasoline, or aviation fuel, for without them his army and air force would have been in big trouble. Texaco was not the only US oil company supplying him. Following Rieber's lead, Shell, Socony, Atlantic Refining, and Standard Oil of New Jersey also found a customer in the Generalissimo, although the bulk of his oil would continue to come from Texaco. Texaco alone would supply the Nationalists with more than twice as much oil as the Republic was able to buy from all sources.

Something also not legally considered armaments were trucks. Those used by Franco's army were largely American—some 12,000 of them, purchased from General Motors, Studebaker, and Ford. (GM did Franco a huge favor by taking its payment in Nationalist pesetas, which could not be exported from Spain during the war and would have value only if Franco won.) Firestone Tires similarly sold its products to the Generalissimo's military. An advertisement in Spain declared, "Victory smiles on the best. The glorious Nationalist army always wins on the field of battle. Firestone Tires has had its nineteenth consecutive victory in the Indianapolis 500."

US law did, however, say that such supposedly nonmilitary products going to a country at war could not be shipped on American vessels. And here, it appeared, there was hope of cutting Franco's oil lifeline from Texaco, for customs agents discovered that Torkild Rieber's tankers were evading this provision of the law. The Texaco ships would leave the company's pipeline terminal in Texas with cargo manifests showing them destined for Antwerp, Rotterdam, or Amsterdam. Only at sea would their captains open sealed instructions redirecting them to ports in Nationalist Spain.

In addition to ordering these manifests falsified, Rieber was violating another part of the law: he was extending credit to a government at war. Nominally, that credit was for 90 days from the date the oil was shipped—itself startlingly lenient terms for the oil business. The real terms were more generous yet. As Rieber's friend the Nationalist oil official Álvarez Alonso later explained, "We paid what we could when we could, and the debt went well over the established limit." In effect, Rieber was serving as Franco's banker.

When FBI agents questioned him about the violations in the spring of 1937, Rieber turned on his deep-voiced sea captain's charm and played the role of a nonpolitical businessman, explaining that he was sure the Nationalists "would be victorious and he did not want to lose the Spaniards' business which amounted to from $3,000,000 to $5,000,000 per year." The FBI apparently did not realize that Rieber's company was also acting as Franco's purchasing agent, when the Nationalists needed goods not in Texaco's inventory. Only decades later, as we shall see, would archives reveal other extraordinary favors the oil company did for Franco.

The young Justice Department official handling the 1937 Texaco investigation seemed timid about moving against Rieber. Only more than three months after receiving news of the falsified manifests did he write his boss, Attorney General Homer Cummings, saying that he was inclined to send the case for prosecution to New York, where Texaco's headquarters were, but "in view of . . . the prominence of some of the offendors . . . you might wish to know of the matter before the case is submitted."

The next week, Cummings brought up the subject at a meeting of the cabinet, mentioning a possible conspiracy indictment against Texaco. President Roosevelt, he reported, declared himself "in favor of prompt and vigorous prosecution." But FDR subsequently changed his mind, for the prosecution was anything but vigorous. Although violators of the neutrality law could be subject to five years in prison, Texaco received only a wrist-slap, eventually paying a $22,000 fine for extending credit to a belligerent government. Years later, when oil companies began issuing credit cards to consumers, a joke made the rounds of industry insiders: Whom did Texaco give its first credit card to? Francisco Franco.

11

Devil's Bargain

DESPITE THEIR DEFEAT at Guadalajara, Nationalist troops made ominous advances elsewhere in the spring of 1937, particularly on Spain's northern coast. There, Basque forces were struggling to hold on to a diminishing band of territory cut off from the rest of the Republic, and a new group fell victim to the Nationalist policy of deliberate terror. For in the Basque country, most of the Catholic clergy had backed the Republic, which had given them the freedom to preach and teach in the Basque language. (Indeed, one Basque nationalist said that a sin he acknowledged in the confessional booth was using "Spanish words.") As a result, 16 priests were murdered by Nationalist troops, many more were tortured, and more than 80 sentenced to long prison terms. In territory the Nationalists conquered, there would be no more sermons in Basque.

Before long, the war reached a small inland city, less than ten miles from the front lines and filled with refugees fleeing the Nationalists, their belongings piled in ox carts. Guernica (today usually called by its Basque name, Gernika) had long had a special place in the history of the independent-minded Basques. Legend has it that Ferdinand and Isabella, the monarchs who helped to unify Spain, came to Guernica in 1476 and, standing beneath an oak tree, pledged to preserve ancient Basque privileges. A poet wrote a famous song dedicated to the tree. Two trees later but in the same spot, delegates had assembled in 1936 to swear in the president of an autonomous Basque territory allied with the Republic.

Late on the afternoon of April 26, 1937, a church bell tolled an air-raid warning. Some people rushed to their cellars; others, including farmers who had brought their cattle and sheep to Guernica for market day, fled to the fields outside of town. A single Nazi plane flew overhead, dropping its load of bombs on the city, and when nothing more happened, people again emerged onto the streets. At just that moment—now that the lack of fire on the first flight had revealed that Guernica had little in the way of antiaircraft defenses—the real attack came. Twenty-three Ju-52 bombers from the Condor Legion, accompanied by some two dozen other aircraft, flying in relays from bases close by, began dropping antipersonnel bombs, high explosives, and incendiaries in aluminum tubes designed to set exposed wood in smashed buildings on fire. German pilots nicknamed this mixture *Generalstabsmischung*, or General Staff's Blend, and they dropped more than 30 tons of it over some three hours.

Families were buried in their houses; clouds of smoke and dust rose into the air; sheep and cattle, covered in flaming chemicals from the incendiaries, stampeded in terror through streets filled with shattered masonry. At the Santa María church, the priest managed to use communion wine to put out an incendiary, but it was a rare piece of luck on a day of destruction. As people realized that cellars would not save them from collapsing buildings and began to flee, waves of Heinkel He-51 fighter planes zoomed in low, strafing every human or animal in sight. Some 200 people were killed and many more wounded. The greater part of the city was reduced to charred, smoldering ruins. As night fell, an eerie orange glow filled the sky.

In a sense, Guernica was a military target, as retreating Republican troops and their equipment were about to pass through the town, but their route could have been disrupted far more easily if the bombers had concentrated on a nearby bridge. It escaped the massive air raid undamaged; in fact, people took shelter beneath it. The one indisputably military installation in town, an arms factory, was not harmed. Essentially the raid was an experiment in what highly concentrated aerial bombing could do to a town or city. For some time, Condor Legion officers had been impatient to test their firepower in this way. "It would be welcomed if the Spanish side at last explicitly asked for attacks on built-up areas," read a German internal memo five months earlier. The bomber force "was targeted at Guernica," wrote the legion's chief of staff, the Prussian aristocrat Lieutenant Colonel Wolfram von Richthofen (cousin and flying mate of the First World War's famous "Red Baron"), in his war diary on April 26. His blue eyes, crewcut blond hair, erect military bearing, and love of physical fitness made him the very picture of the "Aryan" type Hitler so valued.

The carpet bombing of Guernica represented the first near-total destruction of a European city from the air. Although the civilian death toll was actually smaller than that in some less noticed Nationalist attacks on a nearby town several weeks earlier, it had a powerful impact on a world that had not yet seen the London blitz or the obliteration of Dresden and Hiroshima. The attack, of course, also inspired the century's most famous painting. Pablo Picasso, already deeply angered by the bombing of Madrid, had been commissioned to do a mural for the Republic's pavilion at a world's fair in Paris that summer. After the raid on Guernica he dropped his original plan and instead worked on his knees, standing, and on a ladder to cover a canvas 11 feet high and more than 25 feet wide with images of the bombing, including its animal victims. Other expressions of outrage came from all over the world.

Although the bombing of Guernica has long been a historical landmark, we forget one reason it first inspired such outrage: Franco and the hierarchy of Spain's Catholic Church vigorously denied that it had ever taken place. When the word "Garnika" was found on the April 26 page of the diary of a German pilot shot down by the Basques, he claimed that this was the name of a girlfriend in Hamburg. Franco's denials were accepted by the British foreign secretary and the American secretary of state, both determined not to get drawn into the Spanish war. Guernica, the Nationalist propaganda apparatus claimed, had been burned to the ground by retreating Republican troops. In response, the French satirical weekly *Le Canard Enchaîné* published the news that Joan of Arc herself had lit the fire that burned her to death at the stake.

For nearly 40 years, the Franco regime continued to maintain that the Basques themselves had blown up Guernica. Several foreign correspondents, however, reached the town only six hours after the bombing, when the ruins were still on fire, and a vivid, powerful account by one from the London *Times*, filled with precise detail on types of bombs and aircraft, was reprinted by newspapers in many countries. The Franco enthusiast William P. Carney of the *New York Times*, on the other hand, not only reported the Nationalist denials, but visited what was left of the town once it was captured by Franco's forces a few days after the bombing. He maintained that he found no bomb craters in the streets and concluded that "most of the destruction here could have been the result of fires and dynamiting, as the Nationalists claim, because the roofless shells of many buildings are still standing and huge shells dropped from [planes] do not hollow out buildings, leaving their four walls standing." Exactly why fires and dynamiting would hollow out a building while a bomb would not, he did not explain.

For this and other services to the Nationalist cause, Carney would be rewarded long after the war and his retirement from the *Times* with a job as a lobbyist and PR man in the United States for Franco's regime.

As the news from Guernica reached the latest American volunteers to arrive in Spain, most were in training several hundred miles to the south, under Bob Merriman's supervision. His diary is filled with crisp evaluations of their performance, and disapproval of those who were drunk or undisciplined. Although he insisted that the men salute him, he ate with them and corrected them when they called him "sir," as if he were an officer in a conventional army. Traditional military men would have raised their eyebrows at something else as well: on one training exercise, Bob brought Marion with him. As she described it: "An eleven-mile march was planned. . . . So, wearing my hemp-soled espadrilles, I joined the men and we headed down the dusty road to where machine gun exercises would be held with live ammunition. Real machine gun bullets over their heads drove home exactly what it would be like when the men went into combat. . . . Bob and I slept together that night on a bed of scrub pine branches in an open field." His diary was as usual all business, and the only apparent reference to this march was a brief "Marion doing well in field."

Most of the time, however, they were apart, Marion working at the International Brigades headquarters in Albacete, and Bob at a nearby camp where the Americans he was training were quartered in a vine-covered convent and ate their meals in what had once been a church. When the two both had time off, they swam in the Jucar River near Albacete. At one point they went to Madrid together so Bob, Hemingway, Dr. Pike, and others could make a shortwave radio broadcast for the Republic to the United States. Marion got a taste of what it was like to be under shellfire in the besieged city, its shops almost bare of food, its streets littered with rubble. Back in Albacete, her room at the city's Hotel Regina was a haven for off-duty American volunteers, as well as doctors and nurses from the US medical unit, who knew they could always find a cup of George Washington instant coffee there and—if she had any luck at the local shops—some crackers and sardines as well. At work, she typed, ran errands, wrote for the International Brigades newspaper, copied US Army manuals, and dealt with visiting notables like the writer Dorothy Parker. She followed Bob's lead and joined the Communist Party. Her job proved as much an education about the United States as about Spain. It was the first time, for example, that she had ever known any blacks or Jews.

The American volunteers accepted her presence, but, she wrote, "sometimes I was accepted a little too much. Occasionally, the men made advances. . . . I told one such enterprising young man that . . . if I slept with him as he suggested I'd have to sleep with the other two thousand men to be fair and that I wasn't up to it." One ardent

American tried to convice her "that it was my Party duty to go to bed with him since I was a Party member & he needed me."

Gathering material for his newspaper and magazine articles, Louis Fischer visited Bob's training camp, writing, "There, in the center of the dry Castilian plateau, the accents of Mississippi, the Bronx, New England, Philadelphia, Chicago and West Coast wharfs mingled with the Spanish of the folks round about. . . . 'A year ago this afternoon,' I thought, 'I played tennis with Merriman on the Petrovka [a street in Moscow].'" Now that Bob was deadly serious about fighting a war, however, his feelings toward his former tennis partner seemed to cool, for he described Fischer in his diary as the "same old self—with pretty girl and same inside air."

Still in the trenches as the Lincoln Battalion's lone Englishman, Pat Gurney showed the usual contempt of frontline soldiers for those in the rear. Of the "nabobs" of Albacete, he wrote, "Most of them were dressed in the most extraordinary collection of self-invented uniforms—leather coats in many lengths and colours, breeches with an assortment of spectacular-looking highboots of all kinds, and a beret. They all wore Sam Browne belts of varying and elaborate design, with large, business-like pistols. No one would forgo this last status symbol, although they were useless in the city and urgently needed at the Front."

One volunteer penned some doggerel:

On the front of Albacete
Meet the generals of the rear
Oh! They fight the grandest battles
Though the shells they never hear,
For the wind is in their make-up.
You can hear the generals say:
"Yes, we're going to Jarama
Mañana or next day."

The front the Lincolns continued to hold some 20 miles southeast of Madrid was stable, but intermittent shelling and rifle fire meant, as Gurney wrote, "it was never possible to relax." One of his jobs was to make a daily trip over the bare, rocky ground from the Lincoln trenches to XV Brigade headquarters, and his route took him past what was known as the "meat yard. . . . It was here that the day's quota of corpses were deposited while awaiting removal. The numbers varied between two and twenty. Snipers and mortar fire took a small but regular toll, and every morning a number of these utterly forlorn objects were laid out there under their blankets."

The recollections of other Lincolns also offer a depressing picture of boredom, squalor, bad food, and incompetent higher commanders in what seemed like endless months in the trenches. This did not stop correspondents determined to portray a different mood, and no one was more so inclined than Herbert Matthews. When he paid a quick visit in May 1937, he wrote in the *New York Times* that the Americans were "a healthy, happy lot with plenty of zest for fighting. One chap, who said he had been in a seamen's strike last Winter, told me he was getting much better food here than he got in New York." By contrast, Virginia Cowles, who also visited these trenches around the same time, was far more realistic: "the men looked strained and sick and I learned they had been in the front line for seventy-four days without a break. . . . Their faces [were] lined and worn."

Gurney's time in the field had deflated his previous euphoria over the Spanish Revolution, and he now felt that the anarchists and the POUM were "criminally naïve" in their belief that military matters could be put to a vote of the soldiers involved. Nonetheless, he was appalled by the hatred of these groups promoted by the commissars of the International Brigades. "The official Party . . . produced a mass of palpably absurd propaganda, claiming that the POUM were in alliance with Franco who, for all his faults, certainly would not have allied himself with a small party of dissident Marxists." As spring moved into summer, Gurney began "looking for an opportunity to get out of the whole show. . . . I was prepared to be killed fighting to achieve a form of social justice for Spain, but not to achieve a talking point for the Communist Party or anybody else."

His political distress, however, was generally not shared by his comrades. The International Brigade troops at the front were separated by language and distance from the growing political feuding in places like Barcelona, and few seemed to pay much attention to it. The many Lincolns who would break with the Communist Party nearly all did so only years or decades later. Despite his frustrations, Gurney never doubted that he had been right to come to Spain. "The tragic part of the situation was that the vast majority of us still felt convinced of the justice of our cause and were anxious to fight for it."

The political tension Gurney saw was not unique to the Spanish Republic. Other societies in turmoil have faced the same question: can you have a revolution and fight a war at the same time? After King Charles I was captured in the English Civil War, in the celebrated Putney Debates of 1647 radicals put forth ideas far ahead of their time, like universal manhood suffrage. But then Charles escaped, the war resumed, and universal suffrage, even for men, was not achieved for several more centuries. In the 1790s, when the people of Haiti seized their freedom in history's greatest slave revolt, they carved out small plots for themselves from the large plantations they had previously worked in bondage, so that as free men and women they could grow their own food at last. But such a system did not produce the sugar and coffee that could buy the foreign arms desperately needed to fight off France's attempt to recapture its former colony. As a result, the Haitian leader Toussaint L'Ouverture forced his reluctant people back onto the old plantations, under harsh discipline, to grow cash crops once again.

A similar friction bedeviled Republican Spain. For all their allure, the qualities that made the infant Spanish Revolution so attractive to its admirers—egalitarianism, decentralized power, exuberant defiance of authority—have never been the building blocks of strong armies. With the revolution-minded anarchists and the POUM on one side and the increasingly powerful Communists and their mainstream allies on the other, conflict over what kind of society the Republic was to be steadily mounted. In Madrid, Barcelona, and elsewhere, the two sides clashed, people were killed, and one prominent Communist politician was assassinated.

Beyond the differences over whether revolutionary change should be postponed until the war was won lay other divisions: the anarchists retained their profound suspicion of government of any kind, while the Communists, using the leverage of Soviet arms, maneuvered Party members into key security and military staff positions. "Our influence in the army . . . is growing by leaps and bounds," reported a commissar in the Lincolns in a letter to his wife this spring. Paranoia was rife on both sides. The Communist Party put up posters showing a POUM mask half lifted, with a swastika underneath, while Lois Orr believed the Communists and their allies were "allowing known Fifth Columnists to walk the streets of Madrid."

The anarchist stronghold of Barcelona was where things reached the breaking point. Historians still argue about just who was to blame, but the final trigger was several telephone calls.

The red-and-black anarchist flag had flown for months over the city's telephone exchange, a triumphant symbol of revolutionary power because it had been seized from the American-owned International Telephone and Telegraph Corporation. Anarchist militiamen manned sandbagged guard posts at the building's doors. The anarchists regarded the phone system as essential to people's control of the economy—and, resembling many a regime past and present, also as a convenient way of monitoring their political opponents. On May 2, 1937, a Republican cabinet minister in Valencia tried to telephone an official of the Catalan regional government in Barcelona, only to be told by the anarchist operator that there was no such government—the anarchist dream—only a "defense committee." When the Republic's president, Manuel Azaña, called Lluís Companys, the president of Catalonia, the same day, an anarchist operator broke into their call and insisted that they stop talking. Officials in both governments were furious, and Catalonia's security minister ordered the police to take over the telephone building. The anarchist guards were armed, and began firing.

"The shots frightened clouds of birds into the grey overcast sky," Lois Orr remembered, "and sped word through the city: IT had finally begun." The fighting quickly escalated into a tragic war-within-the-war that would take many lives. It was the decisive show-down over just who would control Spain's second-largest city, and indeed the whole northeastern corner of the country all the way to the French frontier. Would ultimate power belong to the Republic's cabinet in Valencia and the Catalan regional government under it, or be in the hands of the thousands of armed anarchist militiamen who for months had been guarding buildings, roadblocks, and even—as the Orrs had discovered when they entered Spain—border control posts?

George Orwell, on leave in Barcelona, found himself in the middle of the fighting. Although aware of the political tensions within the Republican side, he had not until now grasped how lethal they were. In fact, he had hoped to use his leave to transfer from the POUM militia to the International Brigades. Despite distrusting the Communist Party, he knew its units were better equipped and defending Madrid, which, in contrast to the relatively sleepy Aragon front, seemed to be the crucial fight. "The revolutionary purism of the P.O.U.M.," he wrote, "though I saw its logic, seemed to me rather futile. After all, the one thing that mattered was to win the war."

British Communists in Spain knew of Orwell as an author and felt that it would be a coup to recruit him to the International Brigades. They had several undercover agents in Barcelona, including at least one whom Orwell and his wife believed to be a POUM comrade. One report to brigades headquarters at Albacete said that Orwell "has little political understanding" but was "the leading personality and most respected man in the contingent" of Britons fighting with the POUM and "wishes to fight on the Madrid front and states that in a few days he will formally apply to us for enlistment."

Events, however, intervened:

"About midday on 3 May," as Orwell later wrote in *Homage to Catalonia*, "a friend crossing the lounge of the hotel said casually: 'There's been some kind of trouble at the Telephone Exchange, I hear. . . .' That afternoon, between three and four, I was halfway down the Ramblas when I heard several rifle-shots behind me. . . . Up and down the street you could hear snap–snap–snap as the shopkeepers slammed the steel shutters over their windows."

With the police cracking down on the anarchists and the POUM, Orwell was immediately sent to protect the POUM office building where his wife Eileen and Charles Orr worked. For three days and nights, he and a small group of others, including Harry Milton, a New Yorker from his militia unit, were stationed on the roof of a movie theater that overlooked the building from across the tree-lined Ramblas.

"I used to sit on the roof marvelling at the folly of it all," he wrote. ". . . You could see for miles around—vista after vista of tall slender buildings, glass domes and fantastic curly roofs with brilliant green and copper tiles; over to eastward the glittering pale blue sea—the first glimpse of the sea that I had had since coming to Spain. And the whole huge town of a million people was locked in a sort of violent inertia. . . . Nothing was happening except the streaming of bullets from barricades and sand-bagged windows. . . . Here and there along the Ramblas the trams stood motionless where their drivers had jumped out of them when the fighting started. And all the while the devilish noise, echoing from thousands of stone buildings, went on and on, like a tropical rainstorm."

Several days later, his group of militiamen was put to work fortifying POUM headquarters with stone blocks. Counting their weaponry, they found they had only 20 working rifles, about 50 bullets, plus a few pistols and grenades. Eileen joined him, to be on hand to help nurse any wounded. But they had no medical supplies. Meanwhile, more armed men from both sides occupied more roofs. "The position was so complicated," he wrote, "that it would have been quite unintelligible if every building had not flown a party flag." Some Assault Guards, the Republican government's paramilitary urban police, took over a roof diagonally across the street from Orwell's.

"It was infuriating. I had been a hundred and fifteen days in the line and had come back to Barcelona ravenous for a bit of rest and comfort; and instead I had to spend my time sitting on a roof opposite Assault Guards as bored as myself, who periodically waved to me and assured me that they were 'workers' (meaning that they hoped I would not shoot them), but who would certainly open fire if they got the order to do so."

They did not open fire, but tens of thousands of shots were exchanged elsewhere in the city, in street fighting that lasted nearly a week. After it ended—but before he understood all the consequences—Orwell, distressed at finding the factionalism so bitter, and angry that the Communist-backed police had used their guns against the anarchists and the POUM, abandoned his plan to transfer to the International Brigades. Despite everything, he still believed the war was worth fighting, and he returned to his militia unit at the front.

Lois Orr was sick at home when the firing started. Orwell's Scottish comrade Bob Smillie, also in Barcelona on leave and a friend of the Orrs, had just brought her some eggs, bread, and strawberries. The moment the fighting began, however, she was out of bed. "10 minutes after she heard about it, she was out with me helping build barricades," Charles Orr wrote proudly to his mother on May 8. "I am an expert now—worked on 5 or 6 wounded and 1 killed in my principle [*sic*] station. My neck was grazed. But it would be worth dying for. . . . We are quite o.k.—a little hungry. The fighting is evidently finished—but no one has won."

He was wrong about that. The Republic's government had won, establishing its rule over the city and region for the duration of the war. One recent study puts the toll of known dead at 218, the great majority of them anarchists. Although they probably had the support of most Catalans, the anarchists faced a painful choice: to control Barcelona they would have had to withdraw their militia from the front and use it against the Republican paramilitary forces in the streets. This might have temporarily won the battle for the city, but could well have doomed the war effort against Franco. Despite being accused of betrayal by many of their more fervent followers, the anarchist leaders ordered an end to armed resistance.

Charles Orr soon realized how things stood. "We have seen and learned a lot during the last few days," he wrote his mother, "and expect to be driven underground at any time now." From this point on, he began signing most of his letters home with a false name. Militant to the end, Lois had nothing but contempt for what she regarded as an anarchist surrender. "The revolution was over," she wrote, "but the counter-revolution had not yet shown what it would do. We waited."

After months with few customers, Barcelona's hat shops suddenly found business booming. By June, the Orrs noted another sign that the old ways of life were returning. Still sharing the apartment of the former Nazi consul with other foreigners, they found their electricity and hot water turned off. "I'm writing you by candle light," Charles told his mother, "because the Electric Co. tried to make us pay for the German Consul's bill. We offered to pay our part since Feb. 15 even, but they wouldn't bargain. So—no more hot baths." With no press releases about revolutionary changes to write, Lois had quit her job with the Catalan government's propaganda office. Eileen Blair tried to raise her spirits by finding her extra food.

Anarchist power was broken, but, fueled by Stalin's venom against heretics, the prime target of the increasingly influential Communist Party remained the relatively small POUM. The Communists insisted that the Republican prime minister, the left-wing Socialist Francisco Largo Caballero, ban the POUM and arrest its leadership. When he refused, an alliance of Communists, mainstream liberals, and moderate Socialists forced him to resign, and Dr. Juan Negrín was installed in his place. He was a portly, multilingual physiologist famous for his gargantuan appetite—he sometimes ate two or three dinners a night, in different restaurants—who supported the push for a unified military and a centrally controlled war economy. "It would be wrong, however," says Hugh Thomas in his comprehensive history of the war, "to conclude that Negrín was a mere instrument of Russian policy."

Negrín and his cabinet faced a devil's bargain. Thanks to the American, British, and French refusal to sell weapons, the Soviet

Union remained the Republic's only significant source of arms, not to mention military advisors and training for specialists like tank crews and fighter pilots. In return, the Communists continued to demand key posts in the police and the army, and were now also insisting on a Moscow-style show trial of the POUM leadership. Negrín navigated these treacherous waters as best he could, giving Stalin some, although by no means all, of what he wanted. A few years later, of course, in another war, it would be the United States and Britain that faced exactly the same devil's bargain. They could not defeat Hitler without allying with the Soviet Union and granting some of Stalin's demands, such as for postwar domination of Eastern Europe.

At 8 a.m. on June 17, 1937, four men in uniform, one of them a Russian, and four plainclothesmen from the Republic's Soviet-controlled military intelligence service arrived at the Orrs' front door. They "showed us," Lois later wrote, "a floor plan of our apartment and a list of everyone who had lived or even visited there." They arrested the couple and seized all their letters, journals, and other possessions, even the red-and-yellow cloth—monarchist colors—with which they had decorated the bathroom door. These items would not be seen again.

More than half a century later, when some Soviet intelligence files were at last opened, it was clear that the Orrs had been under close surveillance, enough so that agents knew Lois was more militant than Charles. "Her fanatical approach to various political issues," reads a report, "was particularly striking during her work in Barcelona."

The Comintern undercover agents in the city were a multinational crew. The comment on Lois and notes about other foreign POUM supporters are in German. We know the name of one German Communist agent in Barcelona, Hubert von Ranke, because before the end of 1937 he would have a change of heart: he left Spain, left the Party, and declared that the people he had spied on and interrogated "were not 'agents of Franco' but honest revolutionaries." Also on the scene was a British Communist, David Crook, who pretended to be a POUM sympathizer and had gone picnicking at the beach with the Orrs less than two weeks before their arrest. In his memoirs Crook claimed that during the long Spanish siesta hour he would slip into the office used by Charles Orr and Eileen Blair and purloin documents, to be quickly photographed at a Soviet safe house. Some surveillance reports in the Soviet files are in French, which suggests that International Brigades commissar André Marty may also have had operatives in Barcelona.

The police station to which the Orrs were taken was so crowded that some prisoners were left sitting in stairwells. Charles recognized Spanish POUM leaders and anti-Stalinists of various stripes from the United States, Canada, Scotland, Holland, Germany, Switzerland, and Poland who had been part of their circle. He and 100 other prisoners were crowded into a cellblock with only 35 cots and fed two bowls of soup and two pieces of bread a day. Bedbugs crawled the walls.

One midnight shortly thereafter, Charles, Lois, and some 30 other foreigners were marched through narrow streets illuminated only by the flashlights of their guards to what had once been a local right-winger's home. The servants' quarters had been converted into cells. There, as the days passed, some prisoners began a hunger strike. Both men and women, housed separately, recognized undercover police in the cells with them, which put a damper on conversations.

These anti-Stalinists found themselves sharing their prison with International Brigades soldiers who had deserted or otherwise run afoul of the authorities. "Stalin's terror was at its height," Lois wrote. "Some loyal stalinist had drawn on the wall of our room a beautiful map of the Soviet Union, lovingly detailed with mineral deposits, industrial centers, mountain ranges and tundras. The men told us their quarters had a big picture of Stalin on the wall. These carefully executed wall drawings brought me much too close to the horror of the Moscow Trials, where you cravenly protest your love and faithfulness to those who falsely accuse and then murder you. Would I come to that?"

She found the Spanish guards friendly. "They were not sadists, but quite human, and easy on us because we were women. We were lucky the Russians had to use Spaniards to do their dirty work. . . . They let us talk to the men through the doors, handed notes and papers back and forth between our cells, and even went out to buy us soap, which was at a premium in Barcelona." Lois tried to keep her spirits up by taking language lessons from a German cellmate and learning dress design from one from Poland. "They called me 'the baby' because my life story was so short, and mothered me kindly. . . . We sang every day. French, German and even American songs from our room joined the far-off songs from the other cells." The prisoners she worried about most were the Germans and Italians, who, if released, would face prison or worse if they were sent home. When the acting American consul in Barcelona heard that the Orrs and another American had been arrested, he called the police but was told—falsely—that they refused to see him.

A Russian who spoke good English was present when Charles and then Lois were summoned for fingerprinting and interrogation. "You will never escape your fascist crimes," he told her. It did not help their morale to notice in a Communist newspaper—all they were allowed to read—that the POUM was accused of being part of a Nationalist spy ring.

As the Orrs and many other POUM supporters remained in their cells, this absurd charge was dutifully repeated by various foreign correspondents, who, in a hurry to meet deadlines as journalists always are, simply reported what officials told them. The United Press reporter was told the tale—as insider information, not to be attributed to anyone—by an intelligence attaché at the Soviet embassy in Valencia. Similar anonymously sourced stories appeared in the *Times* of London ("it is stated"), the *Manchester Guardian* ("details . . . were made public"), and the *New York Times* ("it is claimed"). None of the four journalists were even in Barcelona. The *New York Times* article was by Herbert Matthews and was headlined "Plot Uncovered in Spain. . . . Message to Franco Found on Back of a Map." It went on to speak of 200 army officers, Fascists, and POUM members accused of using secret radio transmitters to send coded information to Nationalist forces, as well as a message for the Generalissimo himself in invisible ink. In another article hailing, bizarrely, the government's "bloodless victory" in the bloody Barcelona fighting, Matthews reported that the POUM and the anarchist labor federation, the CNT, had been "at the bottom of the trouble. It was definitely treason." In a book he published the next year, he declared that the fighting by the POUM and the anarchists was "engineered partly with Fascist money."

Franco was delighted to be given credit for having instigated the fratricidal conflict in Barcelona. He began boasting, according to the German ambassador, that "the street fighting had been started by his agents." On this point, Communist and Nationalist propaganda coincided.

"Such unbelievable lies," Lois Orr fumed, "and about *me*. It was unreal."

George Orwell survived Barcelona's week of street fighting unscathed, but returned to the front deeply disheartened. He was further upset by the news that his young Scottish friend Bob Smillie had been arrested and thrown in prison. Yet he kept his eye on the bigger picture. "Whichever way you took it," Orwell wrote, "it was a depressing outlook. But it did not follow that the Government was not worth fighting for as against the more naked and developed Fascism of Franco and Hitler. Whatever faults the post-war Government might have, Franco's régime would certainly be worse."

His militia unit was manning the front line just outside the town of Huesca, some 500 feet from the enemy. The Nationalist troops were on higher ground, leaving one projecting bend in the POUM trench dangerously exposed to sniper fire. Supervising a change of sentries, one being his American comrade Harry Milton, Orwell found himself at this spot at five o'clock one morning. Six feet three inches tall to begin with—a distinct hazard in trench warfare—he also, according to Milton, had a reckless habit of looking over the top of the parapet.

The writer's powers of observation did not fail him even at this moment:

> The whole experience of being hit by a bullet is very interesting and I think it is worth describing in detail. . . . Roughly speaking it was the sensation of being *at the centre* of an explosion. There seemed to be . . . a blinding flash of light all round me, and I felt a tremendous shock—no pain, only a violent shock, such as you get from an electric terminal; with it a sense of utter weakness, a feeling of being stricken and shrivelled up to nothing. The sand-bags in front of me receded into immense distance. I fancy you would feel much the same if you were struck by lightning. . . .
>
> They laid me down . . . while somebody fetched a stretcher. As soon as I knew that the bullet had gone clean through my neck I took it for granted that I was done for. . . . There must have been about two minutes during which I assumed that I was killed. And that too was interesting—I mean it is interesting to know what your thoughts would be at such a time. My first thought, conventionally enough, was for my wife. My second was a violent resentment at having to leave this world which, when all is said and done, suits me so well. . . . The stupid mischance infuriated me. The meaninglessness of it! To be bumped off, not even in battle, but in this stale corner of the trenches, thanks to a moment's carelessness!

Milton cut Orwell's shirt open, and four men carried him a mile and a half on a stretcher. From there, an ambulance took him to a dressing station in a wooden hut. Soon, two friends from his unit showed up, to ask for his watch, pistol, and flashlight—all items in short supply. A few days later he found himself on a hospital train to Tarragona, south of Barcelona on the Mediterranean coast. As the train pulled into the station, another was pulling out, filled with Italian volunteers of the International Brigades, heading for the front.

> It was . . . packed to the bursting-point with men, with field-guns lashed on the open trucks and more men clustering round the guns. I remember with particular vividness the spectacle of that train passing in the yellow evening light; window after window full of dark, smiling faces, the long tilted barrels of the guns, the scarlet scarves fluttering—all this gliding slowly past us against a turquoise-coloured sea.
>
> . . . The men who were well enough to stand had moved across the carriage to cheer the Italians as they went past. A crutch waved out of the window; bandaged forearms made the Red Salute. It was like an allegorical picture of war; the trainload of fresh men gliding proudly up the line, the maimed men sliding slowly down, and all the while the guns on the open trucks making one's heart leap as guns always do, and reviving that pernicious feeling, so difficult to get rid of, that war *is* glorious after all.

The bullet had missed Orwell's carotid artery by just a few millimeters. Recovering slowly, he was able to speak only in a hoarse whisper that his commanding officer likened to the grinding of brakes on a Model T Ford. He was shunted to various towns, first for treatment, then to obtain the necessary paperwork for a medical discharge. In one hospital, "in the next bed to me there was an Assault Guard wounded over the left eye. He was friendly and gave me cigarettes. I said: 'In Barcelona we should have been shooting one another,' and we laughed over this. It was queer how the general spirit seemed to change when you got anywhere near the front line. All or nearly all of the vicious hatreds of the political parties evaporated."

Away from the front, however, the campaign of wild accusations against the POUM continued. Its sympathizers were being accused by the Communist press around the world of flying the monarchist flag from Barcelona balconies and being in secret contact with Berlin. POUM militia units were said to while away their time playing soccer with Franco's troops in no-man's-land (something repeated in print by both Hemingway and Matthews), "at a time," Orwell wrote, "when, as a matter of fact, the . . . troops were suffering heavy casualties and a number of my personal friends were killed and wounded."

Orwell himself would shortly be accused in the London *Daily Worker* of leaving the POUM trenches to make furtive visits to a hut suspiciously near the Nationalist front lines. He had already been well aware of how propaganda permeated the world he lived in, but the blatant lies he now heard about the war in which he had nearly died had a profound impact on him. They would be reflected more than a decade later in the portrait of the Ministry of Truth in his novel *1984*.

With his neck wound slowly healing, he returned to Barcelona to meet Eileen and prepare to leave Spain. "When I got to the hotel my wife was sitting in the lounge. She got up and came towards me in what struck me as a very unconcerned manner; then she put an arm round my neck and, with a sweet smile for the benefit of the other people in the lounge, hissed in my ear:

"'*Get out!*'

"'What?'

"'Get out of here *at once!*'

"'What?'

"'Don't keep standing here! You must get outside quickly!'

"'What? Why? What do you mean?'

"She had me by the arm and was already leading me."

On the sidewalk outside, Eileen quickly told him: the POUM had been banned; the Orrs and other foreign sympathizers had been arrested, along with POUM leader Andreu Nin and other senior party officials. Bob Smillie, arrested earlier, was still behind bars. Just two days before, six plainclothes police had barged into her room at the hotel, spent nearly two hours searching it, and had taken away all the couple's letters and papers—among them the diary Orwell had meticulously kept during his first four months at the front.

(These documents are believed to still be in a closed archive in Moscow. One file that became accessible after the collapse of the Soviet Union, however, does contain a two-page inventory of all the material confiscated from Eileen's room that day, including "correspondence of G. ORWELL (alias Eric BLAIR) concerning his book, 'The Road to Wigan Pier,'" "letters from families," "checkbook for the months of October and Nov 1936," a list of people the couple exchanged letters with, and "various papers with drawings and doodles.")

Orwell did not dare go back to the hotel, for Eileen believed she had been left at liberty only as bait to catch him. He slept that night in the ruins of a church. The next morning, he was dismayed to learn that Smillie had died in prison, a few days short of his twenty-first birthday, apparently of untreated appendicitis. Rumors—which later turned out to be true—were spreading that Andreu Nin was also dead. Orwell and two British comrades spent several days lying low, sleeping one night in a vacant lot. Several times they crossed paths with other foreign POUM sympathizers also on the run, among them the youthful Willy Brandt.

A few days later, the couple were reunited and were able to slip across the frontier to France. Although Orwell had left Spain fearing arrest by the very government he had been fighting for, his mind remained on the larger war he felt certain would come. He would end the memoir he finished early the following year with this prescient scene from the train window on his return home: "outer London, the barges on the miry river, the familiar streets, the posters telling of cricket matches and Royal weddings, the men in bowler hats, the pigeons in Trafalgar Square, the red buses, the blue policemen—all sleeping the deep, deep sleep of England, from which I sometimes fear that we shall never wake till we are jerked out of it by the roar of bombs."

PART III

12

"I Don't Think I Would Write about That If I Were You"

THE WOUNDED ORWELL would not return to Spain. But someone else was determined to do so: Virginia Cowles still wanted to see what the war looked like from the Nationalist side. This would be a difficult feat for a reporter known to have covered the fighting from the Republic. "I was told I didn't stand a chance of getting a visa. . . . Nevertheless, I decided to try." She made her base of operations the elegant French resort of Saint-Jean-de-Luz. On the Atlantic coast just a few miles from Spain, the town was a nest of intrigue, with Republican and Francoist Spaniards eyeing each other uneasily from nearby café tables. Most of the foreign embassies to the Spanish Republic had moved here to be safe from Franco's shells and bombs. But since the adjoining part of Spain had now been conquered by the Nationalists, German officers from the Condor Legion frequently drove across the border for a French dinner.

Cowles put to work the social connections of her debutante's world. In New York she had known the daughter of the current British ambassador to Spain. Like so many Britons of his class, he was an unabashed Franco enthusiast who contemptuously referred to Republicans as "Reds." Through him, Cowles wrote, "I met Franco's agent, the Conde de Mamblas. On looking back I suppose I took an unfair advantage of the Count, for he was an aristocrat of the old school whose view on the war was confined to the simple philosophy that General Franco had the support of 'ladies and gentlemen.' Having met me under the auspices he did, I suppose he bracketed me as 'safe.'" The Count went to work to get her a visa. While waiting, she found it unnerving to look across the border and see the Nationalist frontier guards in their three-cornered, black patent-leather hats. "These were the people whose machine-gun-fire we had ducked, whose shells we had cursed, and whose planes we had run from."

Finally her visa came through. Although Nationalist territory was largely free of the Republic's food shortages, it was a far harder place for a correspondent to work. On the Republican side, there was considerable press freedom for a country at war and remarkably few restrictions on where journalists could go; no foreign reporter was ever expelled during the conflict. In the other Spain, however, for a foreign correspondent to travel anywhere required permission and a chaperone. The hallways of Nationalist press offices were crowded day and night with journalists impatiently waiting for travel passes, and the authorities were particularly suspicious of reporters from abroad. During the course of the war, they arrested a dozen foreign correspondents, holding two from France for several months. More than 30 foreign journalists were expelled because of official objections to their stories. When Guy de Traversay of the center-right French newspaper *L'Intransigeant* was captured by Franco's forces along with some Republican troops he had been accompanying, he was shot with them, and his body doused in gasoline and burned.

Forbidden in reporting from Nationalist Spain was any mention of German or Italian soldiers, of executions of POWs or Republican sympathizers, and of Franco's troops being anything other than well-behaved, disciplined soldiers. Even if a foreign correspondent had a car, travel to the front was allowed only with Nationalist press office vehicles at the front and rear of a caravan. Journalists with Jewish names often found themselves subject to extra scrutiny. Cowles was assigned a minder, a wealthy English-speaker named Ignacio Rosalles. He was a true believer in Franco's cause, and this proved an advantage: Rosalles offered to take Cowles to Guernica, because he was confident that, just as Franco claimed, it was the retreating Republicans who had burned the city to the ground. "Now you can see for yourself," he told her.

"We arrived in Guernica," she wrote, "to find it a lonely chaos of timber and brick, like an ancient civilization in the process of being excavated. There were only three or four people in the streets. One old man was standing inside an apartment house that had four sides to it but an interior that was only a sea of bricks. . . . I went up to him and asked if he had been in the town during the destruction. He nodded his head and when I asked what had happened, waved his arms in the air and declared that the sky had been black with planes—'*Aviones*,' he said: '*Italianos y Alemanes.*' Rosalles was astonished.

"'Guernica was burned,' he contradicted heatedly. The old man, however, stuck to his point, insisting that after a four-hour bombardment there was little left to burn. Rosalles moved me away. 'He's a Red,' he explained indignantly." But two other people they talked to in Guernica confirmed the old man's account.

A short time later, they dropped in on a military headquarters whose staff officers Rosalles considered safe for Cowles to interview. "They were tall, good-looking Spaniards who spoke enthusiastically . . . and predicted the end of the war by the spring. One of them said he had heard that America was anti-Franco and prophesied that unless the United States mended its ways the sickle and hammer would soon be flying over the White House. 'There's only one way to treat a Red,' he said, 'shoot him.'

"Rosalles described our drive along the coast and told them of the incident at Guernica. 'The town was full of Reds,' he said. 'They tried to tell us it was bombed, not burnt.' The tall staff officer replied: 'But, of course, it was bombed. We bombed it and bombed it and bombed it, and *bueno*, why not?'

"Rosalles looked astonished and when we were back in the car again heading for Bilbao, he said: 'I don't think I would write about that if I were you.'"

Shortly after this, Cowles and Rosalles found themselves blocked on a narrow dirt road along the side of a steep ravine. A heavy truck had bogged down, and despite being pushed by a road gang of prisoners, it couldn't be budged. At that moment, Cowles wrote, "a long black car, preceded by a motor-cycle escort, swung up beside us, and the Italian Ambassador stepped out. . . . Dressed in a magnificent black uniform with rows of medals across his chest, his appearance caused the Spaniards considerable excitement. The orders grew louder and more violent, but the wheels still whirled helplessly in the mud.

"It was considered such discourtesy, however, to keep an Italian Ambassador waiting, that the officer in charge finally solved the problem by ordering the road gang to push the truck over the cliff. With the engine still running, the men heaved, and with a deafening roar the truck fell three hundred feet to the ravine below; the Ambassador gave the Fascist salute and climbed back into his car. . . .

"Rosalles said once again: 'I think it is better not to write about that.'"

Cowles missed little in Nationalist Spain, although it was not safe for her to publish much until she had left. At one point she stood on a hill outside Madrid looking across the battlefront and down into the streets she had walked when on the other side. She could even see the tall white Telefónica building where she had filed her dispatches.

In one newly captured town she saw Franco's Moorish troops looting villagers' homes: "They were coming out of the houses, their arms filled with an odd assortment of knick-knacks; one soldier had a kitchen stool over his shoulder and an egg-beater in his pocket; another a child's doll and an old pair of shoes. Several Moors were sitting on the curb, bending around a packet of playing cards, admiring the brightly coloured queens and knaves." (Those ultimately responsible for such looting were Nationalist officers, who saw to it that booty was sent back to the soldiers' home villages in Morocco, where it proved a powerful aid to recruiting.)

What surprised Cowles most was that no one made any attempt to hide where Franco's real firepower was coming from. "German and

Italian flags flew from one end of insurgent Spain to the other." She found posters of Hitler and Mussolini everywhere, and swastika banners on hotels, bars, and restaurants. She saw walls scrawled with *Viva il Duce* and shops with signs in the windows: *Man spricht Deutsch.* In Salamanca, the Italian envoy for whom the truck had been sacrificed was greeted by a crowd holding torches and "a startling demonstration of Moorish cavalry who came thundering through the Square, their white robes flying in the moonlight."

In Santander, on Spain's northern coast, Cowles watched Italian troops, tanks, trucks, and armored cars hold a victory parade while thousands of refugees, all their worldly goods in pitiful bundles, were "gazing on the celebration with tears running down their cheeks." Meanwhile, "in the working-class quarters doors were closed and window shades pulled down." Outside a jail a long line of women and children waited for news of prisoners. "The entrance of the conquering army, with their guns and motor-cycles gaily decorated with flowers and wreaths, struck an almost sinister note."

When Rosalles stepped away from the parade route for a moment to talk to a friend, she turned to a Spaniard next to her who had been conspicuous in his loud cheers and asked him how he liked the Italians. "'Oh, we like them,' he replied. Then he winked and said, '*De otra manera* . . .' ('If we don't . . .'), and here he drew his finger suggestively across his throat."

"The spirit of revenge . . . was far more virulent than that in Madrid," Cowles wrote. "With a system that encouraged people to denounce their neighbours," there were massive waves of arrests. Prisons "were overflowing, and the executions reached staggering figures. As soon as the Nationalists occupied a town they set up military courts and the trials began." In Santander, she watched the prosecution of three captured Republican army officers and a city official. "The trial took about fifteen minutes." All four were sentenced to death, and a young Nationalist captain on the panel of judges cheerfully told Cowles that this had been the fate of 14 of the 16 men tried that morning. Although it would take many years before the figures could be accurately totaled, we know that in Santander alone, in the weeks after its capture 1,267 people were sentenced to die in trials like the ones Cowles saw, 739 more were shot without trial, and at least 389 more died of mistreatment in prison.

When the court adjourned, "the Captain and I walked down the court-room steps into the open. Standing in front of the building was an open lorry filled with men. As we got closer I saw they were the prisoners who had just been tried. The sky was blue and the sun was streaming down, which made the death sentence seem all the more unreal. Some of them sat with bowed heads, but as we came closer they recognized the young captain as one of the judges, and for one brief second I supposed they had a glimmer of hope that he might save them. They stared at him like bewildered animals, then scrambled to their feet and saluted. It was a pathetic and terrible sight, but the young Captain saluted back casually, took a deep breath of fresh air, and said, gaily: 'Let's go down to the café and have a drink.'"

Beneath Cowles's veneer of being a mere upper-class ingénue in jewelry and high heels, she was a shrewd reporter who gleaned far more information than her Nationalist hosts were aware of. Among this was reasonably accurate data on how many German and Italian military personnel were fighting for Franco. When she published these numbers in a long London *Sunday Times* article soon after leaving Spain, it attracted great attention and was mentioned at length in the House of Commons by former prime minister David Lloyd George, a supporter of the Spanish Republic. He assumed that the story, which bore no byline, had been by a man, referring in his speech to the writer as "he." Soon afterward, a mutual friend offered to bring the author of the article to lunch at Lloyd George's country house. "When I stepped out of the car," Cowles wrote, "the old man regarded me with surprise that almost bordered on resentment. I suppose it was a nasty shock to find that the eminent authority he had quoted was just a green young woman. . . . By the time we left, he seemed to have forgiven me for not being a general, and presented me with a jar of honey and a dozen apples from the farm."

• • •

The army staff car that carried Cowles and her escort around Nationalist Spain was likely powered by gasoline refined from Texaco petroleum—as were the aircraft that had bombed Guernica. President Roosevelt summoned Torkild Rieber to Washington to reprimand him for supplying oil to Franco on credit, a meeting that provoked some anxious cable traffic among Texaco and Nationalist officials, but Rieber quietly let the credit arrangement continue. Despite the considerable discretionary powers the president had under the arms embargo legislation, he did little more. A grateful Franco sent a personal letter to Rieber thanking him for his continued help.

Even though they knew little or nothing about where the Generalissimo's oil was coming from, the Republic's supporters everywhere were angry that Hitler and Mussolini could send hundreds of airplanes and tens of thousands of soldiers to aid Franco while the Western democracies did nothing. This seemed especially frustrating when it came to the United States, for Eleanor Roosevelt had lent her name to an event raising funds for milk for Spanish children and in her newspaper columns continued to speak of their suffering. Surely neither she nor her husband wanted fascism to triumph in Europe. The question remained: how best to bring pressure on them?

More than any other presidential couple, the Roosevelts played host to a wide variety of long-term houseguests, and, as it happened, two years earlier someone now in Spain had been one of them. Martha Gellhorn's mother was an old friend of Eleanor's, and the first lady invited Martha to stay in the White House while she was working on a book about poverty. The first evening she had dinner there, she found herself seated next to the president. From the other end of the table, Eleanor called, "Franklin, talk to that child at your left. She says that all the people in the South have pellagra or syphilis."

Eleanor Roosevelt promptly conscripted Gellhorn to help her with her voluminous correspondence, since hundreds of Americans wrote her every day, with complaints, suggestions, or pleas for help. Disciplined and ambitious about her own writing, Gellhorn found she couldn't get much of it done at the White House. After a few weeks she moved out, but her friendship with the first lady endured and the two women exchanged dozens of letters over the coming years. They were still corresponding when Gellhorn and Hemingway returned to New York in May 1937 to work with Joris Ivens editing the film footage they had shot in Spain. Later that month, Gellhorn met Mrs. Roosevelt and some guests at the low-cost-housing community of Greenbelt, Maryland, a New Deal project. "We all listened to Martha Gellhorn," said Eleanor in her column, "while she told us of her experiences in Spain." To Gellhorn, she wrote, "You are right to be trying to make people realize that what is happening in Spain might happen anywhere."

Beyond the excitement of her romance with Hemingway, Gellhorn had been profoundly affected by wartime Madrid. "It is surprising," she wrote to him, "that only six weeks should so uproot one's life . . . and now life is just a painful wait between morning and evening newspapers, and a terror of what is happening to all of them there."

She threw herself into work on *The Spanish Earth*. The documentary was shaping up as a mixture of footage from Fuentidueña deTajo, the farming village near Madrid that Virginia Cowles had visited with the camera crew, shots of Spanish and International Brigades luminaries, battle scenes, and air raids. Tying the movie's disparate parts together was a fictionalized young man from Fuentidueña who returns from the front to train other villagers to fight.

"Two nights ago," Gellhorn wrote to Eleanor Roosevelt, "we worked with three sound engineers in the lab at the Columbia Broadcasting, and we made the sound of incoming shells with a football bladder and an air hose and fingernails snapping against a screen, all tremendously magnified and it sounds so like a shell that we were scared out of our wits." The film was to be aimed at as wide as possible a public, but there was also an audience of two that would be crucial. Gellhorn suggested to the first lady a private showing at the White House, and Mrs. Roosevelt promptly named a date.

• • •

An increasingly restless and frustrated Pat Gurney was still at the front, on Madrid's southeastern defenses. "We weren't helping anyone by sitting around on the Jarama hills being gradually whittled away by snipers and dysentery. I didn't like fighting, though I was prepared to have another go at it if anybody wanted me to. But powerless inaction was futile. As it happened, the whole problem was solved for me quite simply on a fine summer's morning."

The Lincoln Battalion received orders to rechart the locations of all the Nationalist machine-gun posts in the opposing trenches. Gurney, whose sketching skills had made him the unit's mapmaker, picked up his compass and notebook and went to work. "I was in no hurry and stopped off to gossip with friends in various dugouts as I worked my way along the trench. There was no firing from either side, the vines and the flowers were flowering very prettily in no-man's-land; I was possessed of a particularly happy and carefree attitude towards life in general. I set up the compass at intervals in the small firing-holes in the parapet."

He had nearly finished the job when he came to one firing port where the dirt embankment on the back side of the trench was unusually low, which meant that an alert Nationalist sniper could see a patch of sky through the port, and, if the sky was blocked, would know that someone was standing there. However, the enemy trench was more than 200 yards away, and the firing port only about five inches square, so Gurney wasn't worried as he took his compass bearing.

The bullet that hit him knocked "a hole large enough to take a hen's egg" through his hand, which had been shading the compass, and sent metal splinters into his face and eyes. When he regained consciousness he was in the dugout dressing station of Dr. William Pike, who had worked with him some months before. The physician patched him up as best he could and dispatched him by ambulance to the rear. As he was taken into an operating room, Gurney heard voices talking a foreign language. "I did not wake up until the following morning. . . . My right hand appeared to be done up in a mass of dressings about the size of a boxing glove and felt like one great ball of pain. My face was also covered in dressings so that I could not see." Gurney gradually realized that he was in a small military clinic with a Czech doctor and four untrained Spanish nurses who had no concept of keeping wounds sterile.

"I was determined to get myself shifted to the American Hospital as quickly as I could manage it." Three days later, as some of his sight returned, he was in the clinic's courtyard when he saw an American ambulance driver he knew. The driver said "'Jump in,' and he whirled me away before anyone noticed."

As an awed Gurney described it, the former royal residence of Villa Paz was "a large red-brick structure whose only entrance was a huge, arched tunnel driven through the centre of the south wall into a cobbled courtyard about an acre in extent." The hospital that now occupied the buildings felt like paradise to him, located in "one of the most beautiful areas in the whole of Spain, vast farmlands and wooded country with streams running through it." There was a curving staircase, a library, and portraits of grandees on the walls.

Gurney was given a sedative and put to bed. When he woke in the middle of the night, it was through his sculptor's eyes that he saw the scene:

> Near the foot of the bed sat a nurse reading with a dim light at a small table. She was a fairly tall and very slim girl, sitting in a peculiar position with one upper arm wound around the other supporting her head, and one leg wound around the other to balance herself upon the small chair on which she sat. Her elbows rested on the small table. . . . The whole head had a strangely classical and antique quality. A good forehead with strong, black eyebrows and large, dark eyes. A determined nose that could easily have come from a Florentine portrait, high cheek-bones and a firm chin. A largish mouth with a faintly Dionysiac twist at the corners, almost black hair, parted in the centre and drawn back with only the faint sign of a wave, to a small knot low on a long

and slender neck. It was a most memorable and striking head, set off by the strangeness of the pose and the character of the light.

The nurse, twenty-six-year-old Toby Jensky, had been born to immigrants from Russia and grew up speaking Yiddish at home, which was, paradoxically, a former parsonage in rural Massachusetts. She had worked at Beth Israel Hospital in New York City and arrived in Spain only a few weeks before Gurney appeared in her ward. "She told me all about this," he wrote, "in her strangely deep contralto voice, which contrasted strongly with the delicacy of her appearance. Finally she put me down to sleep, switched off the light . . . and I slept in utter peace and contentment, for the first time in a long while."

Gurney had another operation to undergo, which frightened him, because it involved removing fragments of metal around his eyes. He woke up unable to see or to use either hand, but "I felt perfectly calm and knew that Toby was somewhere close at hand. She must have seen me move and put her hand on my shoulder. 'Don't worry. They've done a swell job on you and everything's going to be just fine.'

"'How can they know that?'

"'It seems that there was no damage to the optic nerve and none of the small pieces of metal did any real harm. They've taken some of them out and the rest are harmless.'"

After a few days the bandages came off his eyes for good, and he could again see Jensky as well as talk with her.

This, at least, is Pat Gurney's version of how he and Toby Jensky met, published nearly 40 years later. But Fredericka Martin, the chief nurse and Jensky's supervisor, maintained that it all happened quite differently. "How he embroidered his story," Martin wrote after reading Gurney's memoir. "He and Toby met in the Court yard where, her insect bitten legs spread out ahead of her to let the sun help heal, she sat for tedious hours peeling vegetables, during a kitchen crisis." (The Spanish cooks had not shown up that day.) "So Pat fell in love with a girl with a pixie face and legs with superating [*sic*] sores exposed to the sun, a scene he later turned into a poignant bedside meeting. . . . So all he says about waking up to see her eyes is fancy." Which version is true? We will never know.

His hand mangled, Gurney realized that he could neither fight nor sculpt again. And however idyllic the hospital, the news arriving there was increasingly alarming. The Basque country had now been largely overrun by Franco's forces, and it was only a matter of time before they and their Nazi and Italian allies turned their full strength on the remainder of Republican Spain. And the past few months had revealed new refinements in weaponry: Hitler's Condor Legion had developed a technique for dropping incendiary bombs along with a plane's auxiliary fuel tank, creating something of a precursor to napalm that pilots called the "flambo."

Gurney was convinced the war was lost. "I was desperately sorry. . . . It was a ghastly situation, meeting and talking to all the sweet and friendly Spanish people working around the hospital, while knowing the fate which would be their lot at Franco's hands, in payment for all the kindness and generosity which they were showing to us. Even after thirty years the horror of that situation hangs around me like the odour of sour and decomposing milk. I hadn't achieved very much on their behalf and if I could achieve nothing more, it was time to leave." But he could not bring himself to leave, because he was in love.

The devil's bargain between the Spanish Republic and the Soviet Union had ensured that the Russians would gain control over the government's internal security apparatus. Added to that was the fear sparked by Nationalist boasts about a fifth column of secret agents, and the result was a raft of arrests. The Communists quickly took over the Republic's military counterespionage agency, the Servicio de Investigación Militar, or SIM. Like such forces the world over, SIM attracted its share of sadists, and conditions in its prisons were notoriously harsh. It did break up several important Nationalist spy rings, but no one knows how many of the people it imprisoned and tortured were Franco fifth columnists and how many anti-Stalinist leftists.

The case of one prisoner would echo through the American literary world. José Robles, an idealistic young Spaniard who rejected his country's military dictatorship of the 1920s, had found sanctuary in the United States. As a professor of Spanish at Johns Hopkins University, he had learned Russian in order to read that country's great nineteenth-century novels in the original. He was on a visit to Spain when the civil war broke out and promptly volunteered for the Republican military. The army was glad to have him, for it was critically short of officers, especially any who knew English, French, or Russian. Commissioned a lieutenant colonel, Robles was given a hush-hush post, apparently as liaison officer to General Vladimir Gorev, the Soviet military attaché and military intelligence chief in Spain.

For two decades Robles had known John Dos Passos, one of whose novels he had translated into Spanish. The novelist was sure that Robles would be glad to help him and his old friend Ernest Hemingway in their work on *The Spanish Earth.* But when Dos Passos arrived in Spain in April 1937 and tried to get in touch, people gave him evasive answers. Only when he found Robles's wife did he discover that Robles had been arrested.

Whether Robles was actually guilty of anything is unknown. The only thing certain is that he was in a position to know a great deal about the growing Soviet influence over the Republic. Not a Communist but a lifelong academic, he had no professional expertise in keeping secrets, and rumors circulated that he talked about what he knew more freely than was wise. It is also possible that putting Robles under arrest was a maneuver by the Soviet secret police, the NKVD, against its rival, the military intelligence service represented by General Gorev.

Dos Passos, a man of the left whose masterwork, the *U.S.A.* trilogy, had just put him on the cover of *Time*, was horrified that his friend had been jailed and that no one could tell him why. Robles's wife begged him to help save her husband. Then he had a further shock: Robles, he was told, had been executed.

Hemingway made the wound worse by making clear he thought Dos Passos should stop asking questions. As Josephine Herbst summed up his attitude, "It was going to throw suspicion on all of us and get us into trouble." With his well-known penchant for sudden acts of cruelty toward other writers, Hemingway already felt competitive with Dos Passos. "He wanted to be *the* war writer of his age," wrote Herbst, and he cannot have been pleased that in France Jean-Paul Sartre had just called Dos Passos "the greatest writer of our time." Furthermore, Dos Passos and his wife were close to Hemingway's wife Pauline, and Hemingway was in the midst of an increasingly public affair with Martha Gellhorn.

Although Dos Passos followed through on his work on *The Spanish Earth*, he did keep asking questions. When he left Spain, he was in despair over Robles, at the start of a political journey from left to right, and permanently estranged from Hemingway. As one critic has observed, "Hemingway seems to have needed to destroy a friendship or a marriage every few years just to keep functioning. In Madrid he did both." But however mean-spirited Hemingway could be, on his part more than just personal rivalry was involved. Whatever Republican Spain's flaws or injustices—and he would later show he was abundantly aware of them—he cared above all else that it win the war. He was wary of anything that could be a public distraction, even an unsolved death.

Among SIM's other victims in the spring of 1937 was POUM leader Andreu Nin, the former justice minister of Catalonia and translator into Catalan of Dostoyevsky's *Crime and Punishment.* Nin was a particular object of Soviet wrath because before turning anti-Stalinist he had lived in the Soviet Union for nearly a decade and for a time had been close to Stalin's archenemy, Trotsky. The POUM's newspaper had been virtually alone in Republican Spain in attacking the Purge trials. Stalin's chief secret police agent in the country, Alexander Orlov, himself appears to have overseen Nin's torture and execution.

Despite such deaths, the vast Soviet-scale bloodbath against all non-Stalinist leftists, feared by Orwell and others, did not happen. It is impossible to know what the exact death toll was, but one scholar sympathetic to the POUM estimates that some 30 POUM members,

Trotskyists, and anarchists were deliberately killed by the Communists in SIM prisons or elsewhere, in addition to those who died in events like the Barcelona street fighting.

Orwell ended up feeling that the Negrín government "has shown more political tolerance than anyone expected." To the dismay of both anarchists and Communists, it even began investigations into a few of the killing sprees that had taken place in Republican territory during the early months of the war. Despite their control of the SIM prisons, the Communists did not have similar power over Republican Spain's courts. Imperfect and subject to political pressure though these were, they were more evenhanded than those of many a nation in the grip of war. When, after many delays, the POUM executive committee would finally be put on trial, it was not the Soviet-style show trial Stalin had demanded; although some defendants were sentenced to prison, others were found innocent of all charges. The Comintern representative on the scene reported to Moscow in dismay that the outcome was "scandalous," since "no serious punishment"—that is, death sentences—had been decreed.

Many foreign sympathizers of the POUM and the anarchists were soon released from jail. This is what happened to Lois and Charles Orr, who, after nine days in custody, found themselves abruptly let out onto a Barcelona street at four o'clock one morning. A few days later, they were on board a ship for Marseille. Their ten months in Spain were over, as was the experiment in social transformation they had come to join. When they went belowdecks to eat their first meal in the ship's dining room, Lois felt she was "at a wake."

After mid-1937, anarchist and other dissenting newspapers were intermittently censored and the remaining vestiges of worker control largely suppressed. In Aragon troops under a Communist commander even forced peasants collectively working some estates to return land, tools, and livestock to their former owners. Prime Minister Negrín, eager to gain support abroad and, as he put it, "to persuade the democratic powers of the non-revolutionary nature of [the] Republican struggle," announced plans to privatize industries that had been nationalized. Although the war continued full steam, the Spanish Revolution had now been brought to an end. How should we look back on it?

It is easy to see why the period of revolutionary fervor had such enormous appeal. For a century or more, idealists had dreamed of a world where wealth would be shared, where workers would own factories and peasants land, and where democracy, in yet-to-be-defined ways, would be far more direct. For some months much of this had actually happened, above all in Barcelona, the country's second-largest city, surrounding Catalonia, and nearby Aragon. Imagine a sweeping revolution in the United States centered on Chicago, including all of Illinois and Indiana. The huge changes were deeply tarnished by thousands of killings. But it is still hard to find an example, before or since, where so many ideas normally considered utopian were put into practice on a scale affecting millions of people.

If the Spanish Revolution had continued unhindered, could it have helped win the war? Lois Orr was certain of this: "If only the people would act now to take things back into their own hands, maybe we could end these stupid, senseless defeats." Orwell felt the same way when he published *Homage to Catalonia* the year after he left Spain. The POUM and anarchist slogan, "'The war and the revolution are inseparable,' was less visionary than it sounds," he wrote. If the government "had appealed to the workers of the world in the name not of 'democratic Spain,' but of 'revolutionary Spain,' it is hard to believe that they would not have got a response"—in the form of strikes and boycotts by "tens of millions" in other countries. Furthermore, he argued, had the Republic promised independence to Spanish Morocco, it would have set off uprisings in Franco's rear.

Though today we consider Orwell the patron saint of independent thinking, at this point in his life, like so many leftists of all hues, he romanticized the working class as the world's key revolutionary force. This was—uncharacteristically for him—wildly wishful thinking. Nor, as he thought, was Spanish Morocco a tinderbox awaiting a match to ignite an anticolonial revolt. It was instead a mosaic of highly traditional societies where independence advocates were weak and divided. The Nationalist army had no trouble continuing to recruit Moroccan soldiers; by 1937, one out of seven males from the territory was in Franco's forces.

Surely it would have been vastly better if the Republic's political factions had resolved their differences without hundreds of people being killed and wounded in street fighting, and without Soviet-controlled security forces murdering dissenters in jail. However, to fight a complex, mechanized war, a disciplined army responsible to a central command is far more effective than a range of militias reporting to a crazy quilt of political parties and trade unions. The fact that Spanish Communists were eager to use centralization to gain more power for themselves does not make this any less true. Nor was it unreasonable to hope that if France and the United States, at least, perceived Spain as not revolutionary, they might rethink their unwillingness to sell it arms. The leaders of both nations, in fact, would give tantalizing hints of relenting, and the French once or twice in a small way would actually do so.

The dream of the Spanish anarchists had further problems. It is hard to picture how an abhorrence for any kind of government and for the use of money could long be combined with life in an industrialized society. You can easily imagine bartering eggs for cloth, but what if the goods involved are aircraft parts and x-ray machines? The world the anarchists imagined would have been hard enough to sustain in peacetime, much less in the midst of a backs-to-the-wall war for survival. Nonetheless, doomed though the Spanish Revolution may have been, for a matter of months a stunningly different kind of society grew and flourished in a way it never has since, in Spain or anywhere else. And in a world today where economic inequality is increasing, the short-lived array of cooperatives, land worked in common, and worker-controlled factories and businesses of the Spain of 1936–37 offers a fascinating, tempting example of a path not taken.

Someone in another part of the world trying to learn about this while it was happening, however, would have had a tough time. Although the Spanish Revolution took place amid one of the largest concentrations of foreign correspondents on earth, they virtually never wrote about it.

Reporters easily fall into the comforts of herd behavior. Rare is the journalist, just arrived in a foreign country, who does not immediately gravitate toward others carrying notebooks or cameras and take cues from them. What's happening today? Is there a press conference at the ministry? Have you heard . . . ? And rare is the correspondent already on the scene, proud to have learned how to navigate local waters, who does not offer a newcomer friendly advice.

When reporters are repeatedly under fire—and in Spain several were killed—this sense of comradeship is all the stronger. The foreign press corps in Madrid ate lunch and dinner together at a long table reserved for them in the nightclub-like basement restaurant of the Hotel Gran Vía, where, wrote Josephine Herbst, they "talked learnedly . . . about the number of shells that had come in, the number of people killed." Nearly all of them stayed at the nearby Hotel Florida. Their memoirs are filled with accounts of shared hardships, including the execrable food at the Gran Vía. ("Millet and water soup," as Hemingway described it, "yellow rice with horse meat in it.") Cheers from around the press table would greet a colleague newly arrived from abroad who brought a suitcase of canned food for journalist colleagues; groans met one who did not.

The news a correspondent reports under such circumstances is greatly influenced by what others are reporting. Every journalist on assignment has had the experience of receiving anxious messages from the home office saying that a rival newspaper or network has reported this or that, and why haven't we heard anything about it from you? These days such queries come by email or text message; back then they came by telegram. And wherever journalists keep a close eye on what their colleagues are reporting, an Authorized Version of events tends to develop. It takes an unusually independent, contrarian spirit to see things differently.

"You could learn as much at the Hotel Florida in those years," Hemingway bragged, "as you could learn anywhere in the world."

But could you? The correspondents who passed through the Florida flocked to cover the major battles, above all those for Madrid. A story about a firefight between buildings on the university campus, its classroom blackboards still filled with professors' notes, or about crouching in trenches under shellfire, was much more likely to make the front page than one about a factory taken over by its workers in Barcelona or an estate occupied by peasants in Aragon—especially if someone from a competing newspaper was sending off stories about crouching in those same trenches.

At the heart of the Authorized Version of the Spanish Civil War was an easy-to-understand, heroes-vs.-villains narrative: Spain had a democratically elected government fighting a right-wing military coup backed by Hitler and Mussolini, and a great European city was under siege. This, of course, was also the story that the Republic's government and its supporters urgently wanted told, and the more famous the teller, the better. Of W. H. Auden, for example, the Communist journalist Claud Cockburn said, "What we really wanted him for was to go to the front, write some pieces saying hurrah for the Republic, and then go away and write some poems, also saying hurrah for the Republic."

If you search the American and British press during these years, for every thousand articles about ground gained and lost on the battlefield or bombs falling on Madrid, you are lucky if you can find one that so much as mentions the way Spaniards briefly wrote a new chapter in Europe's centuries-old battle between classes. And seldom did any of the gifted photographers who won fame covering this war with their compact new 35 mm cameras turn their lenses on this story. Most correspondents had little interest in the revolution's epicenter, Catalonia. "The Catalans . . . are sort of fake Spaniards," Martha Gellhorn wrote dismissively to Eleanor Roosevelt.

The fact that a utopian social revolution might have been an impractical and romantic dream even in peacetime, and was surely an impossible one when fighting a terrible war, made it no less worth reporting. Of the many hundreds of correspondents from abroad who passed through Spain during the war, not one showed much interest in the revolution that for months surrounded them—neither the famous, like Hemingway and Gellhorn, nor the obscure, like Milly Bennett, nor the bitter *New York Times* rivals Matthews and Carney, nor those who showed unusual boldness in going after other news, like Virginia Cowles. She noted, at least, that the Hotel Florida itself "was in the hands of elevator boys, doormen and clerks, while the restaurant where I ate was managed jointly by a group of waiters." Rare was the journalist who mentioned such things, even in passing. Not a single one bothered to spend a few days in a Spanish factory or business or estate taken over by its workers, to examine just how the utopian dream was faring in practice.

"It didn't seem possible," Lois Orr said of the correspondents, "that they were describing the same Spain I was in, the one located on the Iberian Peninsula." Has history ever seen a case where such a huge array of talented reporters ignored such a big story right in front of them? The most extensive eyewitness record by any American of Spain's revolutionary moment remains in the letters and unpublished memoir of this nineteen-year-old who had gone to Europe for her honeymoon.

13

"As Good a Method of Getting Married as Any Other"

When she had time off from her nursing, Toby Jensky wrote home from Villa Paz, often reassuring her family that she was far from the front and not in danger: "Tell Mom not to worry—her darling is safe & eating well." On June 27, 1937, came her first reference to Pat Gurney: "There is still plenty of romance in the air here—now its an English sculptor—more about him later."

Although he had had plenty of lovers, Gurney found himself affected by Jensky as by no other woman. Being wounded and seeing comrades killed had changed him deeply: "I was up against something that had never happened to me before or since. I became obsessed with the idea of producing a child. Sex developed an entirely new dimension and we were untiring in our pursuit of it. Something had to be done about the situation." He co-opted a hospital car and a few friends, "to go and find some official who would legally marry us. But the whole thing seemed to be quite hopeless. There had been no law of civil marriage before the War, and now there were no priests, and neither of us would have wanted them if they had existed. . . . The civil bureaucracy was in such chaos that no mayor or other official seemed to know what his powers were or what the procedure was and finally we gave up.

"But if we could not have an official marriage I decided to invent one. . . . [Villa Paz] had a wonderful two-wheeled cart and a pair of most beautiful, creamy, long-horned oxen. . . . We garlanded the oxen with wreaths of flowers, loaded the cart with a barrel of wine and an assortment of food stuffs and set off to hold a feast. Nearby there was a stream with a small cascade, set off in a copse of trees. Everybody off duty joined us: we ate, drank, splashed around in the water and caressed the sweet, docile oxen, all in the dappled shade of the surrounding trees. Finally we wandered home singing and leading the oxen. Toby and I retired to bed amid the plaudits of our friends. All of which was probably as good a method of getting married as any other."

Jensky, however, seems not to have felt quite the same way. Only after five pages of a long letter to her sister and brother-in-law did she even get around to mentioning "my big romance" with "an English sculptor here with a wounded hand—about 6ft 2 blond—very mad." She goes on to say, "He decided he was in love with me & wanted me to go to Eng. with him. I treated it all as a joke—until 2 guys came around with a car. About 6 of us got in and went for a ride. When we got to a town Pat decided he wanted to get married. He annoyed me so long that I said O.K. I'd marry him just to teach him not to go around asking girls to marry him. When we got to the mayor's I really was scared—and walking up the stairs they all burst out laughing. . . . We couldn't get married without a paper from Dr. Pitts so I was saved." She did not mention an ox-cart excursion and feast.

Before long, the couple was separated by the war. On July 6, a new Republican offensive began at Brunete, some hundred miles away. "There were a tremendous number of casualties as a result of this battle," Gurney wrote, "and orders were received at Villa Paz to evacuate any wounded man who was capable of walking to make room for the men from Brunete. . . . Villa Paz had become the centre of my life. Apart from the fact that it contained a number of dear and intimate friends, together with my newly acquired wife, it represented a haven of peace and safety in an exceedingly unsafe world."

But he had no choice: ambulances full of wounded and dying soldiers were arriving in the courtyard. With a letter from the hospital recommending a medical discharge, Gurney hitched a ride and was on his way. A few days later, Jensky wrote home, leaving her own feelings a mystery: "He was still in love with me & if I wouldn't go with him, he wanted to marry me before he left. I didn't. He's on his way to Eng. now hoping I'll join him soon."

The flow of mangled bodies to Villa Paz and other hospitals quickly turned into a flood. Jensky's letters remained light and frothy, as if she were writing her family from a European vacation instead of a brutal civil war. However, she made clear to her sister and brother-in-law why this was so: "Its very hard writing letters from Spain because the mail is censored—and we can't write about the things we see or hear—only about the weather etc." Censors were not merely worried about military secrets; news of Republican setbacks on the battlefield might cut into the fund-raising in the United States that kept medical supplies coming.

Someone else was on Toby Jensky's mind besides her patients and Pat Gurney. It was, in fact, a constant preoccupation. References threaded through the letters she sent home. "I've been inquiring about Phil he's well and working in Barcelona." And then: "I wrote you that I got a letter from Phil. He's busy working in a factory and very well and happy. . . . Seriously don't worry he's O.K. I've got my eye on him."

Phil Schachter was family: his older brother Max was married to Jensky's sister. A New York machinist who had just finished trade school and joined the Young Communist League, Phil left very few written traces. To imagine his young life is like trying to draw a portrait with only a few pencil strokes. He was only twenty-one when he headed off to Spain without daring to tell his widowed father. To one of his brothers he wrote, just after arriving in Europe: "You have probably guessed my destination. . . . I'm very sorry I left the way I did but it was the only [way] I could see my way clear to go. . . . At the first chance I'll write and tell you everything." But to his father, he wrote:

> *Dear Pop,*
> *Well here I am in Paris. I had a fine trip over. I left the ship and am going to Marseilles. From there I may come back or go somewhere else. I don't know where. . . . Please don't worry I'll be all right.*

Phil's father was the proprietor of a laundry that, like so many small businesses, was struggling to stay solvent in the Depression, and his four children had all at times pitched in to help save money. Max had even stayed on in the family apartment after he married Jensky's sister. Phil clearly felt torn between a sense of family responsibility and his belief that Spain was the crucible in a global struggle against fascism.

After making the arduous nighttime climb over the Pyrenees, he first put his machinist's skills to work repairing rifles behind the lines. But, eager to fight, in June 1937 he wrote to his brother Harry, also a machinist who shared his Communist convictions, that he had joined the newly trained George Washington Battalion and was heading for the front. "Try to calm Pop if letters stop coming after this for quite a while. . . . Write and tell me if he is suspicious of anything." To Max he wrote, "I feel fine and do not for a moment have any regrets as to coming over here. The only thing is I've been worried as to how Pop . . . would take it."

Near the end of the month, he wrote Harry again: "We are now in reserve positions. We are now camped in an olive grove listening to the guns on the front." By then, their father had evidently realized that Phil was in Spain, but Phil was still determined to leave the impression that he was merely repairing rifles in the rear, for on July 3 he wrote to Max, "I hope Pop won't get any ideas that I'm in the army."

• • •

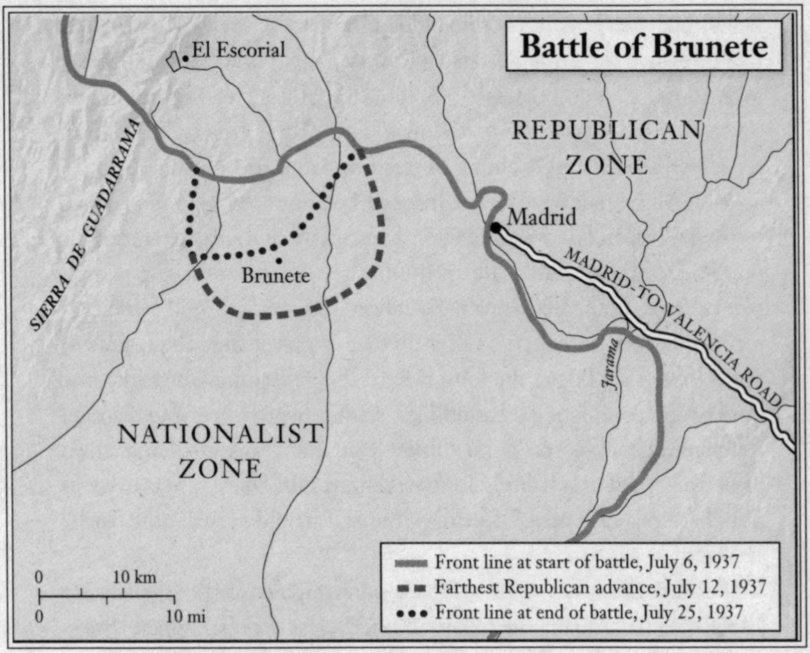

The Battle of Brunete took its name from a village in the arid Guadarrama Mountains west of Madrid. Republican troops aimed to cut off the Nationalist forces that had pushed their way into the city's outskirts, from which they could shell the metropolis relentlessly. With the siege of Madrid on front pages the world over, relieving that pressure would be a stunning Republican victory in propaganda as well as arms. This carefully planned surprise assault involving tanks, artillery, and some 70,000 soldiers was something new: a large-scale offensive by the Republican army, which had spent most of the war's first year coping with attacks by Franco's troops. For many newly arrived Americans, it would be their first time in combat. Phil Schachter's Washington Battalion was dispatched to the front after a sendoff fiesta at its training base featuring music and humorous skits by soldiers poking fun at their superiors.

The Republic's army was still desperately short of experienced officers, but every major commander now had a Soviet advisor. For this offensive the army also had 132 new T-26 Soviet tanks, superior to any that Franco possessed. (Stalin, like Hitler, was finding Spain a useful testing ground.) In the first days of the attack, Republican forces wrested a sizable chunk of territory from the Nationalists.

Bob Merriman was not at Brunete, but hundreds of men he had trained were, and he waited anxiously for news of them. After months of static, uncomfortable life in muddy trenches or training camps, troops from both the Lincoln Battalion and the untested Washington were eager to be part of a battle that might change the course of the war. As they began the long trek to their jumping-off point, "the boys were confident and kidding," wrote twenty-year-old Samuel Levinger, a rabbi's son from Ohio. "But there was a solemn, deep undertone to all the kidding for we realized fully that . . . many would not come out of it alive." Levinger himself would survive this battle, although not the next.

Because this was a surprise attack, no foreign correspondents were allowed to accompany the troops. Nonetheless, Louis Fischer, always adept at pulling the right strings, managed to make himself an exception. Soon after the battle began, he drove out from Madrid to the newly captured village of Brunete in search of his countrymen. "All the streets were empty. I looked into two houses and they were empty. The third was a farmer's hut. As I walked in I called out in Spanish, 'Are there any Americans here?' and then I heard, 'Yeh, whatchya lookin' for?'

"A young man in tin helmet and khaki uniform was sitting on a pile of large tins—jam captured from Franco, writing a letter. . . . He had worked on the main crane at the Republic Steel works in Chicago. How was the Little Steel strike going, he wanted to know.

"We went out into the yard to listen to the shelling. We heard sharp machine gunning. About a half mile to the west of us, an airplane dove to earth. 'They're strafing our men in the trenches out there,' the crane driver explained. A moment later a second airplane dove and then a third."

Despite its initial gains, the offensive soon bogged down. The Republic's Soviet tanks looked impressive as they rolled over the rugged ground, but they were invisibly crippled in two ways. In choosing Spanish tank crews, Soviet advisors had insisted on Communists, refusing to consider the much wider pool of soldiers from other political parties, many of whom had had more experience with driving or machinery. Then there was the long shadow of the Great Purge. Its latest prominent victim was Marshal Mikhail Tukhachevsky, former chief of staff of the Red Army, whom Stalin imagined as a potential rival. He had been tortured into confessing to being a German spy and was executed a few weeks before the battle began. The marshal was noted for his pioneering ideas about armored warfare, including the use of tank columns as highly mobile pincers in just the sort of surprise attack that was under way at Brunete. In the actual battle, however, no Soviet officer dared risk being seen using the disgraced Tukhachevsky's tactics, so Republican tanks were spread out far less effectively in support of infantry.

In addition, the army's supply personnel were completely inexperienced when it came to an operation on this scale. In parching hundred-degree weather, when streams marked on maps turned out to be dry, they couldn't even keep frontline troops supplied with water. Six of the eight men in one Washington Battalion squad collapsed from sunstroke. ("Sun like the thunder of God," Martha Gellhorn had noted of the Spanish heat.) So strong was the sun that some soldiers experienced a kind of snow blindness in which everything looked white. Nationalist incendiary bombs and hot artillery shrapnel set dry grass and brush on fire, and more shrapnel fragments landed in pots of stew on the Americans' cooking fires.

An early target for the XV International Brigade was a Nationalist-held hill known as Mosquito Ridge. Two days into the battle, the Lincolns and Washingtons were advancing toward it through the Duke of Alba's private hunting reserve. They felt a momentary surge of encouragement when they came across the bodies of Nationalist officers shot in the back—evidently by their own men. With no water for their water-cooled Maxim machine guns, men urinated in the cooling jackets that surrounded the barrels. As July 9 dawned, the

Americans and the British tried to take the ridge, but Moors were entrenched on its heights. German and Italian fighters swooped low overhead strafing, while the Americans lay on their backs, fruitlessly firing at the planes with their rifles. Supply parties trying to make their way uphill with food and ammunition were shot down. Muddy drinking water, found by men frantically digging deep holes in a dry riverbed, tasted of dead mule, according to one soldier, and brought back an all too familiar scourge, diarrhea. It came on so swiftly and repeatedly that some men slit their pants to deal with it.

The Lincoln Battalion's newly appointed commander was Oliver Law, a thirty-six-year-old Texan and US Army veteran. He had driven a Yellow Cab and done other blue-collar jobs in Chicago while becoming a Communist Party member. Little is known about his life before Spain—Party propaganda celebrating him is notably bereft of detail—except that working as a labor and tenant organizer apparently led him to at least one arrest and beating at the hands of the Chicago police. An important reason for Law's selection as commander was a fact noted in Spanish in his International Brigades military records: he was black.

The Party was one of the few organizations of any kind eager to show that it welcomed black Americans as equals. It had run blacks for vice president of the United States as well as for state and local public offices throughout the 1930s. Unlike these never-elected candidates, however, Law now had life-and-death authority: this was the first time a black man had ever commanded an integrated military unit of Americans in combat. Simply to meet a black officer had been a startling experience for the American military attaché in Spain, Colonel Stephen Fuqua, a Southerner. He dropped in on the Lincolns and, as a visitor heard the story, "said to Law—'Er, I see you are in a Captain's uniform?' Law replied with dignity, 'Yes, I am, because I *am* a Captain.' . . . Whereupon the Colonel hemmed and hawed and finally came out with: 'I'm sure your people must be proud of you, my boy.'"

Lincoln veterans disagree about how competent Law was and

whether his previous military experience, mainly as an army private stationed on the Mexican border, was relevant. Pat Gurney, however, who had no love for Communist propaganda and a good nose for political humbug, knew him and thought him a "very fine" soldier. Law had been under fire with Merriman at Jarama, but Brunete was his first experience of leadership in battle. At first he faltered badly, showing the same terror as many of his men when confronted with the hail of Nationalist fire. Later, perhaps to make up for his initial fear, he was out in front of his troops, waving a pistol and urging them up Mosquito Ridge, when he was fatally wounded. His career as a black officer commanding a largely white battalion had lasted only a few days, but nothing like it would happen in the US Army for many years to come.

As the Republican drive lost momentum and a Nationalist counterattack began, wary American soldiers saw the skies fill with something ominous and new—a compact, sleek, single-engine monoplane moving at what seemed like unprecedented speed, with a fearsome rate of climb. Germany's Messerschmitt Bf-109 was making its combat debut. This fighter would become the deadly, versatile mainstay of the Luftwaffe during the Second World War. By now, the Nationalists had gained air superiority over the Republic. Franco could field more than 200 planes at a time, flown by well-trained German, Italian, and Spanish pilots, and the Republican air force was quickly overwhelmed. On a single day, the Condor Legion shot down 21 Republican aircraft.

Meanwhile, German bombs pounded Republican infantrymen as they struggled to dig trenches in the hard-baked earth. When troops of the Washington Battalion advanced too closely bunched together, four Italian heavy bombers dropped their loads with terrible consequences. "We passed on," remembered a captain in the nearby British battalion, "making our way between huge craters, round the edges of which the bodies of dozens of Americans were still smoldering. They had turned a curious black."

As machine-gunner David McKelvy White remembered it:

> Time ceased to exist. . . . Sometimes it was light with a fierce sun, sometimes dark and very cold. . . . We saw dull, horrible and ludicrous wounds. We learned that men are not always killed in noble or picturesque postures. We spent hours clutching the good earth while big shells fell all around us, 8 or 10 to the minute. . . . We saw air battles at night, fantastic with tracer bullets. We saw a direct hit at a great German bomber, no staggering plane, no wreckage, only a great cloud of flame and then nothing. . . . Time and again we would march all night and, between fighting and guard duty the next day, work hard at dug-outs we were never to be able to use, for there would be more marching that night.
>
> We went without food; we went, worst of all, without water, because our truck was cut off. . . . We ran in advances where we could see fascists fleeing before us. . . . We fell back once in disorder ourselves, leaving to the enemy our machine gun, much amo, some food, and, worse of all, chocolate and American cigarettes. We heard political speeches when we could hardly keep awake. . . . Once I helped carry a stretcher about 200 meters before we discovered that our charge had died, when we unceremoniously dumped the body and went back for another. . . . We saw tough guys crack up and babble like babies, wild-eyed. We saw boys grow to resolute maturity in a day. We felt the hot air from bomb explosions and saw men burst into flame before our eyes.

When the offensive petered out after three weeks, the Republic had lost some 25,000 troops killed, wounded, or taken prisoner, among them 300 Americans. Jack Shirai, the Japanese-American chef, was dead, as were two American doctors. The British battalion had also been badly hit. Among the casualties was its eccentric but respected chief of staff, Major George Nathan. Openly gay—not an easy thing for a military man in the 1930s—he sported a gold-tipped baton, and, when fatally wounded, asked the soldiers around him to sing until he died.

With close to half of their men as casualties, the Lincoln and Washington Battalions had to be merged. Officially it became the Lincoln-Washington Battalion, but almost everyone soon began referring to it as the Lincoln. Drained and exhausted, some men tried to flee. Among the roughly 2,800 American volunteers in Spain, it is estimated that over the course of the war at least 100 deserted. Some were caught and at least two executed; some managed to cross the mountains into France or stow away on merchant ships.

The offensive had been a costly failure, but for the government of the Spanish Republic, there seemed no alternative but to continue fighting. Back in England, George Orwell wrote during Brunete of the International Brigades as "in some sense fighting for all of us—a thin line of suffering and often ill-armed human beings standing between barbarism and at least comparative decency."

Phil Schachter's family received two letters from him dated July 15, 1937, written during a short lull after the fighting over Mosquito Ridge. To his brother Max and Max's wife, Ida, he mentioned hearing that someone was "trying to get Pop to get the Consul after me. I hope you understand how ridiculous the idea is. . . . I think I'm old enough to know what I'm doing and I would resent it very much if any efforts were made in that direction. . . . So please prevent Pop from taking any such steps." To his brother Harry, he wrote, "We were in action about 7 days and it was no picnic. . . . I still have to clean my rifle and it is getting dark so good-bye. Give my love to everyone." Then the letters stopped coming.

Brunete marked the first appearance on the battlefield of a mysterious American whose full story is still not known. Born in Puerto Rico, Vincent Usera was a tall, striking figure with chiseled, movie-star good looks. Communist Party officials in New York had been delighted when he showed up to enlist, for unlike any other American volunteer, he had recent combat experience. But they were wary too, because Usera had not come from the world of left-wing politics. When he departed for Spain, trusted Party members traveling with him were assigned to keep a close watch.

International Brigades officials in Spain felt the same ambivalence. "He wears a trim moustache and carefully-tailored uniform, which together give him the appearance of a professional military officer," said one report. Yet "he readily admits that before coming to Spain he had had no connection with nor knowledge of the labor movement." The report noted of Usera that "during a discussion he becomes rather nervous and uncertain of his statements; one gets the impression that he is trying to maintain a 'front,' but is having difficulty doing so." Another comment in Usera's file, in Spanish, noted, "Suspected of being an agent."

Usera told people in Spain that he had joined the US Marines at the age of seventeen and served on armored gunboats that patrolled China's Yangtze River against pirates. Then, he said, he fought in Nicaragua, at a time when the marines were occupying the country and battling an uprising led by the guerrilla leader Augusto Sandino. He later transferred for a time to the Nicaraguan military. Although his colorful descriptions of combat with pirates on the Yangtze and with Sandino's guerrillas in the jungle cannot be verified, Usera's official US military records confirm that he enlisted in the marines as a teenager, served for six years in unnamed locations, and then joined the Nicaraguan army. After that point, the full story becomes harder to discern.

To International Brigades officials in Spain, Usera claimed that "his career in the Marine Corps came to an abrupt end when he became involved in a personal way with the wife of somebody 'who had more influence than I did.'" After that, he said, he had spent two years in "show business" in Newport, Rhode Island, helped out by "Mrs. Vanderbilt," whom he had gotten to know while stationed in Newport in the service. After several more years as an insurance broker, he volunteered for Spain.

It was amazingly ill advised to be boasting to Communists in Spain of a friendship with Mrs. Vanderbilt, but whether or not that existed, a 1934 article in a Newport newspaper mentions Usera as the house manager of a theater there. And an oral history of a fellow marine confirms his story of an affair with someone else's wife—indeed, the wives of several officers, it appears. But the course of his later life strongly suggests that when he volunteered for the Spanish Civil War, Usera did so with plans to report back to the US military.

Army intelligence agents in the United States had long kept a close eye on left-wingers at home and knew how eager the Lincoln recruiters were to find men with military experience. "At least one Reserve Officer," an agent in Chicago reported to Washington in 1937, "is known to have been approached with a proposition to instruct in military training." With this in mind, it appears, the army may have sent the Lincolns a military man who could quietly keep Washington informed. Another possibility is that Usera's career in uniform had been stalled by his philandering and that he undertook this mission to Spain on his own, hoping to produce intelligence that would restore him to favor with the US military.

The Lincoln brass remained uneasy: why was this nonpolitical man a volunteer? Perhaps sensing their doubts, Usera boasted that he was friends with a well-known Washington labor activist. But he made this claim in Spain, where it was impossible to check. In military matters he was obviously a consummate professional with experience in training soldiers. Furthermore, very usefully, he was bilingual in English and Spanish. His competence first won him a job instructing new recruits, then a position as company commander, and finally at Brunete the post of adjutant (basically second-in-command) to Oliver Law. At a pivotal moment during the battle, however, shortly before Law was killed, Usera disappeared, finding an excuse to go to brigade headquarters in the rear. "He was a soldier of fortune," concluded the furious battalion commissar Steve Nelson, who had to take command himself when Usera couldn't be found, adding, "But he knew a lot about soldiering, and such men were scarce."

Chewed out and demoted, Usera vanished again, only to be arrested in Barcelona trying to leave Spain without permission. By now his name appeared on a list of "bad elements" in the International Brigades personnel files. Nonetheless, his military experience was so valuable that he was put back to work training new recruits. His language skills proved all the more essential when a company of Spanish soldiers had to be integrated, with considerable difficulty, into the American battalion.

Usera, the files show, had emphatic ideas about proper training and what American volunteers were doing wrong: they needed better discipline; officers should delegate more tasks to subordinates; Bob Merriman was a good supervisor but was trying to do too many things; officers should firmly expect obedience from their men even when they had been friends in civilian life. He set up sophisticated exercises in maneuvering under imaginary enemy fire—as a squad, as a whole company, against trenches, in a forest, with mock casualties among commanders—and his assured, knowledgeable opinions seem to have impressed everyone, including the official who felt he was maintaining a "front." At a graduation ceremony for the men Usera trained, they gave him a hearty round of applause, something that thoroughly disconcerted International Brigades officers who were sure he was not to be trusted.

Early the next year, however, again in the middle of a battle, Usera would desert the American volunteers once more, this time for good. A paper trail shows him traveling by freighter from Antwerp to Weehawken, New Jersey; then he temporarily vanishes from sight.

Most armies of this period were trying to learn all they could from the conflict in Spain about what they might face in the next world war. We know now that for some months the British had an undercover agent in the International Brigades, and some think the same was true for the French, Czech, and Polish intelligence services. US Army files from the 1930s bulge with comments about the fighting in Spain. One 1937 report from an American military attaché in England speaks of Spain as a "war laboratory." And so it was undoubtedly with special interest that an audience at the United States Naval Institute, the in-house think tank on the grounds of the Naval Academy in Annapolis, Maryland, would assemble in 1939 to hear a lecture entitled "Some Lessons from the Spanish War."

The speaker was Vincent Usera. Soon after this lecture, which covered tactics, weapons, training, defense against aerial attacks, and other matters, Usera would successfully resume his US military career, this time joining the army. By 1943 he was a major, and by 1944 the executive officer of an infantry battalion in Europe. Later came several positions in military intelligence (another possible hint at his role in Spain), and study at the elite Command and General Staff College at Fort Leavenworth, Kansas. When Dwight D. Eisenhower was NATO commander in 1951, Usera was an intelligence officer on his staff. He retired as a full colonel in 1963, and went to live in Franco's Spain. One of his last posts before retirement was as a military advisor in Vietnam.

A few days after his visit to the battlefield at Brunete, Louis Fischer traveled to Paris, where he watched an impressive display of arms in the city's annual Bastille Day parade, thinking bitterly of the weapons the Spanish Republic could not buy. It could win the war in three months, he felt, with "twenty percent of the military establishment that paraded that morning."

Then it was back to Moscow after half a year away. The dream that had sustained him emotionally for 15 years was in tatters. The eight-story building where Fischer and his family lived held approximately 160 apartments; in more than half of them people had been arrested. One neighbor sensed his time was coming: "His little bundle of clothing and toilet articles was packed in readiness." Three weeks later, the secret police came for him. They almost always appeared at night. From the American ambassador's residence, surrounded by apartment buildings, could be heard the sound of paddy wagons and then the screams of terrified families as men were taken away in the dark.

Stalin's paranoia always had a xenophobic tinge, and the ax of the Great Purge fell with particular weight on anyone who had served in Spain, where, the dictator feared, Soviet officials might have been corrupted by Western ideas or intelligence agencies. A friend of Fischer's who had been ambassador to Spain was recalled to Moscow and disappeared. The Soviet consul general in Barcelona, a well-known hero of the Russian Revolution, similarly recalled, was sent to the firing squad, along with a lengthy string of other high-ranking diplomats, generals, advisors, and journalists abruptly summoned home. Sometimes their executions took place soon after the men had been publicly welcomed as heroes, given banquets, and awarded medals.

"It was better not to call on Soviet friends and acquaintances," Fischer wrote. "The visit of a foreigner might get them into trouble. Always, literally always in the past, our apartment was filled with Russians when I arrived from abroad. They came . . . to welcome me back, but also to get the latest news and impressions of the international scene. This time nobody came."

With his wife and children unable to leave Russia, Fischer dared not express his dismay in print. He quickly returned to Spain. Hungry as always to be near those in power, he grew close to the new prime minister, Juan Negrín, working as an advisor and at one point living in Negrín's official residence, the Presidencia.

He fired off memos to the prime minister on a variety of subjects and tried to work out a scheme for circumventing the arms embargo by transferring American weapons to Spain through a third country. He purchased arms on the black market, tried to recruit Spanish-speaking officers from Latin America, and approached the French government: wouldn't they like their reserve officers to get some combat experience? Representing the Republic, he spoke to a group of 72 members of Parliament at the House of Commons. He accompanied Negrín on a secret visit to Paris to try, in vain, to get the French to change their minds about arms sales. He also may have had a hand in arranging the travel of Americans joining the Lincolns, for a letter from an International Brigades official discreetly acknowledges "the American merchandise that we could receive thanks to your praiseworthy and indefatigable efforts." At this point the principal "American merchandise" arriving was new volunteers.

Fischer had essentially transferred to the Spanish Republic all the loyalty he had once had for the Soviet Union—and some of the blindness as well. Like other American correspondents, he seems to have barely noticed the now suppressed social revolution. He also ignored the way the Soviets were using their aid to gain control of the Republic's security forces—or perhaps he simply felt that this was a price the country had to pay for Russian arms. On some points, however, he would prove chillingly on target. "If democracy is crushed in Spain," he told readers of the *Nation*, ". . . Rome and Berlin will be convinced that they can with impunity continue their campaigns against small states. The turn of the larger states will come later."

14

Texaco Goes to War

Despite the Spanish war, the rich still considered the Mediterranean a playground, so in the summer of 1937 one of the world's wealthiest women, the American cereals heiress Marjorie Merriweather Post, headed there for a cruise on her yacht, the *Sea Cloud*, a lavish, 350-foot, four-masted barque with a crew of 72. Everything was going smoothly when suddenly the captain found that the ship's radio would not work. The reason: interference from the Italian navy's primitive radar system. Benito Mussolini had put his ships and submarines to work attacking the supply lines to Republican Spain.

A new and deadly front in the war had now opened. Among its early victims were volunteers for the International Brigades who—trying to avoid the arduous climb across the Pyrenees—sailed from Marseille on the passenger vessel *Ciudad de Barcelona*, headed for its namesake city. When the ship was 20 miles short of its destination, recalled an American on board, "a lone Republican seaplane flew alongside. The pilot was gesticulating wildly and pointing." His warning was too late: moments later, torpedoes from a submarine hit the vessel and in seven minutes it was gone. "I remember the screaming faces of men trapped at the portholes."

Ironically, one of the volunteers unable to escape was the former captain of the Brooklyn College swim team. Some 50 volunteers from various countries drowned, including at least ten Americans. "All around the ship was a mass of floating wreckage: barrels, crates, cases, planking, canvas, wooden bedsteads," wrote a Canadian survivor. "And amongst all this debris were bobbing heads, and floating bodies, and around the bodies the sea crimson with blood."

Such attacks escalated dramatically. Franco had sent his brother to Rome to ask Mussolini to sink any ship that might be carrying arms to the Republic, and the Italian dictator was happy to oblige. They agreed that if an Italian submarine had to surface, it would fly the Spanish Nationalist flag. Italy had one of the world's largest fleets of submarines, and 52 of them, plus 41 cruisers and destroyers, began patrolling the Mediterranean, on the lookout for vessels sailing to Republican ports. The Italians also provided some submarines for Franco's navy—it was one of these that sank the *Ciudad de Barcelona*.

In August 1937 alone, Italian submarines, aircraft, and surface warships sank 26 vessels carrying cargo to or from Republican ports. Aviators could see oil slicks dotting the Mediterranean, marking sunken ships like floating gravestones. Some of the lost ships were Russian, so after August the USSR abandoned any attempt to send weapons and ammunition to Spain via the Mediterranean. Soviet vessels instead took the safe but far longer route from Arctic or Baltic ports through the Atlantic to unload their supplies in France, to be transported onward to Spain by land. But this proved undependable because a divided, skittish French government periodically bottled up Soviet cargo in the port of Bordeaux for months at a time. An erratic stream of Soviet arms did get through, but came nowhere near matching the help supplied to Franco by Mussolini and Hitler. Never again would Soviet aid turn the tide of a battle.

• • •

What if help came, instead, from the United States? Might the leader of the world's largest democracy have a change of heart? That was the hope of Martha Gellhorn, Ernest Hemingway, and film director Joris Ivens on the evening of July 8, 1937, when they were invited to show Franklin and Eleanor Roosevelt *The Spanish Earth*. Seldom has a film premiered before a more powerful audience. Gellhorn, who knew from experience that fare from the kitchen of the Roosevelt White House was abysmal, insisted they stop for sandwiches on the way.

The filmmakers had been struggling with their material up to the last minute. Originally, Orson Welles was to be the documentary's narrator, but Hemingway got into a shouting match with him when Welles criticized the novelist's script during the recording. In the final version of the hourlong movie, Hemingway speaks his own text in his flat, mid-American voice. But the documentary turned out to be less than the full success its makers had hoped for. Its dual story lines about besieged Madrid and the village of Fuentidueña fit together clumsily, and its purpose of generating sympathy for the embattled Republic is at times oddly sidetracked by Hemingway's fascination with war and his narration extolling battle as a testing ground: "The ultimate loneliness of what is known as combat. . . . This is the true face of men going into action. It is a little different from any other face that you will ever see."

The Spanish Earth also evades one central point. The citizens of Fuentidueña are shown energetically digging irrigation ditches, through which a stream of water finally gushes triumphantly into Spain's arid soil. The narration never explains that the villagers could do this only because they had formed a union and confiscated the land from a handful of big owners who had previously used it as a hunting reserve. Like so many supporters of the Republic, the filmmakers feared that highlighting such matters might antagonize the audience they hoped to reach.

About her reunion with the Roosevelts, Gellhorn later wrote that she was "trembling with nerves and a desire to have them see with my eyes." Following a dinner that Hemingway described as "rainwater soup followed by rubber squab, a nice wilted salad and a cake some admirer had sent in," about 30 guests joined them as the president in his wheelchair led the way into the White House movie theater. The screening appeared to go well, but Roosevelt, who at first kept silent, seemed aware of the film's political omissions. When he spoke at last, he suggested, as Ivens recalled it, "Why don't you give more stress to the fact that the Spaniards are fighting, not merely for the right to their own government, but also for the right to bring under cultivation those great tracts of land which the old system forcibly left barren?" Perhaps with his eye on the next war, the president also asked about the performance of tanks and the battle of Guadalajara, both of which had been shown on the screen.

Writing to his mother-in-law in his tough-guy mode, Hemingway described FDR as "very Harvard charming and sexless and womanly like a great Woman Secretary of Labor." Without mentioning Gellhorn, he sent a telegram to his wife Pauline: WHITE HOUSE STILL SAME COLOR BUT ENTHUSIASTIC.

If, however, Pauline read Eleanor Roosevelt's newspaper column two days later, she would have seen that her husband and Ivens had been accompanied by Gellhorn. Eleanor's column, too, suggested that the film should be politically more explicit. "In the picture . . . I think they presuppose too much knowledge of old world conditions and I hope before it is shown generally, there will be some way of bringing out the background which is very alien to our own country. Here land is not as yet concentrated in the hands of any groups to such an extent that the people generally can not acquire any for themselves."

On her way to the family retreat at Hyde Park, New York, Mrs. Roosevelt took the midnight sleeper train to New York City with her three guests. From there, Hemingway and Ivens flew on to Hollywood for several star-studded benefit showings that raised pledges of enough money to send 20 new ambulances to Spain (although it is not clear how many actually reached the country). Both men, Gellhorn wrote enthusiastically to Eleanor, "were impressed that you and Mr. Roosevelt said to make it stronger—that's what it amounted to—

by underlining the causes of the conflict." Didn't such suggestions augur well for a change of American policy toward Spain?

Everyone prefers to do business with a winner, and the Republic's leaders hoped that a striking victory on the battlefield might make it easier to buy arms abroad. Brunete was supposed to be that triumph, but had failed. The following month, August 1937, the army tried again, this time with 80,000 troops in Aragon, inland from Barcelona. The attack was planned to wrest the ancient city of Saragossa, where there were many Republican sympathizers, from Franco's hands. The generals also urgently hoped to draw Nationalist troops away from Spain's northern coast before they overran it completely. They had another motive as well for starting an offensive here: anarchist militia units still held much of the line in Aragon, and the increasingly Communist-dominated army was eager to incorporate their men under its command.

Nationalist resistance was stronger than expected, however. The Republicans got bogged down on the way to Saragossa, and ended up focusing their efforts instead on the far smaller town of Belchite. Americans were in the thick of the fighting with Bob Merriman back in action, now promoted to major as chief of staff of the XV International Brigade. The brigade's commander was still Colonel Vladimir Copic, the difficult Yugoslav with a reputation for avoiding the front line. (Merriman found him "scared stiff" during combat, and Hemingway thought he "ran his brigade like a badly-administered pig-sty and handled it . . . like an old apple-woman with locomotor ataxia trying to be a blocking back against the N. Y. Giants.") Merriman's diary, as usual, was full of cryptic notes about supply and morale problems, gasoline shortages, transport breakdowns, and endlessly quarreling commanders—but he confided to it how hard it was to be separated from his wife. "Received note from Marion and sent one. Goodbye another time dear girl—I wanted to see you so mad[ly]."

In a new experience for them, the Lincolns captured nearly 1,000 Nationalist prisoners, most of them trapped in a hilltop fortress whose water pipeline had been cut. "Fortified heights," Merriman

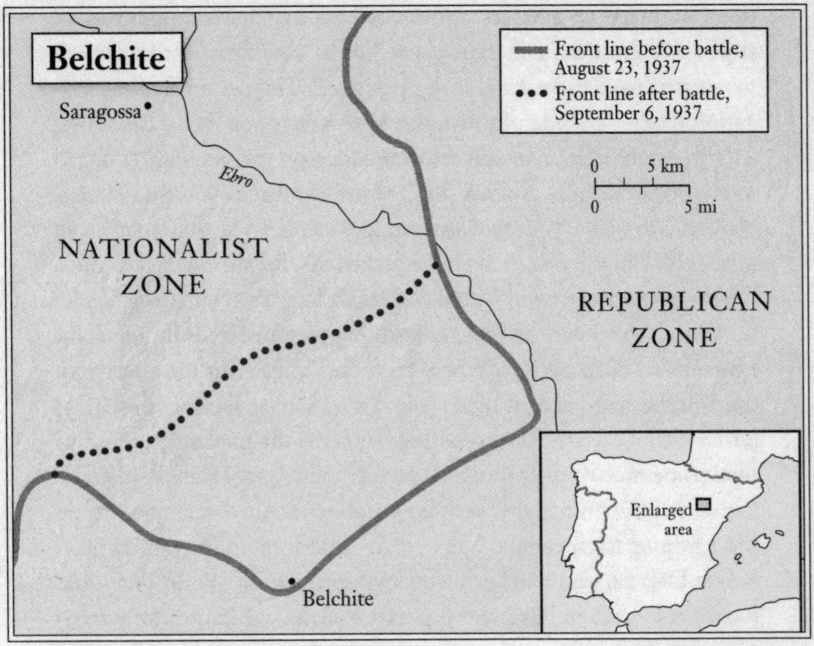

wrote. "Prisoners came in droves wanting water etc. Haggard bad looking lot."

The treatment of prisoners in this war was ruthless. The Republicans routinely shot captured Nationalist officers, regarding them as beyond redemption. But Nationalist enlisted men were considered either deluded by propaganda or forced to fight against their will, and so were generally allowed to live. On the other side, the Nationalists systematically shot captured officers and many enlisted men as well, particularly the Internationals: 173 of the 287 Americans known to have been taken prisoner were killed.

Merriman recorded the shooting of captured officers at Belchite in his diary, but not what he felt about it, except to say "one german comrade unnecessarily taunted a brave young officer." Had his feelings hardened as the war dragged on? Or did he think it unsoldierly to leave a record of any qualms? We do not know.

In Belchite the Lincolns and other Republican troops found Nationalist machine-gunners entrenched in half-buried pillboxes of steel and reinforced concrete, as well as in a seminary and a church tower that gave them good firing positions. Trapped in shallow irrigation ditches outside of town, the Americans took heavy casualties. All three company commanders were killed on the first day. "We had to go forward," Steve Nelson, now commissar for the XV Brigade, explained years later. "Yet that seemed like suicide. On the other hand, if we stayed in the trench, we'd be picked off like sitting ducks. And a retreat over bare ground would cost more lives than an attack."

When Merriman, at brigade headquarters, ordered the reluctant Lincolns to once again advance, he found himself in the reverse of the role he had been in seven months earlier at Jarama: initiating, rather than receiving and resisting, an order that seemed bound to send some men to their deaths. To Merriman's rage, Hans Amlie, the new Lincoln commander, refused to obey it. An older man, Amlie was a mining engineer and Norwegian-American prairie radical from North Dakota, who had been wounded in the First World War, then fought at Jarama and Brunete. A gentle soul, he was known for watching over the welfare of his men. His selection as commander had some politics behind it, for his brother was a congressman from Wisconsin.

Merriman and Nelson erupted at the balky Amlie over the telephone, threatening him with a court-martial, and Nelson headed for the front line to enforce discipline. "What the hell is the matter with you guys?" Amlie shouted at Nelson when he arrived. "Go forward—how *can* we go forward? That town's bristling with machine guns. . . . You want to slaughter the whole damn battalion?"

Nelson, however, noticed an alternative means of attack. A deep ditch ran into Belchite, and he led some of the Lincolns down it and into a vacant olive oil factory at its end. From this foothold, they began infiltrating the town. Nearly a week of grim house-to-house fighting followed, with Merriman himself leading small groups across rooftops to clear buildings of Nationalist defenders. "Broke into houses, cleaned out houses—snipers and threw grenades. . . . Grenade thrown from window into us. Cut several places. . . . Worked too much as a soldier," he wrote self-critically, "and directed too little." Told by their officers that they would all be slaughtered by the Internationals if captured, the Nationalists fought ferociously, making barricades of rubble, cobblestones, mattresses, or anything else they could find. Some officers made their men fight barefoot, to discourage them from running away.

Among the attackers, casualties were high, with both Amlie and the popular Steve Nelson left wounded. The fighting reduced Belchite to smoldering rubble, and by the time the Americans and other Republican troops prevailed, they had conquered a wasteland. Although officially it was a severe offense for Republican soldiers to loot, Merriman gave in to temptation and from the town's ruins took two red bedspreads. "Looting is still going on in great fashion and even picked up nice present for Marion," he noted. But the taking of tiny Belchite, a place of no military significance except for having been the site of a battle in the Napoleonic Wars, was a hollow conquest. The offensive had stalled before reaching its intended target, Saragossa. As at Brunete, the battle ended with the Republic gaining a small piece of territory while losing far too many tanks, aircraft, and men.

After the fighting stopped, Bob sent word for Marion to come. They were of course eager to see each other, but the ostensible reason for her trip was that the brigade's paperwork had to be put in order. A record was needed of men killed or wounded in the fighting—in part so relatives in the United States and Britain could claim life insurance for the dead.

Late one afternoon, he walked her through the narrow, crooked streets of Belchite, showing her the places where Steve Nelson had been wounded and others killed, the skeletons of houses where he and his men had chased enemy soldiers from room to room with grenades, and the church tower against which he had led an assault. In the summer heat, Marion noticed sewer rats "as large as cats," attracted by decaying corpses. Darkness fell. By the light of a full moon, inside a ruined church, she read Nationalist posters still on the walls. "There were posted rules for the modesty of young women, rules requiring long skirts and long sleeves, saying sin is a woman's because she tempts man." As they were leaving the church, "suddenly, we heard piano music. . . . There, across a street in half a house, the front walls blown away, the inside looking like a stage, sat a Spanish soldier at a grand piano, playing Beethoven."

Although those on the ground knew better, the capture of Belchite was presented to the world as a stirring success. Most American correspondents, glad for the chance to portray the Lincolns as fighting heroically, ignored the failure of the overall offensive and the fact that the Republic was gradually losing ground to the Nationalists. "The Government won a victory . . . greater than has been realized," Herbert Matthews wrote in the *Times*, calling the battle one of the Republic's "biggest triumphs."

Hemingway and Gellhorn, back from their visit to the White House, traveled to Belchite with Matthews. In *Collier's*, Gellhorn described the town as "caved in. . . . You couldn't get through those streets, where the houses had slumped sideways. There were only a few soldiers in Belchite now, cleaning up. They were digging for the dead, under the piles of mortar, bricks and fallen beams. You would pass a high pile of rubbish, and smell suddenly the sharp rotting smell of the dead. Farther on would be a half-decayed carcass of a mule, with flies thick on it. And then a sewing machine, by itself, blown out into the street."

Bob Merriman, she wrote, "explained the offensive to us, drawing the plan of it on the dirt of the floor, going over every point carefully as if we were his freshmen class in economics back in California. Forty kilometers march . . . the dead piled eight feet high in the streets . . . 'The boys did well,' Merriman said. There was dust on his glasses and he had very white teeth. He was a big man, but shy and stiff, and his voice made you want to call him 'Professor.'"

Hemingway also waxed effusive about the Lincolns. "Since I had seen them last spring they have become soldiers. The romantics have pulled out, the cowards have gone home along with the badly wounded . . . after seven months they knew their trade." Their house-to-house combat was "old Indian fighting tactics"—a peculiar image, since few American Indians fought among stone buildings. Merriman "was a leader in the final assault. Unshaven, his face smoke blackened, his men tell how he bombed his way forwards, wounded six times slightly by hand-grenade splinters in the hands and face, but refusing to have his wounds dressed until the cathedral was taken."

Also on hand, writing for the Associated Press, was Milly Bennett, who always enjoyed the chance to see Merriman. She had long felt more wary of Stalin's scythe than he, and it sounds as if they may have had another of their political arguments in Belchite, for in his diary he noted that Bennett told him "about arrests in Moscow—foreign department." This referred to Stalin's sweeping purge of Soviet diplomats, some of whom the two of them knew. Whether the news gave him any qualms we do not know; it is the sole reference to such matters in his diary or letters.

Bennett had a particular interest in reaching Belchite, because Wallace Burton, the old boyfriend she pursued to Spain, had gone there with the Lincolns. Although she had been describing him to everyone as her fiancé, this had come as news to Burton, an Indiana-born seaman. ("Milly wrote that she and Burton may get married after he comes out," Bob Merriman had told Marion some time earlier in a letter from the front. "Burton says that it is the first he heard of it but he'll do it if it will get him a long leave.")

In a field hospital, however, Bennett learned that Burton had just been killed by a sniper. She left for Valencia to write her story about the battle, only to return a week or so later, hitching a ride on an antitank gun, to see if she could find more about how he died. At a hospital, she came upon the tall, blond, likable Hans Amlie, whom she already knew. He was recovering from his wound and waiting to be sent home. It did not take her long to set her sights on him. "Should I marry him here?" she asked her friend Marion. "Or should I wait until we get back to the States?"

"You better nab him while you can," Marion responded.

Before Amlie was sent home to rally support for the Lincolns, the two of them asked a Spanish judge to marry them. The judge told them that he was not allowed to perform a marriage unless both people involved presented birth certificates. These, of course, they did not have. Then, just as the downcast couple left the judge's chambers, a friendly clerk whispered a suggestion: birth certificates were not required if it was a deathbed marriage. Neither bride nor groom was anywhere near a deathbed, but the clerk knew a doctor who would provide the right paperwork. Successfully married, Bennett told the story to a New York newspaper once they arrived home. Amlie was her third husband, she acknowledged, but she vowed he would be the last.

Meanwhile, another wartime romance was foundering. Pat Gurney had returned to England in midsummer, considering himself married to Toby Jensky. On September 7, 1937, she wrote to her sister from the hospital at Villa Paz, "I was beginning to feel like a woman scorned till a few days ago when I got a cable from HIM asking me to join him in London and make an honest man of him. I'm still not ready to pack up and leave, but whether or not I'll go there I don't know—can't seem to decide."

A month later, she was still uncertain: "I'm in a jam—don't know what to do about my love in England. He wants me to join him. I want to go—then what?" A month after that came signs that Gurney's hopes might be threatened. Writing her sister again, Jensky cryptically mentioned "another romance, this time it is an American."

Despite the Roosevelt administration's failure so far to help the Republic, the Lincolns took encouragement from any indication that an official of the US government felt differently. One such sign came soon after Belchite and a later, failed attack that left close to 80 Americans dead, when an unexpected visitor appeared at XV Brigade headquarters with a small American flag flying from the hood of his car.

He was Colonel Stephen Fuqua, the American military attaché in Spain, a stocky, balding man of sixty-two who had attended West Point and fought in the Philippine-American War and the First World War. His daughter would soon marry a British volunteer for Franco. This lifelong army officer from Louisiana was the last person anyone might expect to be supportive of the American volunteers. Yet when he gave an informal speech in his Southern accent to the XV Brigade's soldiers, he told them, "I am glad Americans are among [you]." He noted that Republican Spain was a democracy, and added, "I cannot speak officially. You must read between the lines to see how glad I am to be here with you." It was an extraordinary statement coming from the military representative of a government that had stamped the passports of these men "Not Valid for Travel to Spain."

In the 15-page report he sent to Washington describing his visit, Fuqua lamented the brigade's deficiencies in equipment—"Blanket issue, one to each man—hardly enough for winter"—and "pitiful" attempts at close-order drill. At the same time, he reported that its "fighting spirit is evidently high. . . . What battle successes these men have attained seemingly have come to them through their strong conviction of the rightness of their cause, of their physical courage, of their personal bravery and through their indomitable spirit."

He had favorable things to say about several Americans, but the one who impressed him most was the chief of staff. "Major Merriman . . . is the backbone and moving spirit of the XV Brigade. . . . He is a fine manly type, over six feet in height, physically sound with the endurance of an ox, pleasing personality, filled with initiative, overflowing with energy, he moves about everywhere in the command honored and respected by all, he is unquestionably the domina[n]t figure in the brigade."

Before he departed, Fuqua made Merriman a present of a leather jacket that he had worn in the First World War. Unmentioned in his report is something else the colonel did at this moment when there was a strict embargo on delivering American arms of any kind to Spain. He quietly left the Lincoln-Washington Battalion a box containing some US Army manuals—and, hidden beneath them, two pistols.

Fuqua's present of pistols may have momentarily cheered the Lincolns, but another American, Torkild Rieber, was giving Franco a vastly greater gift: an unstinting stream of Texaco oil. The American press continued to ignore the story. For correspondents in Spain, discovering the details would have required more dogged and less glamorous reporting than making day trips to the front in a car full of colleagues. And in the United States, although journalists sometimes wrote about "Cap" Rieber's opening of new oil fields and colorful accounts of his seafaring past, his supply line of Texas oil on credit to Nationalist Spain went unnoticed. Virtually the only mention throughout the war appeared in the newspaper of the "Wobblies"—the venerable radical group the Industrial Workers of the World—whose editor was apparently tipped off by a sailor on one of Rieber's tankers. Not a word on the subject appeared in the *New York Times* or any other major American daily.

Ironically, the one mainstream reporter who almost certainly knew the whole story never wrote about it. This was William P. Carney, the *Times*'s man in Nationalist Spain. Referring to Carney as "a good friend of mine," Rieber's Paris associate William M. Brewster wrote to the head of the Nationalist oil monopoly asking if he or José Antonio Álvarez Alonso—the young official there who so admired Rieber—would invite Carney to lunch or dinner, saying of Carney that "of all newspaper correspondents he has done so far the most effective propaganda for the cause in the American Press." The men clearly trusted Carney to keep quiet about Texaco's central role in Franco's war effort, and he did, not once mentioning the company in his stories.

No reporter ever learned of some astonishing additional help the company gave Franco. The US government knew that Texaco's lifeline of oil was being shipped, in violation of the American neutrality law, in the company's own fleet of oceangoing tankers, one of the largest in the business. But decades later, in the archives of the Nationalist oil monopoly, a Spanish scholar who had worked for some years as a petrochemical engineer, Guillem Martínez Molinos, discovered something more. Rieber did not charge for this service. The oil was priced as if Franco were transporting it in his own ships. Not only did Washington know nothing of this large hidden subsidy to

Toby Jensky (left) and Pat Gurney,
a British-American romance in the midst of war.

Nationalist troops by a bomb crater in Guernica.

Captured Republican militiamen, September 1936.
Such prisoners were often executed.

Hitler and Franco meet.

Republic sympathizer Eleanor Roosevelt and her husband Franklin, who too late declared his embargo on arms to Spain a "grave mistake."

July 1938: a Lincoln volunteer gets a haircut just before the Battle of the Ebro.

Vincent Usera (in striped suit), suspected US military intelligence agent, under watch en route to Spain by Lincoln volunteer Saul Wellman.

A victim of the aerial bombing of Madrid.

Teruel, the coldest battle of the war.

Republican troops advance through the city's ruined buildings.

Celebrated and celebrating. Ernest Hemingway in newly captured Teruel, with XV International Brigade chief of operations Malcolm Dunbar (left), Herbert Matthews (in beret), and Republican General Enrique Líster (right).

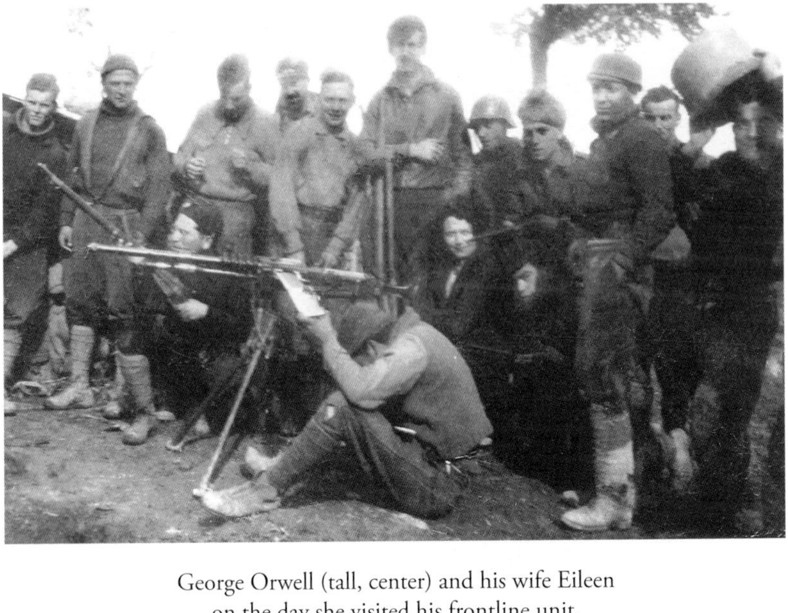

George Orwell (tall, center) and his wife Eileen on the day she visited his frontline unit.

Two eloquent witnesses to the fighting of 1938: James Neugass (shaving) and Alvah Bessie.

The last, desperate push against the Nationalists: Republican troops cross the Ebro.

War's end. Half a million Republican refugees
stream across the Pyrenees into France.

the Nationalists, but neither did Texaco's shareholders, for no mention of it appears in the company's annual reports. Nor, as far as we can tell, did Rieber bother to inform his board of directors, for it is not recorded in the minutes of their meetings.

The corporation made a further remarkable gift to Franco, Martínez has found. Commanders directing the bombers, surface ships, and attack submarines of Franco and his German and Italian allies were always well informed. Tankers carrying oil to the Republic were one of their prime targets: during the war at least 29 of them were attacked, damaged, sunk, or captured. The risk was so high that in the summer of 1937 insurance rates for tankers in the Mediterranean abruptly quadrupled. Something that may have helped make these waters so dangerous, it turns out, is that the Nationalists had the aid of an international maritime intelligence network. It belonged to Texaco.

The oil company had offices, installations, and sales agents across the world. Quietly, thanks to Rieber, orders went out to them. From port cities came cables to the Texaco office in Paris providing details about oil tankers headed for the Republic. From Paris, Rieber's associate Brewster coordinated this flow of intelligence, passing on to the Nationalists information he received from London, Istanbul, Marseille, and elsewhere. Some of Brewster's messages listed what quantity of oil, gasoline, or diesel fuel a tanker was carrying and how much the Republicans had paid for it—strategic intelligence useful for assessing Republican oil supplies and finances. But whenever he could, he delighted in relaying information that could be used by a bomber pilot or submarine captain looking for targets.

Take, for example, a letter Brewster wrote on July 2, 1937, to José Arvilla Hernandez, the head of the Nationalist oil monopoly in Burgos, Franco's capital, about a Republican tanker observed at a French port near Bordeaux:

> *My dear friend:*
>
> *. . . this will confirm that the s/s "CAMPOAMOR" arrived at Le Verdon on May 9th at 7 a.m. fully loaded with a cargo of gasoline . . .*

> *this, you will remember, I had already advised you of. The captain is Julio Pineda . . .*
>
> *Twice since her arrival, the s/s "CAMPOAMOR" has put to sea, but each time she has returned to Le Verdon without touching at any port. Her name and port of registry have been painted out and no new name substituted, while her hull and funnel are now painted black. She is lying at anchor in Le Verdon roads, but a few days ago she came alongside the quay and took on board a large store of food supplies, which seems to indicate an early departure. . . . [The ship] is actually expected to sail in a few days using the British flag.*
>
> *I felt it was extremely urgent to get this information to you as soon as possible and have to-day sent you a telegram endeavouring to give you the gist. . . .*
>
> *. . . the moment the vessel puts to sea I will telegraph you urgently.*
>
> *Have you no one you could send up to work on Pineda as it would seem that he is a very half-hearted Red and, perhaps, with a little persuasion he might be induced to deliberately give himself up with his ship.*

With his letter Brewster included a report in French from his man on the docks at Le Verdon with more detail, including the license number of a car from Republican Spain seen coming from the waterfront. That the *Campoamor* had twice left its anchorage and then returned without unloading, we know now from naval records, is due to Nationalist ships and submarines patrolling the coast off Santander—then still in Republican hands—where the tanker was supposed to deliver its cargo of 10,000 tons of aviation fuel. Indeed, in one attempt to reach Santander, only the cover of darkness had enabled the *Campoamor* to escape a Nationalist cruiser. The information about its repainting and reflagging would have been highly valuable to Nationalist naval commanders.

As it happened, they did not need to put it to use. More important was Brewster's belief that the *Campoamor*'s captain might be persuaded to join the Nationalist cause—and word he included from his French agent that in Le Verdon much of the crew left the ship "almost every evening." We do not know if the Nationalists had other sources of intelligence that may have confirmed what they heard from Texaco, but these last two pieces of information proved crucial. Four days after Brewster's letter and telegram, with many of the crew attending a dance onshore, the *Campoamor*, still at anchor, was boarded near midnight by an armed Nationalist raiding party. With the aid of the ship's captain, the raiders quickly sailed it to a port held by Franco.

The United States might be neutral, but Texaco had gone to war.

15

"In My Book You'll Be an American"

In some places, like the outskirts of Madrid, the front in this war resembled the fixed, opposing rows of trenches that Europe had come to know so well from 1914 to 1918. Elsewhere, however, the dividing line between Republican and Nationalist forces snaked through mountainous, thinly populated terrain. In such places the front line was ragged and porous, and many Republican guerrilla bands staged raids across it into Nationalist territory. By the summer of 1937, some 1,600 men had been taught guerrilla tactics by Soviet trainers in half a dozen camps.

One guerrilla unit was headed by Antoni Chrost, a Polish Communist of working-class origins who had been among the first foreign volunteers to reach Spain. His base was the village of Alfambra, midway between Madrid and Barcelona. A mountain range separated Alfambra from a long salient of Nationalist territory that pointed like a dagger into the Republican zone. Inside this strip of land lay a road and railway line that reached the provincial capital of Teruel, at the dagger's tip. These important supply routes, only 15 miles across the mountains from Alfambra, were a target for Chrost's guerrilla raids.

One day, according to Chrost, he arrived at his headquarters to find a stranger chatting with a political commissar. Tall, burly, and mustachioed, the visitor seemed to enjoy displaying his repertoire of Spanish curses. "*Me cago en la leche de la madre que te parió* [I shit in the milk of the mother who bore you]," he was saying jovially when Chrost asked for his identification. The newcomer promptly produced the proper safe-conduct document from a high army command. It asked that the bearer—whose name Chrost did not recognize—be given any help he needed. The visitor then proceeded to ask a stream of questions about how the guerrillas operated. Who, for instance, guided them through and behind Nationalist lines?

"These guides are recruited from the region where the action will occur," Chrost explained. "They know every road, every path. . . . When the action is close to the lines, we use only one. When it is farther away, we use many. . . . Guerrillas call them living compasses."

"I'm hungry as a dog!" the stranger interrupted, smelling a meal in preparation. The two men continued talking over dinner, which ended with his offering to introduce Chrost to a girl he knew in Valencia. Chrost declined, and his guest bid him goodbye, saying, "*Salud*, you distrustful fellow."

Some six weeks later, Chrost says, the visitor returned, with two officers from the army corps that controlled Chrost's unit and with official permission to participate in a guerrilla raid—specifying that during it he would be under Chrost's command. The objective on this one-night foray was to blow up a train as it crossed a bridge on the line to Teruel.

The night of the raid provided more than 12½ hours of mostly moonless darkness, sufficient time to get across the mountains to the railway and most of the way back. The men divided up the supplies they would carry and the visitor was assigned his share, lighter than those of the others: food, a revolver, hand grenades. The group headed off cautiously into the darkness and finally located the railway bridge they were to blow up, hiding first in some willow bushes and then in a culvert. Smoke and sparks visible down the track announced the train's approach. When it reached the bridge, where the men had set their dynamite, the explosion went off as planned, destroying some of the cars completely.

After a rapid return trek across the mountains, the guerrillas reached Alfambra. Chrost ordered all of them, including the visitor—who at first objected grumpily—to soak their feet in warm salt water, a Polish folk remedy said to reduce blisters. Then they sat down for a celebratory feast of roast lamb and wine. For the first time, Chrost recalled, his enigmatic guest asked Chrost about himself: was he a Russian?

"No, a Pole," Chrost said.

"But in my book," the man replied, "you'll be an American."

The stranger, of course, was Ernest Hemingway. Like many novelists, he rarely spoke of the research—sometimes surprisingly extensive—that lay behind his fiction. Both Martha Gellhorn and Herbert Matthews were with him on his first trip to Alfambra, in September 1937; Gellhorn noted the stop in her diary. Hemingway, however, never wrote or publicly said anything about the second visit. (We know from other witnesses that he also spent a day that autumn observing guerrillas being trained at a base not far from Alfambra.) Gellhorn made no diary entries during the week of the writer's foray behind the lines and, if she knew about it, never revealed it. Chrost did not tell his side of the story until 20 years later. Hence readers did not know that the central episode in the novel that would appear three years after that nighttime raid, *For Whom the Bell Tolls*, was based on more than the novelist's imagination.

Throughout 1937, news reached hundreds of Americans about loved ones killed or wounded in Spain. For some, however, there was no word. In New York, Phil Schachter's family had heard nothing since his letters in the midst of the bloody fighting at Brunete. Some weeks after that battle, Toby Jensky, who was receiving anxious queries, wrote to her sister from Villa Paz: "Now for Phil and his pop—if you can, impress upon him the fact that not getting letters from here doesn't mean a thing—very often all our mail is held up for a few weeks, especially when troops are being transported—then they use every train, truck and what not."

But to the family back home, Jensky's assurances began to sound hollow. "I am trying desperately to get some information regarding my brother," Max Schachter wrote to an official at the International Brigades base at Albacete. "It is now 13 weeks since we have heard from him. . . . My family is frantic with worry and definite word of him would be a Godsend. . . . Let us hear from you as soon as humanly possible."

Finally Jensky was able to communicate frankly to her sister Ida, Max's wife: "I am writing this with the permission of the political commissar. Phil disappeared last July 24. I heard about it at the time from his commander—Walter Garland [a black US military veteran from Brooklyn, Garland was a patient at Villa Paz after being wounded at Brunete]. . . . To date nothing has been heard from or about him. . . . So far I must have spoken to about 75 people who were near him on that day or who saw him earlier but their stories are all the same. He was sent on an errand and was never heard of since. I don't know what the papers wrote about the battle at Brunete—but it was a pretty tough and chaotic time. . . . I am still doing all I can to get hold of any news. . . . I didn't write about this before because I kept hoping every day that I would hear something more definite. . . . I realize that this is inadequate and not much help—but it is all that anyone knows."

One of the letters Jensky received must have asked if Phil had been taken prisoner, because she added: "Whoever started the rumor about him being captured must have been dreaming. . . . There is no record of it."

In August 1937, the Vatican joined Italy and Germany in officially recognizing Franco's regime as the legitimate government of Spain. The Republic continued to suffer military setbacks, and October brought more grim news: the last remaining section of the country's north coast had fallen to Franco.

Nearly two thirds of Spain's industry and most of its agricultural and mineral wealth were now in Nationalist hands, including the coal fields of Asturias and the important munitions plants, iron mines, and steel mills of the Basque country. The Republic still held a large swath of eastern and central Spain, including the biggest cities—Madrid, Barcelona, and Valencia—but factories in them were largely cut off from their traditional sources of raw materials. The flow of foreign military supplies to the two Spains had long been in favor of the Nationalists, and now the balance of industry and natural resources was tilting strongly their way as well.

With the war news increasingly somber, Bob Merriman was acutely aware of the envy among his men that Marion was in the country and often with him. Other American volunteers, wrote the Merrimans' British friend Kate Mangan in the Republic's press office, felt that it was "very unfair for Bob to have his wife in Spain when the rest of them could not."

Some months earlier, the Merrimans had spent a rare few days of leave in Valencia, its palm-shaded streets and Mediterranean breezes a refuge from the harsher landscape of the interior. "Marion," Mangan remembered, "though a tall girl, looked frail and small by comparison as he was very tall." On the first night, Marion said "she had a presentiment that Bob would be killed and she desperately wanted to have a baby so that she would have something left to her."

On the second day of their brief leave, the Merrimans went to the beach with Mangan and several others. "When we were all on the beach Bob presented Marion with a cardboard box he had been carrying. It contained an embroidered Spanish shawl of yellow silk, a very handsome thing. They both stood up and he wrapped it round her to see how it looked and the fringe fluttered in the wind. Marion flung her arms round him. It was the anniversary of their wedding day. They had been married five years. They were so spontaneous, happy and fond of one another, and looked so young and handsome."

They all lay on the sand and watched the approach of a cargo ship with white sails.

"It shouldn't be like that," said Bob.

"What shouldn't be?"

"Oh, the sun and the blue sky and the green waves, and then that

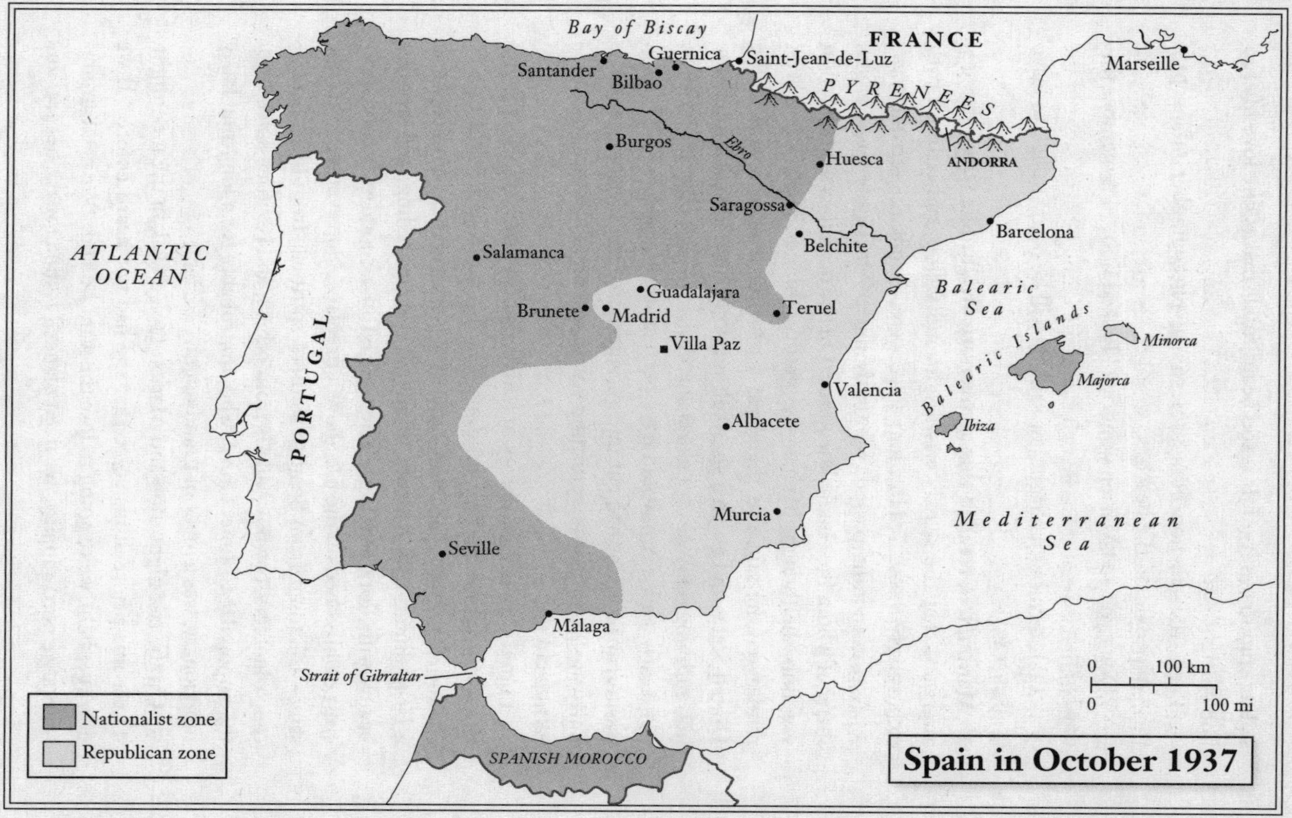
Spain in October 1937
Nationalist zone
Republican zone
Bay of Biscay
FRANCE
Marseille
Guernica
Saint-Jean-de-Luz
Santander
Bilbao
PYRENEES
Burgos
Ebro
Huesca
ANDORRA
Saragossa
Barcelona
Belchite
ATLANTIC
OCEAN
Salamanca
Guadalajara
Balearic
Sea
Brunete
Madrid
Teruel
PORTUGAL
Villa Paz
Balearic Islands
Minorca
Majorca
Valencia
Ibiza
Albacete
Murcia
Mediterranean
Sea
Seville
Málaga
Strait of Gibraltar
SPANISH MOROCCO
0
100 km
0
100 mi

sailing ship to top it off. It is too beautiful. It makes one love life too much."

Then Mangan noticed a professional photographer taking pictures of people on the beach:

"'Don't you and Marion want one,' I asked Bob, 'to remember this day by?'

"'I'll remember it alright,' he said. 'It will be hard enough to leave it all as it is.'"

Marion, too, recalled this anniversary vividly. She wrote decades afterward that the shawl "was bright and yellow and covered with rich, velvety roses. . . . How happy we were, despite the terrible war."

As the months passed, hundreds more Americans were killed, many of whom the couple knew well. On the occasions when Marion saw Bob, she thought his hair was getting thinner. During one brief rendezvous, he said that there was a plan for her "to return to the United States and go on a six-week speaking tour." At such moments her autobiography always skirts mention of the Communist Party, but clearly such a trip would have been at its orders. Franco's relentless territorial gains had cut into recruiting for the Lincolns, and the Party was putting some returning volunteers on the lecture and fundraising circuit.

In mid-November, she spent a final few days with Bob, in the XV Brigade's new temporary headquarters in an old grain mill east of Madrid. Its owner had built himself a grand home, complete with a large dining hall, frescoes of animals on the ceiling, and wooden beams with floral carvings. They stayed in a room with the family crest emblazoned on the tile above a fireplace. One evening everyone sang—folksongs from Spanish soldiers, spirituals from black American volunteers, cowboy ballads from others, and baritone solos from the unpopular Colonel Copic, who, improbably for a longtime Party functionary, was a lover of grand opera.

On the last night, Bob and Marion took a walk in the moonlight. There was a note in his voice that she had not heard before: "If we don't get help, we're going to lose the war," he said. "We need ammunition, we need supplies, we need planes." It didn't make her feel any better when he added, "I want you to promise me one thing. If I'm killed, you'll marry again." He turned her wedding ring round and round on her finger, a familiar gesture between them, and then gave her the two leather-bound pocket diaries, each page printed with the Spanish name of the saint whose day it was, in which he had been jotting in microscopic handwriting since he arrived in Spain. They had one last night together, and then an army car was waiting for her next to the mill. She wept, and was on her way.

The train she took from the French border to Paris was filled with drunken wounded Americans, relieved to be out of the war at last. On the ship across the Atlantic she found Louis Fischer—unlike her, he was traveling in first class—"and we spent many hours discussing the war." He, too, was on his way to lecture and lobby for the Republic, and, as always, had plenty of advice, suggesting what Marion could say on her speaking tour. She began practicing every day in front of the mirror in her cabin.

When they landed in New York a few days before Christmas, "word apparently had spread that the wife of the American commander was en route; a small gathering greeted me at the pier with questions. Had I seen a husband, a father, a brother, a boyfriend? . . . I had so little to offer. It broke my heart to look into the eyes of a young woman and say, no." One man at the pier asked, "How did my son die?" Marion knew the volunteer had been shot as a deserter but replied, "Like a soldier." The Friends of the Lincoln Brigade set up a busy round of interviews with reporters, who were happy to write favorable profiles of the twenty-eight-year-old, good-looking wife of a wounded American battle hero who had stayed in Spain to fight on. The main message she had for them, however, was one she no longer fully believed: that Franco would be defeated.

Then, suddenly, it seemed that he might be. "Just when the whole world knew the fascists planned an attack we staged a fine one ourselves," Bob wrote Marion jubilantly from Spain. "Furthermore, it is the first one we have completed just as we planned it. Teruel is our Christmas present to all the anti-fascists of the world."

Begun in mid-December 1937, the battle was a damaging blow to the Nationalists, distracting Franco from his prolonged attempt to encircle and capture Madrid. In high mountain country, surrounded by bleak rocky peaks and ravines, the ancient walled city of Teruel lay at the end of the Nationalist salient whose railway line Hemingway had helped sabotage. The city itself had been the site of the kind of atrocities that took place whenever the Nationalists captured new territory and flaunted their power. In one case, 13 people judged subversive, including a twenty-year-old woman and the director of a teacher training college—teachers were always suspect—were shot in Teruel's central square, after which people danced to band music in the victims' blood.

The local bishop, Anselmo Polanco, objected—but only to the dancing. Otherwise, he was a fierce backer of the Nationalist cause and apparently gave permission for Franco's troops to shoot two of his priests considered too friendly to the Republic. In August, from the balcony of his palace he had reviewed a parade by a battalion of Foreign Legionnaires who passed by carrying the noses, ears, and other body parts of murdered Republican prisoners speared on their bayonets. As an object of public humiliation, one prisoner had been left alive and forced to parade carrying a heavy load and wearing an ox's yoke, as if he were a pack animal.

At an altitude of 3,000 feet, Teruel was known for its near-arctic winters. One December day recorded the century's lowest temperature for this region. Both armies suffered miserably. Pipes froze and men had to light fires to melt snow for water. On the Nationalist side, a single division reported 3,500 frostbite cases. A four-day blizzard left behind a new layer of snow. Nonetheless, Republican forces launched a successful surprise attack, occupying most of Teruel, although their advance was slowed as hungry troops, blankets wrapped around their heads and upper bodies against the cold, stopped to loot food supplies along the way. They had a temporary advantage: the terrible weather had grounded the Condor Legion. Although street fighting in the frozen city still raged, the attack made headlines around the globe. For the first time, the Republic was on its way to capturing a provincial capital, a triumph that would be complete by early January. Hemingway, Herbert Matthews, and the photographer Robert Capa all rushed to cover the story. With the Republic's red, yellow, and purple flag flying over the town, Hemingway declared it "the biggest upset expert opinion has received since Max Schmeling knocked out Joe Louis."

Matthews, in the more restrained language of the *New York Times*, called Teruel's capture "a surprising and dramatic development . . . carried out with complete surprise and so far with equal success." In a later memoir, unconstrained by *Times* prose, he referred to it as "one of the most thrilling days of my life." The cold, he wrote, was overwhelming: "Nothing is protection against those icy blasts that come shrieking down from the north, penetrating any amount of clothes. Your eyes fill with constant tears from the sting of it; your fingers swell and become numb and all feeling goes out of your feet except an overwhelming iciness; you gasp for breath and cannot stand in one spot . . . for the wind buffets you like a fighter boring in."

Hemingway's dispatches were one more arena for his public performance as a warrior-writer, and he always liked to show off how close to the action he was. At Teruel, "the soldier I was lying next to was having trouble with his rifle. It jammed after every shot and I showed him how to knock the bolt open with a rock. Then suddenly we heard cheering run along the line and across the next ridge we could see the Fascists running from their first line." A Capa photograph captured the moment, showing Hemingway, hatless and with glasses, lying on the ground next to the helmeted Republican infantryman. In his enthusiasm for combat, the novelist was sending the North American Newspaper Alliance more stories than they wanted. "Had most godwonderful housetohouse fighting story ready to put on wire," he complained bitterly in a letter to his first wife, Hadley Mowrer, "when Nana cabled they didn't want anymore."

The battle, he said in a dispatch that did make it into print, "may be the decisive one of this war." Although she was no less sympathetic to the Republican cause, the young Virginia Cowles would prove wiser on this score. Not at all swept away by the fall of Te-

Spain in … as a wh…
ruel, while the battle still raged she wrote about the war … that there seemed "little hope" of a victory by the Republican army, which was "a poor match for Franco's trained forces."

The struggle for Teruel ignited another round of internal warfare at the *New York Times*. On December 31, 1937, William P. Carney, well behind Nationalist lines, filed an upbeat report claiming that a massive counteroffensive had recaptured the city: "Smashing through the entire fifteen-mile-front established by the government west and north of Teruel only sixteen days ago, General Francisco Franco's 'relief army' this afternoon entered the besieged town."

"The Times retook the town for Franco," Hemingway raged. Matthews, who had just been in Teruel, was furious. He knew that Carney was relying only on Franco's press releases. His anger was all the greater because Hemingway, who had just left Spain, told him by telephone from Paris, where the *Times* was available, that the paper was shortening the lengthy dispatches he was sending them. Though it meant a long journey from Valencia, Matthews immediately returned to the embattled city and sent the newspaper a story that would make the front page, headlined "Teruel Still Held by Loyalist Army, Visit There Shows."

"From your correspondent's inquiry on the spot yesterday, it seems certain that the Rebels [Nationalists] never reached the city . . . and in short never really menaced the provincial capital, which remains firmly in Government hands." In the same story, in a blatant dig at the unnamed Carney, he declared, "It has been axiomatic in this war that nothing can be learned with certainty unless one goes to the spot and sees with his own eyes."

As the year ended, a mobile team from the American hospital at Villa Paz was sent into the field. Toby Jensky wrote her sister and brother-in-law, "We're off to the front. . . . Up mountains and down only to climb others. . . . A large ambulance, 1 small one & a station wagon. The trucks left a day before." They drove past the windmills of Don Quixote's La Mancha country while warplanes cruised overhead, then moved on, Jensky sleeping on a stretcher in the ambulance. "Seemed I had slept through 2 flats, and the chauffeur was now working on his third." Then came another move to "this little town," which could not be named in her letter for security reasons, but Jensky gave a hint of which front the mobile hospital was serving: "By now you've probably read of the great victory of our army at Teruel."

PART IV

16

"A Letter to My *Novia*"

In the battered remains of a barracks in snow-covered Teruel one frigid night in mid-January 1938, a tall, broad-shouldered, thirty-two-year-old American with a high forehead, prominent nose, and face that wrinkled easily into a smile sat writing by firelight. The zippered binding of his leather notebook intrigued several Spanish soldiers. When they asked what he was composing, he said, "A letter to my *novia*." But it was not a letter to his fiancée; it was a diary.

An ambulance driver in the same mobile American medical team as Toby Jensky, James Neugass, like so many American volunteers, was Jewish, but there the similarities stopped. He was from a long-established clan in New Orleans, where his family were bankers and philanthropists; a grandfather had been president of the city's stock exchange. His education included stints at Harvard, Yale, and Oxford, but not enough time at any of them to graduate. He would later say, "I got . . . my master's degree at Teruel."

After leaving college, Neugass had been something of a dilettante: traveling widely on family money, publishing poetry in the *Atlantic Monthly* and other magazines, and working as a merchant seaman, reporter, fencing teacher, cook, and social worker. Swept up in the political heat of the 1930s, he joined the Communist Party and was an editor and organizer for several left-wing labor unions, ending up jailed during one strike. His poetry reflected the times and, despite his background, had been included in anthologies with titles like *Proletarian Writers in the United States.* In 1935, addressing his fellow poets, he wrote:

> *Gentlemen, we have spoken about these things before,*
> *Yet in a thousand years there will still be sunsets. . . .*
> *But in the meantime, boys, we have a little job to do.*
> *We have powder to pour, fuses to set, sparks to strike.*

It was neither as a would-be proletarian nor as an activist striking sparks that he wrote in that leather-bound notebook. It was, instead, as a self-deprecating observer with a distinctive sense of irony. Friends knew Jim Neugass had kept a diary in Spain, but for decades it was believed lost. A copy was only discovered more than half a century after his death.

When his unit had been ordered to move to the Teruel front, Neugass—someone who had never "heard a more lethal noise than the backfiring of a car"—seemed amused to find himself in a combat zone. The ambulance he drove, "a long low limousine with the lines and glass windows of a hearse," held two wounded patients on stretchers or nine sitting up, and brought up the rear of a convoy headed by a larger ambulance, which bore the inscription "Donated by the Students and Faculty of Harvard University."

"Hacking night-coughs, jaundice, sores, itches, diarrhea and constipation are the occupational diseases of war in Spain," he noted as they drew closer to Teruel. "Constipation is the least serious of them, since it is often cured by the sight and sound of planes."

Franco's air force continued to dominate the skies, so the medical detachment was careful to show no lights at night. As they rolled through the Spanish countryside, Neugass was struck again and again by the abject poverty, underlining the words in his diary: "What crime did these peasants commit? What is their guilt? Why did their Pope turn against them?"

Quartered one night in the dirt-floored house of a family of 12, he found that all they had to burn for heat and cooking was thorn bushes, "tough little plants the size and shape of coral branches. . . . Every thirty seconds a new thorn bush must be thrown on the flames." The family offered to share their meal with him, but "when I looked at the size of the single earthenware jug in the fireplace, I answered that I had already had supper."

It wasn't merely food the peasants lacked. On another occasion, "as we stopped for gas, a little girl ran up to my car and asked for a newspaper. I had none. Then she asked for 'anything printed.' I finally found a torn three-weeks' old part of a Madrid paper. The little girl was quite contented."

Of the village where the medical unit first set up its mobile hospital he wrote: "I have not yet seen a single gabled roof in Alcorisa. Wood is rare, money scarce, and ridge-poles much too expensive. The average house is built of sun-baked strawed mud or a weakly mortared rubble, with no cement or stucco." Only the Church had fine buildings: "The village convent is an immense, solidly-built structure, not too large for the hospital which now houses, instead of the soft prayers of nuns, the cries of [the] dying. The river-bottom land, best in Alcorisa, also belonged to the church. Off on the hill, in a clump of soaring blue-black cedars, is the former sanctuary which the former bishop used as a summer home."

Neugass kept a wry eye on his comrades. He noted, for instance, the "five-foot, hundred and fifty-pound American pharmacist and laboratory technician, who is said to lose twenty pounds every time she falls in love, and to gain an exactly similar amount whenever the object of her affection gets well and leaves for the Front." A British nurse was known as the "Stowaway Nightingale," because she kept appearing at the front against orders, elegantly attired in beret and high boots, in search of her boyfriend.

"I have seen Bob Merriman a good deal," he wrote. "He has the

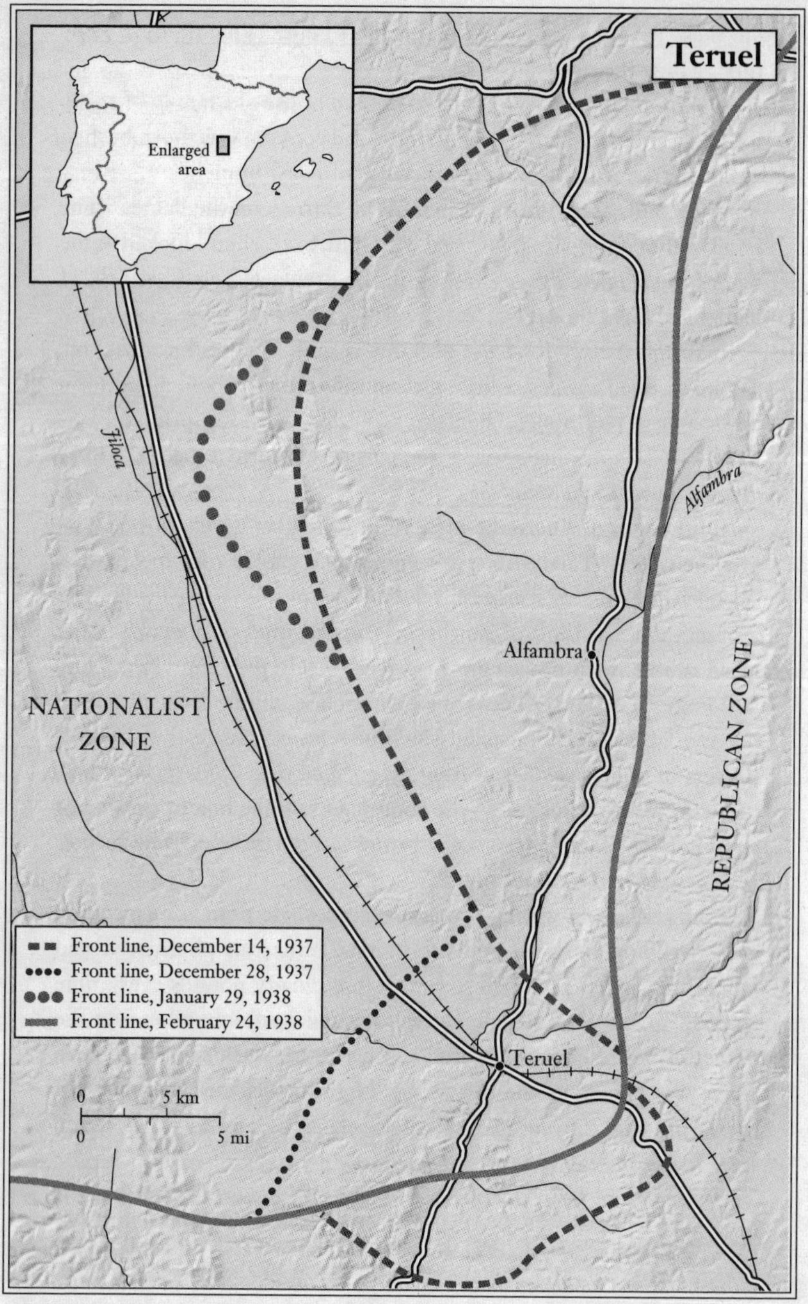
Teruel
Enlarged area
Jiloca
Alfambra
Alfambra
NATIONALIST ZONE
REPUBLICAN ZONE
Teruel
Front line, December 14, 1937
Front line, December 28, 1937
Front line, January 29, 1938
Front line, February 24, 1938
0 5 km
0 5 mi

physique of an Oregon crew-man. Pale gray eyes flash through horn-rims. He is perpetually agitated but never nervous. Everything and everyone interests him. He has a way of infecting the entire brigade with his almost too boyish charisma." Others often remarked on Merriman's charisma; only Neugass's "too" captures the Boy Scout quality that went with it.

A prime enemy was Teruel's legendary cold. Without antifreeze, drivers like Neugass were given orders "for every radiator to be drained no later than ten o'clock each evening. . . . I open my valves, run my engine until dashboard thermometer shows 200, and shut off engine. . . . In the morning, icicles have to be chipped off the butterfly nuts before valves can be closed.

"We break the ice in the river before we can brush our teeth. . . . The hands of the girls and women who wash laundry . . . in the river are blue as turkey feet and almost as hard and gnarled. . . . Little charcoal remains for the braziers which for centuries have been the town's sources of heat." The presence of so many soldiers had exhausted the already scant supply of fuel. "All but the top branches of the former Bishop's incredible cedars have disappeared into the village fireplaces."

Normal sleeping quarters were scarce, and American volunteers often had to make do with floors, stretchers, and tables. If beds were available, they sometimes held two or three men. At one point Neugass found himself about to share a bed with Arnold Donowa, his unit's oral surgeon. The first dean of the Howard University dental school, Donowa was born in Trinidad. "For a century my family has had its laundry done by negroes, and its cooking. Negro women have taken care of the men's overflow sexual desires and the children they had with their wives," Neugass wrote in his diary. "This was the first time I had shared a room, much less a bed, with a negro. My grandfather had been a slaveholder. Two ancestors had fought with the Confederates. The eyes of three generations of New Orleans private bankers and their women were on me as I stood in the room with D. He sensed this but made no comment."

• • •

A drive by Franco's troops to reverse the humiliating loss of Teruel hammered on through January and February 1938. Republican soldiers continued to hold the city, even though snow clogged their trenches and blizzards frequently stopped their supply convoys. On cloudless days German and Italian planes so dominated the air that fighter pilots would taunt Teruel's defenders by skywriting the Nationalist yoke-and-arrows symbol. This aerial armada dropped incendiaries to set the city's wooden buildings on fire, and Nationalist artillery on nearby hills fired shells timed to burst just above the ground, hurling fragments at the Republican soldiers huddled in ruins, ditches, and trenches. They could hear the hot metal hissing into snowbanks on all sides. Dead mules and burnt-out trucks littered the roads. Americans and Canadians of the Mackenzie-Papineau Battalion were stationed on a ridge of chalk, which the incessant Nationalist artillery barrage pulverized into white dust that clogged their throats and jammed their machine guns.

The medical unit had little respite. Neugass, constantly on the road, watched truckloads of fresh soldiers heading for the embattled city. "Wonder how the troops who pass us feel about seeing ambulances," he wrote. "Something like seeing an undertaker's on your way to the hospital." The temperature fell to −18° F. Nonetheless, engines boiled away their water as ambulances roared up steep mountain roads in low gear, wheels spinning in the snow. Frustrated drivers tried to jam snow into their radiators. Neugass stole a pitcher to hold extra water, but liquid sloshing from it mixed with the blood on the floor of his ambulance and froze into something that looked like raspberry sherbet. The vehicles, so essential to the mobile unit, were looked after as carefully as patients. "We came to regard our cars as Cossacks regard their horses. . . . Spare parts were almost unknown; spare tires more precious than gold," wrote Neugass's commander, the New York surgeon Dr. Edward Barsky, who had treated Bob Merriman's shattered shoulder after Jarama and hundreds more International Brigades soldiers since then. He added, "We had plenty of money. It can be very useless stuff."

Neugass doubled as Barsky's driver. The surgeon, who seemed to live on nothing but bread and cigarettes, had a sardonic edge, but the pair got along well. Traveling to Teruel in the first place had been an ordeal. After driving one entire night, Neugass could stay awake no longer. "I handed the wheel over to the Major. 'I'm a surgeon and he's supposed to be a driver,' I heard him say, as my eyelids sank inexorably as the jaws of a hydraulic press. 'I watch the road for him while he drives. Now that I'm doing his work, he has to sleep.'"

An hour later, the blizzard they were in turned into a gale, and they had no tire chains and no windshield wipers. Neugass "got out and walked ahead of my car, to show B. where the road was. Had to stamp hard through the twelve-inch minimum of the drifts so that I could tell, with my heels, the hard surface of the road from the bottomless snow of the ditch. . . . My mustache and hair were stiff as shredded wheat with snow. Have to shave that mustache. No use carrying all that extra weight."

They reached a point where a wrecked truck blocked the highway, and they had to reverse their course. "Nurses and doctors, pushing like tugboats at the sides of an ocean liner, turned our car in her length." After backtracking to a village where they were given some rope made of rawhide—the nearest thing to tire chains—they tried the road again, but soon it became too steep and snowy and their trucks and ambulances bogged down. Neugass was ordered to stay with the vehicles while Barsky, Toby Jensky, and the other medical staff walked seven miles over the mountains to a town, where they were able to trade scarce cigarettes for some bread and persuade the mayor to send men to dig out the convoy.

Things grew worse as the weeks passed. There were no defrosters. "I now wipe ice off the inside of my windshield at night with my bare hand," wrote Neugass. "The glove wore out."

In villages, church bells were the signal for air raids. The unit's operating tables treated those who didn't find shelter in time. "Truckloads of what first looked like snow-covered sacks of wheat pulled up in front of the village hospital. Blood dripped out of the tailboard into the snow. Planes had caught a battalion . . . fifteen miles from Teruel, where they had gone 'on rest.'"

Such experiences and the exhaustion of all-night driving began to wear Neugass down. "The need for sleep . . . dulled the edge of my memory. I know: I ought to be able to recall what I have seen and done. Phrases smooth as oil should roll off the end of my pencil."

When the unit set up camp in a new village, Toby Jensky wrote her sister and brother-in-law, "We heat the place with kerosene stoves, carry water from the center of town and empty bed pans in a ditch. . . . I don't take my clothes off very often these days because it's too cold—just take my boots off and dive under the blankets." Then, in the typically jaunty fashion of her letters, she added, "It's fun taking these shacks . . . with no water or toilets & turning them into hospitals—with operating room and all."

Recording the same new encampment for his diary, without needing to keep an eye on the mail censor, Neugass wrote: "The engine of the shower-truck furnished power for the lights. Two operating tables were going full blast. A door would open, with a vision of silent figures dressed in white, and naked bare skin and the bandaged stumps of arms and legs, rags floating in slop jars of reddish liquid. . . . Why was it that nothing was being done to ease the occasional low whimpers that came from the figures under the blankets? I helped with the stretchers until the Major told me to go back to Mezquita for additional instruments. I would have done anything, so ashamed was I to be unwounded." Meanwhile, Dr. Barsky and another surgeon, dealing with a flood of injured men, operated for 50 hours without sleep.

On such occasions, sometimes nurses would substitute for doctors. One night, nurse Esther Silverstein went to an operating room to borrow an instrument and was startled to find the doctor asleep in a chair and his nurse performing surgery. "She said, 'Shshsh!' And I was very quiet and I said, 'What are you doing?' And she said, 'Oh, I'm just finishing this up, the poor doctor is just so tired.' And I said, 'Do you do this often?' and she said, 'Oh, frequently, but don't tell anybody.'"

Nurses learned not to put instruments near a table's edge, because bomb explosions might jar them to the floor. American doctors, when teamed up with those from other countries, learned to operate together without a language in common. Equipment was scarce; nurses had to sharpen hypodermic needles on stones. Years later, Jensky remembered those weeks: "Bodies coming in & going out. . . . Pandemonium. . . . Along corridors bodies lay. Some were dead; others waiting to go to the operating room. Some dead bodies were stacked up—cordwood style." At one point she leaned out a window when she heard a noise. Someone grabbed her and pulled her back inside, saying, "They are strafing the building, dope." She tried to relax by crocheting and knitting in her time off, at one point making a scarf for Dr. Barsky.

Neugass's diary entries reflected a pride in his driving, in his ambulance (which he referred to as "my sweetheart"), and in the very fact that he was writing every day, sometimes using an empty operating table as a desk. Behind all this was an unspoken satisfaction in leaving his privileged background behind. He always stopped on the highway to trade information with other drivers, and felt that collectively they knew more about the war than anybody. He learned to eat whatever was available—chocolate made with mule fat and dried codfish that tasted like "rawhide soaked in glue then boiled in machine oil"; he learned how to plug a leaky ambulance radiator by pouring in a raw egg—and also jotted down this recipe for using a radiator to cook an egg: "First get the egg. Then wrap it in gauze, drop down radiator of car and race engine, with blanket over hood, until water boils. Egg may be withdrawn by means of gauze."

Most of the time, though, Neugass struck a more somber note. At first he was shocked when he saw a British doctor, Reginald Saxton, using a big syringe to draw blood out of the vein of a Republican soldier who had just been killed. "What do you think you're doing, Saxton?" he asked. The doctor explained, "We're running short on donors." The soldier had been asphyxiated in a Teruel dugout by a shell burst and had died without losing blood, unusual in combat. The doctor would determine the corpse's blood type and then use it for transfusions. (Another XV Brigade doctor, Jacques Grunblatt, once gave his own blood to a patient, a double amputee, when no one else's matched.)

Before long, little surprised Neugass. "My job was to cut off clothing," he wrote. "This must be done because of the danger of infection and because we must find out very quickly all the places where a man has been hit. Very few of the wounded I saw last night or at any other time were hit in only one place. Modern shrapnel breaks into fine metal spray that spreads as efficiently as water over an expensively-groomed lawn. . . . You cannot pull off a man's clothing because this motion, however careful and slight, would grind the broken ends of his bones into his muscle."

After one particularly grueling night of driving and a day of being shelled, an exhausted Neugass went looking for a place to sleep at a time when the unit's operating rooms were sheltered from bombers in a large cave. "Crawled into the deepest end of the Post cave to a stiff blood-stained stretcher. With relief I observed by the light of a candle stuck into the clay wall that both men in the stretchers alongside of me were dead. If they were alive, they would have been making too much noise." On another day he wrote: "You can get used to everything. Two weeks more of this life and I could sleep inside a long dead whale and not notice the smell."

As the weeks went by, the odds were turning ever more grim. "You can be very sure, if no one is in sight," he wrote of the highway to Teruel, "that the avions are on you. More and more and more of them. Flying fields at Berlin and Rome must be empty as a baseball park at night." Watching one dogfight, he kept track as Nationalist aircraft with black X's on their white tails battled Republican fighters with red wingtips. "We lost one plane and They three. This we count a defeat. Tonight Their commander will telegraph Hitler and in twenty-four hours Their three lost planes will be replaced with six brand-new ones. Last night I looted the ignition diagrams from the dashboard of a Fiat [fighter plane] we had knocked down. All the writing on it was in Italian." Attacks by Mussolini's navy had reduced the flow of Soviet aircraft and artillery, including much-needed 75 mm howitzers. "Where are those planes, and acres of 75's?"

On the Teruel front, as at Jarama, VIPs paid lightning visits. Neugass had little use for them: "Literary men, visiting members of

Parliament, trade union leaders and lady novelists in search of a story for *The New Yorker* run through the bowels of the Front . . . like a dose of Epsom salts. . . . They arrive, ask a few questions, look up at the sky, then jump back into their cars." About only one visiting journalist did he feel differently: "We love Herbert Matthews . . . as much as we hate Carney. A few hours ago he brought us a carton of cigarettes and a bottle of whiskey. We drank half and sent the rest to Merriman."

Most of the Americans involved survived the combat in Teruel, but the Republican army suffered heavy casualties while trying to hold the city. Supplies were short and clothing in tatters. Neugass had to mend the toes of his shoes with adhesive tape. One night he watched soldiers from the British battalion head for positions in the frontline trenches: "The English . . . came up the road in the moonlight. Too tired to swear, the men were wordless. The torn blankets over heads and shoulders and tied like skirts around the waist, the shoes wrapped with rags, the rifles on their shoulders gave them the appearance of a battalion of women beggars. Ranks of stretcher-bearers with eight-foot spearlike poles added to the Biblical quality of the scene."

In the other direction flowed a sometimes overwhelming stream of wounded. Toby Jensky had no more hairpins for the dark tresses that had so attracted Pat Gurney, so she had to braid her hair and tie the end with a bandage. In one place the medical unit was stationed, a group of sheep sheds, Dr. Barsky ordered sheets "nailed to the walls and the ceiling," wrote Neugass. "These linens will keep dirt from falling onto the operating table when we are bombed."

Although the drained Neugass kept writing in his diary, question marks began appearing next to dates. To escape bombing, ambulance runs took place only at night, without headlights, while enemy tracer bullets made showers of sparks in the sky. At one point, leaving Teruel, he feared he had chosen the wrong road, one that could take him into Nationalist territory. After turning his ambulance around, readying himself to step on the gas for a quick getaway, he took the risk of hailing several men sitting by a fire 200 yards away, whose uniforms he could not see in the dark. When the answer came back, "*¿Qué quieres tú?*" he relaxed, knowing they were Republicans. "If I had been answered '*Usted*' instead of '*Tú*,' I should have been speaking to fascists."

Increasingly he was worn down by the daily evidence of the battle's toll: "the human leg which had somehow gotten into the garbage pail in the kitchen," the howling of civilian mental patients who could not be evacuated because their hospital was now in no-man's-land, and the impossible choices that seemed to face him at all times. "Driving a belly case faster than twelve miles an hour over the best road in Spain will kill him, but if you do not run fast enough to get away from the planes, he will be killed anyway and take yourself and your car with him. . . . Ether poured into a dying man is ether wasted but we cannot let our men die without helping them up to the last moment and with our last material."

The air raids became worse. At one point, 15 trimotor Nationalist planes bombed a town where the mobile American hospital had set up. Shrapnel hit the building, and wounded men pulled blankets over their heads in case windows shattered. Jensky and another ward nurse stayed with the patients but dove beneath beds. Dr. Barsky and his operating room team were in midsurgery and did not stop. "'Get out of here, Jim,' said the Major to me, 'you are not on duty. Beat it before They come back.'"

A few minutes later, Neugass and four other drivers—*chóferes*—heard the roar of the next wave of approaching bombers. He jumped into a dugout; the others ran to a house "where they could be protected from everything but a direct hit."

The house took a direct hit. Neugass spent half an hour digging in the ruins. "Eventually we loaded enough arms and legs and torsos on a stretcher to establish the names of the four chóferes and the fact that they were all dead. No one has ever been more dead." The blast completely beheaded one driver, who had worked behind the counter at a Childs restaurant in New York City.

Jim Neugass's diary says little about politics, yet he was fully aware that Spain's fate was being decided elsewhere: "Washington, London and Paris are the real battlefields, not Teruel."

Everyone understood this, and the American volunteers all hoped that even if events in Spain were not dire enough to spur Washington to sell arms to the Republic, what was happening elsewhere in Europe might be. In February 1938, in a last-ditch attempt to forestall a threatened German invasion of his country, Chancellor Kurt Schuschnigg of Austria went to meet Hitler at Berchtesgaden, the Führer's Bavarian mountaintop chalet. Hitler had at his side Hugo Sperrle, the former commander of the Condor Legion, and asked him to describe the effects of his bombers in Spain. "Do you want to make another Spain out of Austria?" Hitler asked Schuschnigg. On February 20, escalating the pressure on the country, Hitler grandiosely promised "protection" to ethnic Germans living outside the Reich.

"Tired of explaining to good admirable ignorant seemingly sleepy people about Fascism & democracy," Martha Gellhorn wrote to Eleanor Roosevelt from a monthlong American lecture tour. "Hate our foreign policy, why is it like that? Please tell me. Love, Marty." But Mrs. Roosevelt had no good answer, and even when writing in private to her beloved protégée, she was careful never to directly criticize her husband's actions.

On February 24, Louis Fischer, now more of a lobbyist for Republican Spain than a journalist, spent an hour with the first lady at the White House. "Please don't tell me about Spain," she said. "Martha Gellhorn has already talked to me about it." But he doggedly described air raids he had seen and argued for ending the arms embargo. Fischer's pleas were all the more desperate because he was in a position to know how sharply the flow of Soviet arms to the Republic was diminishing. They had tea and then "as I stood up to go, she promised to tell the President what I had said." In a grim article Fischer published that same week, for once bereft of his usual name-dropping, he underlined the impact of American neutrality: "We take sides by doing nothing."

At the front, most of the American medical team was once again ordered to move—a bad sign. Neugass soon found himself driving his ambulance over the same road on which he had been caught in the blizzard nearly two months before. "All towns along the way have now been bombed. House where I slept New Year's night in Aliaga was down on its knees. . . . Rubble drools from the doorway mouths of the village hearths. Clods and stones lie blown across the streets," he wrote by candlelight in an abandoned hospital ward, periodically feeding a fire with pieces of broken chairs. "Something has gone very very wrong. Don't know what it is, yet, but I think it must have been Teruel."

Two days later, the unit set up operations at a mountain farm, only to be overwhelmed with a cascade of maimed men. There was no fuel for the sterilizers, and Neugass had to boil surgical instruments over a fire of sticks. "Don't feel well today," he jotted after 36 hours of driving and unloading beds, mattresses, stretchers, and other equipment. "No energy. Battery is running low." And then he added the news they all knew was coming: "Teruel is Theirs."

17

"Only a Few Grains of Sand Left in the Hourglass"

HERBERT MATTHEWS WAS getting a shave in the barbershop of the Hotel Majestic, the base for foreign correspondents in Barcelona, when an unending series of explosions made him realize that a more deadly stage of the war was under way. The Republic's government had recently moved to that city from Valencia. "By March, 1938," he wrote, "we thought we knew all about bombing and shelling, but we were innocents. It took eighteen raids in forty-four hours on Barcelona to show us."

The heaviest the world had yet seen, these raids were executed mainly by Mussolini's bombers based on Majorca. With a port and three airfields, that Spanish island had in effect become an Italian military base, conveniently within 15 minutes' flying time of Barcelona and Valencia. German aircraft joined the raids as well, and some of the bombs they dropped may have been manufactured in Delaware by DuPont. Starting in January, the American chemical behemoth sold at least 40,000 bombs to Germany. Since that country was not officially at war with anyone, the sale was not considered a violation of the porous US neutrality law.

What Matthews did not know was that in launching these round-the-clock attacks, Mussolini had not bothered to consult his ally Franco. The Generalissimo was furious, for he wanted to be the one to choose bombing targets—left-wing neighborhoods, and not factories once owned by his supporters, who hoped to soon reclaim them. The Italian dictator, however, had bigger fish to fry: strengthening his bargaining power in his relationship with Hitler. The Barcelona raids killed at least 1,000 people and injured some 2,000 more. When one bomb hit a truckload of explosives and caused an enormous blast, frantic rumors spread through the city that Italy had invented some new kind of superbomb. Mussolini "was pleased by the fact that the Italians have managed to provoke horror by their aggression instead of complacency with their mandolins," Count Galeazzo Ciano, the Italian foreign minister and the dictator's playboy son-in-law, wrote in his diary. "This will send up our stock in Germany, where they love total and ruthless war."

Although he had to restrain himself in what he wrote for the *Times*, the raids made Matthews feel that "my pen was dipped in blood." In a reference to the Barcelona raids that surfaced later, even the German ambassador to Franco's Spain acknowledged that "there was no evidence of any attempt to hit military objectives." In the streets, Matthews found "ambulances dashing up with men on the footboards blowing whistles, women screaming and struggling hysterically, men shouting." From wrecked buildings came the desperate cries of those trapped inside; in the morgue of one hospital alone, he counted 328 bodies.

"The news from Spain has been terrible, too terrible," Martha Gellhorn wrote to Eleanor Roosevelt from the liner taking her to Europe, "and I felt I had to get back. . . . It makes me helpless and crazy with anger to watch the next Great War hurtling towards us. . . . Why don't we lift our embargo to Spain. . . . I wish I could see you. But you wouldn't like me much. I have gone angry to the bone."

Barcelona was running low on food. Hotel waiters scraped plates to take scraps home to their families. People ate chickpeas and lentils (nicknamed "Dr. Negrín's pills") and raised vegetables and chickens on apartment balconies. Cats and pigeons found their way into cooking pots. To flaunt how much there was to eat on their side of the lines, the Nationalists from time to time sent planes over the city to drop loaves of bread.

After a visit that took her close to the front, Gellhorn wrote again: "I was out on the road and watched for fifty minutes twelve black German planes, flying in a perfect circle, not varying their position, flying and bombing and diving to machine gun: and they were working on one company of Government soldiers, who had no planes or anti-aircraft to protect them but who were standing there, holding up the advance so as to permit an orderly retreat. That same day we watched thirty three silver Italian bombers fly in wedges over the mountains across the hot clear sky to bomb Tortosa."

Only Eleanor Roosevelt read this description. When Gellhorn proposed an article to *Collier's*, the magazine replied by telegram: NOT INTERESTED BARCELONA STORY STOP STALE BY THE TIME WE PUBLISH.

Editors' eyes were elsewhere. Just four days before the bombings, Germany invaded Austria. Hitler followed his troops, and the next day officially annexed the country as part of the Third Reich. "Not as tyrants have we come, but as liberators," he declared, although some Austrians felt otherwise. Tens of thousands of Jews and Nazi opponents were promptly arrested. Mobs rampaged through Vienna's streets, smashing and looting Jewish-owned shops, beating their owners, and forcing them to eat grass or scrub toilets. The Führer had been issuing threats for years, but now, for the first time since 1914, German troops had actually crossed a national frontier.

Backers of the Republic hoped that such blatant aggression might at last move the Western powers to change their stance about Spain. There seemed reason for optimism when a new government in Paris opened the border, allowing transit of Soviet arms and even of a few weapons bought in France. But without support from Britain, France would go no further. And Britain was firmly fixed on the path of appeasement. In April, Prime Minister Neville Chamberlain went to Rome to sign agreements with Italy that in effect recognized its sovereignty over Ethiopia. In return, among other things, Mussolini agreed to withdraw his "volunteers" from Spain—by the end of the war.

In the United States, millions of people favored letting Republican Spain buy weapons. The Communist Party and the Friends of the Abraham Lincoln Brigade, which it controlled, were the best organized, but plenty of others with no connection to communism felt the same way. Speakers supporting the Republic and raising funds for Spanish relief toured the country. In early 1938, Marion Merriman joined them, beginning in New York and working her way west. When she reached Reno, where she and Bob had graduated from college less than six years before, the funeral director who had once hired them both arranged for his onetime kitchen helper to talk to the local Rotary Club.

Soon afterward, Marion found herself in Hollywood for two weeks, at the home of Dorothy Parker, the author and screenwriter whom she had met in Spain. Gradually she became more at ease speaking at fundraisers, even when they included celebrities like Ira Gershwin, Lillian Hellman, and Dashiell Hammett. In time she settled in a $20-a-month apartment in San Francisco, with a job raising money for Dr. Barsky's medical unit and other Spanish aid efforts. Where she and Bob had once ridden ferries across the bay to go dancing on Nob Hill, the water was now spanned by the San Francisco–Oakland Bay Bridge, which, with its newly opened sister span across the Golden Gate, had changed the look of the city forever.

Marion gave talks to campus meetings, women's clubs, labor rallies, and business groups. Her two younger sisters once again moved in with her. A letter from Bob said, "I wait every day for your handwriting." If conditions improved, she hoped to return to Spain.

But things were going badly there. In late March 1938, she was horrified to read that Franco's advancing troops had overrun a XV Brigade command post abandoned so hastily that Bob had left personal effects behind. Triumphant Nationalist officers displayed to correspondents his diary and a photograph of Marion. For a few days she feared that he had been captured or killed. But then word came that he was safe.

After the loss of Teruel, the exhausted International Brigades retreated to new positions. In a house where the American medical unit set up operations, a portable generator lit a single light bulb, and an iron stove boiled water and supplied heat. "Two tables poorly stocked with bandages and drugs and instruments, but clean as plaster, stand out in the dim light," wrote Jim Neugass. "Surgeon with a flashlight changes dressings." Wounded men groaned and shouted. "So long as I can write I don't suppose I am completely gone. I do not feel well. . . . Through an open window over the bed on which I write I see white soundless flashes on top of the nearest hill. Snow begins to fall."

A few days later he was down with a fever, in a hospital bed himself for several nights, his dreams haunted by driving. "I dodge a truck, duck a plane, dive into a ditch, pass a truck, dodge a plane, dive into a ditch, dodge a plane, until each second of the ward alarm clock raps out like a machine-gun bullet and there is no time left and then I dodge another truck and another plane. If we only had as many planes as we have trucks!"

Eight days later, back at work, he wrote, "My speedometer has registered a thousand miles of road since I last wrote into this journal." Neugass felt increasingly worried: "Something big must be coming off. . . . Never saw Them bomb so heavily so far back of the lines."

A quick look at a map made clear to anyone what the something big would be. With Teruel back in their hands and Nationalist troops making other gains as well, the territory they occupied at one point bulged to within 60 miles of the Mediterranean. A strong offensive that reached the sea would split Republican Spain in two.

Dr. Edward Barsky was worried. He went to XV Brigade headquarters to talk to Bob Merriman, who was happy to have his superior, the much-loathed Colonel Copic, on leave. Barsky had known Merriman since he had first appeared on the surgeon's operating table a year earlier. "'Well, Bob,' I said, 'what's going to happen here?'"

Doggedly upbeat as ever, Merriman told him: "Well, if they don't attack, we are going to attack." But with the nearby Nationalists overwhelmingly stronger in men and weapons, it was hard to imagine how that could happen.

On the drive back to his unit, Barsky was struck by the poor preparations for any Nationalist assault—no trenches or fortifications were to be seen, and many senior Republican commanders were on leave. At one point he and the others with him fled their ambulance when they spotted a German plane so close that Barsky could see the face of a crewman in helmet and sunglasses. "Never stay on a road or near your car," he wrote, "when a plane is passing. . . . Make sure that you are perpendicular to the route of the plane and then as the machine gun bullets sweep at you, you will offer the smallest possible target. Instead of your whole body from head to foot being the target, just your body from side to side will be the target."

When the American hospital moved again, Barsky ordered zigzag trenches dug between its tents for shelter against bombs. "We were fairly busy, and the times we weren't operating or on service we spent in the trenches. . . . Something forces you to look up and watch those planes. You feel a little better if you can see them because if that plane, which is right over you now, has not dropped a bomb at this second you can see that you're safe. By the time he drops the next one he is 100 yards past you."

One bomb, however, covered Barsky's trench with dirt, wrecked the hospital generator, and killed a driver and two patients. The blast also fractured the upper arm and skull of an operating room nurse, twenty-three-year-old Helen Freeman, formerly of Brooklyn Jewish Hospital. Blood streamed down her side and a fellow nurse could see the pulsing of an artery in the smashed arm. Barsky operated on her and then installed her in a trench. "Every now and then when I had a minute I would jump into the trench and see how Helen was," he remembered. He did not dare send her off to a larger Spanish hospital, as he normally would the severely wounded, fearing what would be

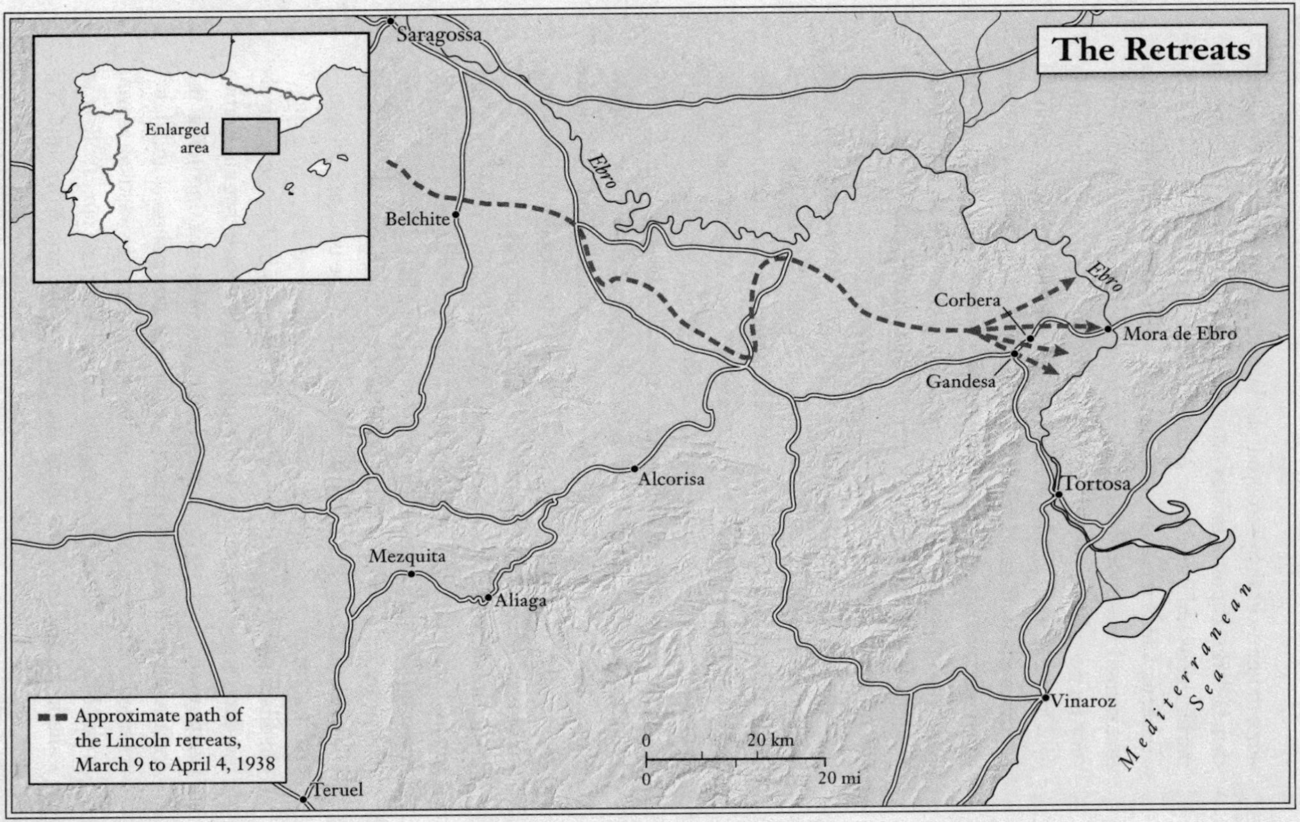
The Retreats
Enlarged area
Saragossa
Belchite
Ebro
Ebro
Corbera
Mora de Ebro
Gandesa
Alcorisa
Tortosa
Mezquita
Aliaga
Vinaroz
Teruel
Mediterranean Sea
0 20 km
0 20 mi
Approximate path of the Lincoln retreats, March 9 to April 4, 1938

done to her by Franco's troops if the hospital was captured. "I decided that Helen was going to stay with us and when orders did come to move, she would move back with us."

Barsky's unit was soon ordered to pull back another ten miles, but that proved not enough to get away from Nationalist aircraft. "Here they let us have it with hand-grenades dropped from planes along with the bombs. . . . The artillery was almost upon us. It sounded just over the next small hill." He waited frantically for more orders, worrying how his 50 wounded patients would fare. At last a motorcycle messenger brought the command to evacuate. The ambulances headed off with other military vehicles in a convoy that was funneled down the narrow main street of a small town.

"Through this tunnel," Barsky wrote, "all, everything, the army and the moving hospital had to pass. . . . And I saw the last thing in the way of an obstacle I expected. The street of that little town was packed solid with sheep! A solid agglomeration of wool and meat as impassable as lava. . . . The artillery of the enemy was din in our ears. All my patients were in the ambulances well in back of me. . . . Then I thought of something. About five of us opened all the doors of the houses and like sheep-dogs we herded those animals inside. We broke in doors that we couldn't open and left a man in each doorway to keep the sheep inside, while the army and the hospital passed by."

Soon afterward, when the convoy halted beside a river, the chief medical officer of the division to which the XV Brigade was attached, a young British physician, found them. "'It's bad, Barsky,' he said, with tears in his eyes, and his voice broke a bit. 'Very bad. I'm glad you didn't unpack. I'm afraid it's the end here, the lines are broken.'"

On March 9, 1938, the day before Jim Neugass had noted his feeling that "something big" was coming, it had already begun. Franco threw more than 150,000 troops into the offensive, including the crack Army of Africa. Streams of Condor Legion bombers and fighters filled the skies, some of them brazenly sporting swastikas as well as the black X of the Nationalists. As many as 120 aircraft flew in a single formation. Directly in the path of the attack was the XV

Brigade, battered from the ferocious fighting at Teruel and a more recent battle since then. The Americans, British, and Canadians in the brigade felt a chill when Nationalist planes swooped overhead dropping propaganda leaflets—in English.

"This meant the fascists knew where we were," remembered Lincoln communications technician Harry Fisher. And something else was new. On the day the big Nationalist assault was launched, "we saw three planes circling . . . about a mile away. Suddenly one plane started to dive almost straight down. We thought it had been hit and began cheering, but after almost reaching the ground, it dropped its load and started to climb again. The second and third planes did the same thing. We were baffled, having never seen anything like this."

Fisher was one of the first Americans to observe in action the brand-new German Stuka JU-87 dive bomber. In the Second World War, millions of soldiers and civilians would come to dread the way this single-engine monoplane could use the trajectory of its dive to plant a bomb of more than 1,000 pounds on a tank, a bridge, or a building with far greater accuracy than a normal bomber, while wind-driven sirens mounted on the landing gear terrified those on the ground with their unearthly wail. In the months to come, the Germans would test several different models of Stukas in Spain.

As the XV Brigade's chief of staff, Bob Merriman looms large in the memories of the survivors of those frightening days. Photographs almost always show him as a commanding presence: erect, confident, feet planted slightly apart, wearing a brimmed military cap and a long greatcoat against the Spanish winter. As a soldier, he had found himself. All these years later, what are we to make of this man?

Physically fearless, he inspired such loyalty that at least two Lincoln veterans would name children after him. Yet even his private diary reveals no thoughts that deviate from the Party line, speaking, for instance, of the need "to openly fight Trotskyite and bad elements." Just before he went into action for the first time at Jarama, he wrote in it, "Long Live Communism! Long Live the Soviet Union!" And this after living there for two years in the aftermath of the great famine and at the beginning of the Great Purge.

Perhaps, however intellectually crippling, his very nature as a true believer was what made him, from all accounts, an inspiring military commander. Skeptics, or those trying to parse political complexities, seldom make good warriors. George Orwell, better than anyone at such parsing, wrote after returning from Spain, "I came to the conclusion, somewhat against my will, that in the long run 'good party men' make the best soldiers." Ernest Hemingway, notably, felt the same way. "I like Communists when they're soldiers," he told a *Daily Worker* correspondent. "When they're priests I hate them."

It was soldiers and not priests that the outnumbered Republican troops needed as the fierce Nationalist juggernaut pushed them east toward the sea. A messenger Merriman sent late one night from XV Brigade headquarters to the Lincolns with an order to take up new positions never arrived. So he stormed off to the Lincoln command post himself at three o'clock in the morning: "I sent a runner at ten last night. Why the hell are you still here?" The volunteers had never before seen him unshaven and upset. He traveled on, sometimes in a small car, sometimes in an armored truck, finally on foot, collecting stragglers, looking for separated units of the brigade and trying to grasp the shape of what was obviously a major enemy breakthrough. Nationalist spearheads were penetrating deep into territory the Republicans thought was their own. He escaped one of them only because his driver turned off the road and tore across a field. His inner feelings remained as invisible as ever; if he knew any panic, he showed it to no one, for despite this chaos, he still seemed to call forth devotion in his men. "They had told us he was gone, missing, maybe dead," remembered one American. Suddenly Merriman appeared. "When I approached him I felt as if I were approaching someone risen from the dead. I felt so good to see him I threw my arms around him and kissed him."

In the vanguard of the Nationalist forces pushing back the Lincolns was the British Franco enthusiast Peter Kemp. To his immense pride, he now wore the forage cap with the red-and-gold tassel of a Foreign Legion officer. The legion was "an élite brotherhood—the finest fighting force in the world. . . . The thrill of serving with and commanding such troops in action was one of the greatest experiences of my life." He was profoundly moved to hear his fellow legionnaires sing their hymn, "Bridegroom of Death."

Unknown to Kemp, on the other side of the lines from him was his contemporary from Trinity College, Cambridge, Malcolm Dunbar, chief of operations for the XV International Brigade. Kemp's advancing unit captured a hilltop monastery that American volunteers had just evacuated. "In their flight they had abandoned their personal belongings, including a large quantity of mail from home, some of it unopened . . . letters from sweethearts, wives and even, in one or two cases, children. It was horrible to feel that many of these men, who spoke my own language and who had come even further from home to fight for a cause in which they believed as deeply as I believed in ours, would never return to enjoy the love that glowed so warmly from the pages I was reading.

"'The radio is on,' a girl from Brooklyn had written, 'and I'm writing letters. Yours comes first of course. They are playing the Seventh Symphony. You know how that music brings us together, how often we've heard it together. Please, oh please, come back to me soon.'"

With the retreating Republican army, Jim Neugass noted in his diary: "Lecera, the town in which we slept last night, was pounded to pieces today. We are still ahead of Them. How long can our luck last?" During the daytime there was the additional agony of knowing that badly injured men were waiting for help, but that any ambulance sent for them would be attacked from the air. Until dark, only those who could hobble in on foot made it to the tent that served as a temporary operating room.

Morphine and other supplies were nearly gone. The husky Neugass was often called on by the nurses to lift the wounded on and off the operating table. "When they are in my arms, I can hear their shattered bones grinding inside of their flesh." At night, when not driving, he slept in one of the ambulances.

Neugass was delivering patients to a larger hospital at a railhead behind the lines when it was bombed. "A hundred and five wounded were killed in their beds." But he never ceased trying to capture the feel of what he experienced: "When [the bombing] comes near, you do not hear it with your ears. The sound reaches your eardrums through the ground and then through your body, as does a dentist's drill or the sound of a surgeons' saw cutting through one of your bones. . . . I think our time must just about have run out. Only a few grains of sand left in the hourglass."

Returning to his unit, he found a crevice between rocks for shelter. "My hole is nine feet long and from twelve to eighteen inches high. A twenty-ton boulder is the canopy. . . . In case of a direct hit, my comrades would be spared the nuisance of digging a grave. 'Here lies a chófer who took the wrong road.'"

He began to see retreating soldiers who had thrown away their rifles. Refugees clogged the road as well: "Passed families of peasants marching like queues of mourners behind carts loaded with all that was mortal of their destroyed homes. . . . Copper and majolica pots, casseroles and pans, half a dozen cheap bentwood chairs, pine chests almost worn out with scrubbing, crowned by huge mattresses."

Back at the unit's post, Neugass went to check on the wounded nurse, Helen Freeman. "Helen lay in the deepest part of the zigzag ditch, bandages on her head. 'How are you, Helen?' I asked. There was no answer." Despite nearly losing an arm, however, Helen Freeman would survive, and be evacuated to the United States two months later.

As the tempo and panic of the Republican retreat increased, the entries in Neugass's diary grew elliptical and ever shorter. Some of what he wrote was probably added later. He ceased noting dates. Sometimes he referred to himself as "the Chófer." He was now armed. In one town, the main street was "clogged with peasants, carts, refugees. . . . Clots of unarmed soldiers, their hair white with dust of the road, crowded at the well." The traffic jam "filled the street with the shouts of drivers, racing of engines and cries of peasants. The bells in the church-tower ceaselessly jangled a warning that planes were coming."

His vehicle was packed with the unit's nurses. As they drove on, panicked civilians and soldiers tried to climb on board. "A woman ran up and down the road, hands in her red hair, screaming that the fascists were coming.

"The Chófer's car sagged to the iron rims of his wheels as peasants and rifleless militiamen jumped to the running board. Groaning from the chassis gave notice that the car was about to break down. The Chófer shoved the nose of his gun into the stomach of a woman. She jumped back to the road. The other peasants and militiamen stepped from the running board when they saw the Chófer's gun."

No one in the medical unit knew where the front was, only that it was rapidly catching up with them. When their sole escape route was through a field too rough for one large ambulance, they blew it up, along with other equipment, so it would not fall into Nationalist hands. At night, with all headlights off for fear of Nationalist planes, Dr. Barsky stood on the ambulance running board with a flashlight, directing Neugass along rutted dirt roads. When they met small fleeing groups of Americans and Canadians, wild rumors flew: Madrid had fallen, 600 Nazi planes had bombed Vienna to smithereens, escape routes over the Pyrenees were blocked.

As in a scene from a phantasmagoric film, Neugass came across 60 uniformed members of a Barcelona marching band, sheltering with their dusty instruments in a roadside ditch. "The musicians could not understand why they had suddenly been loaded, like so many sacks of flour, into open trucks, carted across Catalonia and then dumped into this lonely ditch where there were no civilians, no microphones, no audience." In another misbegotten attempt to raise morale, the government had sent a giant truck with two men in the back, waist-deep in leaflets they were tossing out as more dropped from aircraft above. "*Milicianos de la Republica! Oficiales! Chóferes! Trabajadores! Campesinos!* . . . One hundred men, well entrenched, can stand off a thousand fascists . . . the rumors spread by the Fifth Column that Madrid has been taken and that Barcelona has decided to capitulate are false. . . . Not One Step Back! To Resist Is to Conquer!"

Still the frantic flight continued until, in the middle of one night, Neugass realized he was lost. "The Chófer was afraid to stop, afraid to move, afraid to call out to the many men who he just knew must be up in the hills at each side of the road.

"The sounds of the battle were on all sides of him."

In the dark he crossed paths with a soldier from the British battalion who shared with him a supply of Mills bombs—hand grenades. A moment later, Neugass, writing of himself in the third person, "lifted out a Mills bomb, pulled the pin and pitched it at the three, five, six, black shapes who were running at him. He threw himself on the ground as the shrapnel of his bomb and something very soft and wet skipped along the earth near him; knelt, drew another grenade, pulled the pin, threw and bent to the ground.

"As he rose to go back to his car a desire to count the dark bundles of clothing that lay on the field came over him.

"He never knew if it was one of the dead who had gotten up or if it was still another fascist who came at him, but the shape that ran onto the knife in his left hand and dropped off the broad blade lay, afterwards, as quietly as any of them."

A fragment of writing separate from the leather-bound diary seems to refer to this same night, which was apparently also when he received a piece of shrapnel in his thigh. "Killed three, five, eight of them. One with knife, others with bombs. At night. May have to kill more. Still have my car. Eat olives off the trees. Hard to find in moonlight. Not sure where I am. Separated from unit. With infantry. Looking for the lines. Are there lines? Everything all mixed up. Very, very bad. Wound hurts. Have to move on, somewhere."

18

At the River's Edge

As his foreign legion unit remained in the forefront of Franco's powerful drive to reach the Mediterranean, Peter Kemp at one point found "about a dozen prisoners were huddled together, while some of our tank crews stood in front of them loading rifles. As I approached there was a series of shots, and the prisoners slumped to the ground.

"'My God!' I said to Cancela [the company commander], feeling slightly sick. 'What do they think they're doing, shooting those prisoners?'

"Cancela looked at me. 'They're from the International Brigades,' he said grimly."

Shortly after came an incident that "I can scarcely bear to write of." When an Irish deserter from the International Brigades crossed into Nationalist territory, soldiers brought him to Kemp so he could be interrogated in English. The two talked, and the deserter told Kemp he was a seaman from Belfast. With Cancela, Kemp then pleaded for the man's life, on grounds that he had deserted the Republicans. He was referred up the chain of command to a colonel.

"I found Colonel Peñaredonda sitting cross-legged with a plate of fried eggs on his knee. . . . 'No, Peter,' he said casually, his mouth full of egg, '. . . Just take him away and shoot him.'

"I was so astonished that my mouth dropped open; my heart seemed to stop beating. Peñaredonda looked up, his eyes full of hatred:

"'Get out!' he snarled. 'You heard what I said.' As I withdrew he shouted after me: 'I warn you, I intend to see that this order is carried out.'" As Kemp walked away, he noticed that the colonel had ordered two Foreign Legionnaires to follow him at a distance.

"It was almost more than I could bear to face the prisoner. . . . I forced myself to look at him. I am sure he knew what I was going to say.

"'I've got to shoot you.' A barely audible 'Oh my God!' escaped him."

Kemp asked the Irishman if he wanted a priest or if he wanted any messages delivered.

"'Nothing,' he whispered, 'please make it quick.'"

In an attempt to stem the offensive, new American volunteers who had barely started training were rushed to the front. One of them was Alvah Bessie. A former stage actor in New York City, he had also published fiction, worked as a newspaper reporter, and learned to fly—something he hoped to do in Spain. He had left two children and a wife, from whom he was separated, in Brooklyn. In a photo of him—bearded, a cigarette dangling from his lips, a pen and a notebook in the pocket of his rumpled military jacket, his weathered eyes squinting against the sun—he looks far older than his thirty-three years. Another American volunteer took to calling him "grampa."

"There were two major reasons for my being there," Bessie wrote. "To achieve self-integration, and to lend my individual strength (such as it was) to the fight against our eternal enemy—oppression; and the validity of the second reason was not impaired by the fact that it was a shade weaker than the first." Few other loyal Communists would have been so honest about motives that fellow Party members might have labeled bourgeois. In February 1938, Bessie made the exhausting hike over the Pyrenees—30 miles in 11 hours—and then noted in his diary, "First sense of fear from planes, instead of beauty."

Most of Spain's coal was now in the Nationalist zone and locomotives burned wood, so his journey to the International Brigades base at Albacete was a slow one. Once there, he heard voices call out, "Any guys from Chicago? Manchester, Leeds?" New recruits were welcomed in English, French, German, Spanish, and Polish. In the showers, he noticed that the bodies of some older volunteers bore wounds from the First World War. At a courtyard ceremony, a band played the national anthems of the various countries the recruits came from, all of which, of course, had refused to sell the Republic arms. Americans gave the clenched-fist salute while listening to "The Star-Spangled Banner."

A large banner read 1938—AÑO DE LA VICTORIA—1938. But victory seemed nowhere in sight as Bessie looked at the Spanish newspapers: "You had to read between the lines: '... Fighting with unusual brilliance, our troops retired to previously determined positions.'" Food was meager—burnt barley as a substitute for coffee, and rice or beans with burro meat—and never enough to stave off hunger. There was not much bread, for the country's wheat was now mostly behind Nationalist lines too. On the black market, only tobacco and soap had any trading value; by itself, money could buy nothing edible except nuts and marmalade. At this time on the other side of the lines Peter Kemp and his fellow officers in his Foreign Legion unit were eating smoked ham.

Less than a week after Franco's new assault began, Bessie and other newly arrived Internationals were taken to the front in a roundabout journey of several days in boxcars and trucks. At last came the moment he and other new American volunteers had long dreamed of: joining the Lincoln-Washington Battalion in the field. "All of us had blankets neatly rolled and slung over our shoulders." But the occasion was far from what they had imagined.

"Scattered over the side of this wooded hill that commanded a magnificent view of the mountain scenery ... we found a little over a hundred men, disorganized, sitting, lying, sprawling on the ground.

They had week-old beards; they were filthy and lousy; they stank; their clothes were in rags; they had no rifles, no blankets, no ammunition, no mess kits. . . . They did not speak to us at first; they ignored us; they did not answer our questions except in grunts or with expletives." The retreating Lincolns had received no food for five days.

Only a few seemed to retain any sense of order. "Major Merriman, tall, scholarly, wearing horn-rimmed glasses, spoke to us: 'We will go into action again soon,' he said. 'In this action we will be expected to retake terrain lost previously, and the sacrifice of every life may be asked.'" Dave Doran, a labor union organizer from Albany, New York, and the XV International Brigade's commissar, followed him: "Any man seen mistreating a rifle or machine-gun, or throwing it away . . . is to be shot on sight." But there were no rifles left to throw away.

For several days, both the bruised American survivors and the new arrivals slept on the hillside waiting for weapons and orders, throwing themselves flat on the ground when German and Italian planes flew overhead. A food truck brought coffee and garbanzo beans, both cold. Another truck carried those who wanted to bathe to an icy river. Then the battalion continued its retreat, but at night, so as not to present a target for the planes. "The rainy season came on, suddenly and with a vengeance. . . . Then we marched again, our feet sucking and squelching in the mud, our faces streaming with rain, our blankets, draped over our heads, heavy with water."

Only after Bessie had been on the move for more than a week did arms arrive. "My rifle, whose metal-work bore the stamp of the Russian Imperial Eagle, was numbered 59034. Under the partly obliterated Imperial emblem was a new stamp, the hammer-and-sickle of the Soviet Union."

Soldiers of the XV Brigade, along with tens of thousands of other Republican troops, streamed in a haphazard, zigzag flight from west to east, drawing ever closer to the Ebro River. Flowing in this part of Spain from north to south, the river was the last great natural barrier before the Mediterranean. As they straggled on, Bessie recalled later, "the more experienced men shed what little equipment they had: tin cans and blankets, plates and spoons, extra underwear, placing the shining objects carefully under bushes so they could not be seen from the air." But "many men threw away ponchos and blankets, to regret it at night. Cold." Some fleeing American and Canadian machine-gunners left behind their weapons, so heavy to carry, first taking them apart and scattering the pieces widely over the fields so the guns couldn't be used against them. Discipline completely broke down, as men deserted and fled, a few eventually making it across the border to France.

One night, someone in Bessie's unit found a box of long, cylindrical objects wrapped in paper. Thinking it was Spanish chocolate, the hungry Americans eagerly tore off the paper, only to find sticks of dynamite. Lying in the darkness next to Bessie, a soldier talked in his sleep: "Hamburger on rye with onions on the side."

Bessie was worried about how he would fare in combat. In his diary, less polished but sometimes more frank than the memoir he would publish after his return from Spain, he wrote, "Will I be a coward?" Soon his squad was exchanging bullets and machine-gun fire with the pursuing Nationalists.

On the night of April 1, 1938, he caught sight of Merriman for the last time when Bob drove up in a staff car pockmarked by bullets to confer with other officers before ordering the brigade to begin moving again. As the men got ready to march, an explosion sent them racing for the roadside ditches. It was the supply staff blowing up an ammunition dump to prevent it from falling into enemy hands. As the Lincolns marched off into the darkness, behind them they could see in the distance something that had never before been visible in any combat zone: headlights. It was an ominous sign for their own blacked-out units. Franco's vehicles could now display themselves as brazenly as they wanted, for they faced little danger from skies nearly bare of Republican warplanes.

Surviving the chaotic nightmare of the retreat, Jim Neugass, Edward Barsky, and their medical colleagues finally managed to reach Barcelona. About Barsky another doctor wrote, "He looks like a wreck, so tired that he can scarcely drag himself about, and with all his old spirit gone out of him, but sticking on and helping."

Neugass had been hit in the back by a bomb fragment—"a disc of hot iron, half an inch thick and as big as a fifty-cent piece," he wrote—and shrapnel had also scarred his left thigh and scalp. He was spitting up blood and found it hard to walk. Barsky knew his driver's nerves were shattered.

"'What do you want to do?' the Major asked me, 'Stay here and drive my car or go back to the States and write that book?'"

Neugass said he wanted to go home. Barsky replied:

"O.K., I'll send you out. But who the hell is going to send me out?"

Dismayed by Franco's offensive and eager to get back to the front, Ernest Hemingway was starting to squabble with the North American Newspaper Alliance, which had reduced the rate it was paying him and now asked him to cover the war from Franco's side as well. Not surprisingly, the Nationalists refused to admit Republican Spain's most famous literary champion. Then, wanting to ensure that the *New York Times* would carry his syndicated dispatches, NANA asked that he stop traveling with Herbert Matthews, so their stories would not overlap. Although not an unreasonable request, it left the novelist enraged. Certain that the Catholic pro-Franco editors at the *Times* were conspiring to separate him from his friend Matthews, he fired off a cable denouncing this "Jesuit manoeuvre." Meanwhile, his marriage was fraying under the impact of his ever more visible relationship with Martha Gellhorn. She was again in Spain with him, although their journalist friends discreetly omitted her presence from stories they wrote mentioning Hemingway.

Beneath his swagger, however, was a man who cared deeply. He talked with US Ambassador Claude Bowers about saving American medical staff and the men they were looking after in the event of a Franco victory, in which he feared the wounded would be slaughtered and the nurses raped—as had already happened when the Nationalists captured Republican military hospitals. He found out how many American wounded were in which hospitals and began planning which ports they could be evacuated from. He and several reporter friends also assured the ambassador that a French hospital had agreed to care for Americans too severely wounded to travel all the way home. "These correspondents and Hemingway will take on themselves the task of assembling these people at the port," Bowers reported to Washington. The ambassador's apparent openness to this plan fed Hemingway's delusions of power. "Why the hell let our guys get trapped by the Fascists?" he held forth to a group of American journalists and medical volunteers at Barcelona's Hotel Majestic. "If it has to be done, I'll get an American warship and we'll evacuate every single American."

Ignoring his NANA editors, Hemingway set out for the front with Matthews in a black, two-seater Matford roadster. Like the fleeing Lincolns they were trying to find, they watched for Nationalist planes. "As this correspondent dove headforward into a ditch he looked up sideways," he reported, "watching a mon[o]plane come down and wing over and then evidently decide a single car was not worth turning his eight machine guns loose on." Before long the two reporters ran into a mass of refugees, including a woman on muleback holding a baby that she had given birth to the day before, its skull gray with dust. Then came soldiers, trucks, guns, and "we began seeing people that we knew, officers you had met before, soldiers from New York and Chicago who told how the enemy had broken through and taken Gandesa, that Americans were fighting and holding the bridge at Mora across the Ebro River."

The retreating, disoriented members of the XV Brigade had split into several groups. Bob Merriman was leading one, which would subdivide again in an attempt to break out of a Nationalist encirclement; Alvah Bessie was with another, a column of 80 exhausted men. An hour before dawn on April 2, they were trudging forward when he suddenly saw the Americans ahead of him start to run.

"We were in a field now, and the field was full of sleeping men; men sleeping in blankets on the ground, and officers sleeping in pup-tents under the olive trees. *We* didn't have any pup-tents, even for our officers. There were horses tethered among the trees, restless in the dark. I tripped over a sleeping man and he sat up and said, '*Coño!*' . . . and then I heard the voices behind, crying '*Alto. ¡Los Rojos! ¡Alto Los Rojos!*' and lengthened my stride." Franco's forces had leapfrogged ahead of the retreating Americans, who had unwittingly stumbled into a camp of the Nationalist 1st Division.

Bessie dropped his extra blankets and a mess kit, and, separated from the others, he and three friends scrambled up a terraced hillside in panic. "I could hear the voices plain now and the rifles and pistols and the bullets snapping overhead . . . my body was getting heavier by the minute; it wanted to sink; it wanted to drop onto the ground, but my legs kept going." Finally, at dawn, the four reached the shelter of a forest with thick underbrush. There they heard singing in an unfamiliar language in the distance and realized it was from a contingent of Moors. The fleeing Americans stripped the red star of the International Brigades off their caps and moved on.

Drained of all energy, sleepless for several days, with little food except for berries and green almonds on the trees, the quartet headed for the Ebro River, whose far bank, in Republican hands, promised safety. Avoiding roads and sticking to fields and slopes, they drew closer until, from a hilltop, they looked down and saw "straggling columns of men, moving through the mountains, climbing the hills ahead, winding toward the Ebro." Luke Hinman, a California longshoreman and one of Bessie's companions, recognized them as French and German International Brigaders. "'They're ours,' Luke said, and we moved down the hill and joined the men."

The retreating troops converged on Mora de Ebro, a small town beneath a medieval castle where a bridge crossed the river. The streets, wrote Bessie, "were jammed with ragged and demoralized men, wandering idly about in the utmost confusion. 'Where's the British?' '*Où est la Quatorzième?*' '*Wo ist die Elfte?*' . . . We lay in a small fenced-in enclosure that was practically covered with human excrement. . . . There was no command, there was no authority, there was not even a point to which you could report." When some Canadians asked, "'Where's the Lincoln?' 'We're the Lincoln,' we said. . . .

Soldiers were sitting on the pavement, too exhausted to go on. It was strange to see men, in the streets of a civilized town, urinating on the pavement." A little girl of about six sat on the tailgate of a truck, crying, over and over, "*¡Mamá perdida! ¡Mamá perdida!*"

When a field telephone brought word of Nationalist tanks approaching, the Republican soldiers poured eastward across the bridge, on which boxes of dynamite were already wired together so it could be blown up behind them. On the far side, they reached a larger town that had some semblance of order. Survivors were being separated according to their units, and supplies were arriving from the rear, including letters from home for the Americans—these came by courier one night. "We sat crouched around a lighted match under a blanket in a deep ditch, while he went through the mail. He read hundreds of names, but only about fifteen men claimed letters. It took him half an hour to read all the names on the letters, and after the first few times nobody would say, 'Dead' or 'Missing'; we just kept silent."

Issues of the International Brigades' *Volunteer for Liberty* also reached them. What had previously been a newspaper full of upbeat articles ("Christmas at the Brigade," "Dombrowski Brigade Helps Peasants Gather Olive Crop," "Canadians in Spain") had become a two-page leaflet filled with exhortations: "Do Not Yield an Inch of Ground to the Enemy!," "Drive Out the Invaders of Spain!," "Now Is the Time to Strike Back!," and "Discipline: The Difference Between Troops and Rabble."

As the battered survivors gathered, Bessie wrote, "no one had heard any news of Merriman."

At a headquarters behind the lines, Sandor Voros, the Hungarian-American volunteer who left such a vivid account of crossing the Pyrenees, was assigned as commissar for the multinational column of XV Brigade soldiers Bob Merriman was leading as it tried to fight off the advancing Nationalists, and Voros set off for the front to find him. Voros admired Merriman immensely, although this had not stopped him from once making a pass at Marion when Bob was not around. He hiked for several hours, along the way organizing some British soldiers into a battle police unit to try to stop the flow of panicked men to the rear, many of whom had abandoned their rifles. "The British are tough about it, they threaten to shoot those who don't want to turn back. They mean business, they fire after two men who refuse to stop."

Finally he found the knoll where he expected Merriman to be. "I learn that having designated that spot as Command Post, Merriman had gone ahead with the troops to place them in position.... The runner sent back by Merriman told me that the last he saw of him, Major Merriman was leading the last troops personally into line under intense rifle and machine gun fire. No word had been received from him since."

Voros sent two runners out to find Merriman; neither returned. He could hear rifle fire in the rugged hills, then Nationalist artillery. Men were streaming to the rear. "[A] husky boy, an American, broad-shouldered and athletic, I doubt if he is twenty . . . walks unseeing, his eyes bulging and unblinking in a fixed stare, his mouth wide open . . . he won't respond to inquiries about his name and unit, only mumbles: 'I wanttogohome, Iwanttogohome.'"

Voros's watch had stopped and nobody else had one. He leapt into a foxhole to escape strafing and bombing from Nationalist planes. Still desperate to find Merriman, he cursed the "egalitarian streak" that had led Bob to remain under fire with his men—knowing that the men perhaps would not have stayed in position otherwise. Shells bursting all around Voros made clear the Nationalists were fast approaching. A Spanish officer, his face streaked with blood, told him the Republican troops trying to hold the area were almost out of ammunition. Commandeering a truck, Voros raced back to a supply dump on the east side of the Ebro for more. By the time he got the truck loaded and returned to the bridge that Alvah Bessie had just crossed, they were "halted by Spanish troops.... They won't let us proceed, the bridge is about to be blasted. I plead with the Spanish major in charge to let us dash through. He insists it is too late, the dynamite charges are all in place, they will be set off *momentito*."

And then they were. "A tremendous explosion shakes the ground, followed by other detonations. A column of flame envelops the middle span of the bridge, a huge section of it rises, steel girders float into the sky riding on tongues of flame. . . . A large steel fragment whizzes by my head, the air is full of hissing shrapnel, I throw myself to the ground until the air is clear of flying fragments. . . . An awed hush settles on the night." The last quick escape route for Merriman and for hundreds of fleeing Lincolns and other Republican troops trapped on the west side of the river had been closed. "The Ebro is too wide and deep to ford, too swift for most men to swim."

Franco's drive to the sea received massive news coverage, but for family members anxious about Americans caught up in the fighting, details were scarce. From France came reports of thousands of Spanish refugees, and some Republican deserters, streaming across the frontier. On April 4, 1938, Herbert Matthews wrote in the *Times* that "nobody knows yet what happened" to the American battalion or to the XV Brigade's staff officers, including Merriman. The destruction of the bridge over the Ebro at Mora did not bode well for surviving Lincolns trapped on the other side, most of whom were working-class city boys who had never had the chance to learn to swim.

Matthews and Hemingway tried once more to locate the missing Americans. It was then, driving along the Ebro's Republican-held east bank, that they encountered two Americans who had swum the river—haggard, barefoot, and naked except for blankets that had been tossed to them from a passing truck—George Watt and John Gates.

Tall and handsome with reddish blond hair, Watt was a former Communist student leader from New York whose warm smile, intensity, and boyish fervor for the cause of Spain led other soldiers to dub him "Kilowatt." "He was a gentle man, not a typical Party functionary," remembered one person who knew him years later, "the sort of guy who, if he was talking to a little kid, would get down on his knees to be at the same level." By contrast, Gates was emotionally contained and much less liked by his fellow soldiers, a short, wiry figure capable of intimidating many a larger man by his air of authority. Alvah Bessie found him "hard-boiled." He was a Party stalwart and commissar whose comments on who was or was not "a good comrade" appear in dozens of Lincoln personnel records. Rising rapidly to become one of the senior Americans in Spain, Gates had a reputation as a fast-talking, humorless disciplinarian. At this moment, however, there was no one left to discipline.

After the four men embraced, delighted to have found one another, Watt and Gates told the two writers the harrowing story of how they had swum the river, while several of their comrades, all nonswimmers and some wounded, had been swept downstream clinging to a homemade raft and had disappeared. Before crossing, they had trekked for three days and two nights, finding their way by the North Star. Spotter planes flew overhead in the daytime, and the rumble of Franco's tanks could often be heard in the distance. Spanish villagers had given them food and told them that some Internationals had been executed by the Nationalists in a town plaza.

After telling the two survivors what news they had, Hemingway and Matthews headed off in search of more Lincolns. Soon after, Gates and Watt found a comrade who had waded into the river with them but had landed farther downstream, as well as Bessie and two companions, who had made it across the bridge before it was blown up. The swimmers finally acquired some clothes, and Hemingway and Matthews returned to talk to all six Americans at length as, Matthews wrote, they sat "shivering on the ground in the warm sunlight."

The swimmers, who were clearly the ones shivering, told Matthews that the night before they had—like Bessie—accidentally stumbled into a Nationalist camp, which apparently included some Nazi tank crews. Unlike Bessie and his group, however, they weren't recognized. "When challenged, they answered in Spanish. . . . The three Americans did not know who the other soldiers were," wrote Matthews. "One asked and, he related, got the answer in German, 'Eighth Division.' They knew what that meant, but none of them lost his head and all trudged calmly on."

Alvah Bessie described Matthews as "tall, thin, dressed in brown corduroy, wearing horn-shelled glasses. He had a long, ascetic face, firm lips, a gloomy look about him." Hemingway was "taller, heavy, red-faced, one of the largest men you will ever see; he wore steel-rimmed glasses and a bushy mustache . . . they were just as relieved to see us as we were to see them."

The two correspondents gave the cigarette-starved volunteers a supply of Lucky Strikes and Chesterfields. "Hemingway was eager as a child . . . he was like a big kid, and you liked him," wrote Bessie. "He asked questions like a kid: 'What then? What happened then? And what did *you* do? And what did *he* say? And *then* what did you do?' Matthews said nothing, but he took notes on a folded sheet of paper."

A few days later, Matthews wrote to his father: "I never had a sadder story to write than the smashing of the Lincoln-Washington. It made me positively sick. I knew all those men very well and they were some of the finest chaps I ever hope to meet. I would have given a year's salary not to have had to write that story."

The crash of artillery in the distance was a reminder that Franco might reach the Mediterranean in a matter of days. "Hemingway did not seem to be discouraged, but Matthews was," Bessie recalled. "Hemingway said, Sure they would get to the sea, but that was nothing to worry about. It had been foreseen; it would be taken care of; methods had already been worked out for communication between Catalonia and the rest of Spain; by ship, by plane, everything would be all right." Hemingway reported a deal Roosevelt had made: he would give 200 planes to France, so France could give 200 planes to the Spanish Republic. (In this he was mistaking the wish for the deed. A few days earlier, Hemingway and Matthews had cabled Roosevelt proposing such a deal.)

Bessie was skeptical about the planes. "But where were they?" Even as a disorderly mass of refugees and retreating troops streamed by them on the highway, the novelist remained unreservedly optimistic: "The war will enter a new phase now, Hemingway said: the Government's resistance will redouble . . . decent people everywhere were putting pressure on their governments to come to the assistance of Spain."

What had happened to the rest of the Americans? No one really knew, but Matthews summarized for *Times* readers one survivor's story. Merriman had been leading a group of International Brigades soldiers toward the Ebro, the man said, when they encountered Nationalist troops in the dark. They tried to bluff their way through, still hoping to reach the river.

"The answer was an abrupt 'Manos arriba!' ['Hands up!'] Then the [Nationalist] soldier shouted to the sergeant of the guard, 'Reds, Reds!'

"When Mr. Merriman and the group behind him heard that, instead of running away they rushed toward the Insurgents." The survivor managed to slip away, but "heard shots behind, and finally a businesslike 'Manos arriba!' shouted in such a way that he decided the men must have been cornered."

"I was alone when the phone rang," Marion Merriman remembered. "A San Francisco newspaper friend called and asked if I had heard the news." Matthews's story mentioning Bob had just come over the wires, as had a similar piece by Hemingway. "The reporter eased himself out of the conversation, saying he was awfully sorry to give such news to me." Marion called another journalist, and then the office of the Friends of the Abraham Lincoln Brigade in New York, the Red Cross, and the Communist Party. No one had any more information. Milly Bennett, now living in nearby Marin County, came over immediately.

A few days later, a United Press dispatch from Barcelona appeared in San Francisco Bay Area newspapers. The Americans had been "cut to pieces," it said. "Among those missing was Maj. Robert Merriman of Berkeley, Calif. . . . Captured officers of the International Brigade are shot at once."

19

A Change of Heart?

It was not Herbert Matthews but William P. Carney, traveling behind Franco's troops, whose story led the front page of the *New York Times.* The Nationalists, he reported, "confounded their enemy today and reached the Mediterranean, thus finally dividing Republican Spain into two parts."

It happened on April 15, 1938, at the seaside village of Vinaroz. Barcelona and surrounding Catalonia were now separated from a larger swath of Republican territory that included Valencia and Madrid. Photographs flashed across the globe of jubilant, helmeted Nationalist troops brandishing flags and rifles, racing into the sea and giving the palm-outward Fascist salute. Disappointed that day was Benito Mussolini, who had hoped that his Italians would be the first to reach the sea.

The journalists who backed the Republic tried to put the best face on things. In the *Nation*, Louis Fischer claimed that Franco's offensive "has failed. Its purpose was to end the war. It merely succeeded in investing a few unimportant fishing villages along the Mediterranean coast and galvanizing a harried people into heightened resistance."

But the elevator in his Barcelona hotel was not working; the city was short of electricity, other Nationalist advances having cut the power lines from hydroelectric plants in the Pyrenees—perhaps an even more serious blow than slicing the Republic in two.

And the Republican military was in bad shape. The day the country was divided, the Lincoln-Washington Battalion could muster just 120 men out of the 400 it had had several weeks before. Only help from abroad, it seemed, could save things. An American truck driver who gave Alvah Bessie a lift in the aftermath of the great retreats expressed what many felt: "If France don't come in now, we're fucked ducks."

The month after Franco's troops reached the sea, Adolf Hitler visited Italy. It was a state visit to end all state visits. The Nazi dictator's entourage of some 500 officials, guards, and journalists filled three trains. More than 22,000 German and Italian flags were planted along their route to Rome. When the Führer disembarked at a special station built for the occasion, he was driven along the new Viale Adolfo Hitler. More swastika banners blossomed on the capital's streets, and garbage dumps and rundown buildings he might see from his train window were cleaned up or masked by billboards. At night, batteries of extra floodlights lit up the city's monuments.

He and Mussolini watched ceremonial wreath-layings, a procession of 50,000 Fascist youths, a performance of Wagner's *Lohengrin*, a huge parade of Italian soldiers goose-stepping in newly learned Nazi style, and military demonstrations outside the city with live bombs and artillery shells. Hitler seemed especially interested in the Pantheon, paying a second, private visit after a ceremonial one, evidently gathering ideas for the grand rebuilding of Berlin he planned. At a state banquet, the two dictators spoke soaringly of the eternal solidarity between their two peoples. As a sign of tighter ties between the two Fascist states, Mussolini shortly arranged for a group of prominent Italian scientists to issue a statement declaring Italy to be an "Aryan civilization" defined by "ancient purity of blood." Anti-Semitic laws would soon follow.

After Hitler returned to Germany, Virginia Cowles would witness his ability to mesmerize a huge crowd at a Nazi rally in Nuremberg:

> The power of the spectacles lay not so much in their ingeniousness but in their immensity. . . . Instead of a few gilt eagles there were hundreds; instead of hundreds of flags there were thousands. . . . At night the mystic quality of the ritual was exaggerated by huge burning urns at the top of the stadium, their orange flames leaping into the blackness, while the flood-lighting effect of hundreds of powerful searchlights played eerily against the sky. The music had an almost religious solemnity, timed by the steady beat of drums that sounded like the distant throb of tom-toms. . . .
>
> Then came motorcycles with yellow flags, a fleet of black cars, and Hitler standing in one, his arm outstretched. Behind him followed thousands of disciplined supporters. In the silver light they seemed to pour into the bowl like a flood of water. Each of them carried a Nazi flag and when they were assembled in mass formation, the bowl looked like a shimmering sea of swastikas.
>
> Then Hitler began to speak. The crowd hushed into silence, but the drums continued their steady beat. Hitler's voice rasped into the night. . . . Some of the audience began swaying back and forth, chanting "*Sieg Heil*" over and over in a frenzy of delirium. I looked at the faces round me and saw tears streaming down people's cheeks. The drums had grown louder and I suddenly felt frightened.

Nationalist Spain, meanwhile, had requested German help for its security services. Hitler was happy to oblige, sending SS Colonel Heinz Jost (later to command one of the Nazi Einsatzgruppe killing squads in Eastern Europe) to Salamanca at the head of a team of officers to help organize a vast archive of captured Republican documents and other data on some two million people considered subversive. The Gestapo stationed interrogators in Spain, and any captured German International Brigade volunteers were handed over to them. Franco awarded SS chief Heinrich Himmler the Nationalists' highest medal, the Grand Cross of the Imperial Order of the Yoke and Arrows.

After Hitler's incorporation of Austria, his sights were next fixed on Czechoslovakia, where he claimed to be coming to the aid of ethnic Germans suffering discrimination. Reporting from that country, Cowles, as always, found a man eager to escort her to the center of the action, in this case a pro-Nazi Sudeten German, as the ethnic Germans of the Czech borderlands were called. A Nazi rally, just two miles inside Czechoslovakia from the German frontier, was "a nightmare of flags, swastikas, banners . . . posters of Hitler, and ear-splitting 'Heils.' It was held in the Town Hall which was packed by over 6,500 Germans. The crowded corridors were lined with uniformed Sudeten guards." Germany mobilized troops along the border, and the Czechs called up 400,000 soldiers in response. The crisis was temporarily defused, but few doubted that it would flare up again.

Across the Atlantic, meanwhile, it suddenly seemed as if events like this might be influencing the leader of the most powerful country of all.

"Roosevelt Backs Lifting Arms Embargo on Spain," read a two-column front-page *New York Times* headline on May 5, 1938. "The administration has decided to throw its support behind the resolution of Senator Gerald P. Nye of North Dakota for lifting the arms embargo against Spain," began the story. "The prospect is that the legislation will be passed before adjournment of the present session." Roosevelt was on holiday, fishing from a navy vessel in the Caribbean. He was to return to Washington shortly, and everyone awaited a more formal announcement then. At last, it appeared, Republican forces could begin buying the American arms they so urgently needed.

For Marion Merriman, Roosevelt's apparent change of heart had come too late. Most painful was the uncertainty. Although the Nationalists routinely shot prisoners of war, especially officers and foreign volunteers, for a short period this spring Franco halted the practice, wanting to have International Brigades prisoners he could exchange for Italian POWs in Republican hands. Carney of the *Times* was even allowed to interview some captured Americans; wasn't that a sign that such men might be allowed to live? But no one was certain, or knew just what had happened to the Americans reported missing in the chaotic retreat at the Ebro.

Herbert Matthews reflected the uncertainty in his stories. A friend in New York called Marion every day that a Matthews piece mentioned Bob. On April 10, the correspondent wrote that Merriman and XV Brigade Commissar Dave Doran "are still missing," but that the sudden appearance of three other American officers who made their way out of Nationalist territory "has raised hopes that they may yet show up. . . . Merriman and Doran, like their comrades, are men of great resourcefulness, courage and strength, and if anybody can get out of such a scrape, it is felt, those two could."

"Berkeley Volunteer Now Reported Safe," ran a headline in the *Oakland Tribune* on April 14, based on a rumor that Bob was in a Nationalist prison near Bilbao. In May, American diplomats in both Madrid and Barcelona sent Marion messages that they had heard the same news. On May 29 Carney reported that 18 Americans were in a concentration camp near Burgos, but Nationalist officials would not confirm the rumor that Merriman was one of them. Carney went on to say that "unofficial but usually well-informed sources" had told him that "some Americans . . . had been shot without trial shortly after having been captured."

Marion's fear turned to anger when her New York friend read her the end of the story over the phone: "Charles Bay, the United States Consul in Seville, came to Burgos to confer with officials here about commercial affairs, but said that he had no instructions to inquire about the status of the American war prisoners here. 'When Americans enlist to fight under a foreign flag,' he said, 'they cannot expect our government to worry about what happens to them thereafter.'"

"The bastard!" she shouted into the phone.

She would have been even more outraged had she known that

several months earlier not only Bay, but his boss, Secretary of State Cordell Hull, had swiftly and successfully intervened with Franco to win the freedom of Guy Castle, an American volunteer in the Nationalists' Foreign Legion who had been caught trying to desert and was facing the death penalty.

More than 100 University of California professors signed a letter to Hull asking for his help, which produced little more than a statement insisting that Consul Bay had been misquoted. Bob's mother wrote to Mrs. Roosevelt, who passed the letter on to the State Department. A group of scholars in Britain sent a telegram to Franco on Bob's behalf. In June, an inch-high four-column headline in a Nevada newspaper read, "Merriman Is Believed Safe." But it was only the same Bilbao rumor again. "After months of searching in every possible way," Marion wrote, "I finally had to accept that Bob was not in a prison camp in Bilbao nor was he anywhere else."

She found some comfort, at least, in being with people who had known him. That November, she would give a Thanksgiving dinner for Lincoln veterans in San Francisco. In the months to come, she would piece together accounts of Bob's fate from Americans who managed to survive the great retreat. As far as she could tell, the last time anyone had seen Bob was on April 2, 1938—two days before Hemingway and Matthews ran into the men who swam the Ebro. Bob was leading retreating troops toward the town of Corbera, some six miles west of the river, when they found Nationalist soldiers in their path. Here the stories of the survivors diverged. The account Matthews reported had the Nationalists shouting, "Hands up!" Other witnesses, however, heard only rifle shots in the darkness.

Of the moment when Bob disappeared, this was all Marion was able to discover—until, that is, she would unexpectedly receive a letter half a century later.

When Franklin D. Roosevelt returned from his fishing holiday, it became clear that the report that he favored scrapping the arms embargo was false—at least for now. How the rumor originated is still not known, for behind his bonhomie, rimless glasses, and ivory cigarette holder, Roosevelt was one of the most inscrutable of American presidents.

Many members of Congress from both parties wanted to lift the embargo, as did a cluster of anti-Nazi State Department officials, among them the ambassador to Spain, Claude Bowers, who was still writing the president long-winded letters pleading the Republic's case. It was thought at first that someone from one of these groups might have planted the story in the *Times* to put pressure on FDR. Arthur Krock, the journalist who wrote the article, was a frequent conduit for the opinions of influential officials. Several decades later, Krock told a historian that either Secretary of State Hull or Undersecretary Sumner Welles—he could not remember which—had given him the story, hoping to spur an end to the embargo. On another occasion, he claimed the leak came from Secretary of the Interior Harold L. Ickes, well known as the cabinet's most ardent backer of the Spanish Republic. For months Ickes had been pressing FDR on the issue, once telling him that the failure to sell arms to Spain was "a black page in American history." But Ickes's diary shows him as surprised as everyone else by the *Times* story.

One historian suggests a darker explanation: that the leaker was Roosevelt himself. Possibly, the theory goes, he used Welles—an old friend who had been an usher at FDR's wedding—as his intermediary. The president had a habit of occasionally planting a rumor about a change of policy he knew would please part of his constituency; if he later decided not to follow through, he could then blame the obstruction of his plans on some other group.

It seems likely that he never intended to openly change course on Spain. This was politically too risky a step to take when other problems loomed larger. The troubled American economy was suffering another dip in what his opponents were calling the "Roosevelt Recession." FDR's popularity ratings were down, and he was worrying about his party's prospects in the upcoming midterm elections. And for America to help the Republic would mean greatly antagonizing the British allies Roosevelt so valued, as well as overriding entrenched conservatives in his own State Department. Moreover, however much the president might dislike the prospect of a Franco-controlled Spain, it posed little direct threat as a potential enemy of the United States, something he was starting to fear when it came to Germany and Japan.

For the time being, Roosevelt wanted to use his limited political capital on a crucial but stalled piece of New Deal legislation, the Fair Labor Standards Act. If he leaked the story to the *Times*, the speculation goes, it was to spur an outcry in favor of maintaining the embargo—something he could then point to in order to get the pro-Republic liberals off his back. Indeed, this is exactly what happened: Krock's story produced a flood of speeches and lobbying from the American Catholic hierarchy demanding that the prohibition on arms for Spain be kept in place.

Just how heavily Catholic pressure really weighed on Roosevelt is debatable. Then as now, many American Catholics did not vote the way their bishops wanted them to. More than 70 percent of the nation's Catholics had voted for Roosevelt in 1936, and most surely would have continued to support him whatever he did about Spain. Still, being able to blame the Catholics was convenient, because the liberals pressing the president to sell arms to the Republic were willing to believe anything ill of the Catholic Church, as were Roosevelt's fellow upper-class WASPs. "Dammit . . . if I lift the embargo," FDR said to one person who came to lobby him for the Republic, "the Catholics will crucify me!" He told the ardently pro-Republic Harold Ickes that "to raise the embargo would mean the loss of every Catholic vote next fall, which was nonsense." Such claims, however, convinced Martha Gellhorn, who believed that even though FDR "was completely sympathetic . . . he knew that there wasn't anything that could be done; the Roman Catholics had that one sewed up."

Although he worried about Communist influence in the Republic, abundant evidence suggests that Roosevelt was quietly having second thoughts about the arms embargo. On several occasions he discussed ways of covertly circumventing it. Yet he always found excuses for stopping short of doing so—telling Ickes, for instance, "that if we

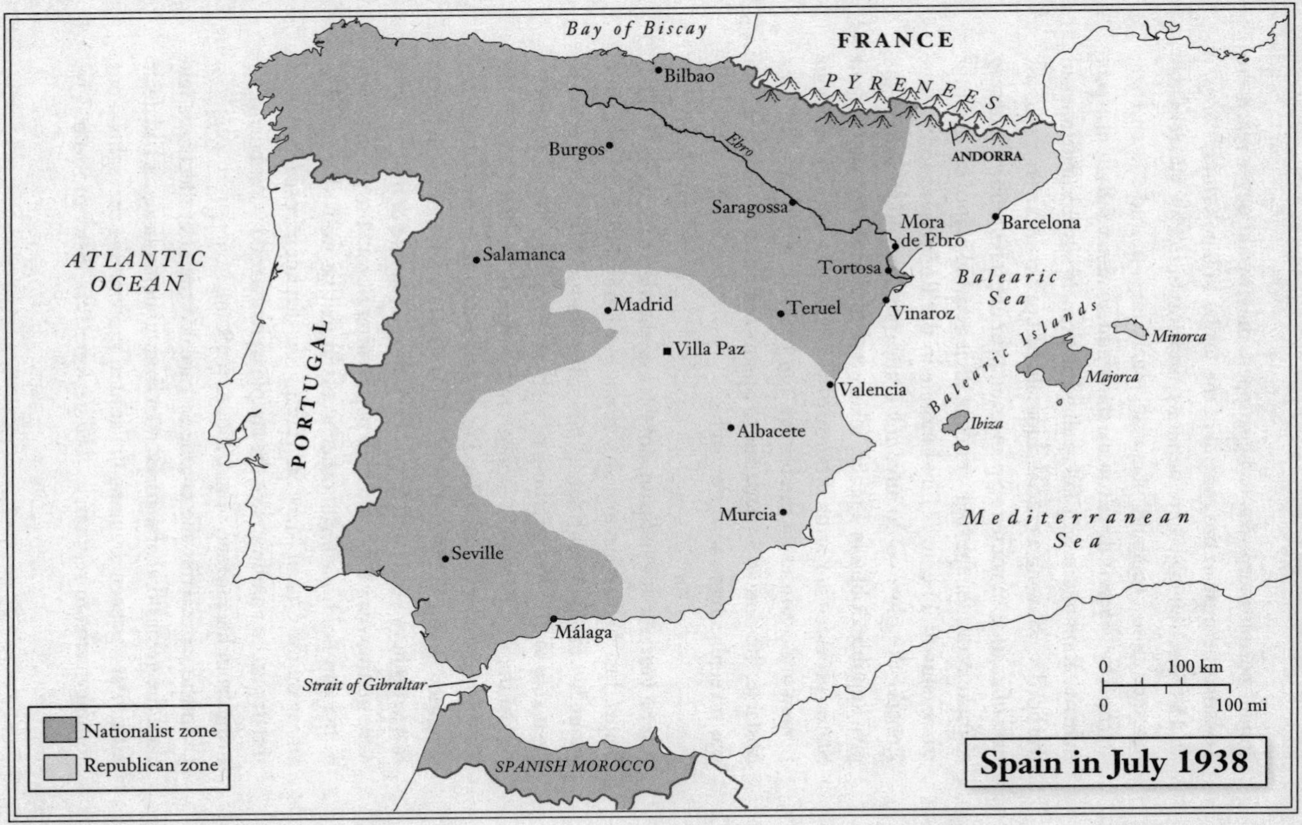
Bay of Biscay
FRANCE
PYRENEES
Bilbao
Ebro
Burgos
ANDORRA
Saragossa
Mora
de Ebro
Barcelona
ATLANTIC
OCEAN
Salamanca
Tortosa
Balearic
Sea
Madrid
Teruel
Vinaroz
Balearic Islands
Minorca
PORTUGAL
Villa Paz
Majorca
Valencia
Ibiza
Albacete
Murcia
Mediterranean
Sea
Seville
Málaga
Strait of Gibraltar
0
100 km
0
100 mi
Nationalist zone
Republican zone
SPANISH MOROCCO
Spain in July 1938

should permit munitions to be shipped, they would never reach the Loyalists because of the control of the sea by Franco's ships."

His inaction had a tremendous ripple effect. The Western democracy closest to Spain, of course, was France. In mid-March 1938, alarmed by Franco's drive toward the Mediterranean and the prospect that the Republic might fall, a divided French government opened the border, allowing a crucial shipment of 152 Soviet aircraft to cross part of France en route to Spain, even pruning trees along a highway to make room for the high crates of disassembled planes carried by a truck convoy. The news lifted morale in the Republican forces. But Roosevelt's failure to do anything comparable fatally weakened the pro-Republic lobby in France. Ickes warned him that if the United States provided no arms, France would succumb to pressure from Britain and again close the border. On June 13, it did so. With this obstacle, the flow of Soviet arms to Spain continued to shrink. There was no replacement source in sight.

After a year nursing in Spain, Toby Jensky headed back to the United States. Just before leaving, she wrote her sister and brother-in-law about his brother, Phil Schachter, still missing: "To date have not been able to discover anything new about Phil, but I'm still trying."

On the way home, she stopped in London to see Pat Gurney. He considered himself married to her, but for good measure, he was determined to repeat the ceremony in England. "Pat's mother, relatives & friends have been swell to me. He pulled a fast one & told them we were getting married—and they pay no attention to me when I deny it. If I can hold out for another week all will be well—because I'm sailing on the Queen Mary on May 4." She did not succeed, however, and despite her ambivalence the couple were married—Pat borrowed a ring from his mother—on April 29, 1938.

In the same letter she guardedly revealed the aftereffects she felt from the great flood of maimed men she and her colleagues had dealt with: "Pat has been dragging me around showing me the sights—but nothing seems to register. . . . We get very little news of Spain. The news we do get is bad and I'm worried—about a million friends there." Pat Gurney must have wondered how long the marriage would last when his new wife sailed for home just a week after the wedding.

As reports that Franco was holding American prisoners appeared in the press, the hopes of Phil Schachter's family remained alive. His brother Max wrote to New York Senator Robert F. Wagner, to the Spanish Republic's Ministry of Defense (whose reply claimed that Phil had been taken prisoner), and, repeatedly, to the State Department. From the latter, an official responded stiffly, "I regret to inform you that a despatch has been received from the American Vice Consul at Valencia . . . reporting that Mr. Schachter is unknown to the Vice Consul's informants."

20

Gambling for Time

In May 1938, Louis Fischer traveled to Moscow to see his family. The Soviets had just finished staging the third big show trial of the Great Purge. All but three of the 21 defendants were promptly sentenced to death; the others would perish later in the *gulag*. Six of those on trial were friends of Fischer's.

He dared write nothing, in part because he was still trying to arrange new shipments of desperately needed Soviet arms to Spain. He also knew his family was vulnerable: not only was his wife, Markoosha, a Soviet citizen, but in the flush of their earlier enthusiasm for communism, they had never bothered to register their two sons' births with the US embassy. The USSR might therefore consider the boys Soviet nationals as well. Neither his wife nor sons had exit visas.

"Markoosha and the boys met me on my arrival in Moscow, and straightaway Markoosha started pouring dark news into my ear. 'How is So-and-So?' I asked. Disappeared. 'And X?' He had been shot. His wife? In exile." Fischer knew he could never report from Moscow again. Before returning to Spain, he wrote to the head of the secret police, "telling him that my work would henceforth keep me abroad and that I therefore wanted my family to emigrate." Months passed.

From Spain, ever more anxious, he twice wrote to Stalin himself. There were no replies.

Although the Nationalists now controlled the major part of Spain's territory, the Republic still held Madrid. On the western side of town, the front line continued to snake through the university campus, with both sides dug into trenches sometimes less than 50 yards apart. When a *New York Herald Tribune* reporter walked through the Republican ones in the spring of 1938, he found that "illiteracy and rats were the enemies most vigorously pursued. . . . Each company had its school for reading and writing. . . . In those dark galleries beneath the earth the work of the university was going on in a way its founders could not have dreamed."

Two other Americans visited exactly this same part of the front at about this time—on the other side. They were Torkild Rieber and his Paris associate William M. Brewster. As Rieber made his second wartime trip to a Nationalist Spain deeply grateful for Texaco oil, he and Brewster were given a VIP tour of the front, which included a lunch with Franco's commanders in the portion of the university their troops controlled. Military and civilian officials escorted the Rieber party, which traveled in an eight-passenger American Vultee V-1A, a favorite executive transport of the era. It was one of the aircraft the Nationalists had gained the previous year when they captured the ship *Mar Cantábrico* once it had left New York with a cargo destined for the Republic. In Saragossa, one stop on the tour, Rieber noticed that most of the Nationalist army's trucks were Fords. He joked that he should telegraph his friend Walter Chrysler: "Walter: I don't see any Chryslers; only Ford is doing something for civilization." After the trip, Rieber sent a thank-you telegram to his hosts: HAVING RETURNED TO PARIS BREWSTER AND I ARE REFLECTING ON EXTRAORDINARY CONSIDERATIONS AND COURTESIES EXTENDED US DURING OUR TRAVEL YOUR GLORIOUS COUNTRY.

Brewster was continuing to forward a stream of intelligence messages about Republican oil supplies to Nationalist headquarters in Burgos. There would be more than 50 of these over the course of the war. One, for instance, reported an explosion that apparently destroyed a Republic-bound tanker in the Dardanelles: "the Reds will be missing a cargo of gasoline which they are so badly in need of." Nationalist attacks were making maritime traffic to the Republic ever more dangerous, leaving, in total, some 300 cargo ships going to or from Republican ports sunk, damaged, or captured. Because of this, the freight rates shipping companies charged for such voyages were triple those for routes to Nationalist Spain. Some sailors balked at even making the trip. When the crew of a British tanker, the *Arlon*, loading gasoline at the Romanian port of Constanța, learned the ship would sail for Republican Spain, they refused to work. They went to the British consul, demanded passage home, and were replaced by a Romanian crew. This, too, was one of the ships Texaco was tracking. After the same vessel made another voyage from Constanța, a message from Brewster named the *Arlon*, the port it was heading for, Valencia, and what it was carrying—"7,000 Tons of Gasoline." (Several voyages later, the *Arlon* would be destroyed in a Nationalist bombing raid while in port at Valencia.) Seldom has a corporation based in a neutral nation provided this sort of intelligence to the military of a country at war.

The Republic still held Barcelona and Valencia, but these two Mediterranean cities were separated by a widening isthmus of Nationalist territory. Mail between them had to be carried by submarine. The army was short of rifles, and draftees were ever younger—the *quinta del biberón*, the Spaniards called it, the baby-bottle call-up. Few new foreign volunteers were arriving, and in the Lincoln-Washington Battalion Americans were now outnumbered by Spaniards.

Divided in two, with millions of refugee mouths to feed, the Republic faced grim choices. Some in the government advocated a compromise peace, though Franco had sworn he would accept only all-out victory. Before long, however, the embattled leaders agreed on a different strategy. For the Americans and other International Brigades troops who had survived the spring's calamitous retreats, it brought to an end an all-too-brief period of recuperation in a picturesque rural district of Catalonia, with vineyards, ancient stone villages, and a creek where you could swim to escape the summer heat. Alvah Bessie first understood what was in store when, on maneuvers, the Lincolns were sent on a night march to the shore of a dry riverbed. There they divided into small squads, with as many men in each as would fill a small boat, and traversed the pebbled riverbed on foot while making wry comments like "You gotta row harder." Then they were drilled in climbing and attacking a terraced mountain slope. "'Aha!' the men said, 'we're going to cross a river. Now what river do you suppose *that* could be?' But I think we knew the river; we had crossed it once before, in the opposite direction."

The last part of the Ebro's course to the sea still divided Nationalist and Republican troops. Soon after the practice assault, Bessie and his comrades were again marched off at night and ordered to put into knapsacks or blankets any tin plates or other equipment that might rattle. Trucks heading in the same direction had their headlights off.

After nearly all his predecessors in the post had been killed or wounded, the latest battalion commander, Milton Wolff, was a mere twenty-two years old. Until a photograph of him appeared in a Yiddish newspaper in New York, he had convinced his mother that he was merely working in a factory to free up a Spaniard to be a soldier. He called the wary, dispirited men together and, in his Brooklyn accent, explained the plan: "We are going to cross the Ebro, travel fast and light, penetrate deep into Fascist territory and hold positions while other troops come over on bridges that will be constructed while we're marching inland." Republican intelligence, he explained, knew where the Nationalist food and ammunition dumps were. It became clear to Bessie that this surprise offensive was supposed to sustain itself on captured supplies.

No one needed to tell the 80,000 troops secretly transported to the east bank of the Ebro about the risks they faced. Even if the first waves successfully advanced, they would then have the river at their backs, jagged, rocky mountain country ahead of them, and supply lines crossing flimsy wooden pontoon bridges vulnerable to the Condor Legion. They were also up against a far larger number of Nationalist troops. And, after losses during the rout of March and early April, the entire Republican army had a mere 150 artillery pieces, some from the nineteenth century.

The Republic's leaders were launching an attack that, in purely military terms, was foolhardy. But more than ever, Prime Minister Juan Negrín and his cabinet were playing to an audience beyond Spain. They were gambling for time. If they could seize ground, albeit temporarily, and if Hitler made another aggressive move that set off a wider war, then everything could change. The Republic might find itself allied with Britain and France at last. To believe that a war engulfing the whole continent was in the offing was not unrealistic; it would, in fact, begin the next year. Even without that, Negrín and those around him calculated, a swift, dramatic gain of territory might persuade major countries to sell Spain arms at last. "Not a day passed . . . when we did not have fresh reasons to hope," wrote Foreign Minister Julio Álvarez del Vayo later, "that the Western democracies would come to their senses and restore us our rights to buy from them."

The attack was well prepared and the first stages went well. With the help of local sympathizers, scouts had quietly located Nationalist positions, most of them held by inexperienced troops. Before dawn on July 25, 1938, advance units slipped across the Ebro. Then, in a fleet of small wooden rowboats that had been camouflaged with tree branches—some laboriously transported overland from Mediterranean fishing villages, others built on the scene in a church-turned-workshop—came additional soldiers and engineers who quickly set up a dozen pontoon bridges. Some of these were crude assemblies of planks lashed together on top of barrels, making a boardwalk barely wide enough to accommodate a single file of soldiers on foot—or of stretcher bearers carrying back the wounded. The Nationalists, however, were shocked and dismayed, for they had not expected an attack here. Through the thin walls of the Generalissimo's Pullman compartment bedroom in his mobile headquarters, an aide was startled to hear Franco sobbing.

The American and Canadian volunteers crossed the Ebro in the first boatloads of troops. The mules that would carry their supplies were herded, protesting, into the water behind them. Leonard Lamb, a New York schoolteacher, stood in the prow of one boat in a pose meant to spoof the famous portrait of George Washington crossing the Delaware. Also in the first wave of this offensive was the British battalion. We can only guess what ran through the mind of one of its company commanders, Lewis Clive, as he traversed the river in a heavily laden rowboat. In 1932, he had won a gold medal for Britain in the Summer Olympics—in rowing.

Alvah Bessie wrote in his diary after the first night, "No food . . . slept in straw, in stone barn; dead tired, hungry, wet with perspiration." The next day, he and his fellow soldiers ravenously consumed an odd assortment of captured goods: Italian canned fish in tomato sauce, cookies, rock-hard chocolate, and cigars, which they broke up, to roll the tobacco into cigarettes.

That same day, a Lincoln lieutenant and seven Spanish conscripts were captured and disarmed, but the lieutenant then bluffed a Nationalist officer into thinking he was surrounded by a far larger number of Republican troops. A few hours later, the officer surrendered to his own prisoner—who then marched back to XV Brigade headquarters with an astonishing 208 Nationalists in tow, six of them officers. "We were startled to see that they looked so much like us," wrote Bessie. "Spanish, dressed in nondescript pickup uniforms, dirty and uncombed, unshaved, exhausted and patently terrified."

The Nationalists struck back at the offensive with fierce counterattacks. It was a full week before Bessie took his boots off for the first time, even when sleeping. More than 140 Nationalist bombers and dive bombers were unleashed, not to mention 100 fighters that strafed concentrations of troops as they bunched up to cross the Ebro. At times the lines of trucks waiting to traverse the few floating bridges large enough for them stretched back several miles, making inviting targets. Then Franco's engineers opened upriver dams in the Pyrenees, and the resulting flood swept away some of the lighter pontoon bridges.

Two weeks into the offensive, Louis Fischer visited the troops in the Republican bridgehead. For the diminishing number of correspondents in Spain, however, it was no longer an easy drive to the front lines and then back to a hotel, as had been the case in Madrid. To avoid Nationalist bombers, he had to travel at night. "The river bank and the river beaches were pocked with deep bomb holes which sometimes filled with water," Fischer wrote. "The engineers labored up to the waist in the river fastening new tow-ropes and replacing broken pontoons. The work proceeded in complete darkness lest a light attract hostile bombers."

Fischer began searching for the Americans. "Each time our driver flashed on a dim light to avoid hitting someone, the soldiers yelled, '*Apagar la luz.*'" But at last "we heard New Yorkese and Chicagoese in the Spanish blackout . . . men [who] had been in battle since the first day of the offensive. Thirteen days of constant combat without undressing, without bathing, sleeping on rocks and hard ground." He slept the rest of the night in the back seat of the car, and the next morning "we found the Americans in an olive grove . . . and when they got up there was nothing to eat or drink, not even water, and one could see them massaging the insides of their mouths with their tongues."

After talking to Alvah Bessie and others, Fischer headed back to Barcelona. "Usually, one was guided by the trucks. If a truck ahead of you stopped with a jerk and its occupants dashed out into the fields you knew they had sighted a plane. . . . As we approached a spot where a side road intersected our main highway I noticed that a soldier and a boy who had been sitting on a culvert quickly jumped up and ran. We threw open the doors and bolted. . . . We all lay in the stinking ditch by the side of the road." A Nationalist plane dropped four bombs one after another, but curiously none of them exploded. The next day, Fischer mentioned this to Negrín over lunch. The prime minister told him it was common: "We have opened dud bombs made for Franco in Portugal in which the workingmen inserted notes saying, 'Friend, this bomb won't hurt you.'" There were many similar accounts, certainly too many to all be true, but such stories provided small flashes of hope in a dark time.

On the Ebro battlefront, the summer heat was overwhelming. One August day saw recorded temperatures of 98° F in the shade and 134° in the sun. Many men had no helmets. Bessie wrote: "I showed the Spanish boys . . . how to put leaves inside their caps to ward off sun-stroke, but worse than the heat was the lack of water. . . . The men ran back and forth a dozen times with loads of canteens, but no one got enough. We were wet from head to foot with sweat." In addition, the rocky terrain made digging trenches or foxholes nearly impossible. "You'd ruin a diamond drill trying to dig a hole," remembered one man who had been a miner. Digging a grave was no less difficult, and for many a Lincoln burial simply meant having rocks piled on top of what was left of him. Food appeared erratically and was odd at best: "dried *bacalao* (codfish, very salty)," Bessie remembered, "and a petrified sort of blood-sausage that was more gristle than meat." The Americans' old nemesis, diarrhea, returned in full force. "I could hit a dime at ten meters!" one man joked. Sometimes, to rub in the disparity in the rival armies' food supplies, loudspeakers in the Nationalist trenches broadcast their daily menu.

His side outgunned, the skies full of German and Italian planes, Bessie still kept a shrewd eye on his own emotions, an ability he shared with Orwell and Neugass. "At such times the tension is intolerable," he wrote of an afternoon when his unit was sheltering in a pitiful two-foot trench scratched out of a stony hillcrest, waiting nervously to go into action. Machine-gun fire rattled nearby. "Your mouth dries up and you spit cotton; your stomach clenches and unclenches, your bowels writhe and there is a deep ache in your chest. You look around and you see other men sitting, talking calmly, showing no fear in their faces, acting as though they were on a picnic in the woods; and you realize with astonishment that if you could see yourself, that is exactly what you would see. For men do not like to show fear in the presence of other men, and they put on a good act."

The new Spanish recruits filling the battalion's ranks failed badly

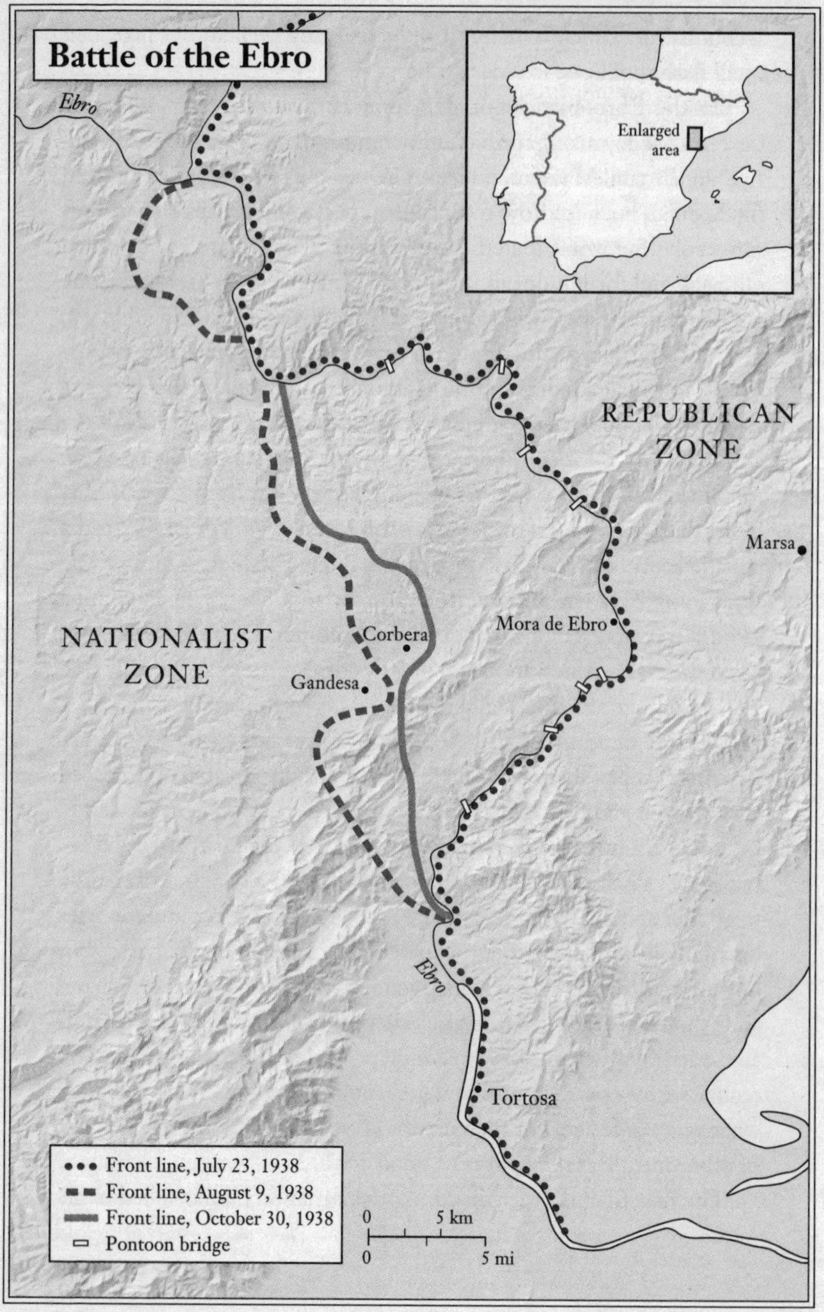
Battle of the Ebro
Ebro
Enlarged area
REPUBLICAN ZONE
Marsa
NATIONALIST ZONE
Corbera
Mora de Ebro
Gandesa
Ebro
Tortosa
Front line, July 23, 1938
Front line, August 9, 1938
Front line, October 30, 1938
Pontoon bridge
0
5 km
0
5 mi

when they came under fire. "They could not be urged, threatened, kicked or shot (two of them were) into advancing." This was not surprising, for unlike the American volunteers, the Spaniards were draftees—who must have been apprehensive at landing in the International Brigades, which were widely known, in battle after battle, for being thrown into the forefront of the deadliest fighting. As Bessie watched reinforcements arrive, it was clear that the government was down to the bottom of the manpower barrel: men too old or too young, ex-convicts, former deserters.

Nationalist aircraft were dropping leaflets urging them to surrender: "In Franco's Spain, justice reigns; there is abundance, peace and liberty. No one is hungry. . . . Come over to your brothers." Of the leaflets, one American commented, "Ain't got no union label." Some Spanish soldiers, however, did desert. But for Americans there was no abundance, peace, or liberty on the other side. When some 40 members of the Lincoln-Washington Battalion, 14 of them American, were taken prisoner in September, Nationalist troops marched them to the rear. When an officer heard men talking English, he stopped the march, separated out the Americans, and ordered them machine-gunned.

The Republican army had received new antiaircraft guns, but, Bessie wrote, "we had so few that . . . seventy-five planes merely sailed with exasperating ease through their sparse fire; then when ten of ours appeared they had to run a gauntlet of fire that blackened the sky for hundreds of acres. It was heart-breaking."

Intense shelling filled the air not just with shrapnel but also with chips of rock blasted off the mountainsides. Bessie found a different sort of horror when the shelling paused. "After all these hours, eight in all, when you tried to walk, rising from the narrow niche in which you had been lying all that day, it was almost impossible. Your legs refused to obey your mind, and you had to look at them to assure yourself that they were there, and *will* them to move. . . . Trying to relieve yourself some distance from the shelter—ready to jump and run at the sound of a distant gun—you tottered on your feet and fell back into your excrement. You wondered how much of this it would be possible to bear." One American sergeant clenched a short stick between his teeth to keep them from chattering.

When his best friend was wounded and lost an eye, Bessie inherited his pistol, sticky with blood—and soon after got word that he had died in a hospital. A Nationalist shell hit a food truck and the men had no food that night. A month after they crossed the river, the 768 men in the battalion had been reduced to 380. A visiting journalist brought word that Nazi Germany had mobilized huge numbers of troops on the Czech and French frontiers for "maneuvers."

The steady trickle of news reaching the Lincolns made clear that France and Britain, led by Prime Minister Neville Chamberlain, were eager to soothe Hitler. This crushed any hope of Western arms sales to the Republic. "Mr. Chamberlain is going to sell the Czechs down the river," a friend of Bessie's at the front told him in August 1938, "mark my words."

In September, Bessie was at XV Brigade headquarters in the Ebro bridgehead when some of the details of concessions Chamberlain was offering came through. "The news from Europe was worse than ever, with England and France agreeing to the dismemberment of Czechoslovakia and presenting a 'plan' of compromise." Hitler would gain large areas of the country, and the plan would include "the usual 'guarantees' of her frontiers by England, France, Germany and Italy. The murderers were guaranteeing to respect the corpse!"

The Czech crisis escalated throughout the month. On September 12, Hitler gave a fiery speech demanding self-determination for Czechoslovakia's ethnic Germans. Three days later, Chamberlain rushed to confer with the Führer at his Alpine retreat of Berchtesgaden. A week later, the British prime minister paid a second visit to Hitler, whose demands only escalated. Finally, on September 29 came the Munich conference, in which the leaders of Europe's major nations, sitting in a semicircle of armchairs around a large fireplace in the city's palatial new Nazi Party headquarters, essentially dismembered Czechoslovakia. The others gave Hitler all he wanted—10,000 square miles of Czech territory containing some 3.5 million people, some of whom were not even ethnic Germans.

Although Chamberlain returned to London in his striped trousers and starched wing collar to claim that he had achieved "peace in our time," it was an enormous, cost-free victory for Hitler. Czechoslovakia's fate was all the more poignant because, almost alone among the states of Eastern Europe, it had been a thriving democracy. Franco promptly sent Chamberlain his "warmest congratulations" for his "magnificent efforts for the preservation of peace in Europe."

Virginia Cowles, covering the crisis, found Prague "chilled by an air of menace, with the centuries-old buildings looking sad and grey beneath an overcast sky." The country's president announced the results of the Munich conference over loudspeakers to a huge, somber crowd gathered in Wenceslas Square. One reporter brought a Czech secretary to translate for the small group of foreign correspondents watching. "The broadcast was a short one," Cowles wrote, "telling the nation of the final decision to partition the country. Then the pathetic words: 'Our State will not be the smallest. There are smaller States than we shall be.' The Czech stenographer put down her pencil, buried her head in her hands and wept."

Someone who keenly watched the making of the Munich agreement was Joseph Stalin, who, for all his vengeance against imaginary enemies, knew that he faced a real one in Hitler. He now realized that Britain and France would never step in to prevent a Franco victory. Mussolini's submarines continued to make it dangerous to ship Soviet arms to Spain. Stalin began to lose interest in the war, and people noticed that Spanish news no longer ran on the front pages of *Pravda* and *Izvestia*. It had been a year since the dictator had recalled his ambassador to Spain in order to have him shot, and he had never bothered to appoint a new one. Stalin gradually withdrew most of the Russian and Eastern European officers he had lent to the Republic's military, and, for good measure, he continued to order many of them executed. Among those recalled to the Soviet Union and never seen again was the XV Brigade's commander, the opera-singing Colonel Vladimir Copic. Soviet military personnel in the Republic, once close to a thousand, would drop to a quarter of that by the end of 1938.

Convinced that Britain and France were unlikely to join with the Soviet Union in the alliance against Germany he wanted, Stalin began to pursue a different strategy. Before the year was over, the newspaper of the Socialist Party, USA—the party to which Lois and Charles Orr had belonged—would carry a prescient headline: "Will Hitler and Stalin Make a Deal?"

In Spain, Prime Minister Negrín and his cabinet knew that the majority of International Brigades volunteers had now been killed or wounded, and that Communist parties around the world were no longer recruiting more. So the government took a modest chance, hoping against hope that by publicly withdrawing the Internationals, it might pressure the democracies to insist that Franco do the same with Hitler's and Mussolini's soldiers and airmen. In a dramatic speech before the League of Nations in Geneva, Negrín announced that all members of the International Brigades would be pulled out of combat and would leave Spain.

Fearing a collapse of discipline before the men could be withdrawn in an orderly fashion, some brigade officers tried—in vain—to prevent word from reaching the front lines. Alvah Bessie heard the news on a day when a bomb blast from a German Junkers knocked him flat. He and his fellow soldiers knew that this gamble was not one of high stakes, for only a few thousand exhausted Internationals were left. Of the several hundred Americans still in Spain, many were in hospitals; only about 80 were at the front. Three days after Negrín's announcement, having just retreated in bloodied disarray from a devastating Nationalist artillery barrage, the remaining Americans in the combat zone left it for good, crossing the Ebro River for the last time on the crude planks of a pontoon bridge.

PART V

21

The Taste of Tears

From packed sidewalks, from windows and crowded balconies draped with flags, and from precarious footholds on sycamore trees and lampposts, 300,000 Spaniards wept, cheered, waved, and threw flowers, confetti, and notes of thanks. It was October 28, 1938, and 2,500 troops from what was left of the International Brigades were marching down the Diagonal, one of Barcelona's grand avenues, for an official farewell. Along the boulevard were signs with names of the battles in which the volunteers had fought. The brigades had borne the brunt of so much combat that their soldiers had been killed at nearly three times the rate of the rest of the Republican army.

Many of the Internationals still in Spain were in hospitals, but men from 26 countries made it to the parade. The gaunt files of marchers could barely be seen over the heads of the vast crowds who turned out to cheer them. The 200 Americans who marched included a handful of nurses from the medical detachment. The rest were men, who came along the avenue with blanket rolls slung over their right shoulders, the shabbiest of uniforms, and mismatched footgear. They walked nine abreast, sometimes ankle-deep in flowers.

"Those men had learned to fight before they had learned to parade. . . . They could not seem to keep in step or in line," wrote Herbert Matthews in his memoirs. He was in Barcelona that day, but the *New York Times* understandably did not print the extravagant dispatch he sent by cable. The Internationals, he said, in defiance of reality, "leave undefeated and their last battle was the victory of the Ebro."

As the volunteers marched through the city, they could see the gutted buildings and peeled-away apartment house walls that bore testimony to Mussolini's intensive bombing raids earlier in the year. Republican fighter planes flew overhead, on guard against new attacks. Bands played but could barely be heard. "The women and children were jumping into our arms," remembered a New York volunteer, "calling us sons, brothers, calling 'come back.' . . . I never had such an experience . . . because these men, such tough fighters, every last one of them was crying." Milton Robertson, a medical student wounded at the Ebro, was in a group of Internationals who were driven to the parade from a hospital. "The roar of cheering was continuous," he wrote home the next day. "It was like a wave that never broke, but poured on. . . . A little boy, nine or ten years old, stood on the corner. Tears streaked a dirty line down his face. He saw our truck bearing down, saw the bandages flash about. He dashed out, met the truck, and clambered up the side. Tears still streaming down his face, he thrust his arms about me and kissed me on both cheeks. I kissed him tasting his tears."

Finally the troops were drawn up in formation for the playing of the Republic's national anthem and speeches by the nation's leaders. With great emotion, Prime Minister Negrín promised Spanish citizenship to any International soldier who returned to Spain after the war. Then the country's greatest orator, Dolores Ibárruri, La Pasionaria, took the podium.

"Mothers! Women!" she began. "When the years pass by and the wounds of war are stanched . . . when pride in a free country is felt equally by all Spaniards—then speak to your children. Tell them of the International Brigades. Tell them how, coming over seas and mountains, crossing frontiers bristling with bayonets . . . these men reached our country as crusaders for freedom. They gave up everything, their loves, their country, home and fortune . . . they came and told us: 'We are here, your cause, Spain's cause is ours. It is the cause of all advanced and progressive mankind. Today they are going away. Many of them, thousands of them, are staying here with the Spanish earth for their shroud."

Then she spoke directly to the volunteers:

"Comrades of the International Brigades! Political reasons, reasons of state . . . are sending you back, some of you to your own countries and others to forced exile. You can go proudly. You are history. You are legend. You are the heroic example of democracy's solidarity and universality. We shall not forget you, and, when the olive tree of peace puts forth its leaves again, mingled with the Spanish Republic's victory—come back!"

La Pasionaria's words have themselves passed into history and legend, finding their way into book titles and inscriptions on monuments. The farewell to the International Brigades marked the end of an almost unparalleled moment. Never before had so many men, from so many countries, against the will of their own governments, come to a place foreign to all of them to fight for what they believed in. One British newspaper primly reported, "Even black-skinned volunteers had their kisses." Everyone who was in Barcelona that day would remember it for the rest of their lives. "It was our day," wrote John Gates. "Women rushed into our lines to kiss us. Men shook our hands and embraced us. Children rode on our shoulders."

As the volunteers marched through the city, Hemingway and Gellhorn were in Paris, on their way to Spain one last time, although neither of them had a journalistic assignment. For Hemingway, the news that the government had withdrawn the Internationals was a huge blow. The Spanish Civil War "was the only time in his life," Gellhorn later said, "when he was not the most important thing there was." In their Paris hotel, she found him leaning against a wall, repeating, "They can't do it! They can't do it!"

It was the only time she ever saw him weep.

• • •

Nothing could save the hard-won bridgehead on the Ebro's west bank. The Nationalists now had close to a million men in uniform, and they relentlessly pushed back the Republic's outnumbered forces. German Stukas dive-bombed convoys of troops as they bunched up to retreat across the river. Several weeks after the farewell parade, Republican soldiers blew up the last bridge. With snow now replacing the summer's unbearable heat, the 113-day Battle of the Ebro was over.

For nearly four months, the soldiers crammed into the bridgehead had been on the receiving end of an average of 13,500 artillery shells a day. Estimates of the Republican toll range up to 30,000 deaths. As always, the number of wounded was far larger. Nationalist artillery fire in those months was the heaviest seen anywhere since the First World War. Spanish civilians in the region would be killed for years to come whenever an unlucky farmer's shovel or plow struck a buried unexploded shell.

After Munich, Hitler, Mussolini, and Franco knew that the path to victory was clear. Previously, Hitler had been in no great hurry for the Spanish war to end, since it distracted Western attention from his ambitions in the east. But with Munich behind him, he sent the Nationalists a massive new wave of arms and supplies, in return for which Franco gave Germany control of mining concessions far beyond those allowed to any other foreign companies.

The United States had not been a party to Munich. President Roosevelt continued to drop hints that he was rethinking his refusal to sell arms. The flood of letters lobbying him included one that read, "For God's sake! Lift that embargo on Spain. Look what happened to us!" It was signed, "Ghost of Czechoslovakia." But then came the November 1938 midterm elections, in which the Democrats lost more than 70 House seats, including those of some of the Spanish Republic's strongest backers. FDR did not want to risk losing further ground with the electorate by changing American policy. This is the only point in the long stream of personally warm but politically guarded letters Eleanor Roosevelt sent to Martha Gellhorn when the first lady struck a different note. "Dear Marty," she wrote. "I not only read your report but I gave it to the president. I hope the day will come when you can write something that will not make one really feel ashamed to read it."

Two weeks after La Pasionaria's farewell to the International Brigades, Franco's German allies offered a sign of what Europe would face under Nazi domination. On the night of November 9, throughout Germany, Austria, and the parts of Czechoslovakia Hitler now controlled, Nazi storm troopers attacked more than 1,000 synagogues and 7,000 Jewish-owned businesses, setting fires, smashing windows with axes and sledgehammers, and killing more than 90 Jews. Homes, schools, and hospitals were vandalized and tombstones in Jewish cemeteries smashed or uprooted. Laughing Nazis threw prayer books and Torah scrolls on bonfires. During *Kristallnacht*, as it was called because of all the broken glass, including stained-glass windows from centuries-old synagogues, fire departments were ordered to let buildings burn, and to douse the flames only if nearby "Aryan" property was threatened. A few days later, all Jewish children were barred from German schools, and some 30,000 Jewish men were taken off to Dachau, Buchenwald, and other concentration camps.

On a snowy morning six weeks later, Franco launched his last offensive. His armies were flush with new German weaponry, and his air force was bolstered by 400 German-trained pilots to whom the Condor Legion began to hand over some of its Messerschmitt fighters. In a desperate secret trip to Paris Negrín pleaded with the French foreign minister and the British and American ambassadors for help, but in vain. He had also been seeking a compromise peace through the Vatican and other channels, but Franco was not interested. Nor was he interested in attempts to mitigate the war's toll. When the British sent a special envoy to encourage both sides in Spain to suspend executions, the Republic readily agreed, and halted all of them for some four months. Nationalist Spain, where the number of political prisoners facing the death sentence ran into the thousands, refused to do likewise.

Critically short of everything from rifles to aircraft, the Republic sent its air force commander to Moscow to beg for aid. Despite having largely lost interest in Spain, Stalin was concerned at the prospect of immediate defeat and dispatched some munitions. The direct Mediterranean route remained too dangerous, and the ships had to go to a French port. France delayed sending on these weapons until it was too late. When a Republican officer went to inspect crates that had finally been brought across the Spanish frontier and left in a field, he found they contained disassembled late-model Soviet fighters and bombers. But by this point no airfields were left where they could be put together, and there were not enough surviving crews to fly them.

In Madrid, the average person was consuming less than 800 calories per day. Without coal, shivering families in candlelit apartments broke up furniture, interior doors, window shutters, and tree branches to burn in their fireplaces. Men newly conscripted into the army were told to bring their own boots and blankets. In Barcelona, swollen with refugees, scurvy raged and the official food ration was 3.5 ounces of lentils per day. The lucky might also be able to find a small dried codfish.

Little of such privation was visible in Herbert Matthews's dispatches. "On the whole, there is no discouragement here," Matthews wrote from Barcelona on January 1, 1939. When he had to report yet another Republican retreat two weeks later, the withdrawal was "a quick and efficient job." A few days after, he had to admit that several towns had been lost, but, he insisted, the morale of the Republic's troops "appears to be excellent. . . . No one here doubts the government's ability to carry on for many more months." As Nationalist troops closed in on Barcelona, he ended an article telegraphed to the *Times* on January 25 by reminding readers that in 1936 Republican soldiers had "performed the miracle of Madrid and perhaps they can perform another." Franco's army entered the outlying districts of Barcelona the next day.

In the Catalan capital torn-up scraps of party and trade union membership cards littered the streets as people destroyed anything that might mark them for retaliation by the Nationalists. Hundreds of thousands fled for the French border with suitcases and cloth bundles, wheeling these on carts if they were lucky. The 20,000 wounded Republican soldiers in the city, unable to leave, feared the worst, because their missing limbs and shrapnel scars would fatally identify them to Franco's troops. "I will never be able to forget the wounded who crawled out of the Vallcarca hospital," wrote one woman. "Mutilated and covered in bandages, half-naked despite the cold, they pushed themselves towards the road, yelling pleas that they should not be left behind. . . . Those who had lost their legs crawled along the ground, those who had lost an arm raised the other with a clenched fist, the youngest crying in fear, the older ones shouting in rage and cursing those of us who were fleeing and were abandoning them." They might not necessarily have been better off had they joined the vast exodus of refugees plodding along the roads for France; in between snow and sleet storms, Nationalist aircraft bombed and strafed these enormous, tattered columns mercilessly.

Marching into Barcelona, Franco's troops first knelt in prayer in one of its grand plazas as long-silent church bells rang, then enjoyed several days of unrestrained looting. Losing the city, Martha Gellhorn wrote Eleanor Roosevelt, was "like having a death in the family, only worse." The street down which the Internationals had paraded three months earlier was renamed the Avenida del Generalissimo. Barcelona, declared a Nationalist general, "is a city which has sinned greatly, and now it must be cleansed." Prisons filled, forbidden books were heaped on bonfires, and thousands of teachers lost their jobs. Meanwhile, on the other side of Europe, his appetite whetted by his gains at Munich, Hitler ignored that agreement and sent his army into Prague.

In the shrinking territory held by an army in which many soldiers had no winter coats, Republican Spain went through one final, tragic spasm of internal fighting that cost hundreds of lives. This time it was between Negrín and his supporters, determined to hold on as long as possible in hopes that a wider European war might bring British and French help, and rebellious army commanders who hoped to save lives with a negotiated peace. Neither side gained what it wanted:

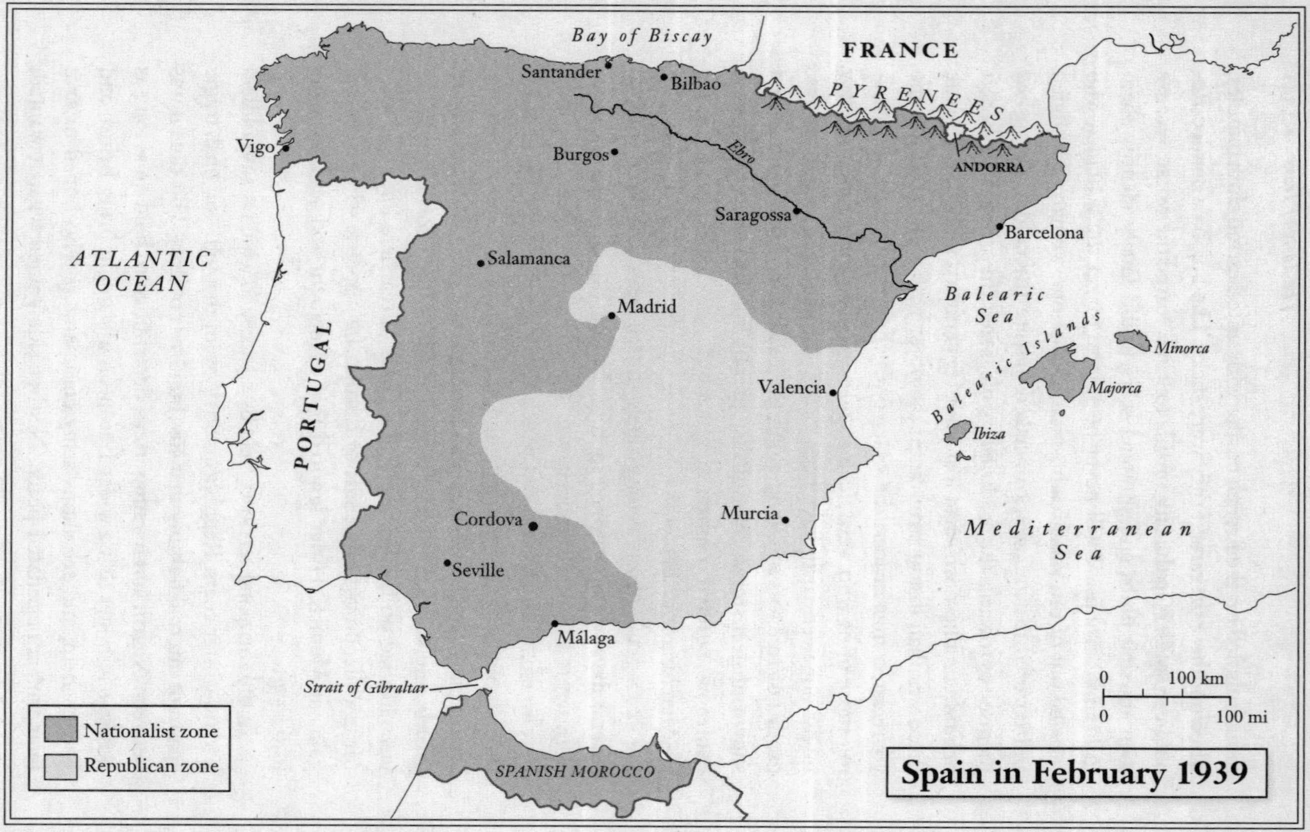
Spain in February 1939
Nationalist zone
Republican zone
Bay of Biscay
FRANCE
PYRENEES
ANDORRA
Santander
Bilbao
Vigo
Burgos
Ebro
Saragossa
Barcelona
ATLANTIC
OCEAN
Salamanca
Madrid
PORTUGAL
Valencia
Balearic
Sea
Balearic Islands
Minorca
Majorca
Ibiza
Cordova
Murcia
Seville
Mediterranean
Sea
Málaga
Strait of Gibraltar
SPANISH MOROCCO
0
100 km
0
100 mi

Britain and France recognized Nationalist Spain on February 27, while combat continued, with France soon handing over a large supply of gold the Republic had banked there—a great boon for Franco, who had no gold reserves. And Franco had no interest in negotiations, only in unconditional surrender. By March 31, 1939, the Nationalists occupied all of Spain, and the fighting was over. In addition to the estimated 200,000 political killings that took place during the war, one conservative calculation puts a similar figure on the number of soldiers killed or fatally wounded in combat, adding to it some 10,000 civilian deaths from bombing raids and another 25,000 from war-related malnutrition or disease in the Republican zone. Other estimates are higher. And, as Spaniards would discover, mass deaths would not end with the war.

In Madrid, Nationalist troops, plus units of their German and Italian allies, marched through the city in a victory parade, while warplanes were arrayed in formation to spell out *Viva Franco* in the sky. The exodus of refugees, mostly on foot, grew to half a million. "Lifting our hearts to God," said a telegram of congratulations to Franco from Pope Pius XII, "we give sincere thanks with your Excellency for the victory of Catholic Spain."

Doubtless also thankful was Torkild Rieber, who knew that Texaco would at last be fully paid for all the oil he had supplied on credit. In total, Rieber sold the Nationalists at least $20 million worth of oil during the civil war, the equivalent, by the most conservative calculation, of some $325 million today. Texaco's tankers made 225 trips to Spain, and ships the company chartered another 156. A grateful Franco continued to buy Texaco oil long after the war, and later made Rieber a Knight of the Grand Cross of Isabella the Catholic, one of Spain's highest honors.

Although the American press had ignored Texaco's oil lifeline, the Nationalists knew how essential it had been. After the war, the Franco government's oil monopoly publicly acknowledged the "enthusiasm shown for our cause" by Rieber and Brewster and the way Texaco had "offered its assistance without reservations of any kind." A few years later the undersecretary of the Spanish foreign ministry went further.

"Without American petroleum and American trucks and American credits," he told a journalist, "we could never have won the civil war."

The refugees had good reason to flee, for Franco's victory brought not reconciliation but vengeance. If, during the war, Nationalist supporters in a particular town or village had been killed or had their property confiscated, people from that town were executed in retaliation, whether or not they had anything to do with the original events. If the regime couldn't lay its hands on someone, his family paid the price. Camil Companys i Jover, for example, was a prominent Barcelona lawyer and head of the city's bar association. Although his parish priest would later testify that he had protected many members of the clergy during the war, his brother was president of Catalonia—soon to be executed by Franco—so he knew he was a marked man. At the end of the war he fled to France, where he committed suicide. Even this did not prevent him from being posthumously sentenced to 15 years' disbarment and a fine, which his widow was forced to pay.

At every level of society, Franco aimed to rid Spain of what he considered alien influences. Anyone speaking Basque or Catalan in public or in church was subject to arrest; Catalan Christian names and Catalan dancing were forbidden. Though there had been few Jews in Spain for centuries, the Generalissimo railed against the "Jewish spirit." He proclaimed a "Law of Political Responsibilities" which, by a logic worthy of *1984*, declared that because his seizure of power had been legitimate, anyone who opposed it was guilty of military rebellion. Similarly guilty was anyone who had, in the two years prior to the 1936 coup, "opposed the Nationalist movement with clear acts or grave passivity."

That law was put into effect by a tribunal headed by Enrique Suñer Ordóñez, a paranoid of the first rank, who condemned the Republic's politicians as "wild boars and cloven-hoofed beasts running through parliament, in search of sacrificial victims to bite with their fangs or smash with their hooves. . . . Spain has been before and is again the theater of an epic combat between Titans and apocalyptic monsters. The programmes laid out in the *Protocols of the Elders of Zion* are beginning to become reality."

Before being dispatched to firing squads, prisoners were often tortured, beaten, or starved until they confessed their sins. Routine torture methods included immersing someone's head in a toilet bowl; forcing him or her to sing Nationalist hymns, right arm outstretched in salute, for hours at a time; and giving electric shocks to the ears, nipples, and genitals. If someone failed to confess, the regime still found ways to proclaim its triumph. For example, Matilde Landa was a secular, educated, professional woman and a Communist (four strikes against her) who found herself a political prisoner in Majorca. The authorities demanded that she recant her beliefs and have a public baptism. Unable to endure more interrogation, she threw herself off a prison balcony. During the 45 minutes it took her to die, a priest was summoned to give her last rites, and the government did not return her body to her family but instead gave her a Catholic burial.

Republican women like Landa drew particular fury. Oliva Cabezas García, a nurse, had tried to escape across the Pyrenees with her lover, Polish volunteer Dr. Jacques Grunblatt. The two had worked together in a XV Brigade hospital. After two days of walking, pregnant with Grunblatt's child, she was unable to go further. She returned to her sister in Madrid and gave birth to a son just as the war ended. To mark Franco's victory, she was forced to dance—while in labor. The news made Grunblatt, a refugee in France, "cry as I never cried in my adult life."

A women's penitentiary in Madrid saw its population swell to almost 14,000. Many women were raped and impregnated in prison, and some 12,000 children of Republican prisoners, some of them babies literally taken from their mothers' arms, were placed in orphanages. These seizures were justified by Spain's chief military psychiatrist, Antonio Vallejo Nágera, a Franco favorite, who believed that otherwise "Marxist fanaticism" would be transmitted like a germ from parent to child.

Because identifying men and women who had supported the Republic was not always easy, denunciations became important, and—as in Stalin's Russia—to fail to denounce anybody was in itself cause for suspicion. "You have no right to deprive the justice system of any enemy of the Fatherland," warned a newspaper in Santander. Priests made note of those who did not attend Mass.

Altogether, at least 20,000 Republicans were executed after Franco's victory. An additional number, unknown but possibly larger, died in the country's packed prisons. In 1940, by the Franco regime's own admission, some 270,000 convicted prisoners were jammed into cells built for 20,000, and another 100,000 were in jail awaiting trial. Food was abysmal, disease rife, and prisoners were sometimes deprived of water for a day or two at a time. In 1941, in just one city, Cordova, 502 inmates died behind bars.

The statistics for those in custody do not include at least 90,000 people in "militarized penal colonies" who were put to work on a variety of projects, including a 110-mile canal to irrigate the land of some large estate owners who had backed Franco. Many prisoners were also rented out to private companies as manual labor, whose low cost had the added effect of keeping free labor's wages down. Some 20,000 forced laborers built the Valley of the Fallen, a gigantic monument, cross, and basilica honoring the Nationalist dead that took nearly 20 years to complete. There were, of course, no such public memorials for Franco's victims. If a labor unionist was simply tossed down a mineshaft, for instance, there would not even be a death certificate, which would mean his wife could never remarry because she wasn't legally a widow. For decades, people who had lost a loved one at such a spot might leave flowers at night. To do anything more was too risky.

Above all, the regime rested on the life-and-death power wielded by Franco. As the historian Antony Beevor writes, "The Caudillo used to read through the sentences of death when taking his coffee after a meal, often in the presence of his personal priest. . . . He would write an 'E' against those he decided should be executed, and a 'C' when commuting the sentence. For those who he considered needed to be made a conspicuous example, he wrote '*garrote y prensa*' (garroting and press coverage)." Once the lists reached each of the country's penal institutions, "the sentences would then be read out in the central gallery of the prison. Some officials enjoyed reading out the first name, then pausing if it was a common one, such as José or Juan, to strike fear into all those who bore it, before adding the family name. In the women's prison of Amorebieta one of the nuns who acted as warders would perform this duty."

Francisco Franco ruled all of Spain for more than 36 years, until he died, amid signs of senility, at the age of eighty-two, a reign longer than that of Hitler, Mussolini, or Stalin. Eventually he adopted some of the trappings of Spanish royalty: entering and leaving church under a canopy, receiving ambassadors on a raised dais, and having coins struck with his image. To some of his favorites, including generals from the war, Franco passed out titles in royal fashion, creating a string of counts, marquises, and dukes. A few of these new noblemen, in a bizarre twist reminiscent of Catholic sainthood, received their titles posthumously.

His rule was, as George Orwell had observed early on, "an attempt not so much to impose Fascism as to restore feudalism." The Catholic Church remained immensely powerful, and the position of women was far worse than in Hitler's Germany. Women were legally considered dependents of their fathers or husbands, whose permission they needed to open a bank account, own property, file a lawsuit, apply for a job, or take a trip away from home. A husband had the right to kill his wife if he caught her committing adultery. Franco's rule became less murderous and repressive in its later decades; Spain eventually enjoyed an economic rise and eased some of the restrictions on women and cultural expression. But torture was routine, the regime remained a police state, and until 1974, a year before the dictator's death, it continued to execute prisoners with the garrote.

22

Kaddish

When 148 returning American volunteers arrived at New York on the liner *Paris* on December 15, 1938, awaiting them seemed to be, in the words of Lincoln commander Milton Wolff, "more cops than people." Police on foot and horseback kept a throng of well-wishers a good distance from the French Line pier on West 48th Street. And immediately came other signs of the hostility with which the government would treat these veterans for decades to come. Men who a year or two earlier had seen their American passports confiscated by André Marty now had their new passports, issued grudgingly by US consulates in Europe, confiscated at dockside. One volunteer asked an official when he would get his back. "Never—I hope" was the reply.

Behind the police lines, the crowd of friends and family members in winter coats, including the Brighton Beach Community Center Drum and Bugle Corps, were a pale echo of the weeping, cheering hundreds of thousands who had lined the parade route through Barcelona seven weeks earlier. Relatives of volunteers missing and unaccounted for, like Phil Schachter, were desperate for news; some of those waiting at the pier held up homemade signs with names or photographs of vanished men.

The vets slipped back into their old lives uneasily. They had seen their friends killed or maimed for a cause about which many Americans had only the dimmest idea. In later years, some volunteers would be told that they looked mighty young to be veterans of the Spanish-American War. With Franco victorious, public interest in the lost struggle against him soon waned. Jim Neugass, for instance, had good contacts in the literary world, but no one wanted to publish his wartime diary.

Some survivors quickly came face to face with what had not changed at home. When James Yates's ship docked in New York, he was taken to a hotel where Lincoln supporters had reserved a block of rooms. "Several of the men had signed for their rooms, but when my turn came the clerk didn't even seem to look at me. 'Sorry,' he said. 'No vacancy.'" Yates was black. His white comrades then moved to another hotel in solidarity with him, which was some comfort, but still "the pain went deeply as any bullet could have done." The equality that he felt he had experienced in Spain was still decades away in the United States. A fellow black Lincoln told him, "Spain was the first place that I ever felt like a free man."

The continent the Lincolns had left sped toward war. Of the returning volunteers Hemingway wrote, "No good men will be at home for long." On August 23, 1939, Stalin and Hitler made the infamous pact that divided Eastern Europe between them. The Nazis invaded western Poland after an aerial blitzkrieg orchestrated by former Condor Legion chief of staff Wolfram von Richthofen, who took to the sky himself in a small observation plane to survey the destruction. The Soviet Union similarly occupied eastern Poland, the Baltic states, part of Romania, and, after bitter fighting, parts of Finland. Britain and France declared hostilities against Germany. The opening round of the Second World War had begun. In June 1941, Hitler threw aside his pact with Stalin and invaded the Soviet Union. Six months later, the Japanese bombed Pearl Harbor, and the United States entered the war.

Although Franco never formally joined the Axis (Hitler wouldn't promise him the slice of France and the huge swath of Africa he wanted), he cooperated closely with the Führer, granting important naval bases that far extended the range of German U-boats. The port of Vigo, where Torkild Rieber's tankers had often unloaded, became a supply and fuel depot for 21 Nazi submarines that raided Allied convoys in the North Atlantic, and German submarines refueled in Spanish Morocco and the Canary Islands as well. Spain also supplied Germany with crucial metals, such as the tungsten used to harden both tank armor and armor-piercing shells, with radio listening stations, bases for reconnaissance aircraft, and outposts for observing maritime traffic in the Strait of Gibraltar. Once the Nazis invaded the USSR, Franco encouraged Spaniards to fight for the cause in a "Blue Division" of volunteers, as well as a "Blue Squadron" of fighter pilots. Some 45,000 Spanish soldiers would join Hitler's doomed war, taking part in the siege of Leningrad and other battles in Russia. (Some who were taken prisoner found themselves sharing quarters in the Soviet *gulag* with Spanish Republican refugees who had run afoul of Stalin's paranoia.)

The greatest aid Spain provided the Nazis, however, had already been given: the wealth of experience that German aviators and other military men gained in nearly three years of the civil war. Twenty-seven different models of Nazi aircraft were tested in Spanish skies. As air force chief Hermann Göring later put it when on trial at Nuremberg, the Spanish war was an opportunity "to test my young *Luftwaffe*. . . . In order that the personnel, too, might gather a certain amount of experience, I saw to it that . . . new people were constantly being sent and others recalled."

The Germans learned many vital lessons from their involvement in Spain: that when you have long-distance supply lines for spare parts you should minimize the number of different types of vehicles, that bombers require fighter escorts, that pilots need extra training for bad weather and nighttime navigation, and that to match Soviet models, Nazi tanks needed improvement. After every large bombing raid, Condor Legion pilots took aerial photographs, studied the results of different tactics, and sent home detailed reports. Sometimes the legion deliberately attacked isolated Spanish towns in the path of an advance, so that as soon as the area was captured, a team on the ground could assess the effectiveness of the bombing. In 1938, residents of four villages near Valencia who survived murderous raids wondered why they had been targeted: the towns had no Republican troop concentrations, factories, or military bases. Discovered decades later in a German archive, a 50-page report with 65 photographs—taken before, during, and after the attacks—made clear the reason. The Condor Legion was testing a new model of the Stuka dive bomber, dropping 500 kg (1,100 lb) bombs.

After the United States entered the Second World War, more than 425 Lincoln vets served in the American armed forces, and roughly 100 more in the merchant marine. At least 21 were killed—in the skies over Germany, on the Murmansk supply route to Russia, on South Pacific islands, behind Japanese lines in the Philippines, and elsewhere. Thousands of International Brigades veterans from other countries also fought for the Allies. Bernard Knox, an Englishman who immigrated to the United States and would later become a distinguished professor of classics at Yale, was sent by the US Army in Italy as liaison to a group of anti-Nazi partisans. At first he found he was "sometimes getting my newly acquired Italian mixed up with my half-forgotten Spanish. . . . Suddenly, after another such fumble, the . . . commander stood up, smiling, walked over to me and patted me on the shoulder. 'Spagna, no?' he said." The two discovered they had fought in adjoining units defending Madrid. "From that point on, relations with the partisans were no problem."

Although the Spanish Civil War ended in 1939, a war of a different sort has raged ever since among writers about this period. At issue is the question: what would have happened if the Spanish Republic had won?

Many on the right argue that a victorious Republic would have become, like Hungary or Bulgaria a decade later, a Soviet satellite. Given the influence Soviet officers had over its secret police and military, some claim, it virtually already *was* a Soviet satellite. The journalist and historian Sam Tanenhaus refers to the Lincoln Brigaders as "conscripts in Stalin's army, and as expendable as the millions of Soviet citizens who died during the Great Terror of the 1930s." He and others point to documents from that era, revealed after the collapse of the USSR, in which Soviet agents in Spain crow over the influence they or Spanish Communists had gained, or urge the "liquidation" of rivals on the Spanish left.

The Soviets did have a powerful presence in Republican Spain. When La Pasionaria gave her eloquent speech of farewell to the International Brigades, one of the huge portraits looking down on the speakers' platform was of Stalin. But whatever its ambitions, it is extremely unlikely that the Kremlin ever could have controlled a victorious Spanish Republic. Maintaining client states almost always depends on wielding the threat of occupation troops. For much of the twentieth century, for instance, the United States dominated Central America and the Caribbean by repeatedly sending in the marines. The USSR similarly kept Eastern Europe under its thumb after 1945 by stationing hundreds of thousands of soldiers there—and deploying them when a country threatened to go its own way, as in Hungary in 1956 or Czechoslovakia in 1968. Without a large occupation force, making Spain, on the far side of Europe, follow Moscow's dictates would have been difficult indeed.

Many supporters of the Spanish Republic maintain that if it had prevailed, the course of European history might have been dramatically altered for the better. "A different outcome of the Spanish Civil War would have certainly weakened the position of Hitler and Mussolini," wrote Willy Brandt, for example, "and maybe prevented World War II."

But this claim, too, is improbable. Despite his support for Franco, Spain was never more than a sideshow for Hitler. His driving obsession had always been to expand German power to the east—over

Poland, the rich farmland of Ukraine and parts of southern Russia, the Balkan and Caspian oil fields. It is hard to imagine a Republican victory in Spain dimming that dream. If, however, the democracies had helped the Republic prevail, in the larger war to come this would have deprived the Nazis of a source of strategic raw materials for weapons production like iron, copper, mercury, tungsten, and pyrites, of important submarine bases, and of the 45,000 troops of the Blue Division.

The fate of all Europe did not rest on the Spanish Civil War, but the fate of one country did. If the Republic had won, Spaniards would not have had to endure 36 years of Franco's ruthless dictatorship. Someone who came to regret—too late—that the Western democracies had turned their backs was Franklin D. Roosevelt. On January 27, 1939, he told a cabinet meeting that he now felt the arms embargo to have been "a grave mistake."

Two years after Marion Merriman returned from Spain she married again, as Bob had urged her to do when he feared he might not survive. Decades later, she told a reporter that at first she was haunted by a nightmare in which Bob returned and she was forced to choose between her two husbands. She gave birth to three sons, worked in the administration at Stanford University, and, like almost all others who volunteered for Spain—no matter whether they were still Party members, ex-Communists, or anti-Communists—endured periodic visits from the FBI. The vigilance of the bureau's suspicious chief, J. Edgar Hoover, extended even to the dead. Robert Merriam, a special assistant to President Eisenhower and a Republican candidate for mayor of Chicago, found himself under investigation when the FBI confused his name with Bob's.

Decades after the war, Marion visited Spain with her second husband, and twice more with fellow veterans after he died, trying to pinpoint the spot where Bob disappeared. But she was frustrated to be able to find out nothing certain: records of the desperate, chaotic retreat in the spring of 1938 were fragmentary, and the passage of time had thinned out the ranks of survivors. "Where went the years?" she wrote to Alvah Bessie just after the fiftieth anniversary of her wedding to Bob.

She remained friends with Milly Bennett, who still seemed at home in a milieu of true-believing Communists while taking satisfaction in not quite being one herself. At one point Bennett wrote proudly of how she could not resist arguing with Party loyalists at Marion's. "She cant have her dear friends . . . in the house . . . because I fight with them!" Bennett tried to find a publisher for her autobiography, *Live Hard, Die Hard*, of which she had written only the first volume, covering her time in revolutionary China in the 1920s. With her files filled with rejection letters, she never went on to write about Russia and Spain. Her husband, former Lincoln commander Hans Amlie, was killed in an industrial accident in 1949, and she fell ill with cancer a decade later. Marion helped care for her in her last months, and was with her when she died in 1960.

The marriage between Toby Jensky and Pat Gurney did not last. He remained in London when she returned to New York, and soon the Second World War made civilian travel between the two countries almost impossible. We can trace the troubled relationship through letters that each sent to a mutual confidant, Fredericka Martin, chief nurse and administrator of the American medical unit in Spain. In 1941, Jensky told Martin about a new boyfriend who, like Gurney, seemed more smitten with her than she with him, then added, "As for Pat . . . I don't know that I want him here or what I want." Still hoping, in 1949 Gurney wrote to Martin, "I am very unhappy about Toby but do not know what I can do about it. Life stinks." Gurney and Jensky tried living together briefly in New York, but on her part the old flame, always uncertain, did not relight, and they divorced. To an interviewer years later, she said that because she "grew up in an unhappy household" she had never wanted to marry anyone. When curious family members asked her about her wartime romance, said a niece, "she refused to talk about him." Jensky continued working as a nurse, and died single in 1995.

Since the bullet wound to his hand made sculpting impossible,

Gurney turned to painting. He also fished and dove for pearls in the Red Sea and the Gulf of Aden, wrote a book about it, farmed, and taught English in Greece, Turkey, and Portugal. He married again. Just before his memoir of Spain was published, he died of a heart attack at the age of sixty-two.

Although more than 15 million Americans donned uniforms to fight fascism in the Second World War, those who had decided to do so earlier continued to live under suspicion. Martin Dies, a beefy, red-faced Texan who built his political career on denouncing Reds, labor unionists, and immigrants, was the first chair of the House Un-American Activities Committee. According to another member of Congress, Dies declared that "if you were against Hitler and Mussolini before Dec. 7, 1941, you were a premature anti-fascist." Although the label was proudly embraced by many Lincoln veterans, some found themselves summoned before legislative committees or fired from jobs after the FBI visited their employers.

Soviet atomic espionage, the Cold War, and the coming of McCarthyism only increased the official paranoia. One American veteran of Spain to fall victim to it was Dr. Edward Barsky. After returning to the United States, he became chair of the Joint Anti-Fascist Refugee Committee, which lobbied against Franco and provided aid for those who had fled Spain. The House Un-American Activities Committee summoned Barsky and others from the group to testify, demanding, among other things, the names of all who received such help. Barsky and his colleagues refused: naming Spaniards could put them or their families at risk. In 1950, Barsky was sentenced to six months in federal prison for contempt of Congress. When released, he found his New York State medical license suspended for another six months. He fought the suspension all the way to the Supreme Court, which ruled against him. Justice William O. Douglas dissented: "When a doctor cannot save lives in America because he is opposed to Franco in Spain, it is time to call a halt and look critically at the neurosis that has possessed us."

In this climate, many Lincolns feared arrest. Machine-gunner Hy

Tabb, one of those who accidentally stumbled through a Nationalist camp at night with Alvah Bessie, later became a printer and proofreader at the *New York Times*. After being subpoenaed by a state legislative committee, he burned all his war memorabilia at his weekend cottage one day, even a collection of posters. Alabama-born Jack Penrod, who led a sniper squad at Teruel and later became professor of English at the University of Florida, destroyed a memoir of the war he had written because "at one time I didn't know whether they might actually get a search warrant to search our house."

Jim Neugass married after returning from Spain and became the father of two boys, but the family's New York City landlord tried to evict them when he discovered Neugass had fought for the Republic. The landlord was happy to cooperate with the FBI, the bureau's files show. He told agents whom Neugass received mail from and said that he "did not know where the subject worked at the present time, but knew that he did a great deal of typewriting, apparently writing a book." The book was a novel, published in 1949 and based on his childhood and youth in New Orleans and New York. But one sign of the times is that in the biographical information he supplied his publisher for the book jacket, he omitted any mention of Spain. The only civil war in the novel is the American one. Neugass even told his older son that the wide shrapnel scar on his thigh was the result of a skiing accident.

Just weeks after his book appeared, Neugass died at the age of forty-four, suffering a heart attack as he left a Greenwich Village subway station. A thief then stole his wallet, leaving his body with no identification; it took his frantic widow four days to find out what had happened. She always believed that all his unpublished writings had been destroyed when a heavy storm flooded her basement some years after his death. A typescript of the diary was only discovered, in a trove of papers in a Vermont used bookstore, more than half a century later. Neugass's younger son and namesake had been just a year and a half old when his father died. After the diary was found, he told the editors who saw it to publication, "This is the most important thing that has ever happened in my life. This man was a ghost to me." Using the rediscovered diary as a guide, he went to Spain and traveled over the roads and through the villages where his father had driven his ambulance.

If ever asked about the crucial help he gave to Franco, Torkild Rieber merely said that he was a patriotic American and that if the United States were ever at war he would quit his job as Texaco CEO and go back to being a ship's captain, in his country's service. The year after the Spanish Civil War ended, however, Rieber came in for some public embarrassment. During the twilight period between the beginning of the Second World War in September 1939 and America's entry two years later, he made no secret of his enthusiasm for Hitler. The Führer, he said, was just the sort of strong, anti-Communist leader with whom one could do business. This Rieber did, with gusto, selling Texaco oil to the Nazis, ordering tankers from Hamburg shipyards, and traveling to Germany after the Polish blitzkrieg so that Hermann Göring could take him on a tour by air of key industrial sites. On that trip he spent a weekend at the Luftwaffe commander's country estate, Carinhall, soon to be extravagantly decorated with art treasures looted from across Europe.

Back home, "Cap" Rieber found his salty-sailor persona still played well in New York society. A regular at insider social events like California's Bohemian Grove gathering and the annual dinner of Washington's Gridiron Club, he now lived in a thirty-fifth-floor apartment at the elegant Hampshire House on Central Park South. Its other celebrity tenants included Ray Bolger, who played the Scarecrow in *The Wizard of Oz.*

For Göring, Rieber did several significant favors, which included facilitating the operations of Gerhardt Westrick, a high-powered German lobbyist–cum–intelligence agent. Westrick worked out of an office at Texaco headquarters, drove a Buick Rieber loaned him, and entertained American businessmen at a Scarsdale mansion rented from a Texaco lawyer. In June 1940, immediately after France surrendered to the invading Nazis, Rieber and Westrick took part in a celebratory dinner in a private room at New York's Waldorf-Astoria Hotel, where executives of Ford, General Motors, Eastman Kodak, and other companies talked about the prospects for American cooperation with the Nazi regime that seemed certain to dominate Europe for the foreseeable future. Germany would be a good credit risk for American loans, Westrick said, and there should definitely be no more of this nonsense of selling US arms to the British.

Rieber was always happy to hire Nazi sympathizers. As a result, a Texaco representative in Germany received frequent telegrams, supposedly about patent claims, from an associate in the company's New York office. In fact, these proved to contain coded information about ships leaving New York for Britain and what their cargoes were. Other information the Nazis at Texaco transmitted or carried to Germany, some of it disguised as routine business correspondence, included detailed intelligence reports on the American petroleum and aircraft industries. Alert British agents discovered some of these goings-on and tipped off the *New York Herald Tribune*. Westrick was expelled from the country, Texaco shamed, and Rieber forced to resign, his departure eased by a hefty pension. Texaco, alarmed by the bad publicity, moved quickly to clean up its public image. It began sponsoring the Metropolitan Opera's weekly radio broadcasts, a relationship that would last for decades.

Thanks to a grateful Franco, however, the deposed Rieber landed on his feet, for the Generalissimo made him chief American buyer for Spain's oil monopoly. He went on to a succession of high-paying positions and directorships in the oil industry, shipbuilding, and other businesses. Returning from a 1960 trip to finalize the purchase of a tanker from a German shipyard, Rieber rented an entire floor at the Hotel Ritz in Paris for his retinue. One evening a cold prevented him from taking the entourage out to dinner at an elegant restaurant, so he asked a young journalist in the party, Lewis Lapham—later to become the longtime editor of *Harper's Magazine*, with politics quite the opposite of Rieber's—to play host in his place. "He summoned me to his room in the Ritz and said, 'Now Lewis, you're going to be me this evening. Do you know how to tip?' I said, 'I don't think so, Cap.' He said, 'Well, it has to be *a lot*.' And he produced fistfuls of hundred-franc notes and told me how extravagant I had to be."

As Rieber aged, his shock of hair turned white, but his vigorous, sturdy figure, knack for making money, and fondness for authoritarian leaders all remained unchanged. He supported an operation smuggling arms across the border in refrigerated railway freight cars for a planned military coup in Mexico, inspected the oil industry of the Shah's Iran for the World Bank, and played host to Franco's daughter and her husband when they visited the United States, taking them across the country in his private plane. The party enjoyed Niagara Falls, an Indian reservation in New Mexico, a banquet at Houston's exclusive Bayou Club, and a visit to Paramount Studios in Hollywood, where they met Bob Hope, Cary Grant, and Alfred Hitchcock and lunched with Cecil B. DeMille. Rieber died in 1968, at the age of eighty-six, a wealthy man.

Virginia Cowles settled in London on the eve of the Second World War. Once it began, she took to the American lecture circuit to urge her country to enter the fighting. After it did so, she worked for a time for the US ambassador to Britain, then went back into the field as a war correspondent. After the war, she married and had a successful career as a writer of historical biographies. At seventy-three, diagnosed with terminal emphysema and given only weeks to live, she asked her husband to drive her through the Sierra de Guadarrama, the mountainous country northwest of Madrid, where she had reported from both sides of the Spanish war. On their way home, in an auto accident in France, he was badly injured and she was killed.

The war's glamour couple, Ernest Hemingway and Martha Gellhorn, married in 1940. Nine years older, he called her "daughter," as he often did with younger women. In their early months together, she was so star-struck that some of her letters to him unconsciously echoed the words and rhythms of his own distinctive prose. "What will I do in New York," a Hemingwayesque passage from one ran, "with all the people who do not know any of the things we know: how fine the Guadarrama are, and how fine the people, and how handsomely we walked up San Juan Hill . . . and how we lay in bed listening to the machine gun bullets, and the bombardment down the street."

But if he expected this stylish young blonde to be a mere trophy wife, Hemingway was soon disappointed. Before long it became clear that she was determined to continue writing and not live in his shadow. They both covered the Second World War, but Gellhorn scored a coup by stowing away on a hospital ship and reaching Omaha Beach the day after D-day. Hemingway didn't manage to get ashore until much later and was furious. They divorced in 1946. Gellhorn went on to cover many more wars, wrote well-received fiction as well, and, until her death at eighty-nine, was known for swiftly ending any interview if she was asked about Hemingway.

On returning from their last trip to wartime Spain, Hemingway began the novel he had been planning. When *For Whom the Bell Tolls* was published in 1940, the author felt it was "the best goddamn book I have ever written." Others disagree, but whatever its shortcomings, the novel showed a more capacious political understanding of the civil war than his journalism from the front or the narrator's script for *The Spanish Earth*. There are searing scenes of violence against civilians by both Nationalists and Republicans. A massacre of right-wingers—some of whom are forced to jump off a cliff—is evoked with a shrewd sense of mob psychology. Although the author's heart was with the doomed Republic, he portrayed some Nationalist soldiers as decent human beings, painted a harsh portrait of Soviet officials, and an absolutely excoriating one of International Brigades commissar André Marty. At one point in the novel, Marty arrests two Republican couriers, fulminating about traitors, instead of speeding their vitally important message to its destination.

Some former Lincolns were shocked. Alvah Bessie condemned the writer for downplaying crucial Soviet help to Spain and for the "vicious . . . personal attack" on Marty (though privately, writing in his diary in Spain, Bessie had referred to Marty as "the demagogue, old and flabby"). He dismissed the novel as "a *Cosmopolitan* love story." Denunciations by other American volunteers followed. Ironically, former Lincoln commissar Steve Nelson, much higher in the Communist Party hierarchy than Bessie, was enthralled, like many readers, by the novel's vivid and suspenseful narrative. In an enthusiastic review, he called the book "a monument in American literature." The Party's national committee then demanded Nelson retract his opinion, which he dutifully did, writing that "it develops that Hemingway did not tell the truth," and adding that it was no accident "this book is hailed in the literary salons of the bourgeoisie."

The Party had hoped that Hemingway's much-anticipated novel would immortalize working-class men of many nations fighting shoulder-to-shoulder against fascism. Instead, the central character, Robert Jordan, is a scholar of Spanish literature and a lone-wolf saboteur who blows up a railway bridge behind the lines, an episode for which Hemingway drew from his overnight expedition with Antoni Chrost's guerrilla band. Paradoxically, although Jordan is, like all Hemingway heroes, no true believer in any organized creed, he is partly modeled on someone who was. In this tall, courageous, fair-haired university instructor from the American West who dies for his convictions in Spain there was an unmistakable suggestion of Bob Merriman.

The best-known nonfiction book to come out of the Spanish Civil War was George Orwell's memoir *Homage to Catalonia*, which was to experience a peculiar history. When it appeared in England in the spring of 1938, this account by someone who fought Franco was anathema to right-wingers, who shunned it. Most readers on the left, however, had no appetite for Orwell's indictment of the Communist-dominated Republican police for hounding and imprisoning members of the POUM. The work sold a mere 800 copies in the dozen years before Orwell's death in 1950. Only after that, during the Cold War, did it find an audience of millions, when critics were eager to point to an early example of Soviet perfidy.

With friends having been imprisoned in Spain and narrowly escaping a spell in jail himself, Orwell naturally was angry about the persecution of the POUM as he was writing. One virtue of *Homage*, however, is its humility. "It is difficult," he wrote, "to be certain about anything except what you have seen with your own eyes. . . . Beware of . . . the distortion inevitably caused by my having seen only one corner of events." Even after the book was in print, on some points he was not afraid to change his mind. Six months later, he decided that given the larger struggle against fascism, the suppression of the revolution-minded POUM had, as he wrote to a friend in late 1938, "far too much fuss made about it." Five years afterward, in an essay, "Looking Back on the Spanish War," he implicitly disavowed a view he had expressed in the book. He had now become convinced that the belief "that the war could have been won if the revolution had not been sabotaged was probably false. . . . The Fascists won because they were the stronger; they had modern arms and the others hadn't." Most historians today would agree.

The role of outside powers, Orwell declared in that 1943 essay, was decisive. "The outcome of the Spanish War was settled in London, Paris, Rome, Berlin." (He could have accurately added Washington to the list.) Months before he died, he left instructions for *Homage* to be rearranged accordingly. He did not cut anything from the book, but asked that two long chapters about the Republic's internal factional disputes be relegated to appendices, although it would be decades after his death before either his British or American publishers carried out his wishes.

Orwell's encounter with Spain raises the question: should a writer reveal damaging information about a cause he or she believes in? Although both Orwell and Hemingway passionately supported the Republic, they answered differently. The war was still on when *Homage* was published, but Orwell's description of a faction-ridden Republic riven by bloody street fighting was a picture far different from what its government wanted to present to the world. Hemingway, by contrast, said nothing in his wartime newspaper dispatches that might have tarnished the heroic Republican image. He saved his acid portraits of André Marty, incompetent commanders, ruthless Communist secret police officers, and the execution of a deserter for his novel and for a searing short story, "Under the Ridge," both published after the war.

"What can I write on it?" the journalist narrator of that story asks a Republican general who has been ordered to launch a hopeless attack with an inadequate number of troops. "Nothing that is not in the official communiqué," the general answers, and later adds, "You can write it all afterwards." Hemingway made the same distinction in a letter to his editor, Maxwell Perkins: "Me, I am faithful and loyal while under arms, but when it is over I am a writer."

An honest writer and someone "under arms" to any cause, no matter how worthy, of course serve different masters. Sometimes it is impossible to be both. Traditionally, we claim that we value Orwell's choice, and *Homage to Catalonia* is held up, with reason, as an example of courageous truth-telling. But we seldom stop to think how much self-censorship we accept when there is widespread belief that a cause is just. Consider the Second World War, the "Good War," which in many ways was not so good at all. For example, starting in 1945 the Allies forcibly ejected some ten million ethnic Germans from parts of Eastern Europe where they had lived for generations. Half a million or more died in the process. Hundreds of Western journalists knew this was going on, but few wrote anything. (A rare exception was Orwell, who early that year declared that the forced removal of Germans from Poland would be an "enormous crime.") Yet seldom is the Second World War considered a shameful chapter in Western journalism.

A decade and a half after the Spanish war, Hemingway declared that "*Homage to Catalonia* is a first-rate book." Orwell felt the same way about *For Whom the Bell Tolls*. What might they have said to each other about their different decisions about self-censorship? The two appear to have crossed paths briefly in a Paris hotel in 1945, when both were war correspondents, but if they talked about Spain, there is no record of it.

• • •

Charles and Lois Orr lived in Paris after leaving Spain, then returned to the United States. He resumed teaching economics, and she worked as a union organizer. Their differences in temperament already had been visible in Spain, and after having a child they divorced. Charles had a long career as an international labor economist; Lois remarried, had several more children, and became a Quaker as well as an activist in the Waldorf Schools movement, dying at sixty-eight. Her nine and a half months as a newlywed in revolutionary Barcelona remained a highlight of her life. Over the course of more than 35 years she wrote many drafts of a book about that period, but it never found a publisher. Her letters from those months did not appear in print until long after her death.

Other Americans whose lives were touched by the Spanish Civil War followed various paths. Although the Lincoln veterans' organization remained dominated by the Communist Party for many years, loyally changing its positions as Moscow did, most vets sooner or later left the Party. Bitter mutual recriminations erupted between those who left and those who stayed; sometimes men who had fought together in Spain stopped speaking to each other. One large exodus from the Party came in response to the blatant cynicism of the Nazi-Soviet Pact of 1939. A still larger one took place after 1956, when Soviet leader Nikita Khrushchev, in a history-making speech to a Party congress in Russia, confirmed what non-Communists had been saying for years about the staggering scale of Stalin's mass arrests, executions, and prison camp network. It was as if the Pope declared that the Protestants had been right all along. At a meeting of the US Communist Party's national committee and other officials, including several Lincoln veterans, Khrushchev's entire speech was read aloud. Men and women wept as they felt lifelong certainties dissolving.

Among those irrevocably shaken by Khrushchev's revelations were the two men who had swum the Ebro together, John Gates and George Watt. Leaving the Party, Watt said, was "the most traumatic episode of my life." In their later years both would write searchingly and self-critically of their youthful naïveté about communism, which they felt some of their fellow vets still shared. Gates, however, continued working in the labor movement, and both men considered themselves democratic socialists. The two stayed in touch and saw each other last as Gates was dying of heart disease in Florida, more than 50 years after the freezing dawn when they swam the river.

Watt and Gates remained proud that they had fought in Spain, as did virtually every other American volunteer mentioned in this story, despite the different political directions they took. Even the man who became one of the best-known anti-Communists of his generation had no regrets about having supported the Spanish Republic. In early 1939, Louis Fischer was finally able to get his wife and children out of the USSR, after Eleanor Roosevelt personally lobbied the Soviets on his behalf. Only then did he feel safe to voice publicly the disillusionment he had long felt in private. In 1949 he became one of six contributors to a widely distributed anthology, an iconic anti-Communist text of its era, *The God That Failed.* Fischer had once written that he could not "imagine life without something higher than myself in which I can have faith." Replacing the Soviet Union as the object of that faith was Mohandas Gandhi, about whom he wrote several books. Eventually, amicably separated from his wife, he settled in Princeton, New Jersey. Women still flocked to him; love letters from them in at least three languages are scattered among his vast files of papers. One of the last, filled with tempestuous fury at her rivals—at one point the Princeton police had to be called in—was another famous apostate from communism, Svetlana Alliluyeva, the rebellious daughter of Joseph Stalin.

All the 2,800 Americans who fought in the Spanish Civil War are gone now; the last died in 2016. While they still lived, many became activists in other causes. Helen Freeman, the nurse badly injured in a bombing raid at the field hospital where she worked with Jim Neugass and Toby Jensky, retired at eighty-three from medical work with the families of California migrant farm laborers. Edward Barsky, their commander at Villa Paz and on the Teruel front, organized doctors and nurses to go to Mississippi in the "Freedom Summer" civil rights campaign of 1964. That year, wounded Lincoln veteran Abe Osheroff, a carpenter, saw his car blown up when he went to the state to help build a black community center. Hilda Bell Roberts, a nurse for a year and a half in Spain, lived long enough to demonstrate against the US war in Afghanistan. Harry Fisher, a runner and radio-telephone technician on practically every front on which the Lincolns fought, died after suffering a heart attack during a protest against the Bush administration's 2003 invasion of Iraq. Perhaps the best epitaph for all the volunteers could be drawn from a letter written by twenty-three-year-old Hyman Katz, several months before he was killed in the retreat from Teruel. If he had not come to Spain, he told his mother, forever afterward he would ask himself, "Why didn't I wake up when the alarm-clock rang?"

In addition to his other self-bestowed titles, Francisco Franco named himself regent for a monarchy that, once he was gone, was to be restored and would keep Spain on his autocratic path. He groomed Prince Juan Carlos, the grandson of the country's last king, to take the throne. Following Franco's death in 1975, the new king, much to everyone's surprise, supported a widespread national desire to return, after some 40 years, to holding elections. Half a dozen years later, he helped the government swiftly rebuff an attempted military coup. Spain has had its economic ups and downs since then, but its future as a parliamentary democracy seems assured.

As long as Franco was in power, the only contact International Brigades veterans could have with former Spanish comrades was furtive. John McElligott had served in the Mackenzie-Papineau Battalion, where in the latter part of the war many Spanish soldiers replaced killed or wounded Americans and Canadians. In 1947, he was a sailor on a ship that docked in Barcelona. Walking down the street, he was startled to see, working as a bootblack, his former commanding officer. He sat down to have his shoes shined, but in public the two men dared make no sign of recognition. The Spaniard, however, wrote something on a piece of paper and slipped it inside McElligott's pant leg. It was an address, and when the sailor went there that evening, he found waiting for him ten Spanish International Brigades veterans. "Tears," McElligott said, "just rolled down my goddamned cheeks."

After Franco's death, such meetings no longer had to be in secret. In 1996—the sixtieth anniversary of the war's outbreak—the Spanish parliament voted to grant honorary citizenship to all living veterans of the International Brigades. Some 380 of them, including 68 Americans, brought their families to Madrid. They visited the old battlefields—a superhighway now cuts through the one at Jarama—and were received with great emotion. In Barcelona, the thousands of people who welcomed them at the railway station had to be held back with crowd-control ropes. Weeping men in their eighties, some in wheelchairs or with walkers, were showered with flower blossoms by young people a fraction of their age. A circle seemed to be complete.

A circle of another sort had closed for Marion Merriman. In 1987, Bob's alma mater, the University of California at Berkeley, received a letter from Spain, addressed only to "Rectorship."

> *Dear Sirs,*
>
> *I am an ancient spanish man that in other time, when I was young . . . was a member of Lincoln-Washington Battalion of the LINCOLN BRIGADE.*
>
> *On that time, I was made prisoner by the FRANCO horse-troops, same day that ROBERT MERRIMAN was dead in front of his Battalion, on April 2, 1,938 at my side in GANDESA. . . .*
>
> *. . . I want ask for that you send to me, the Postal Address of Mrs. Marión MERRIMAN.*

It was signed "Fausto Villar," and there was a P.S.: "I beg your pardon for my bad english, but I have not another one."

There followed a flurry of letters back and forth, in English, Spanish, and a mixture of the two, between Villar and Marion and a widening circle of Lincoln survivors. Villar listed many names of Americans he had served with and provided more information about how "MERRIMAN fall dead at my side."

A furniture maker from Valencia, Villar had served with the Lincolns for some six months. It was then that he started learning English, trading language lessons with an American volunteer who had been a forest ranger in Washington State. In his letters and in pages from an unpublished memoir in Spanish he sent to Marion, he described how at the beginning of their last day together, "with a voice trembling with emotion," Bob Merriman had told a group of Spanish and American soldiers that they were surrounded, and that he would lead them as they tried to "break out of the noose" and reach the Ebro River, where the Republic held the far bank.

As they fled across a leafless vineyard that morning, Nationalist machine-gunners opened fire, and several of the group fell, including Merriman, a few paces from Villar. "I call out to Merriman once, twice, thrice, I don't know how many times, but there is no response. . . . 'Please, Merriman! Please!'"

Certain that Bob was dead, Villar crossed the vineyard and, with a few exhausted survivors, hid in a barn, where Nationalist cavalrymen captured them that evening. He spent two years in concentration camps and labor battalions, and afterward kept silent through all the decades of dictatorship. Like so many people of varied politics—loyal Party members, Hemingway, the US military attaché Colonel Stephen Fuqua, the anti-Communist Sandor Voros—Villar, a political skeptic from an anarchist family, felt Merriman's personal magnetism, calling him "the man I so admired."

After half a century, anyone's memory can be shaky, and others' recollections of that day differ from Villar's. Although no other survivor claims to have been with Merriman in his final moments, several Lincolns who were part of the column of escaping men he was taking to the river say he was still leading them when darkness fell that evening. It was one of them who heard "Reds! . . . Hands up!" in the night, suggesting that Bob and others with him were taken prisoner. Recently, a local historian interviewing elderly villagers in this district was told that a group of fleeing Internationals were captured by the Nationalists, held overnight, and then shot, two by two. One man remembers being forced to dig a grave for an executed prisoner who was "very tall, with brown hair."

Whatever the truth may be, hearing from Villar seemed to bring Marion peace. "I have written to so many people, so many times, about Bob's death, over the years," she said in a letter to Lincoln veteran Luke Hinman, who had survived the desperate retreats of early 1938. "I knew, very soon, that he was dead. And yet, in the middle of the night, I could hear his voice. For many years, in San Francisco, I would catch a glimpse of him and would run to catch up with him. But he always disappeared in the crowd. . . .

"But no one found his body, no one was with him when he died. This I finally acknowledged—but did not accept. This has happened to so many widows in so many wars." Of Villar, she said, "This is the *first* time anyone has said that he saw Bob killed. . . . It all checks out. Incredible! My friend Pat just looked up all the names Fausto mentions, and they're all there. And the dates are accurate!"

Four years after receiving Fausto Villar's first letter, Marion died in her sleep at the age of eighty-two.

Under brilliant blue skies and a warm summer sun, the Ebro River looks surprisingly peaceful. The spring flood has passed and the current is gentle. On the riverbank near where John Gates and George Watt swam for their lives, the operator of a small cable ferry lounges sleepily in a deck chair, waiting for passengers.

More than three quarters of a century after the war ended, the rugged terrain here is still strewn with evidence of combat: bullet-pocked stone walls, a faintly visible inscription, INTENDENCIA [quartermaster] XV BRIGADA, above a building's door, and a hilltop where a local museum official is excavating trenches from the war with a metal detector and small backhoe—he proudly holds up an Italian bullet and submachine-gun magazine that he has unearthed this very afternoon. During the Franco years, the government destroyed any visible memorials to International Brigades soldiers, but outside the town of Marsa, hidden in a thicket of underbrush where it was secretly cared for by villagers during the dictatorship, stands the only tombstone in Spain of an American killed in the war.

It belongs to John Cookson, a University of Wisconsin assistant professor of physics and a signals officer with the Lincolns, who built himself a shortwave radio at the front. He was fatally wounded at age twenty-five when a piece of shrapnel struck his heart during the Battle of the Ebro, just days before the Internationals were withdrawn. Cookson was from a Methodist farm family, but some of the recent visitors to his modest grave marker have evidently been Jewish, for they have placed small stones atop it. Cookson was killed in 1938, yet right next to his resting place, shaded by the same fir tree, is a similar, more recent stone for Clarence Kailin, 1914–2009. Fellow students in high school, the two enlisted and sailed for Spain together. Kailin fought through the war from Jarama to the Ebro, named his son John after Cookson, came back several times to visit his friend's grave, and asked to be buried here.

A half hour's drive away on small, winding roads is a long stretch of rising ground known, in Catalan, simply as Els Tossals—The Hills. Amid evergreen trees and an almond orchard, a high point commands a spectacular view to the south and east. Bob Merriman and at least 50 International Brigades soldiers with him reached this spot on April 2, 1938. It was dawn. The men—Americans, Spaniards, plus some from other countries—had just made an exhausting nightlong march over rough ground, with no moon, carrying all their equipment. From this pine-scented hilltop the land rolls gently downward, carpeted with more almond groves, green fields, and terraced vineyards, to a wide, bucolic valley. Several miles away on the valley floor, as if spread out in a Cezanne landscape, are the towns of Corbera and Gandesa, stone houses with red-tile roofs. Gandesa has an old church tower as well. Beyond them rises a darkly forested mountain range streaked with cliffs. On the other side of that lies the Ebro River. On its far bank, Merriman and those with him knew, they would be safe.

But as the men scanned this view that day at sunrise, it was alive with menace. Enemy forces were not only on their heels but coming into sight in the valley they had to cross. On the highway that runs through it, truckloads of Franco's troops were sweeping in from one side and the vehicles of Mussolini's Corpo Truppe Volontarie were advancing from the other. Nationalist tanks and artillery were visible as well. Nationalist observation planes circled overhead.

Seeing that they were surrounded, the soldiers broke into smaller bands to try to escape. We can only imagine the desperate talk, in several languages, about how best to do so. Some waited on the hill until the cover of night, though that meant more Nationalist troops would have time to take positions in front of them, while Merriman led a group that set off to cross the valley in daylight. "Life has been full because I made it so," he had written in his diary some months earlier, just before being wounded. "May others live the life I have begun and may they carry it still further as I plan to do myself." If he died in a vineyard, as Villar claims, it was on the downward slopes of this hill. If, as others say, he was taken prisoner after dark and later shot, he was captured near or beyond the road through the two red-roofed towns that now lie so peacefully and beautifully in the summer sunlight.

In another part of Spain, at Brunete, the earth still bears traces of the trenches that Americans and other foreign volunteers, under heavy fire in July 1937, frantically dug in the dry, stony ground. Despite pleas to many authorities over many years, Phil Schachter's family never could learn what happened to him after he went missing in that battle. Until his own death, Phil's brother Harry felt the pain and loss, an anguish only deepened by his own disenchantment with communism. "With the increasing years I have increasing guilt and regret that I colluded in his departure," he wrote more than five decades later to a Lincoln veteran who knew Phil. "He was 21 and I can still hear my father crying."

"My family never knew how to fully grieve Phil," wrote Harry's daughter, Rebecca Schachter. Born long after Phil's death, she is a Massachusetts social worker specializing in caring for victims of trauma. "My father would tear up when he spoke of Phil, remembering Pop learning of Phil's death."

In 2012, Rebecca Schachter went to Spain for the first time, accompanying her fifteen-year-old daughter, a dancer, who was performing in a flamenco festival. Then, with Phil's letters in her backpack, she traveled to Brunete. On top of a scarred ridge where the fighting had been fierce, "there was an old bombed out brick structure, the only one around. . . . Here, kneeling down touching the earth, I felt very close to my Uncle Phil, so I spoke to him. I told him he was never forgotten. . . . I told him we honored his goodness and idealism and that the world turned out to be a much more politically complicated truth than he could have known then. . . .

"I told him that his coming to Spain with the Abraham Lincoln Brigade, his willingness to give everything he had believing it could make the world more fair, more free—that this volunteering, hopeful spirit was a source of profound inspiration. Then I paused, and somehow I managed to say kaddish for this son, brother, uncle. All this brought up enormous emotion. It hardly seemed just my own, or my family's. [It] felt part of a universal sorrow for the human struggle that played out in Spain during those dark days that were just the beginning of the trauma and tragedy that overcame all of Europe and throughout the world. Before leaving, I placed some stones I brought from home on the window wall of the brick structure."

Acknowledgments

Any book of history builds on the work of others, and I hope my bibliography and references make clear who some of them are. There are many more people, however, whom I want to thank. It is a cliché, in notes like this one, to say that those who have helped an author are in no way responsible for his or her errors or opinions. That is especially true here, for few events in recent history have inspired such fierce disagreements as the Spanish Civil War, and I know that several of those I mention below look on that era somewhat differently than I do. Given this, it was all the more generous of them to help me.

First, a bow to the Lincoln veterans I knew, all no longer with us: Hank Rubin and Bill Sennett, friends over several decades; Jim Benet and George Draper, fellow reporters at the *San Francisco Chronicle* long ago; and Luke Hinman and George Kaye, with whom I crossed paths more briefly and wish I had questioned more.

Mostly in person but sometimes long-distance, librarians and archivists at 15 different institutions in the United States and abroad helped find me essential documents, occasionally some I didn't think to ask for. I want to especially acknowledge the staff of the wonderfully easy-to-use Tamiment Library at New York University, where I spent many days in the Lincoln Brigade archives; Vita Paladino of the Howard Gotlieb Archival Research Center at Boston University; and David Jacobs of the Hoover Institution Archives at Stanford University, from whom I learned for the first time about Lois Orr and her unpublished manuscript.

My thanks to Hermann Hatzfeldt for translating documents from German, to Andrea Valencia for doing the same with some from Spanish, and to Vanessa Rancaño for more translations and other help with Spanish sources. On the road in Spain, I learned much from Alan Warren and Nick Lloyd.

An extraordinary variety of people responded to my phone calls or emails, often sharing with me their own notes, unpublished work, or other material. Among them were scholars who have studied the Spanish Civil War or people involved in it, sometimes for years longer than I: Magdalena Bogacka-Rode, Gordon Bowker, James Hopkins, Peter Huber, Jo Labanyi, Warren Lerude, Ana Martí, Ángel Viñas, William Braasch Watson, Robert Whealey, and Glennys Young; George Esenwein both answered questions along the way and read the manuscript when I was almost finished. Nick Townsend loaned me his large collection of books about the war, and Tony Greiner and Rickard Jorgensen supplied useful leads. Sandy Matthews, Martha Gellhorn's literary executor, kindly gave me permission to quote from her papers, and Jeff Wachtel did the same for those of his mother, Marion Merriman Wachtel. Frank Soler checked for Torkild Rieber's trail in the Texaco files that are now part of the Chevron archives.

Those who shared documents or memories with me or helped in other ways also included family members of International Brigades veterans: Ellen Grunblatt, Judith Gurney, Lucia Jacobs, Bernice Jensky, Lucy McDiarmid, Jim Neugass, Rebecca Schachter, David Schankin, Lucy Selligman Schneider, Eric Tabb, Andrew Usera, Ruhama Veltfort, and Josie Nelson Yurek. Lincoln descendants Jane Lazarre and David Wellman also read and commented on the manuscript. And I'm grateful, as well, for aid from others with ties to those who were in Spain at that time: Monica and Laura Orr; Elizabeth

Cusick, Lois Orr's daughter, who read the manuscript, as did Harriet Crawley, Virginia Cowles's daughter; Lewis Lapham, who knew Torkild Rieber; and David Milton, whose father was standing next to George Orwell when he was shot.

Peter N. Carroll not only read the manuscript, but shared documents, suggested leads, and answered innumerable questions over several years. Anyone interested in the Americans in Spain is in his debt, not just for the books on the subject he has written, edited or coedited, but for his longtime editorship of the *Volunteer.* And from Spain, Guillem Martínez Molinos generously shared his knowledge of the oil business and his extraordinary collection of Texaco documents with an American he had never met. When the time came, he too read the manuscript, corrected errors, and added details.

A special thanks to more kind souls who, like some of the people I've already mentioned, gave me the greatest gift anyone can give a writer, which was to read what I wrote, share their reactions, and help me find mistakes or omissions. Sebastiaan Faber and Christopher Brooks brought particular expertise on the Spanish Civil War to this task. Others are friends whose wisdom, usually hard won through their own experience of writing, helped me figure out what the story was I wanted to tell and how to better tell it: Harriet Barlow, Elizabeth Farnsworth, Douglas Foster, Elinor Langer, Michael Meyer, and Zachary Shore.

Several of my debts of gratitude are not for the first time. One is to my literary agent, Georges Borchardt, for thirty years my guide in the trade of writing books. Another is to the many good people at my publisher, Houghton Mifflin Harcourt, particularly Bruce Nichols, Ben Hyman, Megan Wilson, and fine-tuner of prose Larry Cooper. And a third is to the incomparable freelance editor Tom Engelhardt; this is the fifth book of mine he has had a hand in. Only those who have worked with him can fully know the difference between merely being edited and being Tom-edited; it's something like the difference between seeing the world in two dimensions and in three. And finally, with me every step of this four-year journey, encouraging me in low moments, rejoicing in high ones, and reading two drafts of the manuscript, was my wife, Arlie. We added some battlefields in Spain to the collection of places we have visited together as one or the other of us was writing about them: they include Pentecostal churches in Louisiana and a bill collectors' bar in San Francisco for her books, and *gulag* camp ruins and remnants of First World War trenches for mine. As this book went to press, we marked our fiftieth wedding anniversary. No man has been more lucky.

Notes

PROLOGUE

page

xiii *"a model which we will"*: Preston 1, p. 223.

xiv *"We walk stark naked"*: Watt, p. 107.

xv *"The writers gave us"*: Gates, pp. 59–60.

"There are hundreds": Watt, pp. 107–108; Gates, p. 60. There are slight but not significant variations in how each of the four participants recall this meeting, which I have described in more detail in the note to p. 307. See also Hemingway, NANA dispatch 20, 4 April 1938, Matthews's account in the *New York Times* the next day, and the interview with Watt in the John Gerassi Papers, ALBA 018, Box 7, Folder 6, p. 56. Gerassi's book *The Premature Antifascists: North American Volunteers in the Spanish Civil War, 1936–39, An Oral History* (New York: Praeger, 1986) has been criticized by some included in it for allegedly distorting what they said. Hence I have generally not quoted from it. But the verbatim texts of his interviews in ALBA 018—in some cases edited and corrected by the volunteers themselves—are a valuable source. They constitute the largest publicly available collection of transcribed interviews with Lincoln volunteers.

xvi *Roughly 2,800 Americans:* These estimates include the medical volunteers. Christopher Brooks, who maintains the useful ALBA database, has, at this writing, data on 2,644 volunteers and 734 deaths. But he and other scholars of the Lincolns believe there were more of each. Some early battalion records disappeared with the two trucks mentioned on p. 114; more may have been lost on other occasions, especially in the chaotic retreats of March and April 1938.

"Wherever in this world": Matthews 1, p. 67.

sent personal telegrams: For the telegram from Vincent Sheean of the *Tribune,* see Voros, pp. 430–31. Matthews cabled FDR via several intermediaries, saying, "shows over unless have two hundred pursuit planes immediately"; Jay Allen to James Roosevelt, 28 March 1938, James Roosevelt Papers, Box 62.

front-page headlines: Chapman, pp. 226–227.

asking one of them: George Draper. The other veteran on the *Chronicle*'s staff was education correspondent James Benet.

xvii *"Men of my generation": L'Espagne libre* (Paris: Calmann-Lévy, 1946), p. 9.

xix *An estimated 270 Spanish Republicans:* See Adam Hochschild, *The Unquiet Ghost: Russians Remember Stalin* (Boston: Houghton Mifflin, 2003), p. 56. My thanks to Eric Tabb, the son of a Lincoln veteran, for some useful references on this subject. The estimate of 270 comes from Luiza Iordache, *Republicanos españoles en el Gulag, 1939–1956* (Barcelona: Institut de Ciències Polítiques i Socials, 2008), p. 136, quoted in Young, p. 2.

1. CHASING MONEYCHANGERS FROM THE TEMPLE

5 *"Practices of the unscrupulous," "There are so many suffering":* Watkins, p. 13.

"Dearest girl of all": The letters quoted here are all in the Robert Hale Merriman Papers, ALBA 191, Box 1, Folder 1. They are mostly undated, though sometimes there is a date and question mark in pencil, apparently added later.

"The most popular": John Kenneth Galbraith to Warren Lerude, 31 December 1985. My thanks to Prof. Lerude for sending me a copy of this letter.

6 *"Bob invented a mischievous game":* Lerude and Merriman, p. 21.

"You walked in the door": Manny Harriman Video Oral History Collection, ALBA Video 048, Box 11, Container 2, interview with Marion Merriman Wachtel; Lerude and Merriman, p. 21; Wyden, p. 236.

9 *"the most dynamic organization":* "Soviet Espionage in America: An Oft-Told Tale," *Reviews in American History* 38(2), June 2010, p. 359.

10 *"There was an organization":* Fisher, p. 2.

"Read the terrible chapter": To Frances Scott Fitzgerald, 15 March 1940, in *The Crack-Up,* ed. Edmund Wilson (New York: New Directions, 1956), p. 290.

11 *"Spain's 'man of the hour'":* "Socialists' Chief Arrested in Spain," *New York Times,* 14 October 1934.

"In the great financial storm": 11 October 1931. George Bernard Shaw, *A Little Talk on America* (London: Friends of the Soviet Union, 1932), quoted in Tzouliadis, p. 11.

12 *"was awarded one"*: Galbraith, p. 23.

2. PROMISED LAND, BLACK WINGS

13 *"My father worked"*: Fischer 1, p. 47.

14 *"I cannot imagine life"*: Fischer 1, pp. 208, 189.

15 *"As he talked to us"*: Fischer 1, pp. 90–91.

"sallow, ponderous": *Chronicles of Wasted Time*, vol. 1 (London: Collins, 1972), p. 246.

Fischer wrote to Stalin: 7 February 1936, Fischer Papers, Box 12, Folder 9; "Moscow Honors Writers," *New York Times*, 28 September 1932; *Washington Post*, 7 April 1935.

16 *"The Prime Minister"*: Fischer 1, p. 376.

Soviet secret police: Fischer 2, pp. 106, 99.

"smiling, shy, tall person": Fischer 1, p. 403.

17 *"engage in conversation"*: Records of the Department of State, Central Files: Spain, Elbridge Durbrow to the Secretary of State, 13 May 1937, file 852.2221, Record Group 59, National Archives, courtesy of Peter N. Carroll.

upbeat articles: "Moscow, the Soviet Capital," 8 July 1935; "Soviet Collective Farms," 22 July 1935.

18 *"the deliberate lies"*: "Soviet Collective Farms," 22 July 1935.

19 *a series of articles:* In the San Francisco *Daily News.*

"We got along": Lerude and Merriman, pp. 40–41.

20 *"I'm attending classes"*: To "Loo," 22 December 1932, Milly Bennett Papers, Box 2, Folder 1.

"Hair like a Hottentot": Morton Sontheimer, *Newspaperman, a Book about the Business* (New York: Whittlesey, 1941), p. 227.

"i would grab": To "Esther," 3 October 1934, Milly Bennett Papers, Box 2, Folder 2.

"their arguments": Lerude and Merriman, pp. 53–55.

21 *"can be bitter"*: To "Florence," 27 January 193?, Milly Bennett Papers, Box 2, Folder 1.

22 *"Fascism has spread"*: Brendon, p. 302.

"will rank some day": Pierre Berton, *The Great Depression: 1929–1939* (Toronto: Anchor, 2001), p. 468.

"He could carry": Voros, p. 250.

23 *"It has been many months"*: 26 February 1936, p. 234.

24 *"The reactionaries"*: Fischer 1, p. 326.

"As we drove along": Fischer 1, pp. 327–328.

25 *estimated at 275,000:* An Ethiopian estimate for the period January 1, 1935, to May 31, 1936, cited by Angelo Del Boca, *The Ethiopian War, 1935–1941* (Chicago: University of Chicago Press, 1969), p. 206n. Italian estimates, predictably, were much lower.

3. "THOSE WHO DO NOT THINK AS WE DO"

27 *"rather stronger"*: Preston 1, pp. 102–103.

28 *"Without Africa"*: Francisco Franco Bahamonde, *Palabras del Caudillo, 19 abril 1937–31 diciembre 1938* (Barcelona: Ediciones FE, 1939), quoted in Sebastian Balfour, "Colonial War and Civil War: The Spanish Army of Africa," in Baumeister and Schüler-Springorum, p. 185.

"Rif tribesmen": José Sanjurjo, quoted in Preston 3, p. 21.

31 *"It is necessary"*: Preston 1, p. 103.

32 *denounced by an informer:* Howson, p. 12.

Republican doctor: Preston 3, p. 312.

33 *"rich, thrilling and interesting"*: Fischer 3, p. 1.

34 *"could proclaim its independence"*: Fischer 1, pp. 363, 370.

"I understood then": Fischer 1, p. 366; "On Madrid's Front Line," *Nation*, 24 October 1936.

36 *"I never passed"*: Whitaker 1, pp. 111–113.

ear for one peseta: Chicago Daily Tribune, 18 August 1936.

"Files of men": "Slaughter of 4,000 at Badajoz, 'City of Horrors,' Is Told by Tribune Man," *Chicago Daily Tribune*, 30 August 1936.

37 *"Of course we shot"*: Whitaker 1, pp. 113, 108.

"organized peasant hunts": Beevor, p. 77.

39 *"Kicking their legs"*: Preston 1, p. 206.

"had them taken": Whitaker 1, p. 114.

"But they weren't": Noel Monks, *Eyewitness* (London: Frederick Muller, 1955), pp. 78–79, quoted in Preston 3, p. 333.

"The wisdom of this policy": Whitaker 2, pp. 106–107.

45 *supplied them with ammunition:* Voelckers to von Weizsäcker, 16 October 1936, *Documents on German Foreign Policy, 1918–1945, from the Archives of the German Foreign Ministry*, Series D (1937–1945), vol. 3, *Germany and the Spanish Civil War 1936–1939* (Washington, DC: Government Printing Office, 1950), p. 112.

"If there is somewhere": Baxell, p. 44.

The enormous economic might: Hull: Little, p. 26; FDR: speech at Chautauqua, 3 August 1936.

46 *FDR's ambassador to Spain:* Fischer 1, p. 254; Roosevelt to Bowers, 16 September 1936, Franklin D. Roosevelt Papers as President: the President's Secretary's file, Box 50.

47 *"prevent the enemies of Spain"*: Stalin, Molotov, and Voroshilov to Largo Caballero, 21 December 1936, quoted in Bolloten, p. 166.

48 *"I hope . . . that you will"*: Beevor, p. 133.

$432 and $692 million: Viñas 1, pp. 359–363.

49 *equivalent of $7 billion:* Here and elsewhere, for historical currency comparisons I have used purchasing power as a standard of measurement. Almost all other means of calculating 1930s currency values in today's dollars, such as by labor value or percentage of GDP, produce a far higher amount. Correspondence with Prof. Viñas has helped me realize how difficult it is to make such comparisons accurately.

4. A NEW HEAVEN AND EARTH

50 *"The fair red-cheeked"*: Cusick 1, pp. 1–5.

51 *"I held out my pesetas"*: "The Spanish Revolution—as I saw it in Catalonia," ms., Charles A. Orr Papers, p. 5.

52 *children in Barcelona's schools:* Thomas, p. 520.

"Pirates, buccaneers, princes": *Solidaridad Obrera*, 24 July 1936, quoted in Esenwein and Shubert, p. 124.

"the times called golden": Miguel de Cervantes, *Don Quixote*, trans. Edith Grossman (New York: HarperCollins, 2003), p. 76.

53 *"Barcelona's Ramblas"*: Cusick 1, pp. 13–14; "The Spanish Revolution—as I saw it in Catalonia," ms., Charles A. Orr Papers, p. 15.

54 *"The Anarchist trade"*: Undated letter fragment, October? 1936, Orr, pp. 82–83.

two million members: Encyclopedia Britannica, "Anarchism," accessed online, 27 February 2015. Other sources give higher or lower numbers, sometimes varying with the politics of the writer. Given the CNT's determinedly nonbureaucratic structure, precise figures do not exist.

"All governments are detestable": *Tierra y Libertad*, 15 September 1933, quoted in Bolloten, p. 194.

55 *"I was received"*: "The Spanish Revolution—as I saw it in Catalonia," ms., Charles A. Orr Papers, p. 7.

56 *"At one moment"*: Beevor, p. 69.

57 *"If only . . . they would make"*: Cusick 2, p. 14.

"These people here are fiends": 4 February 1937, Orr, p. 48; 7 March 1937, Orr, p. 48.

58 *"Those all-night sessions"*: Cusick 1, p. 164.

"the first money": Lois Orr to Mary De Vries, 24 November 1936, Orr, p. 93.

the Spanish Revolution: This should not be confused with a publication of the same name published in this period by anarchist sympathizers in New York.

meals were free: Cusick 1, p. 89; "The Spanish Revolution—as I saw it in Catalonia," ms., Charles A. Orr Papers, p. 15.

59 *"You should see":* Lois and Charles to Charles's sister Dorothy, 5 March 1937, Orr, p. 140.

"We were living the revolution": Cusick 1, p. 16.

"life in revolutionary Barcelona": Seidman 2, p. 167.

60 *"I'm having the time of my life":* 30 September 1936, Orr, p. 72; 2 November 1936, Orr, p. 83.

"Here in Fraga": This was written during an outburst of anarchist fervor a few years earlier. Isaac Puente in *Tierra y Libertad* supplement, August 1932, quoted in Bolloten, p. 66.

61 *increased by 20 percent:* Beevor, p. 113.

"Four couples have": Gaston Leval in *Cahiers de l'humanisme libertaire*, March 1968, quoted in Bolloten, p. 69.

"The main reason": To Mary De Vries, 24 November 1936, Orr, p. 94.

62 *"We must burn": CNT*, Madrid, 31 July 1936, quoted in Preston 3, p. 262; "The Spanish Revolution—as I saw it in Catalonia," ms., Charles A. Orr Papers, p. 14.

63 *"Churches were closed":* "The Spanish Revolution—as I saw it in Catalonia," ms., Charles A. Orr Papers, p. 16; Lawrence A. Fernsworth, "Catalonia Fights 'Gangster' Terror," *New York Times*, 17 January 1937.

64 *nearly 7,000 clergy:* Preston 3, p. 235.

49,000 civilians: Preston 3, p. xvi; the highest rate of killing of all was in the first two months. See Ruiz, p. 106.

some 150,000: Preston 3, pp. xi, xvi. Somewhat different figures are given by the Spanish historian Julián Casanova: "almost 100,000" murdered by the Nationalists during the civil war; 50,000 more killed after the war ended; "more than 60,000" murdered during the war in the Republic; half a million people in Nationalist prisons and concentration camps at the war's end. See Casanova's "The Spanish Civil War: History and Memory" in Jump, p. 201.

"Early one morning": "Homage to Orwell—As I Knew Him in Catalonia," Orr, pp. 177–178.

65 *a British colleague:* This was John McNair, representative in Spain of Britain's Independent Labour Party, something of a sister party to the POUM. Both he (in an unpublished M.A. thesis, *George Orwell: The Man I Knew*, University of Newcastle, 1965) and Orr describe a guard at the door reporting an Englishman's arrival, and then persuading Orwell to join the POUM militia, but each leaves the other out of his account. Orr and McNair worked in the same building, so it appears that they were both there that day and may well have talked to Orwell together. According to McNair's *Spanish Diary*, Orwell, contrary to the militiaman, did speak some Spanish—which other evidence also suggests.

"Eric . . . was tall, lean and gangling": "Homage to Orwell—As I Knew Him in Catalonia," Orr, p. 179.

"Waiters and shop-walkers": Orwell, pp. 32–33. The volume I am quoting from here, *Orwell in Spain*, includes *Homage to Catalonia* and all letters, articles, and reviews he wrote touching on Spain. Unless otherwise indicated, the notes citing just "Orwell" refer to *Homage*.

66 *"We tried to explain"*: Cusick 1, p. 274.

67 *"This is a gloriously exciting place"*: 27–30 September 1936, Orr, pp. 72–73.

5. "I WILL DESTROY MADRID"

68 *a military dictatorship:* See, for example, "Military Dictatorship Will Follow Rebel Success in Spain, Gen. Franco Declares," *Chicago Daily Tribune*, 29 July 1936.

69 *"Fascist sword"*: Frank Joseph, *Mussolini's War: Fascist Italy's Military Struggles from Africa and Western Europe to the Mediterranean and Soviet Union, 1935–45* (Solihull, West Midlands, UK: Helion, 2010), p. 50.

on their breasts: Preston 3, p. 511.

70 *"the celestial city"*: Preston 1, pp. 220–221; Wyden, p. 135n.

In a dispatch: "On Madrid's Front Line," *Nation*, 24 October 1936.

71 *"Yes . . . Those are the facts"*: Patricia Cockburn, *The Years of the Week* (London: Comedia, 1968), pp. 209–210.

72 *"Streets had been"*: Fischer 1, p. 393.

"Three militia girls": Vernon, p. 180; 10 October 1936, quoted in Hopkins, p. 383, n. 67; Preston 6, p. 44.

"The news infuriated": Preston 3, p. 305.

73 *"it was dangerous"*: *My Last Sigh: The Autobiography of Luis Buñuel* (New York: Vintage, 2013), p. 152.

"The city was nervous": Fischer 1, p. 382.

75 *"were being staged"*: Knoblaugh, p. 107.

77 *"I will destroy Madrid"*: Beevor, p. 181.

"Every evening when": "Under Fire in Madrid," *Nation*, 12 December 1936.

78 *"Automobiles packed with"*: Fischer 1, p. 384.

"Has Madrid fallen?": Carroll 2, p. 30.

79 *"We need a quartermaster"*: Fischer 1, pp. 386–387.

80 *"Who cares?"*: *Volunteer for Liberty*, 7 March 1938, p. 2.

81 *"arms wherever it could"*: Fischer 1, pp. 390–391.

"He muddled up": RGASPI 545/6/889.

83 *"For five hours"*: Cusick 1, p. 203.

84 *the largest such mass murder:* An extensive recent treatment of this episode in Paul Preston, *The Last Stalinist: The Life of Santiago Carillo* (London: William Collins, 2014), pp. 78–88, adds detail to the account in Preston 3.

officials risked their lives: Preston 3, pp. 232–233, 285–286, 370–371, 377.

85 *"The die is not":* "Under Fire in Madrid," *Nation*, 12 December 1936.
"sensed the oncoming night": Richard Crossman, ed., *The God That Failed: Six Studies in Communism* (London: Hamish Hamilton, 1950), p. 218.
Two former high officials: For an interview with Kamenev's son a half century later, see Adam Hochschild, *The Unquiet Ghost: Russians Remember Stalin* (Boston: Houghton Mifflin, 2003), pp. 84–92.

86 *"I did not hesitate":* Wyden, p. 192n.
the actual number seems: Esenwein and Shubert, p. 159.
Everyone talked Spain": Fischer 1, p. 403.

87 *"Can't you organize":* To Freda Kirchwey, 16 December 1936, quoted in Preston 2, p. 239.
"it would have been": Fischer 1, pp. 442–443.

88 *"But why you, Bob?":* Lerude and Merriman, p. 71.
"I'm going": Lerude and Merriman, pp. 73–74.
"Hell's bells": Lerude and Merriman, p. 79.
"Bob said he expected": Untitled, undated fragment, Milly Bennett Papers, Box 9, Folder 5.

89 "Salud España": Merriman Diary, 11 January 1937. I have referenced his diary entries by the date on the page where they appear, although sometimes he clearly was writing them on earlier or later days.

6. "DON'T TRY TO CATCH ME"

93 *"for myself":* Gurney, pp. 18, 31, 22, 35. Although Gurney's memoir is more thoughtful than those of most other Lincolns, it was written decades after the war, and occasional names, dates, and other details are garbled.

94 *"houses which had been":* Gurney, pp. 20, 30, 23, 24, 18.

95 *"unmistakably a revolutionary city":* Gurney, pp. 47, 49.

96 *"The position of":* Gurney, pp. 46–47.
"Like the religions of old": Gurney, pp. 51–55.

97 *"There was no fuel":* Gurney, pp. 58–60.
"Everybody was addressed": Gurney, p. 65.

99 *"We began to feel":* Gurney, p. 87.

100 *About three quarters:* Statistics on this differ from one count to the next, reflecting the date it was made. RGASPI 545/3/455 shows 72 percent. RGASPI 545/6/5 shows 79 percent.
A third or more: Figures on this point are imprecise, because many volunteers used New York addresses in applying for a passport.
"For us it wasn't Franco": John Gerassi, *The Premature Antifascists: North*

American Volunteers in the Spanish Civil War, 1936–39, An Oral History (New York: Praeger, 1986), p. 48.

101 *"One volunteer went"*: Carroll 1, pp. 65–66.

102 "¡Viva la República!": Eby, p. 18.

"How can you tell": "On the Road to Spain," Robert Gladnick Papers.

103 *red banner that read:* Eby, pp. 1–2; U.S. Department of State, *Foreign Relations of the United States, Diplomatic Papers, 1937, General*, pp. 469, 473; Perkins to Hull, 8, 18, 21 January 1937. Gladnick describes this moment as well.

"a soggy black flapjack": Martin Hourihan, quoted in Eby, p. 24.

104 *"By the time"*: Joseph Selligman Jr. to his parents, n.d., Frank Aydelotte Papers, Box 62, Folder 909; 12 December 1936; 21 December 1936. I was able to see the latter two items and, unless otherwise noted, other Selligman family material through the courtesy of Selligman's niece, Lucy McDiarmid, and his sister, Lucy Schneider. Since then, the family has donated these documents to the Tamiment Library, where they can be found as the Selligman Family Papers, ALBA 296. They include copies of most of the material on Selligman in the Frank Aydelotte Papers. (Selligman's mother sent copies of many letters from or about her son to Aydelotte, the president of Swarthmore College.)

105 *"an alias rather adds"*: To his parents, 7 February 1937.

"Quit worrying": 19 December 1936, Frank Aydelotte Papers, Box 62, Folder 909; 22 December 1936.

"we looked magnificent": *Observer*, 22 June 1986, quoted in Hopkins, p. 189.

107 *"not even the Brigade"*: Gurney, p. 101.

"their uniform": Gurney, p. 108.

"Everywhere men are lying": Judith Cook, *Apprentices of Freedom* (London: Quartet, 1979), p. 4, quoted in Hopkins, p. 189.

"to a non-existent field": Gurney, pp. 113–114.

108 *URGENTLY REQUEST:* 12 March 1937, Records of the Department of State, Central files: Spain, file 852.2221, Record Group 59, National Archives microfilm.

"taken to hospital": 2 April 1937, Frank Aydelotte Papers, Box 62, Folder 909.

109 *THERE WERE SOME:* Cordell Hull to Joseph Selligman (Sr.), 5 April 1937; Thurston to State Dept., 3 April 1937. Both in Records of the Department of State, Central files: Spain, file 852.2221, Record Group 59, National Archives microfilm.

"We seem to wade": Una Wilson, 25 February 1937, in Fyrth, p. 110.

"I must": Gurney, pp. 126–127.

110 *"Communist Academy"*: RGASPI 545/6/947.

111 *"Merriman was universally"*: Voros, pp. 338, 344.

"so tough": Voros, p. 322.

112 *"The only time"*: Harry Meloff to Mim Sigel, 6 May 1937, in Nelson and Hendricks, p. 145; Voros, p. 437.

"The Spanish peasants": Unpublished memoir, p. 60, Vaughn Love Papers, ALBA 243.

114 *"Marion dear"*: 16–17 February 1937.

"Steve Daduk cracked up": Merriman Diary, 19 February 1937.

115 *"They pitted"*: Frank Ryan, *The Book of the XV Brigade* (Madrid: Commissariat of War, 1938), p. 74.

116 *"frightening rumors"*: Lerude and Merriman, p. 52.

"the shattering news": Lerude and Merriman, p. 75.

7. RIFLES FROM THE 1860S

118 *"to rid ourselves"*: 2 November 1936, quoted in Howson, p. 127.

"We looked blankly": Sommerfield, pp. 185–186.

119 *A postwar inventory:* Howson, p. 251n.

planned a raid: Bolloten, pp. 149–150.

"This is the heavy": Wyden, p. 150.

120 *"any more than"*: Tierney, p. 22.

purchased in nations: Viñas 1, pp. 118–119.

"If I see your passport": Manny Harriman Video Oral History Collection, ALBA Video 048, Box 11, Container 2, interview with Marion Merriman Wachtel.

121 *"He's in the Hospital"*: Lerude and Merriman, p. 75.

"I'll do my damnedest": Mangan, p. 350.

"encased from waist": Lerude and Merriman, p. 76.

"Marion came": 20–21 March 1937.

"broad as": "Article Three," Milly Bennett Papers, Box 9, Folder 5.

"I even sat": Lerude and Merriman, p. 77.

angry memos: See RGASPI 545/6/947, pp. 38–39, and 545/2/164.

122 *120 killed:* Thomas, p. 578. For a comparison of other estimates, see Eby, p. 78, n. 12.

"to have it out": 1 March 1937.

123 *"Set up one hundred"*: Barsky, p. 26.

"We did not put": de Vries, p. 207.

"Inside the truck": Harry Wilkes to Evelyn Ahrend, 12 April 1937, quoted in Carroll 1, p. 104.

124 *"Each instrument"*: Barsky, p. 5.

"Wounded kept coming": Anne Taft to "T," 16 July 1937, Anne Taft Muldavin Papers, ALBA 077, Box 1, Folder 8; de Vries, p. 207.

"You can say": Carroll 1, p. 114.

125 *"a feeling for adventure"*: Kemp 2, p. 6.

"deeply shocked": Kemp 2, p. 74; Kemp 1, pp. 76, 80, 91.

126 *some 19,000:* Stefanie Schüler-Springorum, "War as Adventure: The Experience of the Condor Legion in Spain," in Baumeister and Schüler-Springorum, p. 209. Somewhat higher than earlier published estimates, the figure is based on the author's comprehensive 2009 book on the Condor Legion.

127 *762 of them:* Viñas 1, pp. 78–79, 82, 91.

"was rusty": Orwell, pp. 42–43.

128 *"was always writing"*: John O'Donovan to Ian Angus, April 1967, quoted in Shelden, p. 308.

"Everyone from general": Orwell, pp. 49–50.

129 *have trouble getting orders obeyed:* See, for example, Bolloten, pp. 256–258.

"the smells of urine": Orwell, pp. 92, 60.

"in water": Orwell, pp. 77, 79.

130 *"I remember feeling"*: Orwell, pp. 83–84.

131 *"I would do anything"*: Lerude and Merriman, p. 78.

8. OVER THE MOUNTAINS

132 *"The government knows"*: Felsen, pp. 38–39.

133 *"the guide stopped"*: Voros, pp. 291–294.

134 *estimated 200 volunteers:* Carroll 1, p. 125, citing the international non-intervention authorities.

"Our boys were victorious": Fisher, p. 30. But Fisher gives a different account on p. 44, where he says they were told that the toll had been 5 killed and 17 wounded. In either case, the figures wildly understated the actual casualties.

135 *"So long cast!"*: 6 May 1937.

"The Infanta's villa": Barsky, pp. 93–94.

136 *"Peasants come to us"*: Neugass, 8 December 1937, p. 29.

"the Infanta's private jail": Neugass, 7 December 1937, p. 18.

"the peasants attached": Fyrth, pp. 151–152.

137 *"He was a tall man"*: Paul Burns to Steve Nelson, 28 September 1977, Steve Nelson Papers, ALBA 008, Box 9, Folder 52; Fredericka Martin Papers, ALBA 001, Box 18, Folder 41.

"Everyone up in the line": Gurney, pp. 134–135.

138 *"is one of my constant"*: Thane Summers to Sophie and Art Krause, 26 August 1937, in Nelson and Hendricks, p. 254.

"We aren't going to": "Pingpong Enlivens Spanish War Lull," *New York Times*, 24 May 1937.

139 *"to cut down"*: Gurney, pp. 139–141.

140 *"Comrades, let us not"*: 10 March 1937, quoted in Eby, p. 102.

"No real attempt": Gurney, pp. 145–146.

141 *"Everybody was there"*: Ted Allan, quoted in Wyden, p. 321.
"The most controversial": Gurney, p. 145.
"He appears": "Homage to Hemingway," *New Republic*, 10 November 1936.

142 *"In Spain maybe"*: Matthew Josephson, *Infidel in the Temple: A Memoir of the Thirties* (New York: Knopf, 1967); Herbst, p. 136.
"He was bigger": "Some Impressions of Hemingway," by William Pike, Benjamin Iceland Papers, ALBA 054, Box 2, Folder 11.

143 *"the dress rehearsal"*: Hemingway to the Pfeiffer family, 9 February 1937, in Hemingway 1, p. 458.
"The train": Orwell, p. 94.

144 *"a round-faced Irish"*: "Homage to Orwell—As I Knew Him in Catalonia," Orr, pp. 179–180; Elisaveta Fen, "George Orwell's First Wife," *Twentieth Century*, August 1960, pp. 115–116.

145 *"The militia uniform"*: Orwell, pp. 95–99.
"It is terrible": To Anne, 6–22 January 1937, Orr, p. 124.
"would take me": Cusick 1, p. 229.
"Simple and obvious": "The Spanish Revolution—as I saw it in Catalonia," ms., Charles A. Orr Papers, pp. 17, 22.

146 *"A people as a whole"*: "The Spanish Revolution—as I saw it in Catalonia," ms., Charles A. Orr Papers, p. 13.
"The woman question": Cusick 1, p. 12.

147 *"I was very sorry"*: To her parents, 11–12 April 1937, Orr, p. 155.
"was friendly": "Homage to Orwell—As I Knew Him in Catalonia," Orr, pp. 179–180.
"I felt as if": Cusick 2, p. 186; Orwell, p. 101.

148 *"Battalion commissars"*: Ralph Bates, "Castilian Drama: An Army Is Born," *New Republic*, 20 October 1937, p. 287; Orwell, p. 102.

149 *"Brothers, the Spanish"*: Regler, p. 306.
"Along the roads": NANA dispatch 4, 22 March 1937.

150 *"will take its place"*: NANA dispatch 5, 26 March 1937.

9. CIVIL WAR AT THE *TIMES*

151 *principal correspondent:* The *Times* also published some stories by Lawrence Fernsworth, a stringer in Barcelona, who shared Matthews's sympathy for the Republic.
"looked and behaved": Gurney, p. 145.

152 *"Newspapers and Periodicals"*: RGASPI 545/6/849. Landis, himself a volunteer, mentions how much this exasperated the troops: Landis, p. 618, n. 3.
"thrilling experience": Matthews 3, p. 16; Matthews 1, p. 28; Matthews 4, p. 304; "Science of War Rewritten by Italy," *New York Times*, 10 May 1936; "Future of Ethiopian Populace Presents a Problem for Italy," *New York Times*, 5 May 1936.

"Such human beings": Matthews 3, pp. 186, 185; Matthews 1, p. 67.

153 *"almost fanatically religious":* Matthews 2, p. 20.

"General Franco is": "Franco Hems in Madrid after Malaga Capture," 14 February 1937.

reporting that Franco's troops: "Madrid Is Warned of Its Great Peril," 13 February 1937.

154 *"The dead bodies":* Matthews 2, p. 26.

lightest of censorship: As published, Matthews's stories about the Battle of Guadalajara include many mentions of Italian troops, sometimes even in headlines. And in the first three months of 1937, which included the battle, the *Times* ran more than twice as many bylined stories by him as by Carney.

155 *"popularity firmly established":* "Regime of Terror Is Denied by Llano," 23 March 1937.

ambassador Claude Bowers: Bowers to Roosevelt, 31 March 1937; Bowers to Hull, 18 May 1937, both in Franklin D. Roosevelt Papers as President: the President's Secretary's file, Box 50; "Madrid Situation Revealed; Uncensored Story of Siege," *New York Times,* 7 December 1936.

"for distinguished services": Knightley, p. 200.

156 *"had a monkey-like face":* Cowles, p. 8.

"the trouble is": "Cowles, Virginia," in *Current Biography,* accessed online, 28 February 2012.

"held one's own": Aidan Crawley, *Leap before You Look: A Memoir* (London: Collins, 1988), p. 207. Crawley married her in 1945; Cowles, p. 285.

157 *"no qualifications":* Cowles, p. 4.

travel around the world: The trip around the world resulted in a wide-eyed, frothy book. By the time it appeared in 1938, however, Cowles was already making a name for herself as a serious reporter in Spain and elsewhere and she published the book, *Men Are So Friendly,* under a pseudonym, Nancy Swift.

"As we were walking": Cowles, pp. 15–16.

159 *"always came with":* Mangan, pp. 413–414.

"all kinds of liaisons": Sefton Delmer to Carlos Baker, n.d., quoted in Preston 2, p. 62.

160 *"black-frocked":* Herbst, p. 158.

"The Dean had": Delmer, p. 318.

161 *"Hemingway's room":* Cowles, p. 31.

"he lectured her": Delmer, pp. 328–329.

"The 'Old Homestead,'": Cowles, pp. 33–34.

"peroxide blondes": Cowles, p. 35.

162 *"You took a tram":* Cowles, pp. 21–23.

163 *"considered [it] a friendly":* Cowles, p. 38.

"Shells were dropping": Cowles, p. 30.

164 *"She is young"*: Herbst, pp. 170–171.
165 *"a few minutes"*: "Spain's Life Goes On," *New York Times*, 10 April 1938.
"For weeks": Cowles, p. 55.

10. THE MAN WHO LOVED DICTATORS

166 *60 percent of the oil:* Martínez Molinos 1, p. 84.
167 *"that's the way"*: author's interview with Lewis Lapham, 14 November 2014.
168 *"He cannot sit"*: Thorndike, p. 57; "Captain & Concession," 4 May 1936.
"If I were dying": Anthony Sampson, *The Seven Sisters: The Great Oil Companies and the World They Shaped* (New York: Viking, 1973), p. 196.
169 *"some of my best friends"*: Farago, p. 400; author's interview with Lewis Lapham, 14 November 2014.
shipped to the Nationalists: Álvarez Alonso, p. 8. Rieber vaguely hinted to *Life*'s Thorndike that he ordered five Texaco tankers on the high seas at the time of the rising to change course for Nationalist Spain, and some scholars have repeated this boast as fact. Despite Rieber's enthusiasm for Franco, that particular claim is not true, according to Guillem Martínez Molinos, who has studied the archives of CAMPSA (Compañía Arrendataria del Monopolio de Petroleos, S.A.), the Spanish state oil company of this era.
170 *COME TO PARIS:* Manuel Aznar, "Ilustre historia de un español ejemplar," *ABC* (Madrid), 14 July 1973.
DON'T WORRY: Álvarez Alonso, pp. 5–6.
Juan March: Sánchez Asiaín, pp. 194–195.
job as president: See Martínez Molinos 1 and 2 for more detail.
171 *"rebel for Christ"*: Tierney, p. 92.
"beneath the crimson": Valaik, p. 81.
"will warm the heart": "America Neutral in Spanish Crisis," *Los Angeles Times*, 14 February 1937.
172 *"When the day came"*: Preston 2, pp. 315–316.
173 *"behaved like"*: Howson, p. 183.
come from Texaco: James W. Cortada, *Historical Dictionary of the Spanish Civil War, 1936–1939* (Westport, CT: Greenwood, 1982), p. 140: "Most of the Nationalists' petroleum was supplied by the Texas Oil Company." Martínez Molinos 1 bears this out and supplies more detail.
twice as much oil: Tierney, p. 68.
"Victory smiles": Tierney, p. 68.
174 *"We paid what we could"*: Álvarez Alonso, p. 9.
"would be victorious": Brien McMahon to Cummings, 7 August 1937, Attor-

ney General Personal File—Texas Company Oil Ships, 1937 Aug., Homer S. Cummings Papers, Box 159.

Rieber's company: Martínez Molinos 1, p. 94.

"in view of": Brien McMahon to Cummings, 7 August 1937, Attorney General Personal File—Texas Company Oil Ships, 1937 Aug., Homer S. Cummings Papers, Box 159.

indictment against Texaco: Ickes, p. 194. The cabinet meeting took place on 13 August 1937.

"in favor of prompt": Cummings to McMahon, 13 August 1937, Attorney General Personal File—Texas Company Oil Ships, 1937 Aug., Box 159, Homer S. Cummings Papers.

11. DEVIL'S BARGAIN

175 *"Spanish words":* Fraser, p. 406.

16 priests were murdered: Preston 3, pp. 431, 440.

176 *Some 200 people:* For many years scholars cited much higher casualty tolls, but the most careful and recent study, Preston 5, although by a historian highly sympathetic to the Republic, uses this lower estimate and explains its sources.

177 *"It would be welcomed":* Estes and Kowalsky, p. 87; quoted in Beevor, p. 233.

178 *"most of the destruction":* "Inquirer Doubtful on Guernica Fire; No Evidence Is Found That Basque Town Was Set Aflame by Bombs from Planes," *New York Times,* 5 May 1937.

Carney would be rewarded: See Drew Pearson's syndicated "Washington Merry-Go-Round" column, 6 November 1955 and 19 December 1959.

179 *"An eleven-mile march":* Lerude and Merriman, p. 126; Merriman Diary, 18 July 1937.

"sometimes I was": Lerude and Merriman, p. 143; Marion Merriman manuscript, Robert Hale Merriman Papers, ALBA 191, Box 2, Folder 1. The suitor who appealed to Party loyalty was Sandor Voros.

180 *"There, in the center":* "Madrid's Foreign Defenders," *Nation,* 4 September 1937; Merriman Diary, 9 July 1937.

"Most of them": Gurney, p. 56.

"On the front": Voros, p. 328.

181 *"it was never possible":* Gurney, pp. 139, 151.

"a healthy, happy lot": "Pingpong Enlivens Spanish War Lull," 24 May 1937; Cowles, p. 43.

"criminally naïve": Gurney, pp. 143, 161–162.

not shared by his comrades: A rare exception was William Herrick. See note to p. 364.

182 *"The tragic part":* Gurney, p. 151.

183 *"Our influence"*: 3 May 1937, Dallet, p. 35; Cusick 2, p. 273.

184 *"The shots frightened"*: Cusick 1, p. 294.

"The revolutionary purism": Orwell, p. 183.

"has little political": Walter Tapsell, "Report on the English Section of the P.O.U.M.," International Brigade Collection, Box C 13/7, Marx Memorial Library, London. For a summary of the milieu in Barcelona, see the chapter on Spain in Bowker. Stradling also covers this ground, although Marc Wildermeersch, *George Orwell's Commander in Spain: The Enigma of Georges Kopp* (London: Thames River Press, 2013) effectively disproves Stradling's suggestion that Kopp was reporting on the Blairs to the Communists.

"About midday": Orwell, pp. 103–104, 111, 112, 119.

186 *"10 minutes after"*: Charles to his mother, 8 May 1937, Orr, p. 161.

toll of known dead: Povedano, p. 799ff.

187 *"We have seen"*: 15 May 1937, Orr, p. 162; Cusick 1, p. 303.

"I'm writing you": 11 June 1937, Orr, pp. 171–172.

"It would be wrong": Thomas, p. 649.

188 *"showed us . . . a floor plan"*: Cusick 1, p. 304.

"Her fanatical approach": RGASPI 545/6/958.

"were not 'agents'": Huber conference paper. I am grateful to Dr. Huber for sharing this and another paper with me.

189 *"Stalin's terror"*: Lois Orr, "The May Days and My Arrest," Orr, pp. 191–193.

190 *"You will never"*: Cusick 1, p. 309.

anonymously sourced stories: See Bolloten, pp. 500–501, for an account of how this information was given to him as the United Press correspondent. *Times* of London, "Valencia Alleges Spy Plot," 19 June 1937; only at the end of the article does the correspondent, Lawrence Fernsworth, hint at some skepticism of the charges by saying, "It is only fair to the P.O.U.M. to state that it has repeatedly given warning through its newspaper that a plot was being prepared against it, whereby it would be accused of being in league with the enemy." *Manchester Guardian*, "200 Arrests in Madrid," 19 June 1937. *New York Times*, "Anti-Loyalist Plot Uncovered in Spain: 200 Arrested in Madrid and in Barcelona, Including Army Men and POUM Members," 19 June 1937; the story has no byline, but was written by Matthews, and the original dispatch is in Box 20 of the Herbert L. Matthews Papers.

In a book: Matthews 3, p. 288.

191 *"the street fighting"*: Faupel to German Foreign Ministry, 11 May 1937, quoted in Beevor, pp. 268–269.

"Such unbelievable lies": Cusick 1, p. 308.

"Whichever way you took it": Orwell, p. 128.

192 *"The whole experience"*: Orwell, pp. 131–132.

"It was . . . packed": Orwell, pp. 136–137.

193 *"in the next bed"*: Orwell, p. 144.

"at a time": Orwell, p. 208.

would shortly be accused: RGASPI 545/6/136, Part 2. The accusation came from Frank Frankford, a Briton in the POUM militia, apparently blackmailed into making these and other charges as the price of escaping a prison term for having looted some paintings from a church or museum.

194 *"When I got to the hotel"*: Orwell, p. 146.

One file: RGASPI 545/6/107, pp. 22–26. The same document, p. 25, brands the couple as "pronounced Trotskyites," making them correct to fear they were likely targets for arrest.

195 *"outer London"*: Orwell, p. 169.

12. "I DON'T THINK I WOULD WRITE ABOUT THAT IF I WERE YOU"

199 *"I was told"*: Cowles, pp. 56, 58.

201 *"Now you can see"*: Cowles, pp. 65, 69–70.

202 *"They were coming"*: Cowles, p. 66.

"German and Italian flags": Cowles, pp. 62, 64.

203 *"gazing on the celebration"*: Cowles, p. 67; "Behind the Fighting Fronts: In the Two Clashing Spains," *New York Times,* 9 January 1938; Cowles, p. 67.

"'Oh, we like them'": Cowles, p. 68.

"The spirit of revenge": Cowles, p. 75; Cowles, p. 76; statistics: Preston 3, p. 438.

204 *"the Captain and I"*: Cowles, pp. 74–76.

published these numbers: "Realities of War in Spain," 17 October 1937. Lloyd George's speech was on 28 October.

"When I stepped": Cowles, p. 107.

205 *President Roosevelt summoned:* A telegram from a Texaco executive to a Franco oil official, intercepted by the Republic's intelligence service and given to FDR by the Spanish ambassador on 8 June 1937, says that "the President called Rieber to Washington last week" to warn him about further shipments of oil on credit. Brewster to Arvilla, 23 April 1937, Franklin D. Roosevelt Papers as President: the President's Secretary's file, Box 50.

"Franklin, talk": Interview with Martha Gellhorn, 20 February 1980, p. 20, Eleanor Roosevelt Oral History Project, Eleanor Roosevelt Papers, Box 2.

206 *"We all listened"*: "My Day" column, 28 May 1937; 1 June 1937, Martha Gellhorn Papers, Box 4, Folder 121.

"It is surprising": 17 June 1937, Martha Gellhorn Papers, not boxed.

"Two nights ago": ? June 1937, Martha Gellhorn Papers, Box 4, Folder 122. This letter also appears in Gellhorn, p. 52.

207 *"We weren't helping"*: Gurney, pp. 164, 166, 168–170.

208 *"a large red-brick structure"*: Gurney, pp. 171–173.

209 *"How he embroidered"*: Fredericka Martin to Peter Wyden, 21 December 1984, and a separate note by Martin, both in Fredericka Martin Papers, ALBA 001, Box 18, Folder 41.

210 *"I was desperately sorry"*: Gurney, p. 176.

211 *It is also possible:* Vaill, p. 176, suggests this.

212 *"It was going to"*: Herbst, pp. 154, 150.

"Hemingway seems to have": George Packer, "The Spanish Prisoner," *New Yorker*, 31 October 2005, p. 85. Because the Robles affair ruptured the bond between two famous writers, much has been written about it, including two entire books, those by Koch and Martínez de Pisón. Koch's book is a frustrating one; among other problems, he makes little distinction between memoirs or diaries and fictionalized accounts of these events in novels by several of the participants. A good short treatment is the chapter on the subject in Preston 2, "The Lost Generation Divided: Hemingway, Dos Passos, and the Disappearance of José Robles."

30 POUM members: Schwartz, p. 115. This is apparently a downward revision of an earlier estimate of "at least fifty killed" in Alba and Schwartz, p. 232. Some sources give higher estimates: cf. Thomas, p. 786, who says 40 people were "apparently" executed in Barcelona alone.

213 *"has shown more"*: Orwell, p. 128.

"no serious punishment": This was Palmiro Togliatti, the Italian Communist leader. *Escritos sobre la Guerra de España* (Barcelona: Critica, 1980), p. 232, quoted in Payne 2, p. 231.

"at a wake": "The May Days and My Arrest," Orr, p. 196.

"to persuade the democratic": Estes and Kowalsky, p. 267.

214 *"If only the people"*: Cusick 2, pp. 245–246; Orwell, pp. 188–189.

215 *one out of seven:* Balfour, pp. 278, 312.

216 *"talked learnedly"*: Herbst, p. 138; "Night Before Battle," Hemingway 2, p. 449.

"You could learn": Hemingway to Benjamin Glazer?, n.d., a newly discovered letter. "Hemingway, Your Letter Has Arrived," *New York Times*, 10 February 2008.

217 *"What we really wanted"*: "A Conversation with Claud Cockburn," *The Review* 11–12, p. 51, quoted in Alex Zwerdling, *Orwell and the Left* (New Haven: Yale University Press, 1974), p. 8.

"The Catalans": 3 February 1939, Martha Gellhorn Papers, Box 4, Folder 122.

218 *"was in the hands"*: "Behind the Fighting Fronts: In the Two Clashing Spains," *New York Times*, 9 January 1938.

Not a single one: One of the few foreigners who wrote anything remotely approaching this was an Austrian sociologist, Franz Borkenau, who visited

many such enterprises. His book, *The Spanish Cockpit*, was highly praised by Orwell. Another foreign eyewitness account, less judicious and more starry-eyed, is H.-E. Kaminski, *Ceux de Barcelone* (Paris: Edition Denoël, 1937). The Republic had a vigorous propaganda operation and its censors were under orders to cut news of revolutionary events from foreign correspondents' stories. But this does not explain the lack of reporting on the subject, because for most of the war censorship was relatively porous and reporters easily made their way around it. Herbert Matthews, for instance, found that if his Paris bureau telephoned him at the right time, "the Spanish censor who usually listened in would be out to dinner" (Matthews 1, p. 119).
"It didn't seem possible": Cusick 2, p. 193.

13. "AS GOOD A METHOD OF GETTING MARRIED AS ANY OTHER"

219 *"Tell Mom"*: To Ida and Max Schachter, 12 May 1937 and 27 June 1937, Toby Jensky and Philip Schachter Papers, ALBA 055, Folder 1.
"I was up against": Gurney, pp. 177–178.
220 *"my big romance"*: 17 July 1937, Toby Jensky and Philip Schachter Papers, ALBA 055, Folder 1.
"There were a tremendous": Gurney, pp. 180–181.
221 *"He was still in love"*: To Ida and Max Schachter, 17 July 1937 and 2 May 1937. Toby Jensky and Philip Schachter Papers, ALBA 055, Folder 1.
"I've been inquiring": To Ida and Max Schachter, 17 July 1937 and 2 August 1937, Toby Jensky and Philip Schachter Papers, ALBA 055, Folder 2. See Labanyi for a thoughtful reading of these letters. My thanks to Prof. Labanyi for sharing with me a longer version of the essay on which her article is based.
"You have probably": 2 May 1937, Toby Jensky and Philip Schachter Papers, ALBA 055, Folder 15.
222 *"Dear Pop"*: 28 April 1937, Toby Jensky and Philip Schachter Papers, ALBA 055, Folder 15.
"Try to calm Pop": 5 June 1937 and 19 June 1937, Toby Jensky and Philip Schachter Papers, ALBA 055, Folder 16.
"We are now in reserve": 24 June 1937 and 3 July 1937, Toby Jensky and Philip Schachter Papers, ALBA 055, Folder 16.
224 *"the boys were confident"*: Carroll 1, p. 141.
"All the streets": Fischer 1, p. 425.
225 *Tukhachevsky's tactics:* Beevor, pp. 282–283.
"Sun like the thunder": 4 April 1937, Notes, War in Spain, 1937–38, Martha Gellhorn Papers, Box 1, Folder 7.

226 *arrest and beating:* After his death, the Party worked hard to promote Law as a heroic fighter for justice at home and abroad, and Paul Robeson hoped to make a film about him. Both Yates and Nelson refer to his arrest and beating by the Chicago police, but only in passing.

"said to Law": Eslanda Goode Robeson Diary, 31 January 1938, quoted in Fyrth, p. 305.

227 *"very fine"*: Gurney, p. 136. For a negative view of Law, see D. P. Stephens, *A Memoir of the Spanish Civil War: An Armenian-Canadian in the Lincoln Battalion* (St. John's, Newfoundland: Canadian Committee on Labour History, 2000), pp. 46–48.

fatally wounded: Herrick, pp. 179–180, claims that Law was shot in the back by one of his own men, but his sources for this are all secondhand. There are several firsthand accounts of Law's wounding by enemy fire, summarized in Carroll 1, pp. 138–139. Carroll also points out that two of the people cited by Herrick as sources for his story deny saying anything of the sort.

"We passed on": Fred Copeman, *Reason in Revolt* (London: Blandford, 1948), p. 133.

228 *"Time ceased to exist"*: Diary transcript, pp. 14–15, in Hamilton A. Tyler Papers, Box 3, Folder 27.

229 *at least 100 deserted:* Carroll 1, p. 148.

"in some sense": Review of *The Spanish Cockpit* by Franz Borkenau and *Volunteer in Spain* by John Sommerfield, *Time and Tide*, 31 July 1937, Orwell, p. 231.

"trying to get Pop": 15 July 1937, Toby Jensky and Philip Schachter Papers, ALBA 055, Folder 16.

Vincent Usera: Usera's files from the International Brigades are in RGASPI 545/6/1004. His US military service records were supplied to me under the Freedom of Information Act.

230 *boasting to Communists:* "Casino Theatre Plays for 1934 Announced," *Newport Mercury*, 15 June 1934; *Oral History Transcript, Lieutenant General James P. Berkeley, U.S. Marine Corps (Retired)* (Washington, DC: History and Museums Division, Headquarters, U.S. Marine Corps, 1973), pp. 26–27.

231 *"At least one"*: Records of the War Department General and Special Staffs, Maj. A. L. Hamblen, HQ Sixth Corps Area, Chicago, to Asst. Chief of Staff, G-2, War Department, Washington, 7 December 1937, file 10110.2666-179, Record Group 165, National Archives microfilm. Earlier such reports on Lincoln recruiting can be found in files 10110.2666-143, 10110.2666-155, and 10110.2662-298, Record Group 165.

"He was a soldier": Nelson, p. 153.

"bad elements": RGASPI 545/6/849.

232 *undercover agent:* Stradling, p. 655.

"war laboratory": Records of the War Department General and Special Staffs, Report #38512, 25 January 1937, from Lieutenant Colonel Raymond E. Lee in London, file 2657-S-144-88, Record Group 165, National Archives, College Park, MD; Vincent Usera, "Some Lessons of the Spanish War," *Field Artillery Journal*, September–October 1939, p. 406, reprinted from *United States Naval Institute Proceedings*, July 1939.

233 *"twenty percent"*: Fischer 1, pp. 430, 432, 438, 440.

234 *"American merchandise"*: Gallo to Fischer, 20 September 1937, RGASPI 545/1/11.

235 *"If democracy is crushed"*: "Keeping America Out of War," *Nation*, 27 March 1937.

14. TEXACO GOES TO WAR

236 *"a lone Republican"*: Abe Osheroff, in Bessie and Prago, pp. 84–85.

237 *"All around the ship"*: Liversedge, p. 54.

238 *"trembling with nerves"*: 15 October 1937, Notes, War in Spain, 1937–38, Martha Gellhorn Papers, Box 1, Folder 7; Hemingway to Mrs. Paul Pfeiffer, 2 August 1937, Hemingway 1, p. 460; Ivens, p. 131.

239 *"very Harvard"*: Hemingway to Mrs. Paul Pfeiffer, 2 August 1937, Hemingway 1, p. 460; Moorehead, p. 132.

"In the picture": "My Day," 10 July 1937.

"were impressed": 8 July 1937, Martha Gellhorn Papers, Box 4, Folder 122. This letter also appears in Gellhorn, p. 55.

240 *"ran his brigade"*: Merriman Diary, 29 September 1937; Hemingway to Rolfe, January 1940, Edwin Rolfe Papers, University of Illinois, Box-Folder R1–089; Merriman Diary, 18 August 1937.

"Fortified heights": 26 August 1937.

173 of the 287: Geiser, p. 259.

241 *"one german"*: 26 August 1937.

242 *"We had to go"*: Nelson, Barrett, and Ruck, p. 228.

"What the hell": Landis, p. 289.

"Broke into houses": Merriman Diary, 5 September 1937.

243 *"Looting is still"*: Merriman Diary, 8 September 1937.

"as large as cats": Lerude and Merriman, pp. 172–173.

244 *"The Government won"*: "Belchite Victory Cheers Loyalists," 19 September 1937.

"caved in": "Men Without Medals," *Collier's*, 15 January 1938.

"Since I had seen": NANA dispatch 13, 13 September 1937.

245 *"about arrests in Moscow"*: 19 September 1937.

"Milly wrote": 29 August 1937, Robert Hale Merriman Papers, ALBA 191, Box 1, Folder 2.

"Should I marry": Lerude and Merriman, p. 151.

246 *New York newspaper:* "Two Americans in Spain Managed to Wed by a Ruse," *New York World-Telegram*, 25 January 1938.

"I was beginning": 7 September 1937, Toby Jensky and Philip Schachter Papers, ALBA 055, Folder 2.

"I'm in a jam": To Ida Schachter, 8 October 1938 and 11 November 1937, Toby Jensky and Philip Schachter Papers, ALBA 055, Folder 2.

247 *"I am glad Americans":* Merriman Diary, 27 October 1937. See Burdick for much useful information on Fuqua.

15-page report: Records of the War Department General and Special Staffs, Report No. 6711, from Valencia, 1 November 1937, file 2657-S-144-294, Record Group 165, National Archives, College Park, MD.

248 *two pistols:* Carroll 1, p. 149.

the only mention: "Oil for Lisbon Goes to Franco Let's Stop It!" *Industrial Worker*, 22 May 1937. The cited essay by Chomsky steered me to this.

"a good friend": Brewster to Arvilla, 19 March 1937, CAMPSA (Compañía Arrendataria del Monopolio de Petroleos, S.A.) archives, Madrid, courtesy of Guillem Martínez Molinos.

249 *flow of intelligence:* Martínez Molinos 1, p. 94; Martínez Molinos 2, p. 681. To my knowledge, no other scholar has noticed this remarkable fact.

"My dear friend": CAMPSA archives, Madrid, courtesy of Guillem Martínez Molinos.

250 *returned without unloading:* Fernando Moreno de Alborán y de Reyna and Salvador Moreno de Alborán y de Reyna, *La Guerra silenciosa y silenciada: historia de la compaña naval durante la Guerra de 1936–39*, vol. 2 (Madrid: F. Moreno de Alborán y de Reyna, 1938), pp. 1165–1166.

251 *was boarded near midnight:* "Un Bateau Gouvernemental Disparait à Bordeaux," *Journal du Loiret* (Orléans, France), 9 July 1937; "Rebels Take Oil Tanker as Loyalists Go to Dance," *New York Times*, 9 July 1937.

15. "IN MY BOOK YOU'LL BE AN AMERICAN"

253 *"These guides":* The quotations all come from the record of a 1967 interview with Chrost in Szurek, pp. 144–148. In Watson 2, 3, and 4, the Hemingway scholar Prof. William Braasch Watson describes his travels retracing what he believes to have been Hemingway's journey, first to Alfambra and then behind the lines. No documentation directly confirms the novelist's trip into Nationalist territory, nor is there likely to have ever been any: as Watson points out, written permission to take part in a guerrilla mission would have been a death warrant if the person carrying it were captured. But for the approximate dates Chrost says he took the writer with him on that expedition, Watson found an unusually high-level safe-conduct pass for Hemingway, approved by two separate army

commands, and a trail of bills and receipts confirming that the novelist made a lengthy, otherwise unexplained automobile trip away from Madrid. Watson has also confirmed that International Brigades guerrillas operated from Alfambra, and that in Madrid Hemingway had met the commander of Republican guerrilla forces. Although this evidence is circumstantial rather than direct, Watson found nothing to disprove Chrost's story, and his inclination, like mine and that of Alex Vernon in *Hemingway's Second War*, pp. 169–170, is to accept it as true.

254 *"Now for Phil"*: To Ida Schachter, 7 September 1937, Toby Jensky and Philip Schachter Papers, ALBA 055, Folder 2.

255 *"I am trying desperately"*: To William Lawrence, 16 October 1937, RGASPI 545/6/981.

"I am writing this": 2 September 1937, Toby Jensky and Philip Schachter Papers, ALBA 055, Folder 13.

256 *"very unfair for Bob"*: Mangan, pp. 431–433.

258 *"was bright and yellow"*: Lerude and Merriman, pp. 143, 180.

"If we don't get help": Manny Harriman Video Oral History Collection, ALBA Video 048, Box 11, Container 2, interview with Marion Merriman Wachtel.

259 *"and we spent many hours"*: Lerude and Merriman, p. 188.

"word apparently": Manny Harriman Video Oral History Collection, ALBA Video 048, Box 11, Container 2, interview with Marion Merriman Wachtel.

"Just when the whole": Lerude and Merriman, p. 192.

260 *murdered Republican prisoners:* Preston 3, pp. 451–453.

261 *"the biggest upset"*: NANA dispatch 17, 19 December 1937.

"a surprising and dramatic": "Spanish Loyalists Drive into Teruel after Big Air Raid," *New York Times*, 20 December 1937; Matthews 2, p. 29; "Spanish Loyalists Drive into Teruel after Big Air Raid," *New York Times*, 20 December 1937.

"the soldier I was lying": NANA dispatch 18, 21 December 1937; to Hadley Mowrer, 31 January 1938, Hemingway 1, p. 462.

"may be the decisive": NANA dispatch 17, 19 December 1937; "Behind the Fighting Fronts: In the Two Clashing Spains," *New York Times*, 9 January 1938.

262 *"Smashing through"*: "Victory at Teruel Is Hailed with Joy in Insurgent Spain," 2 January 1938. The dispatch, datelined Saragossa but without a byline, is dated December 31.

"The Times retook": To Hadley Mowrer, 31 January 1938, Hemingway 1, p. 462.

"From your correspondent's": 5 January 1938. In his memoirs (Matthews 2, p. 29) Matthews exaggerated the sins of his enemy Carney, claiming that

Carney "gave a vivid description of how the citizens of Teruel joyfully received the Insurgent troops, giving them the Fascist salute." Carney's story did no such thing.

"We're off": 9 December 1937 (added to on 12 December) and 23 December 1937, Toby Jensky and Philip Schachter Papers, ALBA 055, Folder 3.

16. "A LETTER TO MY *NOVIA*"

267 *"A letter to my* novia": Neugass, 13 January 1938, p. 126.

"I got . . . my master's": "Poet James Neugass, M.A., Teruel," *Daily Worker*, 15 November 1938.

268 *"Gentlemen, we have"*: "To the Trade," Jack Salzman and Leo Zanderer, eds., *Social Poetry of the 1930s: A Selection* (New York: Burt Franklin, 1978), p. 175.

"heard a more lethal": Neugass, 5 December 1937, pp. 7–8, 10.

"What crime did these": Neugass, 3 and 4 January 1938, pp. 103, 106.

269 *"as we stopped for gas"*: Neugass, 5 December 1937, p. 11.

"I have not yet seen": Neugass, 19? December 1937, pp. 52–53.

"five-foot, hundred and fifty-pound": Neugass, 7 December 1937, p. 22, and 22 and 24 December 1937, p. 77.

271 *"for every radiator"*: Neugass, 19? December 1937, p. 60, and 24 December 1937, p. 78.

"For a century": Neugass, 12 December 1937, p. 47.

272 *"Wonder how the troops"*: Neugass, 31 December 1937, p. 92; Barsky, pp. 111, 125.

273 *"I handed the wheel"*: Neugass, 1 January 1938, p. 97.

"I now wipe ice": Neugass, 5 January 1938, p. 108.

274 *"We heat the place"*: 8 January 1938, Toby Jensky and Philip Schachter Papers, ALBA 055, folder 3.

"The engine of the shower-truck": Neugass, 6 January 1938, p. 109.

"She said, 'Shshsh!'": From Julia Newman's film *Into the Fire: American Women in the Spanish Civil War.*

275 *"Bodies coming in"*: Interview with Fredericka Martin, Fredericka Martin Papers, ALBA 001, Box 9, Folder 25.

"rawhide soaked": Neugass, 4 February 1938, p. 192, and 25 January 1938, p. 171.

"What do you think": Neugass, 14 January 1938, pp. 128–129.

276 *"My job was to cut"*: Neugass, 15? January 1938, pp. 138–139; 22 or 23 January 1938, p. 158; and 14 January 1938, p. 135.

"You can be very sure": Neugass, 14 January 1938, p. 128; 15? January 1938, p. 137; 2 February 1938, p. 187.

"Literary men": Neugass, 4 February 1938, pp. 194–195, and 16 January 1938, p. 147.

277 *"nailed to the walls"*: Neugass, 28? January 1938, pp. 183, 180.

278 *"the human leg"*: Neugass, 24 January 1938, p. 167, and 13 February 1938, pp. 212–213.

"'Get out of here, Jim'": Neugass, 17 February 1938, pp. 223, 226.

"Washington, London": Neugass, 15? January 1938, p. 146.

279 *"Tired of explaining"*: 24 January 1938, Martha Gellhorn Papers, Box 4, Folder 122.

"Please don't tell me": Louis Fischer, "Letters from Mrs. Roosevelt," *Journal of Historical Studies* 1(1), Autumn 1967; "The Road to Peace," *Nation*, 26 February 1938.

"All towns along the way": Neugass, 22 February 1938, p. 245, and 24 February 1938, pp. 246–247.

17. "ONLY A FEW GRAINS OF SAND LEFT IN THE HOURGLASS"

281 *"By March, 1938"*: Matthews 1, p. 122.

40,000 bombs: "German Vessel Sails with Big Bomb Cargo," *New York Times*, 9 May 1938.

282 *choose bombing targets:* Left-wing neighborhoods: see Laia Balcells, "Death Is in the Air: Bombings in Catalonia, 1936–1939," *Reis* 136, October–December 2011. Factories: see Fraser, p. 441.

"was pleased by": Quoted in Beevor, p. 333.

"my pen was dipped": Matthews 1, p. 124; quoted in Thomas, p. 785; Matthews 1, p. 124.

"The news from Spain": ? March 1938, Martha Gellhorn Papers, Box 4, Folder 122. Most, though not all, of this letter also appears in Gellhorn, p. 59.

283 *"I was out"*: 24? or 25? April 1938, Martha Gellhorn Papers, Box 4, Folder 122. This letter also appears in Gellhorn, p. 59.

NOT INTERESTED: Moorehead, p. 145. Decades later, Gellhorn's article about Barcelona at this time, "The Third Winter," appeared in her collection *The Face of War* (New York: Simon & Schuster, 1959). Despite a note on the copyright page of that book, it never appeared in *Collier's*.

284 *"I wait every day"*: 28 March 1938, Lerude and Merriman, p. 208.

285 *"Two tables"*: Neugass, 25 February 1938, pp. 248–249; 1 March 1938, p. 251; 9 March 1938, p. 256; and 10 March 1938, p. 262.

286 *"'Well, Bob'"*: Barsky, pp. 158–172.

289 *"This meant the fascists"*: Fisher, pp. 102–103.

"to openly fight": 29 September 1937 and 17 February 1937.

290 *"I came to the conclusion"*: Orwell, pp. 286–287, "Notes on the Spanish

Militias"; Joseph North, *No Men Are Strangers* (New York: International Publishers, 1976), p. 170.

"I sent a runner": Eby, p. 290; anonymous soldier quoted in Rolfe, p. 192.

291 *"an élite brotherhood"*: Kemp 2, p. 76.

"In their flight": Kemp 1, pp. 164–165.

"Lecera, the town": Neugass, 10 March 1938, p. 264; 11 March 1938, p. 265; and 11 March 1938, p. 266.

292 *"My hole is nine feet"*: Neugass, 11 March 1938, p. 268; 12 March 1938, p. 275; and 12 March 1938, p. 276.

"clogged with peasants": Neugass, p. 283.

293 *"The musicians could not"*: Neugass, p. 296.

"Milicianos de la Republica": Neugass, p. 297.

294 *"The Chófer was afraid"*: Neugass, pp. 289–290, 256.

18. AT THE RIVER'S EDGE

295 *"about a dozen"*: Kemp 1, pp. 162, 170–172.

296 *"There were two major reasons"*: Bessie 1, p. 182; Bessie 2, p. 2.

297 *"Any guys from Chicago?"*: Bessie 1, p. 44.

"You had to read": Bessie 1, p. 67.

"All of us had blankets": Bessie 1, pp. 82–83.

298 *"Major Merriman, tall"*: Bessie 1, pp. 82–86.

"The rainy season": Bessie 1, pp. 89–90, 93.

"the more experienced": Bessie 1, p. 94; Bessie 2, p. 23.

299 *"Hamburger on rye"*: Bessie 1, p. 108; Bessie 2, p. 21.

"He looks like a wreck": Dr. Leo Eloesser to the Medical Bureau to Aid Spanish Democracy, 10 April 1938, in Nelson and Hendricks, pp. 273–274.

300 *"a disc of hot iron"*: Neugass, 12 March 1938 (but apparently written later), p. 277.

"'What do you want to do?'": Neugass, 22 March 1938, p. 300.

301 *"These correspondents"*: Bowers to Hull, 2 April 1938, U.S. Department of State, *Foreign Relations of the United States, 1938*, vol. 1, p. 279; Edward Barsky, quoted in Landis, p. 496.

"As this correspondent": NANA Dispatch 19, 3 April 1938.

"We were in a field": Bessie 1, pp. 116–124.

303 *"We sat crouched"*: Bessie 1, p. 140.

"no one had heard": Bessie 1, p. 131.

304 *"The British are tough"*: Voros, pp. 413–424.

305 *"He was a gentle man"*: Author's interview with David Wellman, 18 November 2013; Bessie 2, p. 63.

306 *"shivering on the ground"*: "Shattering of American Battalion Is Described to Writer by Straggling Men," *New York Times*, 5 April 1938.

"tall, thin, dressed": Bessie 1, pp. 135–136.

307 *"I never had a sadder story"*: 7 April 1938, Matthews 2, p. 34.

"Hemingway did not seem": Bessie 1, pp. 137–138. There appear to have been two encounters between the pair of correspondents and the American survivors this day. Both in their books and in the interview with Watt in the John Gerassi Papers, ALBA 018, Box 7, Folder 6, Watt and Gates describe the first, when the two writers found them, alone, exhausted, and naked except for blankets, soon after they had swum the Ebro. The longer conversation described in Bessie 1 and by Hemingway and Matthews in their dispatches evidently happened later in the day, after all six American survivors had found each other and been supplied with food and the three swimmers with clothing. It was also in a different location, Rasquera, a few miles south of where the men apparently swam the river. Bessie 1, p. 135, refers to a "hillside" where hundreds of British and Canadian survivors also had gathered.

308 *"The answer was"*: "Shattering of American Battalion Is Described to Writer by Straggling Men," 5 April 1938.

"I was alone": Lerude and Merriman, p. 219.

"cut to pieces": "Americans to Fight to End for Spain," *Oakland Tribune*, 10 April 1938.

19. A CHANGE OF HEART?

309 *"confounded their enemy"*: "Vinaroz Captured," 16 April 1938.

"has failed": "Spain Won't Surrender," *Nation*, 30 April 1938.

310 *"If France don't come"*: Bessie 1, p. 133.

311 *"The power of the spectacles"*: Cowles, p. 147.

312 *"a nightmare of flags"*: Cowles, pp. 117–118.

313 *"The bastard!"*: Lerude and Merriman, p. 226.

314 *"After months"*: "Yankee Hero's Widow Tells Story 50 Years after the Spanish Civil War," *Los Angeles Times*, 25 April 1986.

315 *the leak came from:* Krock mentioned Welles and Hull to Hugh Thomas in 1963 (Thomas, p. 803n), and he mentioned Ickes to James Ragland in 1957 (Tierney, pp. 99–100).

"a black page": 12 May 1938, Ickes, p. 389.

One historian: Kanawada, pp. 61–64.

316 *"Dammit"*: Tierney, p. 100; Ickes, p. 390; interview with Martha Gellhorn, 20 February 1980, p. 20, Eleanor Roosevelt Oral History Project, Eleanor Roosevelt Papers, Box 2.

"that if we should": Ickes, p. 380.

318 *"To date have not"*: To Ida and Max Schachter, 20 March 1938 and 23 April 1938, Toby Jensky and Philip Schachter Papers, ALBA 055, Folder 3.

319 *"I regret to inform"*: Nathaniel P. Davis to Max Schachter, 13 July 1938, Toby Jensky and Philip Schachter Papers, ALBA 055, Folder 10.

20. GAMBLING FOR TIME

320 *"Markoosha and the boys"*: Fischer 1, pp. 494, 500.
321 *"illiteracy and rats"*: Sheean, pp. 195–196.
"Walter: I don't see": Álvarez Alonso, p. 11.
HAVING RETURNED: Rieber to Arvilla, 15 February 1938, CAMPSA archives, Madrid, courtesy of Guillem Martínez Molinos.
322 *"the Reds will be"*: Brewster to Arvilla, 22 March 1937, CAMPSA archives, Madrid, courtesy of Guillem Martínez Molinos; *Arlon* crew: "British Crew Bars Voyage," *New York Times*, 2 September 1937; Brewster to Arvilla, 19 November 1937, CAMPSA archives, Madrid, courtesy of Guillem Martínez Molinos.
323 *"You gotta row"*: Angela Jackson, p. 45, interview with Milton Wolff; Bessie 1, p. 195.
"We are going to cross": Bessie 1, p. 205.
324 *"Not a day passed"*: Preston 1, p. 137.
to hear Franco sobbing: Eby, p. 393n.
325 *"No food"*: Bessie 2, p. 70.
"We were startled": Bessie 1, p. 219.
326 *"The river bank"*: Fischer 1, pp. 541–550.
327 *"I showed the Spanish"*: Bessie 1, p. 215; William C. Beeching, *Canadian Volunteers: Spain, 1936–1939* (Regina, SK: Canadian Plains Research Center, 1989), p. 152; Bessie 1, pp. 221, 176.
"At such times": Bessie 1, pp. 222, 257, 264.
329 *"Ain't got no"*: Eby, p. 405.
"we had so few": Bessie 1, pp. 243, 293.
330 *"Mr. Chamberlain is going to"*: Bessie 1, p. 268.
"The news from Europe": Bessie 1, p. 337.
331 *"warmest congratulations"*: Preston 3, p. 313.
"chilled by an air": Cowles, pp. 155, 171.
332 *"Will Hitler and Stalin"*: *Socialist Call*, 10 December 1938.

21. THE TASTE OF TEARS

335 *300,000 Spaniards:* Beevor, p. 366.
2,500 troops: "Volunteers in Spain," *Times* of London, 29 October 1938. Katz, p. 60, uses a lower figure, 2,000.
three times the rate: Payne 1, p. 186.
336 *"Those men had learned"*: Matthews 1, p. 141; Herbert L. Matthews Papers, Box 21, Folder 4.

"The women and children": Katz, pp. 61–62; *Volunteer*, December 2008, p. 6.

"Mothers! Women!": Thomas, pp. 830–831.

337 *"Even black-skinned"*: "Barcelona's Farewell to Volunteers," *Hull Daily Mail*, 29 October 1938; Gates, p. 67.

"was the only time": Bernice Kert, *The Hemingway Women* (New York: Norton, 1999), p. 299; Moorehead, p. 153. Vaill, pp. 330–331, establishes that the couple were still in Paris at the time of the parade and not, contrary to myth and to the implication of one passage in Gellhorn's writing, in Barcelona.

338 *30,000 deaths:* On no other number do three of the most prominent historians of the war differ more widely. Preston 1, p. 291, says 7,150, while Thomas, p. 833, says 10,000 to 15,000, and Beevor, p. 358, says 30,000.

"For God's sake!": Thomas, p. 852.

"Dear Marty": 15 November 1938, Martha Gellhorn Papers, Box 4, Folder 121.

339 *When the British sent:* Preston 3, p. 423.

340 *no airfields were left:* Howson, pp. 242–243. Some histories, relying on an account of the trip to Moscow in late November 1938 by the Republic's air force commander, General Ignacio Hidalgo de Cisneros, and his wife, who were very stirred by Stalin's offer of help at this dark moment, overstate the amount of weapons involved. Working from Soviet records, Howson shows that fewer arms were actually sent, and, due to obstacles posed by the French, still fewer arrived in Spain.

"On the whole": "Planes Raid Barcelona at Night," 1 January 1939; "Retreat Orderly Despite Bombings," 14 January 1939; "Loyalist Defense Held Still Strong," 17 January 1939; "Barcelona's Plans Upset by Apathy," 26 January 1939.

341 *"I will never be able"*: Teresa Pàmies, *Quan érem capitans: memòries d'aquella guerra* (Barcelona: DOPESA, 1974), quoted in Beevor, p. 378.

"like having a death": 3 February 1939, Martha Gellhorn Papers, Box 4, Folder 122; Beevor, p. 378.

343 *200,000 political killings:* See note to p. 64.

one conservative calculation: Thomas, pp. 900–901.

"Lifting our hearts": Beevor, p. 397.

$20 million of oil: Martínez Molinos 1, p. 95. Traina, p. 166, quotes Rieber's associate William M. Brewster, in the center of this trade, as "stating in March 1939 that Texaco 'had already received twenty million dollars in cash' from the Nationalists." If Texaco was at this point still extending credit, the actual total value of oil sold would have been even higher. Historians often cite a lower figure, $6 million, which has its origin in the fawning 1940 profile of Rieber in *Life* by Joseph J. Thorndike Jr. But when Thorndike interviewed Rieber, the Second World War had begun, American hostility to fascism was rising, and Rieber had strong motives to

downplay his dealings with Franco. On the conversion of Texaco's sales to today's dollars, see note to p. 49.

225 trips to Spain: Sánchez Asiaín, p. 399, n. 58.

"enthusiasm shown": CAMPSA annual report, 1936–37 (published in 1940); José Maria Doussinague in Charles Foltz, *The Masquerade in Spain* (Boston: Houghton Mifflin, 1948), p. 52.

344 *posthumously sentenced:* Preston 3, p. 505.

"opposed the Nationalist": Beevor, p. 385.

"wild boars": Enrique Suñer, *Los intelectuales y la tragedia española*, 2nd edition (San Sebastián: Editorial Española, 1938), pp. 166–167, quoted in Preston 3, pp. 505–506.

345 *For example, Matilde Landa:* Graham, pp. 114, 204.

"cry as I never cried": Bessie and Prago, p. 337.

346 *"You have no right":* Preston 3, p. 503.

20,000 Republicans: Preston 3, p. xi. Here, as for many statistics, I am relying on Preston's magisterial *The Spanish Holocaust*, the most recent and extensive tabulation. Stanley Payne uses a higher figure—28,000 (Payne 1, pp. 104 and 110)—for those executed after the war, although a lower one for those killed by the Nationalists during the war: "at least 70,000 (and possibly more)," Payne 1, p. 110. Beevor, p. 405, adds together deaths from "Franquist terror" during and after the war, saying "the total figure probably approaches 200,000"—similar to Preston's numbers.

270,000 convicted prisoners: Beevor, p. 405.

502 inmates died: Preston 3, p. 509.

"militarized penal colonies": Preston 3, pp. 509–510; Beevor, p. 404.

"The Caudillo used": Beevor, p. 406.

347 *"an attempt not so much":* Orwell, p. 171.

22. KADDISH

348 *"more cops than people":* Carroll 1, p. 211; Eby, p. 417.

349 *"Several of the men":* Yates, pp. 160, 164.

"No good men": Ernest Hemingway, "Milton Wolff," in Jo Davidson, *Spanish Portraits* (New York: Georgian Press, 1938), quoted in Carroll 2, p. 80.

350 *"to test my young":* Preston 1, pp. 153–154.

351 *50-page report:* Beevor, p. 426. Spanish readers of Beevor's book found in German archives the report he had referred to. The photographs with it were part of a traveling exhibit in Spain in 2012–2013 under the title "Experiments de la Legió Còndor a l'Alt Maestrat, 1938." My thanks to Guillem Martínez Molinos for pointing this out to me.

"sometimes getting": "Premature Anti-Fascist," *Antioch Review* 57(2), Spring 1999, p. 148.

352 *"conscripts in Stalin's army":* Tanenhaus, p. 301.

"liquidation": See Radosh et al. for an extensive collection of these Soviet documents in English.

"A different outcome": From *My Road to Berlin* (New York: Doubleday, 1960), reprinted in Klaus Harpprecht, *Willy Brandt: Portrait and Self-Portrait* (Los Angeles: Nash, 1971), p. 89.

353 *"a grave mistake"*: Ickes, p. 569.

"Where went": 18 May 1982, Robert Hale Merriman Papers, ALBA 191, Box 1, Folder 13.

354 *being one herself*: Although while in Spain she did apply to join the Communist Party, possibly with the thought that this might gain her access that could improve her always marginal position as a freelance reporter. See RGASPI 545/6/862. We do not know if her application was accepted, or if her well-known penchant for loudly criticizing the Soviet Union made the Party turn her away.

"She cant have": To Hans Amlie, n.d., Milly Bennett Papers, Box 2, Folder 3.

her autobiography: The manuscript about China was found among her papers and published under a different title more than 30 years after her death, receiving several enthusiastic reviews. See Bibliography.

"As for Pat": Jensky to Martin and Samuel Berenberg, 14 September 1941, and Gurney to Martin, 1949, both Fredericka Martin Papers, ALBA 001, Box 9, Folder 21; interview with Jensky, research materials for *Into the Fire: American Women in the Spanish Civil War*, a film by Julia Newman, ALBA 266; author's interview with Bernice Jensky, 13 October 2013.

355 *"if you were against"*: The speaker was Representative Hugh De Lacy of Washington State. "U.S. Has 1,500 Atom Bombs Store, Representative De Lacy Says Here," *New York Times*, 31 March 1946.

"When a doctor cannot": Carroll 1, p. 286.

356 *"at one time"*: John Gerassi Papers, ALBA 018, Box 6, Folder 3.

"did not know where": FBI file NY 100–90413, p. 2. I am grateful to Jim Neugass for sharing this and other documents about his father with me.

unpublished writings: Myra Neugass to Fredericka Martin, 23 July 1968, Fredericka Martin Papers, ALBA 001, Box 10, Folder 18.

"This is the most important": Neugass, p. xviii, introduction by Peter N. Carroll and Peter Glazer. Readers owe these historians a debt for shepherding this book into print.

357 *If ever asked:* For example, Thorndike, p. 57.

358 *"He summoned me"*: Author's interview with Lewis Lapham, 14 November 2014.

359 *"What will I do"*: N.d., early 1937, Martha Gellhorn Papers, not boxed.

"the best goddamn book": Hemingway to Clara Spiegel, 23 August 1940, Hemingway 1, p. 511.

360 *"vicious . . . personal attack"*: Bessie, "Hemingway's 'For Whom the Bell

Tolls,'" *New Masses*, 5 November 1940, pp. 27–29; Bessie 2, p. 130; *People's World*, 30 October 1940 and 12 February 1941, quoted in Carroll 1, pp. 239–240.

362 *"It is difficult"*: Orwell, p. 168; Orwell to Frank Jellinek, 20 December 1938, Orwell, p. 320; Orwell, p. 358, "Looking Back on the Spanish War."

"The outcome": Orwell, p. 357, "Looking Back on the Spanish War."

363 *"What can I write"*: The story first appeared in *Cosmopolitan* in October 1939, contrary to the dating in the publisher's preface to Hemingway 2, where it appears on pp. 460–469. Hemingway to Perkins, c. 15 January 1940, quoted in Watson 1, p. 114.

"enormous crime": "As I Please" column, *Tribune*, 2 February 1945.

"Homage to Catalonia": Hemingway to Harvey Breit, April or May 1952, quoted in Rodden and Rossi, p. 61; Orwell on Hemingway: "Wartime Britain has produced nothing of the caliber of 'For Whom the Bell Tolls' or 'Darkness at Noon,'" review of *Robert Cain*, by William Russell, *Manchester Evening News*, 15 June 1944, in Orwell, *I Have Tried to Tell the Truth: Complete Works*, Volume XVI, edited by Peter Davison, assisted by Ian Angus and Sheila Davison (London: Secker & Warburg, 1998, p. 256).

364 *left the Party:* Very few of them, however, appear to have done so because of their experiences in the Spanish Civil War. William Herrick did not leave the Party until the Hitler-Stalin Pact, but, at least in retrospect, found much to feel bitter about in what he had seen in Spain. His searing but not wholly reliable memoir describes (pp. 201–202) being forced to witness a Communist official shooting three prisoners who were apparently anarchists or POUM members. Nasty as this internecine conflict was, few if any other International Brigades members were directly caught up in it, despite a vivid portrayal to the contrary in the Ken Loach film *Land and Freedom*.

"the most traumatic episode": Carroll 1, pp. 376–377.

365 *"imagine life without something"*: Fischer 1, p. 208.

366 *"Why didn't I wake"*: Hyman Katz, 25 November 1937, in Nelson and Hendricks, p. 32.

"Tears . . . just rolled down": Petrou, p. 182.

367 *honorary citizenship:* Full citizenship would have required them to give up citizenship of another country, but a decade later that requirement was removed, and several of the handful of Lincolns then still alive received Spanish passports.

"Dear Sirs": 6 March 1937. Robert Hale Merriman Papers, Bancroft Library, University of California, Berkeley.

"MERRIMAN fall dead": Fausto Villar to Luke Hinman, 22 January 1987. Robert Hale Merriman Papers, Bancroft Library, University of California, Berkeley.

368 *"with a voice"*: Villar Esteban ms., pp. 75–76. In a letter in the *Volunteer*,

Spring 1998, Villar says this happened at 10 a.m., and Merriman was "two meters or so" away.

"the man I so admired": Villar Esteban to Marion Merriman, 8 April 1987, included in Villar Esteban ms., p. 10.

"Reds!": John R. Gerlach, "Behind Fascist Lines," in Bessie and Prago, p. 242. Gerlach wrote this account years later, but it is consistent with what he told Hemingway and Matthews when they interviewed him on April 4, 1938. Leonard Lamb recounts a similar memory in the John Gerassi Papers, ALBA 018, Box 4, Folder 2, as does Clement Markert in Box 4, Folder 13. If both their recollections and Villar's memory are correct, it is possible that Merriman was alive when Villar shouted to him but kept quiet because he did not want to give his position away to Nationalist snipers. The Swiss volunteer Konrad Schmidt offers yet a third version of Merriman's fate: he says he saw Merriman and his adjutant run into a hut to shelter from Nationalist machine-gun fire as they descended from the hilltop, and that "I found out later that he was arrested in that hut" (Schmidt, p. 289). Conceivably, however, given Villar's account of his own actions that day, it could have been Villar and another soldier whom Schmidt saw taking shelter, mistaking their identity.

"very tall": Martí, p. 15.

"I have written": 28 July 1987. Robert Hale Merriman Papers, Bancroft Library, University of California, Berkeley.

370 *at least 50:* The accounts of how many men were on this hilltop vary wildly, and may indicate that they didn't all arrive at once. John R. Gerlach, in "Behind Fascist Lines," in Bessie and Prago, says 50. Martin Maki, a Lincoln machine-gunner who was shortly captured, in the John Gerassi Papers, ALBA 018, Box 4, Folder 19, places the number at "over 100." Schmidt, p. 289, says there were 700.

371 *"Life has been full":* 17 February 1937. The lines were written on February 27, however.

beyond the road: Gerlach's memoir says they crossed the road, which is consistent with the account in Rolfe, pp. 212–213, written in 1939, for which he ("a Chicagoan named Ivan") appears to have been a source. Albin Ragner, in "An Unpublished Memoir," *Volunteer*, 27 February 2013, places Merriman eight or nine miles east of Gandesa, surely an overstatement but in any event beyond the road.

"With the increasing years": Harry Schachter to Carl Geiser, 15 December 1992, courtesy of Rebecca Schachter.

"My family never knew": "Honoring My Uncle Phil Schachter," *Volunteer*, 2 July 2012.

Bibliography

ARCHIVAL OR UNPUBLISHED MATERIAL

Abraham Lincoln Brigade Archives (ALBA), Tamiment Library, New York University. In the source notes, I have referred separately to many individual, numbered sets of papers within this collection.

The originals of Robert Merriman's diaries are in the Robert Hale Merriman Papers, ALBA 191, Box 1, Folder 3. But the library also has an electronic scan, available on request, which can be enlarged and is much more readable. More accessible yet is a scanned, transcribed, and elaborately annotated edition of the entire diary online at this writing at www.merrimandiary.com.

A useful biographical database of American volunteers can be found at the Abraham Lincoln Brigade Archives website.

Frank Aydelotte Papers, Friends Historical Library, Swarthmore College, Swarthmore, PA.

Barsky, Dr. Edward K., with Elizabeth Waugh. *The Surgeon Goes to War.* Unpublished ms., courtesy of Peter N. Carroll. Also to be found in the Edward K. Barsky Papers, ALBA 125, Box 5, Folders 4–21.

Milly Bennett Papers, Hoover Institution Archives, Stanford University.

Homer S. Cummings Papers, Special Collections, University of Virginia Library.

Cusick, Lois [Orr].

1. "Anarchist Millennium: Memories of the Spanish Revolution of 1936–37." 1979. Unpublished ms., courtesy of Elizabeth Cusick; a copy is at the Hoover Institution Library, Stanford University.
2. "Spain, 1936–1937." 1961. An earlier draft of "Anarchist Millennium," courtesy of Elizabeth Cusick; a copy is at the Labadie Collection, University of Michigan Library.

Louis Fischer Papers, Seeley G. Mudd Manuscript Library, Princeton University.

Martha Gellhorn Papers, Howard Gotlieb Archival Research Center, Boston University.

Robert Gladnick Papers, Hoover Institution Archives, Stanford University.

Huber, Peter. "Surveillance et repression dans les Brigades Internationales (1936–1938)," conference paper, Université de Lausanne, 18–20 December 1997.

Mangan, Kate (sometimes referred to as Kate Mangan Kurzke). "The Good Comrade," unpublished ms., Jan Kurzke Papers, International Institute of Social History, Amsterdam, Netherlands.

Herbert L. Matthews Papers, Rare Book and Manuscript Library, Columbia University.

Robert Hale Merriman Papers, Bancroft Library, University of California, Berkeley.

Charles A. Orr Papers, Hoover Institution Archives, Stanford University.

Torkild Rieber interview, Oral History of the Texas Oil Industry, Box 3K22, Briscoe Center for American History, University of Texas at Austin. At this writing, available online.

RGASPI. Russian State Archive of Social-Political History, Moscow. Microfilms of some of these files are held by the Tamiment Library at New York University and are organized by *fond*, *opis*, and *delo*, which can be translated as "archive," "list," and "file." Those relating to the International Brigades are all in *Fond* 545 of the Comintern archives and are indicated in the source notes with succeeding numbers referring to the *opis* and *delo*, as in: RGASPI 545/3/46.

Eleanor Roosevelt Papers, Franklin D. Roosevelt Presidential Library, Hyde Park, NY.

Franklin D. Roosevelt Papers, Franklin D. Roosevelt Presidential Library, Hyde Park, NY.

James Roosevelt Papers, Franklin D. Roosevelt Presidential Library, Hyde Park, NY.

Hamilton A. Tyler Papers, Bancroft Library, University of California, Berkeley.

Villar Esteban, Fausto. "A Little Valencian in the Lincoln Brigade: An Anti-War and Anti-Heroic Symphony." Trans. Paul Sharkey. Special Collections, University of Michigan Library.

Young, Glennys. "Fashioning Spanish Culture in the Gulag and Its International Significance: The Case of the Karaganda Spaniards." Conference paper, University of Cambridge, 29 June 2012.

THESES

Althaus, Dudley Quentin. *A Correspondent's Commitment: Herbert L. Matthews' Coverage of the Spanish Civil War, 1936–1939.* M.A., University of Texas, 1984.

Bogacka-Rode, Magdalena. *Straight Record and the Paper Trail: From Depression Reporters to Foreign Correspondents.* Ph.D., City University of New York, 2014.

Cooper, Sarah. *Reporting the Spanish Civil War from the Loyalist Side: The Professional and Personal Challenge for American Correspondents.* M.A., University of Wisconsin, 1973.

Johnson, Ashley. *Healing the Wounds of Fascism: The American Medical Brigade and the Spanish Civil War.* B.A., Mount Holyoke College, 2007.

BOOKS AND ARTICLES

Alba, Victor, and Stephen Schwartz. *Spanish Marxism versus Soviet Communism: A History of the P.O.U.M.* New Brunswick, NJ: Transaction, 1988.

Alpert, Michael. *A New International History of the Spanish Civil War.* New York: St. Martin's, 1994.

Álvarez Alonso, José Antonio. *Notas sobre el suministro de petroleo a la España nacional en la guerra civil (1936–1939).* Madrid: Graficas Onofre Alonso, 1970.

Anderson, Peter, and Miguel Ángel del Arco Blanco. *Mass Killings and Violence in Spain, 1936–1952: Grappling with the Past.* New York: Routledge, 2015.

Balfour, Sebastian. *Deadly Embrace: Morocco and the Road to the Spanish Civil War.* Oxford: Oxford University Press, 2002.

Baumeister, Martin, and Stefanie Schüler-Springorum, eds. *"If You Tolerate This . . .": The Spanish Civil War in the Age of Total War.* Frankfurt: Campus, 2008.

Baxell, Richard. *Unlikely Warriors: The British in the Spanish Civil War and the Struggle Against Fascism.* London: Aurum, 2012.

Beevor, Antony. *The Battle for Spain: The Spanish Civil War, 1936–1939.* New York: Penguin, 2006.

Bennett, Milly. *On Her Own: Journalistic Adventures from San Francisco to the Chinese Revolution, 1917–1927.* Ed. A. Tom Grunfeld. Armonk, NY: M. E. Sharpe, 1993.

Bessie, Alvah.

1. *Men in Battle: A Story of Americans in Spain.* New York: Scribner's, 1939.
2. *Alvah Bessie's Spanish Civil War Notebooks.* Ed. Dan Bessie. Lexington, KY: University Press of Kentucky, 2002.

Bessie, Alvah, and Albert Prago, eds. *Our Fight: Writings by Veterans of the Abraham Lincoln Brigade, Spain, 1936–1939.* New York: Monthly Review Press, 1987.

Bolloten, Burnett. *The Spanish Civil War: Revolution and Counterrevolution.* Chapel Hill, NC: University of North Carolina Press, 1991.

Borkenau, Franz. *The Spanish Cockpit: An Eye-Witness Account of the Political and

Social Conflicts of the Spanish Civil War. Ann Arbor: University of Michigan Press, 1963.

Bowker, Gordon. *Inside George Orwell.* New York: Palgrave Macmillan, 2003.

Breá, Juan, and Mary Low. *Red Spanish Notebook: The First Six Months of the Revolution and the Civil War.* San Francisco: City Lights, 1979.

Brendon, Piers. *The Dark Valley: A Panorama of the 1930s.* London: Cape, 2000.

Buchanan, Tom. "Three Lives of *Homage to Catalonia*," *Library Transactions* 3(3), 2002.

Burdick, Charles B. "The American Military Attachés in the Spanish Civil War, 1936–1939," *Militärgeschichtliche Mitteilungen* 46(2), December 1989.

Carroll, Peter N.

1. *The Odyssey of the Abraham Lincoln Brigade.* Stanford, CA: Stanford University Press, 1994.
2. *From Guernica to Human Rights: Essays on the Spanish Civil War.* Kent, OH: Kent State University Press, 2015.

Carroll, Peter N., and James D. Fernandez. *Facing Fascism: New York and the Spanish Civil War.* New York: Museum of the City of New York, 2007.

Chapman, Michael E. *Arguing Americanism: Franco Lobbyists, Roosevelt's Foreign Policy, and the Spanish Civil War.* Kent, OH: Kent State University Press, 2011.

Chomsky, Noam. "Objectivity and Liberal Scholarship," in *American Power and the New Mandarins.* New York: New Press, 2002.

Cowles, Virginia. *Looking for Trouble.* New York: Harper & Brothers, 1941.

Crowl, James William. *Angels in Stalin's Paradise: Western Reporters in Soviet Russia, 1917 to 1937, a Case Study of Louis Fischer and Walter Duranty.* Washington, DC: University Press of America, 1982.

Dallet, Joe. *Letters from Spain.* New York: Workers Library, 1938.

Delmer, Sefton. *Trail Sinister: An Autobiography*, vol. 1. London: Secker & Warburg, 1961.

de Vries, Lini. *Up from the Cellar.* Minneapolis: Vanilla Press, 1979.

Dolgoff, Sam, ed. *The Anarchist Collectives: Workers' Self-Management in the Spanish Revolution, 1936–1939.* New York: Free Life Editions, 1974.

Eby, Cecil D. *Comrades and Commissars: The Lincoln Battalion in the Spanish Civil War.* University Park, PA: Pennsylvania State University Press, 2007.

Esenwein, George, and Adrian Shubert. *Spain at War: The Spanish Civil War in Context, 1931–1939.* New York: Longman, 1995.

Estes, Kenneth W., and Daniel Kowalsky. *The Spanish Civil War.* Detroit: St. James, 2005.

Farago, Ladislas. *Game of the Foxes: The Untold Story of German Espionage in the United States and Great Britain during the Second World War.* New York: David McKay, 1971.

Felsen, Milt. *The Anti-Warrior.* Iowa City: University of Iowa Press, 1989.

Fischer, Louis.

1. *Men and Politics: An Autobiography.* New York: Duell, Sloan and Pearce, 1941.

2. *Soviet Journey.* New York: H. Smith and R. Hass, 1935.

3. "Spanish Diary Sep 18–Oct 16, 1936." Fischer Papers, Box 25, Folder 2.

Fisher, Harry. *Comrades: Tales of a Brigadista in the Spanish Civil War.* Lincoln: University of Nebraska Press, 1998.

Fleming, John V. "The Travails of a Fellow-Traveler," *Princeton University Library Chronicle* 71(2), Winter 2010.

Frank, Willard C., Jr. "The Spanish Civil War and the Coming of the Second World War," *International History Review* 9(3), August 1987.

Fraser, Ronald. *Blood of Spain: An Oral History of the Spanish Civil War.* New York: Pantheon, 1979.

Fyrth, Jim, ed., with Sally Alexander. *Women's Voices from the Spanish Civil War.* London: Lawrence & Wishart, 1991.

Galbraith, John Kenneth. *A Life in Our Times.* Boston: Houghton Mifflin, 1981.

Gates, John. *The Story of an American Communist.* New York: Thomas Nelson & Sons, 1958.

Geiser, Carl. *Prisoners of the Good Fight: The Spanish Civil War, 1936–1939.* Westport, CT: Lawrence Hill, 1986.

Gellhorn, Martha. *Selected Letters of Martha Gellhorn.* Ed. Caroline Moorehead. New York: Holt, 2006.

Graham, Helen. *The War and Its Shadow: Spain's Civil War in Europe's Long Twentieth Century.* Brighton, UK: Sussex Academic Press, 2012.

Gurney, Jason. *Crusade in Spain.* London: Faber and Faber, 1974.

Halstead, Charles R. "A 'Somewhat Machiavellian' Face: Colonel Juan Beigbeder as High Commissioner in Spanish Morocco, 1937–1939," *Historian* 37(1), 1 November 1974.

Hemingway, Ernest.

1. *Selected Letters, 1917–1961.* Ed. Carlos Baker. New York: Scribner's, 1981.

2. *The Complete Short Stories of Ernest Hemingway.* New York: Scribner's, 1987.

Citations to Hemingway's North American Newspaper Alliance (NANA) reports from Spain follow their texts as edited by William Braasch Watson and reproduced as "Hemingway's Spanish Civil War Dispatches," *Hemingway Review* 7(2), Spring 1988.

Herbst, Josephine. *The Starched Blue Sky of Spain and Other Memoirs.* New York: HarperPerennial, 1992.

Herrick, William. *Jumping the Line: The Adventures and Misadventures of an American Radical.* Madison: University of Wisconsin Press, 1998.

Hopkins, James K. *Into the Heart of the Fire: The British in the Spanish Civil War.* Stanford, CA: Stanford University Press, 1998.

Howson, Gerald. *Arms for Spain: The Untold Story of the Spanish Civil War.* New York: St. Martin's, 1998.

Ickes, Harold L. *The Secret Diary of Harold L. Ickes: Volume II, The Inside Struggle, 1936–1939.* New York: Simon & Schuster, 1954.

Ivens, Joris. *The Camera and I.* New York: International Publishers, 1969.

Jackson, Angela. *At the Margins of Mayhem: Prologue and Epilogue to the Last Great Battle of the Spanish Civil War.* Torfaen, Wales: Warren & Pell, 2008.

Jackson, Gabriel.

1. *The Spanish Republic and the Civil War, 1931–1939.* Princeton, NJ: Princeton University Press, 1965.
2. *Juan Negrín: Spanish Republican Wartime Leader.* Eastbourne, UK: Sussex Academic Press, 2010.
3. "Collectivist Experiences in the Spanish Civil War," *Mediterranean Studies* 2 (1990).

Jacobs, John Kedzie. *The Stranger in the Attic: Finding a Lost Brother in His Letters Home.* Privately printed, 2013.

Jump, Jim, ed. *Looking Back at the Spanish Civil War: The International Brigade Memorial Trust's Len Crome Memorial Lectures, 2002–2010.* London: Lawrence & Wishart, 2010.

Kanawada, Leo V., Jr. *Franklin D. Roosevelt's Diplomacy and American Catholics, Italians, and Jews.* Ann Arbor, MI: UMI Research Press, 1982.

Katz, William. *The Lincoln Brigade: A Picture History.* New York: Atheneum, 1989.

Keene, Judith. *Fighting for Franco: International Volunteers in Nationalist Spain during the Spanish Civil War, 1936–39.* London: Hambledon Continuum, 2007.

Kemp, Peter.

1. *Mine Were of Trouble.* London: Cassell, 1957.
2. *The Thorns of Memory: Memoirs.* London: Sinclair-Stevenson, 1990.

Knightley, Phillip. *The First Casualty: From the Crimea to Vietnam: The War Correspondent as Hero, Propagandist, and Myth Maker.* New York: Harcourt Brace Jovanovich, 1975.

Knoblaugh, H. Edward. *Correspondent in Spain.* London: Sheed & Ward, 1937.

Koch, Stephen. *The Breaking Point: Hemingway, Dos Passos, and the Murder of José Robles.* New York: Counterpoint, 2005.

Kowalsky, Daniel. *Stalin and the Spanish Civil War.* New York: Columbia University Press, 2008.

Labanyi, Jo. "Finding Emotions in the Archives," *Volunteer,* June 2007.

Landis, Arthur H. *The Abraham Lincoln Brigade.* New York: Citadel, 1967.

Lash, Joseph P. *Eleanor and Franklin: The Story of Their Relationship, Based on Eleanor Roosevelt's Private Papers.* New York: Norton, 1971.

Lear, Walter J. "American Medical Support for Spanish Democracy, 1936–1938," in Anne-Emanuelle Birn and Theodore M. Brown, eds., *Comrades in Health: U.S. Health Internationalists, Abroad and at Home.* New Brunswick, NJ: Rutgers University Press, 2013.

Lerude, Warren, and Marion Merriman. *American Commander in Spain: Robert Hale Merriman and the Abraham Lincoln Brigade.* Reno: University of Nevada Press, 1986.

Little, Douglas. "Antibolshevism and Appeasement: Great Britain, the United States, and the Spanish Civil War," in David F. Schmitz and Richard D. Challener, eds., *Appeasement in Europe: A Reassessment of U.S. Policies.* New York: Greenwood Press, 1990.

Liversedge, Ronald. *Mac-Pap: Memoir of a Canadian in the Spanish Civil War.* Vancouver: New Star, 2013.

Madariaga, María Rosa de. "The Intervention of Moroccan Troops in the Spanish Civil War: A Reconsideration," *European History Quarterly* 22 (1992).

Martí, Anna. "In the Footsteps of the Lincolns," *Volunteer,* September 2012.

Martínez de Pisón, Ignacio. *To Bury the Dead.* Cardigan, Wales: Carnival/Parthian, 2009.

Martínez Molinos, Guillem.

1. "El suministro de petróleo," in *La Guerra Civil 16: La economia de guerra.* Madrid: Historia 16, 1986.
2. "Ríos de Petróleo. El abastecimiento de esencias y grasas durante la guerra civil," in Francisco Comín Comín and Enrique Fuentes Quintana, eds., *Economía y economistas españoles en la guerra civil I: El contexto politico e internacional.* Barcelona: Real Academia de Ciencias Morales y Políticas, 2008.

Matthews, Herbert L.

1. *The Education of a Correspondent.* New York: Harcourt Brace, 1946.
2. *A World in Revolution: A Newspaperman's Memoir.* New York: Scribner's, 1971.
3. *Two Wars and More to Come.* New York: Carrick & Evans, 1938.
4. *Eyewitness in Abyssinia: With Marshal Badoglio's Forces to Addis Ababa.* London: Martin Secker & Warburg, 1937.

Moorehead, Caroline. *Gellhorn: A Twentieth-Century Life.* New York: Henry Holt, 2003.

Nelson, Cary, and Jefferson Hendricks. *Madrid 1937: Letters of the Abraham Lincoln Brigade from the Spanish Civil War.* New York: Routledge, 1996.

Nelson, Steve. *The Volunteers.* New York: Masses & Mainstream, 1953.

Nelson, Steve, James R. Barrett, and Rob Ruck. *Steve Nelson: American Radical.* Pittsburgh: University of Pittsburgh Press, 1981.

Neugass, James. *War Is Beautiful: An American Ambulance Driver in the Spanish Civil War.* Ed. Peter N. Carroll and Peter Glazer. New York: New Press, 2008.

Orr, Lois. *Letters from Barcelona: An American Woman in Revolution and Civil War.* With some material by Charles Orr. Ed. Gerd-Rainer Horn. Basingstoke, Hampshire, UK: Palgrave Macmillan, 2009.

Orwell, George. *Orwell in Spain: The Full Text of* Homage to Catalonia *with Associated Articles, Reviews, and Letters from* The Complete Works of George Orwell. Ed. Peter Davison. London: Penguin, 2001.

Othen, Christopher. *Franco's International Brigades: Adventurers, Fascists, and Christian Crusaders in the Spanish Civil War.* New York: Columbia University Press, 2013.

Patai, Frances. "Heroines of the Good Fight: Testimonies of U.S. Volunteer Nurses in the Spanish Civil War, 1936–1939," *Nursing History Review* 3 (1995), pp. 79–104.

Payne, Stanley.

1. *The Spanish Civil War.* New York: Cambridge University Press, 2012.
2. *The Spanish Civil War, the Soviet Union, and Communism.* New Haven: Yale University Press, 2004.

Petrou, Michael. *Renegades: Canadians in the Spanish Civil War.* Vancouver: University of British Columbia Press, 2008.

Povedano, Manuel Aguilera. "Los hechos de mayo de 1937: Efectivos y bajas de cada bando," *Hispania* 73(245), September–December 2013.

Preston, Paul.

1. *The Spanish Civil War: Reaction, Revolution, and Revenge.* New York: Norton, 2006.
2. *We Saw Spain Die: Foreign Correspondents in the Spanish Civil War.* New York: Skyhorse, 2009.
3. *The Spanish Holocaust: Inquisition and Extermination in Twentieth-Century Spain.* New York: Norton, 2012.
4. *Franco: A Biography.* New York: Basic Books, 1994.
5. *The Destruction of Guernica.* London: Harper Press, 2012.
6. "The Psychopathology of an Assassin: General Gonzalo Queipo de Llano," in Anderson and Arco Blanco.

Puzzo, Dante A. *Spain and the Great Powers, 1936–1941.* New York: Columbia University Press, 1962.

Radosh, Ronald, Mary R. Habeck, and Grigory Sevostianov. *Spain Betrayed: The Soviet Union in the Spanish Civil War.* New Haven: Yale University Press, 2001.

Raguer, Hilari. *Gunpowder and Incense: The Catholic Church and the Spanish Civil War.* London: Routledge, 2007.

Regler, Gustav. *The Owl of Minerva: The Autobiography of Gustav Regler.* Trans. Norman Denny. New York: Farrar, Straus, 1959.

Reynolds, Michael. *Hemingway: The 1930s.* New York: Norton, 1997.

Rhodes, Richard. *Hell and Good Company: The Spanish Civil War and the World It Made.* New York: Simon & Schuster, 2015.

Richardson, R. Dan. *Comintern Army: The International Brigades and the Spanish Civil War.* Lexington: University Press of Kentucky, 1982.

Rodden, John, and John Rossi. "The Mysterious (Un)meeting of George Orwell and Ernest Hemingway," *Kenyon Review* 31(4), Fall 2009.

Rolfe, Edwin. *The Lincoln Battalion: The Story of the Americans Who Fought in Spain in the International Brigades.* New York: Random House, 1939.

Romerstein, Herbert. *Heroic Victims: Stalin's Foreign Legion in the Spanish Civil War.* Washington, DC: Council for the Defense of Freedom, 1994.

Rosenstone, Robert A. *Crusade of the Left: The Lincoln Battalion in the Spanish Civil War.* New York: Pegasus, 1969.

Rubin, Hank. *Spain's Cause Was Mine: A Memoir of an American Medic in the Spanish Civil War.* Carbondale: Southern Illinois University Press, 1997.

Ruiz, Julius. *The "Red Terror" and the Spanish Civil War: Revolutionary Violence in Madrid.* New York: Cambridge University Press, 2014.

Sánchez Asiaín, José Ángel. *La financiacíon de la guerra civil española: Una aproximacíon histórica.* Barcelona: Crítica, 2012.

Schmidt, Konrad. "In Francos Kriegsgefangenschaft," in Max Wullschleger, ed., *Schweizer kämpfen in Spanien.* Zürich: Buchhandlung Stauffacher, 1939.

Schwartz, Stephen. "Reading the Runes: New Perspectives on the Spanish Civil War," *Arena* 2, February 2011.

Sebba, Anne. *Battling for News: The Rise of the Woman Reporter.* London: Hodder & Stoughton, 1994.

Seidman, Michael.

1. *Republic of Egos: A Social History of the Spanish Civil War.* Madison: University of Wisconsin Press, 2002.
2. "The Unorwellian Barcelona," *European History Quarterly* 20, April 1990.

Sheean, Vincent. *Not Peace but a Sword.* New York: Doubleday, Doran, 1939.

Shelden, Michael. *Orwell: The Authorized Biography.* New York: HarperCollins, 1992.

Smith, Page. *Redeeming the Time: A People's History of the 1920s and the New Deal.* New York: McGraw-Hill, 1987.

Sommerfield, John. *Volunteer in Spain.* London: Lawrence & Wishart, 1937.

Stansky, Peter, and William Abrahams.

1. *Orwell: The Transformation.* New York: Knopf, 1980.
2. *Journey to the Frontier: Julian Bell and John Cornford: Their Lives and the 1930s.* London: Constable, 1966.

Stradling, Rob. "The Spies Who Loved Them: The Blairs in Barcelona, 1937," *Intelligence and National Security* 25(5), October 2010.

Szurek, Alexander. *The Shattered Dream.* Boulder, CO: East European Monographs, 1989.

Tanenhaus, Sam. "Innocents Abroad," *Vanity Fair,* September 2001.

Taylor, D. J. *Orwell: The Life.* New York: Holt, 2003.

Thomas, Hugh. *The Spanish Civil War.* Revised edition. New York: Random House, 2001.

Thorndike, Joseph J., Jr. "'Cap' Rieber: He Came Off a Tanker to Build an Oil Empire and Prove That Industrial Daring Is Not Dead," *Life,* 1 July 1940.

Tierney, Dominic. *FDR and the Spanish Civil War: Neutrality and Commitment in the Struggle That Divided America.* Durham, NC: Duke University Press, 2007.

Tisa, John. *Recalling the Good Fight: An Autobiography of the Spanish Civil War.* South Hadley, MA: Bergin & Garvey, 1985.

Traina, Richard P. *American Diplomacy and the Spanish Civil War.* Bloomington: Indiana University Press, 1968.

Tzouliadis, Tim. *The Forsaken: From the Great Depression to the Gulags: Hope and Betrayal in Stalin's Russia*. London: Little, Brown, 2008.

Vaill, Amanda. *Hotel Florida: Truth, Love, and Death in the Spanish Civil War*. New York: Farrar, Straus and Giroux, 2014.

Valaik, J. David. "Catholics, Neutrality, and the Spanish Embargo, 1937–1939," *Journal of American History* 54(1), June 1967.

Vernon, Alex. *Hemingway's Second War: Bearing Witness to the Spanish Civil War*. Iowa City: University of Iowa Press, 2011.

Viñas, Ángel.

1. *Las armas y el oro: Palancas de la guerra, mitos del franquismo*. Barcelona: Pasado & Presente, 2013.
2. "September 1936: Stalin's Decision to Support the Spanish Republic," in Jump.

Voros, Sandor. *American Commissar*. Philadelphia: Chilton, 1961.

Watkins, T. H. *The Great Depression: America in the 1930s*. Boston: Little, Brown, 1993.

Watson, William Braasch.

1. "Hemingway's Attacks on the Soviets and the Communists in *For Whom the Bell Tolls*," *North Dakota Quarterly* 60(2), Spring 1992.
2. "Investigating Hemingway," *North Dakota Quarterly* 59(1), Winter 1991.
3. "Investigating Hemingway: The Trip," *North Dakota Quarterly* 59(3), Summer 1991.
4. "Investigating Hemingway: The Scene," *North Dakota Quarterly* 62(2), Spring 1994–1995.

Watt, George. *The Comet Connection: Escape from Hitler's Europe*. Lexington: University Press of Kentucky, 1990.

Whealey, Robert H.

1. *Hitler and Spain: The Nazi Role in the Spanish Civil War 1936–1939*. Lexington: University Press of Kentucky, 1989.
2. "How Franco Financed His War—Reconsidered," *Journal of Contemporary History* 12(1), January 1977.
3. "Economic Influence of the Great Powers in the Spanish Civil War: From the Popular Front to the Second World War," *International History Review* 5(2), May 1983.

Whitaker, John T.

1. *We Cannot Escape History*. New York: Macmillan, 1943.
2. "Prelude to World War," *Foreign Affairs* 21(1), October 1942.

Wintringham, Tom. *English Captain*. London: Faber and Faber, 1939.

Wyden, Peter. *The Passionate War: The Narrative History of the Spanish Civil War*. New York: Simon & Schuster, 1983.

Yates, James. *From Mississippi to Madrid: Memoir of a Black American in the Abraham Lincoln Brigade*. Greensboro, NC: Open Hand, 1989.

PHOTO CREDITS

Every effort has been made to trace the copyright holders of the photographs used in this book. We apologize for any inadvertent omissions and would be grateful to be notified of any corrections, which will be incorporated in future printings.

farm workers W. Eugene Smith/The LIFE Picture Collection/Getty Images; **aristocrats** Regine Relang/ullstein bild/Getty Images; **church dignitaries** Album/Oronoz/Newscom; **sandbag fortifications** *Le Patriote Illustré;* **Marion and Bob Merriman with Dave Doran** Harry Randall Fifteenth International Brigade Films and Photographs Collection, Courtesy of the Tamiment Library, New York University; **Moorish troops** akg-images/ullstein bild; **Adam Hochschild and Lucy Selligman Schneider** Lucy McDiarmid; **Lois Orr** Courtesy of Elizabeth Cusick; **Torkild Rieber** Courtesy of DeGolyer Library, Southern Methodist University, Robert Yarnall Richie Photograph Collection; **Barcelona barricade** Universal History Archive/UIG/Getty Images; **wedding** akg-images/Newscom; **militia atop armored car** Hulton-Deutsch Collection/Corbis; **George Watt** International Brigades Archive, Moscow, Selected Images, Courtesy of the Tamiment Library, New York University; **John Gates** Records of the International Brigades, RGASPI, Moscow, Courtesy of the Tamiment Library, New York University; **Louis Fischer** Library of Congress, Prints and Photographs Division, NYWT&S Collection, LC-USZ62-132337; **International Brigade** Robert Capa [The International Brigade, Barcelona, Spain], October 28, 1938; © International Center of Photography, New York; **Toby Jensky** Courtesy of Bernice Jensky and the Tamiment Library, New York University; **Pat Gurney** Courtesy of Judith Gurney, Bernice Jensky and the Tamiment Library, New York University; **bomb crater in Guernica** ullstein bild/Getty Images; **prisoners** akg-images/ullstein bild; **Hitler and Franco** Bettmann/Corbis; **Franklin and Eleanor Roosevelt** Bettmann/Corbis; **Lincoln volunteers** Harry Randall Fifteenth International Brigade Films and Photographs Collection, Courtesy of the Tamiment Library, New York University; **Vincent Usera** Courtesy of David Wellman; **bombing of Madrid** akg-images/Newscom; **Teruel in snow** International Brigades Archive, Moscow, Selected Images, Courtesy of the Tamiment Library, New York University; **Malcolm Dunbar, Herbert Matthews, Ernest Hemingway, and General Enrique Líster** Robert Capa [*New York Times* journalist Herbert Matthews (second from left) and Ernest Hemingway (center), Teruel, Spain], late December 1937; © International Center of Photography, New York; **George Orwell and Eileen O'Shaughnessy Blair** Hoover Institution Archives, Harry Milton Papers, Box 1; **James Neugass** Courtesy of James Neugass; **Alvah Bessie** Harry Randall Fifteenth International Brigade Films and Photographs Collection, Courtesy of the Tamiment Library, New York University; **Republican refugees** Album/Oronoz/Newscom

Maps rendered by Mapping Specialists, Ltd., Fitchburg, Wisconsin

Index

Permissions Acknowledgments

Portions of this book have appeared, in different form, in the *New York Review of Books*, the *American Scholar*, the *Volunteer*, and *California*.

The author is grateful for permission to quote from the following:

The Complete Works of George Orwell edited by Peter Davison © the Estate of the late Sonia Brownell Orwell, reproduced by permission of The Random House Group Ltd and A. M. Heath & Company Ltd.

Crusade in Spain by Jason Gurney © 1974 by Mrs. Judith Gurney, all rights reserved, reprinted by permission of Faber and Faber Limited.

Looking for Trouble by Virgnia Cowles, reprinted by permission of Harriet Crawley.

War Is Beautiful by James Neugass, courtesy of the American Lincoln Brigade Archives (ALBA).